"The great prominence – for both width and depth – of Heinz Kurz and Neri Salvadori's contributions is unanimously recognized by all scholars interested in Piero Sraffa's works (published and unpublished) and in the revival of the classical approach to value and distribution. This volume not only adds to the collections of essays by these authors already published, but by broadening the field of analysis or providing new insights on issues they already dealt with, it completes them. One could say that, because of a sort of positive externality, the new collection of essays by Kurz and Salvadori also increases the importance of the previous ones."

Saverio M. Fratini, Professor of Economics,
Roma Tre University, Italy

Competition, Value and Distribution in Classical Economics

Drawing in particular on the work of Sraffa, Smith, Ricardo and Marx, the essays in this volume explore the characteristic features of the Classical economists' approach to economic problems, and the renewal of interest in that approach in modern times.

In recent years, new material has been made available on both Sraffa and Marx which have made new insights and interpretations possible. The release of Sraffa's hitherto unpublished papers and correspondence has led to reconsideration of doctrinal questions such as to what extent Sraffa built upon, or deviated from, the analyses of Adam Smith, David Ricardo and other representatives of the classical British school and Karl Marx. A major theme is also to what extent we can today, equipped with Sraffa's insights and analytical tools, re-interpret and develop ideas of classical authors, which they could present only in primitive forms, on technological progress, exhaustible resources and other contemporary issues. On Marx, the publication of the MEGA2 edition of the works, papers and correspondence of Marx and Engels also gives rise to a reconsideration of this relationship, given Marx's disenchantment with some of his own work, and return to ideas advocated by Ricardo, especially as regards the long-term tendency of the rate of profits. Finally, the classical notion of competition and monopoly deserve to be scrutinized carefully again and frequent misinterpretations in the literature refuted.

This volume is vital reading for scholars of classical economics, Marx and Sraffa, and the history of economic thought more broadly. It also deals with issues in the areas of machinery and technical progress, joint production and economic development and growth.

Heinz D. Kurz is Emeritus Professor of Economics at the University of Graz, Austria, and Fellow of the Graz Schumpeter Centre.

Neri Salvadori is Professor of Economics at the University of Pisa, Italy and Corresponding Fellow of the Accademia Nazionale dei Lincei.

Routledge Studies in the History of Economics

Poverty in Contemporary Economic Thought
Edited by Mats Lundahl, Daniel Rauhut and Neelambar Hatti

Thomas Aquinas and the Civil Economy Tradition
The Mediterranean Spirit of Capitalism
Paolo Santori

The Macroeconomics of Malthus
John Pullen

Competition, Value and Distribution in Classical Economics
Studies in Long-Period Analysis
Heinz D. Kurz and Neri Salvadori

David Ricardo. An Intellectual Biography
Sergio Cremaschi

Humanity and Nature in Economic Thought
Searching for the Organic Origins of the Economy
Edited by Gábor Bíró

European and Chinese Histories of Economic Thought
Theories and Images of Good Governance
Edited by Iwo Amelung and Bertram Schefold

Adam Smith and *The Wealth of Nations* in Spain
A History of Reception, Dissemination, Adaptation and Application, 1777–1840
Edited by Jesús Astigarraga and Juan Zabalza

For more information about this series, please visit www.routledge.com/series/SE0341

Competition, Value and Distribution in Classical Economics

Studies in Long-Period Analysis

Heinz D. Kurz and Neri Salvadori

Routledge
Taylor & Francis Group
LONDON AND NEW YORK

First published 2022
by Routledge
2 Park Square, Milton Park, Abingdon, Oxon OX14 4RN

and by Routledge
605 Third Avenue, New York, NY 10158

Routledge is an imprint of the Taylor & Francis Group, an informa business

British Library Cataloguing-in-Publication Data
A catalogue record for this book is available from the British Library

Library of Congress Cataloging-in-Publication Data
Names: Kurz, Heinz D., author. | Salvadori, Neri, author.
Title: Competition, value and distribution in classical economics : studies in long-period analysis / Heinz D. Kurz and Neri Salvadori.
Description: 1 Edition. | New York, NY : Routledge, 2022. | Series: Routledge studies in the history of economics | Includes bibliographical references and index.
Identifiers: LCCN 2021015621 (print) | LCCN 2021015622 (ebook) | ISBN 9780367687052 (hardback) | ISBN 9780367687069 (paperback) | ISBN 9781003138709 (ebook)
Subjects: LCSH: Competition. | Value. | Distribution (Economic theory)
Classification: LCC HB238 .K87 2022 (print) | LCC HB238 (ebook) | DDC 338.6/048—dc23
LC record available at https://lccn.loc.gov/2021015621
LC ebook record available at https://lccn.loc.gov/2021015622

ISBN: 978-0-367-68705-2 (hbk)
ISBN: 978-0-367-68706-9 (pbk)
ISBN: 978-1-003-13870-9 (ebk)

DOI: 10.4324/9781003138709

Typeset in Bembo
by codeMantra

Contents

About the authors

Heinz D. Kurz is Emeritus Professor of Economics at the University of Graz, Austria, and Fellow of the Graz Schumpeter Centre. He is the author or editor of several books, including *Theory of Production* (co-authored with Neri Salvadori), *The Elgar Companion to David Ricardo* (co-edited with Neri Salvadori), *Economic Thought: A Brief History*, and the three volumes of *The Handbook on the History of Economic Analysis* (co-edited with Gilbert Faccarello). He currently serves on the editorial boards of several journals, including *Metroeconomica* and *The European Journal of the History of Economic Thought*. Prior to Graz he was Professor at the University of Bremen and Theodor Heuss Professor at the New School for Social Research, New York. He is an honorary professor of the University of Nanjing, China. He was a visiting professor, among others, in Paris (Sorbonne and Panthéon), Rome (La Sapienza), Pisa, the National Autonomous University of Mexico (UNAM), Bogotà, Bangkok, Meiji University (Tokyo), and Osaka University. His main fields of research are production, growth, technical progress, capital and income distribution, and the history of economic analysis. He received the main prize of the Austrian Academy of Sciences in 2000 and an honorary doctorate from Bergische Universität, Wuppertal.

Neri Salvadori is Professor of Economics at the University of Pisa, Italy, and Corresponding Fellow of the Accademia Nazionale dei Lincei. He is the author or editor of several books, including *Theory of Production* (co-authored with Heinz D. Kurz), *Ricardo's Theory of Growth and Accumulation: A Modern View, Elgar Companion to David Ricardo* (co-edited with Heinz D. Kurz), and *Old and New Growth Theories*. He currently serves on the editorial boards of *Metroeconomica, The European Journal of the History of Economic Thought*, and *The Journal of Post Keynesian Economics*. Professor Salvadori has also taught at the Universities of Naples, Catania, Denver, and the Maritime University Institute, Naples. He has held visiting professorships at, among others, the University of Graz, the National Autonomous University of Mexico (UNAM), the University of Santiago de Compostela, the University of Paris-X-Nanterre, the University of Nice, and Meiji University (Tokyo). His main research interests involve theory of production, theory of growth, and theory of competition. In recent years he has also contributed to the history of economic thought, particularly in the field of the history of classical economics and the history of the theory of growth. He got the Premio Linceo in 2004 and was awarded the Ordine del Cherubino in 2002.

Contributors

Giuseppe Freni is Professor of Economics at the University of Naples "Parthenope", Italy. His fields of interest are the theory of growth and distribution, theory of natural resources, dynamical economics, and Classical economics.

Christian Gehrke is Associate Professor of Economics at the University of Graz, Austria. His fields of interest are the theory of growth and distribution, the analysis of structural change, and the history of economic thought.

Rodolfo Signorino is Associate Professor of Economics at the Law Faculty of the University of Palermo, Italy. He has published in the areas of Classical and Sraffian economics and the methodology of economics.

Acknowledgements

We are grateful to the following publications for allowing us to reproduce articles which originally appeared in their pages. *European Journal of the History of Economic Thought* for 'David Ricardo: on the art of "elucidating economic principles" in the face of a "labyrinth of difficulties"' and 'Ricardo on machinery: an analysis of Ricardo's examples'; Palgrave Macmillan for 'The construction of the long-run market supply curves: Some notes on Sraffa's critique of partial equilibrium analysis'; *Cahiers d'economie politique* for 'Classical economics after Sraffa'; Anthem Press for 'On the "photograph" interpretation of Piero Sraffa's production equations. A view from the Sraffa archive'; *Review of Political Economy* for 'Sraffa's constructive and interpretive work, and Marx'; *Cambridge Journal of Economics* for 'Don't treat too ill my Piero! Interpreting Sraffa's papers' and 'Adam Smith on markets, competition and violations of natural liberty'; Routledge for 'Besicovitch, Sraffa, and the existence of the Standard commodity'; Presses universitaires de Paris Ouest for 'Piero Sraffa's early work on joint production: probing into the intricacies of multiple-product systems'; *History of Political Economy* for 'The Classical notion of competition revisited'; and *Scottish Journal of Political Economy* for 'Adam Smith on monopoly theory. Making good a lacuna'.

1 Introduction

Heinz D. Kurz and Neri Salvadori

This volume is the fifth in a series of collections of essays written by the two of us, by one of us alone, or by one or the two of us with some other author. The previously published collections of essays were

- *Understanding 'Classical' Economics. Studies in Long-period Theory* (1998),
- *Classical Economics and Modern Theory. Studies in Long-period Analysis* (2003),
- *Interpreting Classical Economics. Studies in Long-period Analysis* (2007), and
- *Revisiting Classical Economics. Studies in Long-period Analysis* (2015).

Each collection reflects the discussions we were and still are involved in regarding the characteristic features of the Classical economists' approach to economic problems and those working in their tradition and the ongoing relevance of this approach. The focus of attention is on its genuine significance, analytical structure, and explanatory power; its resumption in modern times especially by Piero Sraffa; and its difference from the marginalist or neoclassical approaches. In the course of time these discussions have both deepened and widened, which can be inferred from comparing the contents of the five volumes.

All chapters here presented were previously published in journals or in other books. Only one chapter is a revision of a review article that one of us, jointly with Rodolfo Signorino, has published in a journal. Several chapters in our collections of essays have grown out of controversies and two chapters of previous collections were devoted to exchanges we had with Mark Blaug. Salvadori and Signorino got the opportunity to review a book in honour of Blaug after he had passed away, and we thought that a revised version of that review article would have been appropriate to say good-bye to Mark, who in some respects was an intellectual adversary, but never an enemy.

The material in this volume is subdivided in four parts.

Part I is dedicated to 'Classical economics, old and new' and has three chapters.

Chapter 2 deals with David Ricardo's remarkable capacity to 'elucidate economic principles' in the face of a 'labyrinth of difficulties'. It is first

DOI: 10.4324/9781003138709-1

argued that Ricardo was not a purely abstract theorist who lacked any realism. Next, his method of analysis is scrutinised and the role of numerical examples to illustrate important findings explained. The theory of value and distribution constitutes the core piece of Ricardo's analysis. His consecutive attempts to elaborate a coherent theory are reported, and it is stressed that to Ricardo the labour theory of value was a makeshift solution to a problem he did not manage to master completely. The chapter then shows that the criticism levelled at his analysis of different forms of technical progress in chapter II of the *Principles* (Ricardo, 1951, pp. 80–84) cannot be sustained. It is then argued that Ricardo's treatment of exhaustible resources is perfectly sensible and not incompatible with the analysis put forward by Harold Hotelling. Next, Ricardo's famous investigation of the introduction of (improved) machinery into the economic system is discussed and some misunderstandings in the secondary literature are cleared up. Finally, Ricardo's theorem of comparative advantage is explained, and it is emphasised that it cannot be properly understood without a reference to merchants that exploit arbitrage possibilities and the role of money in trade.

Chapter 3 reconstructs and analyses the examples that are reported in the famous chapter 'On Machinery' added by Ricardo in the third edition of his *Principles*. In this chapter Ricardo considers three examples. One of these, actually the last one, is an historical example. In it, employment actually decreased for a while, but new work opportunities were created a little later, albeit not as a consequence of the same process of innovation. This was due to the fact that the economy was growing. To avoid this circumstance and to make his point crystal clear, Ricardo produced his main examples in conditions in which there is no accumulation: the economy is stationary and the profit rate is at its minimum level. But with a given wage rate, technical change has the typical property of increasing the rate of profit: an innovation usually triggers a phase of accumulation. Ricardo was aware of two special cases in which technical change cannot affect the rate of profit: (i) the case in which the technical change affects neither which type of land is marginal nor the processes of production operated on the marginal land; (ii) the case in which the rate of profit is determined in agriculture and the technical change affects only the technology of manufacturing. Ricardo's examples are fully understood when these two cases are considered.

Chapter 4 is the chapter on Blaug mentioned above. A new section is devoted to the analysis of some of Sraffa's unpublished documents concerning the reconstruction of Classical economics. This allows the authors to clarify Blaug's as well as Sraffa's thoughts on the relationship between rational and historical reconstructions. Sraffa has consciously chosen to elaborate a rational reconstruction of a well-defined part of Classical economics, because he thought that any attempt to propose an historical reconstruction of the totality of Classical theory would be a vain enterprise.

Part II is 'On Sraffa's contribution' and has three chapters.

Chapter 5 proposes a rational reconstruction of Sraffa (1925) that makes use of the tools of modern theory of production in order to serve an immediate didactical purpose. In particular, it reformulates the criticism of Sraffa (1925) concerning the construction of the market supply curves used in partial equilibrium analyses with the help of examples, also numerical ones, and by making use of the analytical tools elaborated by the modern theory of production.

Chapter 6 deals with the impact of Sraffa's contribution, in particular, his edition of Ricardo's works and correspondence and his 1960 book, on our understanding of the Classical economists and especially Ricardo. It is argued that Sraffa managed to bring to our attention the genuine significance of the Classical approach to the theory of value and distribution and to show that it was not flawed beyond remedy, as its marginalist critics contended. Rather, it could be reformulated and elaborated in several directions in a coherent way. This concerns, for example, the problem of scarce natural resources, both renewable and exhaustible, economic development, and growth and foreign trade. Sraffa also showed that removing the deficiencies with which the theory was handed down by the Classical authors and Marx and elaborating on its strengths provided the basis for a criticism of marginalist theory. Sraffa's contribution has not only revived an interest in Classical authors, it also implied that the rise to dominance of marginalism was based on a serious misunderstanding – it strongly underestimated the fecundity of the Classical theory and strongly overestimated that of the marginalist one.

Chapter 7 discusses the view that Sraffa's price equations are best interpreted as a 'photograph' of the economic system taken at a given moment of time, which Alessandro Roncaglia had prominently put forward. The chapter shows that Sraffa himself used the metaphor in his preparatory notes leading up to his 1960 book and did so with the explicit intention to discriminate the Classical approach to the problem of value and distribution from the marginalist one: while the former analyses a *given* system of production with regard to its properties concerning income distribution and relative prices, the latter confronts the given system with an *imagined adjacent system*, as is reflected in concepts such as marginal productivity and marginal cost. The metaphor of the photograph was meant to express the focus on a given system and the absence of change. As Sraffa remarked in the preface of his book, confronting the marginalist and the Classical approach: 'The marginal approach requires attention to be focused on change, for without change either in the scale of an industry or in the "proportions of the factors of production" there can be neither marginal product nor marginal cost' (Sraffa 1960, p. v). He went on:

> In a system in which, day after day, production continued unchanged in those respects, the marginal product of a factor (or alternatively the

> marginal cost of a product) would not merely be hard to find – it just would not be there to be found.
>
> (ibidem)

Part III is on '*Production of Commodities by Means of Commodities* in the Making' and has four chapters.

Chapter 8 provides a summary account of Sraffa's constructive and interpretative work on the Classical approach to the theory of value and distribution and its relationship with Marx's contribution. It is pointed that in the first period of his constructive and interpretative work, extending from 1927 to the beginning of 1931, Sraffa adopted a 'physical real cost' and, therefore, a strictly objectivist approach to his production equations and completely eschewed a labour value-based approach. He called the labour theory of value a 'corruption' of the correct concept of cost, which in his view had been advocated by William Petty, the Physiocrats, and also, in principle, the British Classical economists. In this period, Marx played no prominent role in his investigation. Only at a later stage, beginning in the early 1940s, did he explore systematically the relationship between his own re-formulation of the surplus approach to the theory of value and distribution and Marx's contribution. According to Sraffa, one of Marx's perhaps most important findings is his concept of a maximum rate of profits to describe a given system of production.

Chapter 9 turns to the intricate question of how to go about the literary heritage of an author, who during his lifetime has published relatively little, but has written a lot. The published material relative to the unpublished one may be compared to the visible tip of an iceberg relative to its main body, which is sunk in the dark sea. The considerations in the chapter were provoked by some interpreters of Sraffa's hitherto unpublished papers, who based their interpretations on bits and pieces of evidence from the Sraffa archive, stemming from different periods of his intellectual life. Alas, some interpreters made no effort to find out whether their interpretations reflected what Sraffa intended and whether he still advocated the views ascribed to him at an advanced stage of his work or whether he had abandoned them in the course of time. The chapter therefore begins by formulating criteria that ought to be followed when interpreting an author. This is done against the background of Antonio Gramsci's reflections on the 'question of method'. Sraffa, as is well known, was a close friend of Gramsci's and apparently discussed such matters with him when visiting him in prison and especially with regard to the edition of the works and correspondence of David Ricardo to which Sraffa had been appointed at the beginning of the 1930s. The detrimental effects of neglecting such criteria are then illustrated in a first round of criticisms of several interpretations advocated in the literature on Sraffa. Next, a succinct account of the early developments of Sraffa's interpretive and (re-)constructive work is provided. This sets the stage for a second round of more detailed criticisms of the interpretations under consideration.

Chapter 10 explores the relationship between the proof of the existence of the Standard commodity contained in section 37 of Sraffa's book and the proof supplied to Sraffa by Besicovitch on 21 September 1944, and investigates the completeness and consistency of such a proof. It also postulates some reasons which led Sraffa to omit this proof in his book in favour of an argument that the subsequent literature has recognised to be incomplete. The chapter sheds some more light on the issue of the proof of the existence of the Standard commodity from an historical perspective.

Chapter 11 deals with Sraffa's early work on joint production. It is pointed out that Sraffa had studied cases of joint production as early as the late 1920s, but at the time within a Marshallian framework of supply and demand. Marshall had argued that in the simple case of just two products (mutton and wool) produced jointly by means of a single process of production, there was only one price equation to determine two prices. He closed the system in terms of a given function or schedule of (relative) demand for the two products. The relative demand function was taken to provide the needed extra equation in order to ascertain relative prices. Sraffa had criticised Marshall's partial equilibrium analysis in his 1925 and 1926 papers. Did the case of joint production imply that his physical real cost approach to the problem of value, which he had elaborated in the late 1920s, was unable to cope with the problem at hand and that subjective elements expressed in demand functions had to be introduced? Sraffa's answer was no. He responded to the challenge by pointing out that the requirements for use of the various commodities could be met by operating several joint production processes that used or produced the joint products in different proportions. While Sraffa managed to establish important results as early as 1942, including, for example, the possibility of negative labour values vis-à-vis strictly positive prices, others had to wait until the second half of the 1950s.

Part IV is on 'Competition and monopoly' and has three chapters.

Chapter 12 distinguishes and compares two different conceptions of market competition: the Walrasian notion of perfect competition and the Classical notion of free competition, focusing in particular on Adam Smith and Karl Marx. While the Walrasian notion may be described as an equilibrium state in which atomistic agents treat prices parametrically, the Classical notion is a situation in which agents employ their market power by setting prices strategically. Yet, though for the Classical authors price undercutting or outbidding are typical phenomena occurring in any market characterised by free competition, it is fair to say that they went no further than providing some metaphors and some numerical examples that do not give us much more than some unsystematic guidelines on how to analyse in detail the competitive process of market price determination.

Marx was conscious that between a buyer's market, in which the price is determined by the reservation price of sellers, and a seller's market, in which the price is determined by the reservation price of buyers, there is something in between in which the price is not unique and any equilibrium can concern only distributions of probability (mixed strategies) on the behaviour of the traders. An appendix substantiates this fact by using a formalism derived from the analysis of Bertrand competition.

Chapter 13 analyses Adam Smith's views on monopoly by focusing on Books IV and V of *The Wealth of Nations*. It argues that the majority of scholars have assessed Smith's analysis of monopoly starting from premises different from those actually, though implicitly, used by Smith. The chapter shows that Smith makes use of the word 'monopoly' to refer to a heterogeneous collection of market outcomes, besides that of a single seller market, and that Smith's account of monopolists' behaviour is richer than that provided by later theorists. Smith was also aware of the growth-retarding effect of monopoly and urged state regulation.

Chapter 14 argues that according to Smith markets and trade are in principle good things, provided there is competition and a regulatory framework that prevents ruthless selfishness, greed, and rapacity from leading to socially harmful outcomes. But competition and market regulations are always in danger of being undermined and circumnavigated, giving way to monopolies that are very comfortable and highly profitable to monopolists and may spell great trouble for many people. In Smith's view, political economy – as an important, and perhaps even the most important, part of a kind of master political science, encompassing the *science of the legislator* – has the task to fight superstition and false beliefs in matters of economic policy, to debunk opinions that present individual interests as promoting the general good, and to propose changing regulatory frameworks for markets and institutions that help to ward off threats to the security of society as a whole and provide incentives such that self-seeking behaviour also has socially beneficial effects. The East India Companies of Great Britain and the Netherlands were scary cases in point of the enormous damage that unfettered selfish behaviour endowed with monopolistic powers could bring about. Clearly, selfishness alone did *not* yield socially beneficial outcomes. Checks and balances were needed in order to channel selfish behaviour in directions that were socially beneficial and prevent it from developing its dark and destructive sides. The chapter shows that the ideas of Adam Smith may still resonate and illuminate the problems of today and the theories that try to tackle them.

I

Classical economics, old and new

2 David Ricardo

On the art of 'elucidating economic principles' in the face of a 'labyrinth of difficulties'

Heinz D. Kurz

Original paper: Heinz D. Kurz (2015) David Ricardo: on the art of "elucidating economic principles" in the face of a "labyrinth of difficulties", *The European Journal of the History of Economic Thought*, 22(5), 818–851, DOI: 10.1080/09672567.2015.1074713. London: Taylor & Francis Group.

2.1 Introduction

Major interpreters of David Ricardo assess his contribution to political economy in vastly different terms. Karl Marx praises Ricardo's 'scientific impartiality and love of truth' (Marx 1954, p. 412) and the '*honesty* which so essentially distinguishes him from the vulgar economists' (Marx 1959, p. 555; original emphasis). William Stanley Jevons is one in a row of critics who contends that the doctrine of the Classical authors and especially Ricardo 'is radically fallacious; it involves the attempt to determine two unknown quantities from one equation' (Jevons [1871] 1965, p. 258; see also pp. 258–259): profits and the level of output, given the real wage rate. L, eon Walras reiterates the criticism: 'In the language of mathematics one equation cannot be used to determine two unknowns' (Walras [1874–1877] 1954, §368), while Joseph A. Schumpeter (1954) stokes it up: according to him Ricardo's 'fundamental problem' was that he 'wanted to solve in terms of an equation between four variables: net output equals rent plus profits plus wages' (Schumpeter 1954, p. 569). Schumpeter also accuses Ricardo of 'piling a heavy load of practical conclusions upon a tenuous groundwork' (1954, p. 1171). The 'Ricardian vice' is said to consist of drawing bold policy conclusions from oversimplified and arbitrarily closed models of the economy. Knut Wicksell instead defends Ricardo against this kind of criticism: 'the way in which Ricardo develops his argument … is a model of strictly logical reasoning about a subject which seems, at first glance, to admit of so little precision.' And: 'Ricardo's theory of value is, one finds, developed with a high degree of consistency and strictness' (Wicksell [1893] 1954, pp. 34 and 40). He adds

> Since, according to Ricardo, wages represent a magnitude fixed from the beginning, and since – as he later shows – the level of rent is

DOI: 10.4324/9781003138709-3

> also determined by independent causes, the cause of capital profit is already settled. It is neither possible nor necessary to explain capital profit in other ways, if the other assumptions are sound.
>
> (ibid., pp. 36–37)[1]

Interestingly, a few years earlier Alfred Marshall dubs Ricardo the head of the 'brilliant school of deductive reasoning' (Marshall 1890, p. 629), and explains: 'His strong constructive originality is the mark of the highest genius in all nations. … Ricardo's power of threading his way without slip through intricate paths to new and unexpected results has never been surpassed' (ibid, p. 629, n. 1). On Ricardo's approach to the theory of relative prices, Marshall in Chapter XV of Book V, *General Relations of Demand, Supply, and Value*, writes: 'Ricardo's theory of cost of production in relation to value occupies so important a place in the history of economics that any misunderstanding as to its real character must necessarily be very mischievous.' Contrary to a widespread opinion Marshall insists 'that the foundations of the theory as they were left by Ricardo remain intact' (ibid., pp. 416–417).[2]

John Maynard Keynes is mainly concerned about the 'realism' of Ricardo's theory. To him 'Ricardo was the abstract and *a priori* theorist' – a man 'with his head in the clouds' (Keynes 1972 *CW* X, pp. 95 and 98).[3] Ricardo's failure to understand the *Principle of Effective Demand*, which according to Keynes Thomas Robert Malthus had established, and which governs output as a whole and employment, rendered his analysis not only analytically largely useless but also socially harmful. Keynes sighs: 'If only Malthus, instead of Ricardo, had been the parent stem from which nineteenth-century economics proceeded, what a much wiser and richer place the world would be to-day!' (Keynes 1972 *CW* X, pp. 100–101).

Why is there such a diversity of opinions on Ricardo? Why does the discussion of his doctrines not converge on a widely shared point of view? Put differently: why is your Ricardo different from mine?

In this paper I put forward what in my opinion are some of the main reasons for what I consider to be essentially misunderstandings and misinterpretations of Ricardo. I thus side with Wicksell and other commentators who hold Ricardo in high esteem and praise his analytical capabilities, his originality, and his sense of realism. Ricardo's writings are not easy to understand. They may much more easily be misunderstood, as several examples dealt with below show. Ricardo was not given the time to elaborate his ideas in a fully coherent and comprehensive way. His analysis, for the elaboration of which he had only a few years, remained in *statu nascendi*. Many of his insights he never managed to work out fully. A lack of conceptual clarity is reflected in the formulation of ideas, which increases for readers the barriers to entry in Ricardo's analysis. It also leaves somewhat in the dark how various ideas are interconnected, how the parts make up the whole of Ricardo's economics. One thing the attentive reader will swiftly understand: he cannot expect to learn all that is to be known about a particular theme by turning just to the chapter in the *Principles* that refers to the theme in its title. To come to grips with Ricardo's position on exhaustible resources, for example, it is not good enough to focus attention only on Chapter III, 'On the Rent of Mines', just as it is not good enough to read only Chapter VII, 'On Foreign Trade', in order to get a comprehensive picture of his views on international trade. Major obstacles in the way to a better understanding of Ricardo's views appear to be a lack of awareness of his method of reasoning. He typically begins his reasoning by first contemplating a situation in which capital accumulates and the population grows, but in which there is no technical progress. It is only in a second step that he investigates how various types of 'improvement' modify the results obtained. Also the numerical examples Ricardo constructs in order to illustrate what in his view is the main principle at work in a given case have frequently been misunderstood. The paper seeks to clear up some of the misconceptions encountered in the secondary literature on Ricardo. The emphasis is on the theory of value and distribution, the role of scarce natural resources, various types of technical change, and on foreign trade. It will be argued that while the form in which Ricardo presents his argument is frequently less than optimal and a source of misinterpretation, its content is generally remarkable and rich with insights, several of which have not been fully recovered as yet.[4]

The composition of the paper is the following. Section 2.2 scrutinises the claim that Ricardo was a purely abstract theorist. Section 2.3 summarises his method of analysis and the role of numerical examples in it. Section 2.4 deals with his approach to the theory of value and distribution and the intuition that guided his consecutive attempts at solving the problem. Section 2.5 touches briefly upon the contention that his analysis of different forms of technical progress in Chapter II, 'On Rent', is hopelessly muddled; it is shown that this is not so. Section 2.6 then turns to the case of exhaustible resources and argues that his treatment in terms of differential rent is perfectly sensible: while different from the analysis of Harold Hotelling, it is not inferior to, but compatible with it. Section 2.7 turns to his discussion of machinery and clears up some misunderstandings in the literature on it. Finally, Section 2.8 addresses the Theorem of comparative cost and argues that it cannot be properly understood without a reference to arbitrageurs, that is merchants, and the role of money in trade. Section 2.9 concludes.[5]

2.2 Ricardo – the man 'with his head in the clouds'?

Ricardo has been chastised for his 'abstract reasoning', which allegedly lacked any realism and was not practically applicable. Its barrenness is well expressed, his critics contend, by the purely hypothetical numerical examples he constructs for illustrative purposes, which are said to have little or nothing to do with the 'real world'. Comparing Ricardo and Malthus, Keynes opines: 'In economic discussions Ricardo was the abstract and *a priori* theorist, Malthus the inductive and intuitive investigator who hated to stray too far from what he could test by reference to the facts and his own intuitions' (Keynes *CW* X, p. 95). Keynes adds with reference to the correspondence between the two authors dealing with the determination of output, income distribution, and relative prices:

> One cannot rise from a perusal of this correspondence without a feeling that the almost total obliteration of Malthus's line of approach and the complete domination of Ricardo's for a period of a hundred years has been a disaster to the progress of economics. Time after time in these letters Malthus is talking plain sense, the force of which *Ricardo with his head in the clouds* wholly fails to comprehend. Time after time a crushing refutation by Malthus is met by a mind so completely closed that Ricardo does not even see what Malthus is saying.
>
> (Keynes *CW* X, p. 98; emphasis added)

This verdict clearly does not apply to Ricardo, the stock jobber, whose knowledge about money, finance, and banking probably came second to none in his time. Keynes admits: 'when it came to practical finance, the roles of the Jewish stockbroker and the aristocratic clergyman were, as they should be, reversed' (Keynes *CW* X, p. 95). Ricardo knew even minute technical and organisational details of the banking business of his time and he knew financial mathematics – compound interest, annuities, etc. – a knowledge the majority of contemporary economists lacked. But what about the real side of the economy, production processes in agriculture and manufacturing, the organisation of commerce and trade, the export and import of commodities, technical progress? Was Ricardo really the man 'with his head in the clouds'?

Timothy Davis (2002, 2005) had already shown that Ricardo's theoretical views and economic policy advice were typically based on a thorough knowledge of the available macroeconomic empirical data. Mary Morgan provides further compelling evidence that Ricardo 'was no less informed, or less able to judge, the agricultural realities of his day than Malthus, who was for many years the parson of a rural parish' (Morgan 2012, p. 48). As a matter of fact, Ricardo appears to have known a great deal more about the importance of drainage, new crops and crop rotation, and the gradual beginning of mechanisation in agriculture than most of his contemporaries. Morgan focuses attention on

> the common ground and unexpected connection between the two practical domains of political economy and experimental agriculture, and in particular the fundamental importance of these links in Ricardo's works. His account of distribution depended on substantive elements from practical and experimental farming.

She goes on: 'His political arithmetic, or as I shall suggest, his model and modelling, mirror the numerical expression and content of agricultural experimental work.' And: 'Ricardo knew about all this. He was familiar with the experimental farming activities of his day' (Morgan 2012, pp. 53 and 55). It was only on the basis of such practical knowledge that he could develop his 'law of distribution', that is, his analysis of changes in the sharing out of the products as wages, rents, and profits as capital accumulates, the population grows, and technical progress transforms the methods of production.

As regards the manufacturing sector, Ricardo was one of the first to investigate the sector's mechanisation, especially in Chapter XXXI, 'On Machinery', added to the third edition of the *Principles* (1821). He did so partly as a response to the activities of the Luddites, who took machines to be the source of workers' distress and therefore sought to destroy them. Contrary to Adam Smith ([1776] 1976), Ricardo may be said to have glimpsed the tremendous rise in importance of the manufacturing sector in general and of the machine producing industry in particular for the development of the economic system as a whole. And while he did not yet grasp the sector's elevation to the 'engine of growth' of industrialising economies, he sensed that something important was happening that affected also the production of 'necessaries' and led to the gradual industrialisation of agriculture. As an end state of this development he even contemplated a situation in which machine power had completely replaced labour power, with machines producing machines – a fully automated economic system. This had important consequences with respect to income distribution, as he wrote in a letter to McCulloch on 30 June 1821:

> If machinery could do all the work that labour now does, there would be no demand for labour. Nobody would be entitled to consume any thing who was not a capitalist, and who could not buy or hire a machine.
>
> (*Works* VIII, pp. 399–400)

We may conclude by saying that Ricardo was not the proverbial man with his head in the clouds. When his adversaries in Parliament denounced him as a 'visionary on commercial subjects' (*Works* VIII, p. 197) and as someone who has 'just descended from some other planet' (*Works* V, p. 85), this was not because he lacked practical knowledge and analytical judgement on these matters. It was rather because his proposals were seen to harm his adversaries' interests and to be possessed of a compelling logic. Ricardo understood the financial world of his days better than most of his contemporaries. He was also familiar with some of the technical and organisational revolutions that took place before his eyes in the various sectors of the economy and analysed the consequences of different types of technical progress on development and growth, income distribution and relative prices. A careful scrutiny of his works and correspondence shows that his thinking was not overwhelmed, as is frequently contended, by a concern with diminishing returns in agriculture in combination with Malthus's law of population. This brings us to our next theme: Ricardo's method of analysis and the role of numerical examples in it. These appear to have frequently been misapprehended and have led to assessments of Ricardo that are difficult to sustain.

2.3 Ricardo's method and numerical illustrations

The theory Ricardo sought to elaborate shared with Smith's at least three important features. First, the theory had to be *general*: it had to deal with the economic system as a whole and with the interdependence between its different parts. Second, it had to come to grips with the modern economy's *inherent dynamism*, a system that is continually changing from within due to the accumulation of capital, the growth of population, the scarcity of renewable (land) and exhaustible (mines) resources, technical change in all sectors of the economy, a growing social division of labour both domestically and internationally, an expansion of outputs, and an increasing heterogeneity and diversity of commodities. What are the laws governing the system and, especially, what are the laws governing the *distribution* of a growing product amongst the different classes of society, workers, capitalists, and landlords? Third, the analytical method Smith and Ricardo employed in order to investigate the system is known as the *long-period method*. It focuses attention on situations in which, in the ideal case of *free competition*, a uniform rate of profits and uniform rates of wages and of rents for each particular quality of labour or of land obtain. Competitive forces are taken to let 'market prices' and the distributive variables gravitate towards (or oscillate around) their 'natural' levels. The latter were the theoretical magnitudes on whose explanation, and determination, the Classical authors focused attention.

In a *first step* of the analysis Ricardo typically studied in abstract terms the situation of an economy *in a given place and time*. In a *second step* he then studied the path the economy would take in the case in which it followed the 'natural course of things'. By this he meant a course of events in which capital accumulates, the population grows, etc., but in which there is no further technical progress – there are no further 'improvements' in the methods of production. The order according to which lands of different 'fertility' will be cultivated upon the first settling of a country and the subsequent gradual increase of effectual demand for corn, as discussed in Chapter II, 'On Rent', reflects well this course and Ricardo's *method of counterfactual reasoning*: the system expands, but technical knowledge is taken to be frozen in. It is only in a *third step* that he takes technical progress into account and expounds the different effects different types of it have.

The focus of much of Ricardo's analysis is on steps one and two. Understandably, he was keen to get the foundations of his analysis right.

Setting aside technical progress was also motivated by the fact that little can be known today about future technical breakthroughs. What could at most be done was to assess the impact of different well-specified forms of improvements on the economic system. Alas, his stance in this regard appears to have led some commentators to see in Ricardo a technical pessimist, who expected the stationary state to lurk around the corner (see Kurz 2010, pp. 1184 and 1195). This misinterpretation could only have been amplified by the fact that in his discussions with Malthus, Ricardo variously had recourse to the former's law of population. Since Ricardo repeatedly expressed scepticism as to the validity of this alleged 'law' (see Kurz and Salvadori 2009), the question is why he nevertheless accepted it in some of his debates with his friend. He appears to have invoked it in order to get a firm ground to stand on in his controversy with Malthus about the determinants of the general rate of profits. With a real wage rate that is given and constant thanks to the population mechanism, an explanation of the rate of profits in terms of the surplus product left after the necessary means of production and means of sustenance of workers have been deducted from the social product is straightforward and clear, which it is not in the case in which wages are not fixed.

Ricardo had the habit of illustrating his reasoning in terms of numerical examples; see especially his *Essay on Profits* (*Works* IV), in which the argument is developed around an elaborate numerical example. He was in fact one of the first economists to do so, and to good purpose. The simplicity of several of the numerical illustrations and the derivation of economic policy conclusions from some of them has earned him Schumpeter's accusation of 'Ricardian vice'; and the difficulties besetting some of the examples has prompted critics to call his respective analysis 'a complete and hopeless failure' (Cannan [1893] 1967, p. 260). While there can be no doubt that some of Ricardo's illustrations are somewhat misconstrued, how can this be explained in view of Ricardo's untiring effort to get his argument right? There is no need to speculate in this regard, because Ricardo told the reader how he proceeded. His main concern was with the general thrust of the argument, the basic principle he saw at work in the particular situation under consideration. He left it to the reader to think through any further ramifications the argument might have and also the implications of a change in its setting. He emphasised:

> In all these calculations I have been desirous only *to elucidate the principle*, and it is scarcely necessary to observe, that my whole basis is assumed at random, and merely for the purpose of exemplification. The results though different in degree, would have been the same in principle, however accurately I might have stated the [details]. My object has been to simplify the subject...
>
> (*Works* I, pp. 121–122; emphasis added)

What mattered to him were the economic principles he wished to establish; the numerical examples were simple illustrations, chosen *ad hoc*. To point out slips in the illustrations does not imply that the underlying argument is erroneous. Yet this is what some critics of Ricardo have argued. Below a few examples will be given, with regard to which they tended to throw out the baby with the bathwater. It will be argued that several of Ricardo's examples can easily be rectified and brought into harmony with the economic principle he was desirous to elucidate.

2.4 Ricardo's approach to the theory of value and distribution

The theory of value and distribution forms the backbone of all other economic theory in Ricardo: the theory of capital accumulation and economic development, of scarce natural resources, of foreign trade, of taxation and public debt, and so on. This explains why it was at the centre of debates ever since it saw the light of the day. The comprehension of Ricardo and the Classical authors has dramatically improved with the publication of *The Works and Correspondence of David Ricardo* (Ricardo 1951–1973), Piero Sraffa's introductions, especially to Volume I of the Edition, and Sraffa's 1960 resumption of and elaboration on the 'standpoint of the old classical economists from Adam Smith to Ricardo' (Sraffa 1960, p. v). Sraffa's introductions, Luigi Pasinetti (2012, p. 1310) stressed, 'have opened up the way to a clearer and deeper understanding than has ever been the case before of classical economic theory.' In this state of affairs it suffices to resume important aspects of Ricardo's approach and dispel some misinterpretations in the literature.

Relating to what we called the first step in Ricardo's analysis, Sraffa pointed out that the investigation 'is concerned exclusively with such properties of an economic system as do not depend on changes in the scale of production or in the proportions of "factors"' (Sraffa 1960, p. v). The given *system of production* whose (mathematical) properties were to be studied is characterised in terms of (i) given gross output levels of the various commodities and (ii) given methods of production to produce these outputs.[6] Are the givens (or independent variables) (i) and (ii) both necessary and sufficient to ascertain the range within which the magnitudes can vary in which the Classical economists were most interested – the wage rate(s), the rent(s) of land, the general rate of profits, and relative prices?

Sraffa (1960) demonstrated that the answer to this question is yes.[7] More specifically (and setting aside the problem of scarce natural resources, such as land) he showed that the givens (i) and (ii) suffice to determine the competitive rate of profits and relative prices if *real wages* are given and form a part of the physical real costs of production. This case regards 'wages as consisting of the necessary subsistence of the workers and thus entering the system on the same footing as the fuel for the engine or the feed for the cattle' (1960, p. 9). In the simple case of single-product industries and thus circulating capital only, and normalising gross output levels of the different industries as unity, the price equations of classical derivation can be written as

$$\mathbf{p} = (1+r)(\mathbf{M}+\mathbf{S})\mathbf{p} \text{ or } \mathbf{p} = (1+r)\mathbf{A}\mathbf{p} \tag{2.1}$$

where $\mathbf{p}$ is the n-dimensional price vector $(p_1, p_2, \ldots, p_n)^T$, r is the general rate of profits, $\mathbf{M}$ is the $n \times n$ matrix of material means of production, $\mathbf{S}$ is the matrix of the necessary subsistence of workers, and $\mathbf{A} = \mathbf{M} + \mathbf{S}$. On the simplifying assumption of a uniform real wage per unit of labour employed in production, given by vector $\mathbf{c} = (c_1, c_2, \ldots, c_n)$, and denoting the quantities of (direct) labour needed per unit of output in the different industries by $\mathbf{l} = (l_1, l_2, \ldots, l_n)^T$, $\mathbf{S} = \mathbf{l}\mathbf{c}^T$. With $\mathbf{M}$, $\mathbf{l}$, and $\mathbf{c}$ given, and taking a bundle of non-negative quantities of the different commodities $\mathbf{d} = (d_1, d_2, \ldots, d_n)^T$ as the standard of value, that is, setting its value equal to unity,

$$\mathbf{d}^T\mathbf{p} = 1, \tag{2.2}$$

the general rate of profits r and the prices in terms of the standard $\mathbf{d}$ can be ascertained; see, for example, Kurz and Salvadori (1995, chap. 4). No other data or known variables (and especially no demand and supply functions) are needed to determine the unknowns. Hence, the contention put forward by Jevons, Walras, and Schumpeter that Ricardo tried to determine two (or several) unknowns from a single equation is false.

What applies to the case of a particular level of the real wage rate applies to all levels of the real wage compatible with a non-negative rate of profits. This leads to Ricardo's so-called *fundamental law of distribution*, the inverse relationship between the rate of profits (r) and wages (w), or w–r relationship or *wage curve*, which was arguably one of his most important analytical discoveries. The argument applies also to the case in which 'proportional wages' are given. By this Ricardo meant a given share of wages (see Gehrke 2011). Also in this regard Sraffa proved Ricardo's intuition to be correct.[8]

Ricardo stressed that 'Profits come out of the surplus produce' (*Works* II, p. 128). The *surplus product* consists of the quantities of commodities that are left over after all the necessary means of production and means of subsistence in the support of (productive) workers have been deducted from the quantities actually produced of the various commodities during a year; it is a vector of commodities. Setting aside the rents of land, the surplus product constitutes the commodity content of profits. The *capital advanced* on the other hand consists of the means of production and the means of subsistence employed and (partly) used up; this is another vector of commodities. Physically, the *general rate of profits* is the ratio of the two vectors, with the surplus product (profits) in the numerator and the necessary inputs (capital) in the denominator.

Apparently the two magnitudes can only be compared if the various commodities are rendered commensurable with one another. It is here that the theory of value enters the stage of the Classical surplus-based approach to income distribution, as Garegnani (1984) stressed. It actually seems to be irrefutable that the general rate of profits can only be ascertained in terms of, or simultaneously with, the prices of commodities. It therefore cannot but come as a surprise that Ricardo was *not* of this opinion: he was convinced that the problem of distribution could be dealt with independently of the problem of value. In a letter to McCulloch on 13 June 1820 reflecting upon his previous efforts to elaborate a consistent theory of profits he insisted:

> After all the great questions of Rent, Wages, and Profits must be explained by the proportions in which the whole produce is divided between landlords, capitalists, and labourers, and *which are not essentially connected with the doctrine of value.*
>
> (*Works* VIII, p. 194)

He was clear that he had not yet managed to establish the validity of this bold claim in sufficiently general terms, but he was confident that it could be done: 'The truth of this doctrine I deem to be absolutely demonstrable' (*Works* VIII, p. 195).

These are remarkable statements. How could the laws of distribution *not* be essentially connected with the doctrine of value vis-à-vis the heterogeneity of the bundles of commodities that form the surplus product and social capital? And how could Ricardo hope to be able to convince a Malthus and other contemporaries of the truth of his apparently extravagant doctrine?[9]

Ricardo's view applies, of course, in the case of what became known as the 'corn model' subsequent to the publication of Volume I of the Ricardo edition. In his Introduction to it Sraffa famously put forward the 'corn-ratio' interpretation of Ricardo's theory of profits (Sraffa 1951, pp. xxxi–xxxii). Here we need not dwell on this interpretation and the occasionally heated controversy it triggered. It suffices to point out the following. First, Ricardo was not the only author keen to exemplify his basic intuition as regards the problem under consideration. He was well aware of the fact that he was confronted with a myriad of complex relationships, whose precise form neither he nor anyone else (including Malthus) knew at the time (and for a long time thereafter). In a letter to Malthus on 17 April 1815 he spoke of his 'simple doctrine', designed to 'account for all the phenomena in an easy, natural manner', thus staying away from 'a labyrinth of difficulties' (*Works* VI, p. 214). The corn model in the *Essay on Profits* of 1815 was designed to accomplish this.

As is well known, in the *Principles* Ricardo suggested to render heterogeneous commodities commensurate in terms of the amounts of labour bestowed upon them in their production. The labour theory of value was the device by means of which he intended to overcome as best as he could the impasse in which he found himself, lacking a consistent and general theory of value.[10] However, this did not make him entirely abandon his vision that the question of income distribution could be discussed independently of the theory of value. Interestingly, in all three editions of the *Principles* we encounter a numerical example, which satisfies the *homogeneity condition* of output and capital, but now no longer with regard to a *single* industry (corn production) only, but with regard to the *aggregate* of several industries taken together; see *Works* I, pp. 50 and 64 6. As in other parts of his theory of profits, in the example under consideration, Ricardo for simplicity takes capital to consist only of wages advanced at the beginning of the year.[11]

In the example there are three commodities: in addition to corn there are also hats and coats. All three commodities enter the real wage rate and thus are 'necessaries' or capital goods needed in the production of the three commodities themselves (and also in that of other commodities, about which Ricardo does not speak in the context under consideration). If of 100 units produced of each of them, workers and landlords get 25 (or 22) units each, profits consist of 50 (or 56) units of each of them. If capital consists only of the real wages bill, an assumption Ricardo employs for simplicity in much of his reasoning on profits, the rate of profits can be ascertained independently of values and amounts to 50/25 = 2 (or 56/22 = 28/11). The inverse relationship between the rate of profits and real wages (and rents) is alluded to: if wages fell from 25 to 22 units, profits would increase from 50 to 56 units, and the rate of profits would rise from 200% to approximately 254.55%.

Taking into account a multiplicity of wage (or capital) goods, as Malthus had requested in his debate with Ricardo, does not spell trouble for the latter's grand vision of the factors affecting the general rate of profits and the possibility of conceiving of it in physical terms. The rate depends on the conditions of production in all industries that directly or indirectly contribute to the production of wage goods, while it does not depend on the conditions of production of 'luxuries'. Ricardo's above example thus could be said to elevate the corn-ratio theory from its previous single (and only implicitly composite) commodity conceptualisation to an explicitly multi-commodity one.

We may conclude by pointing out how Sraffa in terms of the concept of the 'Standard system' and 'Standard commodity' succeeded in corroborating Ricardo's basic intuition under consideration within a framework in which commodities are produced by means of commodities (and wages are paid *post factum*). Starting from any actual economy (with single production) a hypothetical system may be constructed by re-proportioning the industries of the actual economy until the requested *homogeneity condition* of output and capital is met. As Sraffa (1960, p. 23) emphasised, the particular proportions of the Standard system 'give transparency to a system and render visible what was hidden, but they cannot alter its mathematical properties.' Sraffa (1960, p. 22) thus succeeded in demonstrating the truth of Ricardo's doctrine that 'the rate of profits [can be understood] as a ratio between quantities of commodities irrespective of their prices.'

In the following we deal with a number of propositions contained in the *Principles*, which met with reactions ranging from incomprehension to misinterpretation, criticism, and rejection. It will be shown, however, that in each case the substance of Ricardo's argument is perfectly sound and only the form in which it is presented leaves something to be desired. For the most part we follow Ricardo in assuming that natural prices or 'prices of production' are approximated with sufficient precision by labour values. We begin with his discussion of different forms of improvements in agriculture and their implications for the distribution of the product between workers, capitalists, and landlords in the latter part of Chapter II, 'On Rent'.

2.5 Different forms of technical progress in agriculture

Ricardo's respective discussion was scrutinised by major economists, including John Stuart Mill, Karl Marx, Alfred Marshall, Knut Wicksell, and Paul Samuelson. The numerical examples Ricardo put forward to illustrate the cases of land saving and capital (*alias* labour saving) improvements were generally rejected by commentators. Edwin Cannan ([1893] 1967, pp. 259–260) formulated perhaps the strongest verdict by calling Ricardo's argument 'absolutely and almost obviously wrong' and ending 'in complete and hopeless failure'. Similar judgements came from Harry Johnson (1948, p. 792), Mark Blaug ([1967] 1997, p. 113), Denis O'Brien (1975, pp. 128–129), and Samuelson (1977, p. 521).

A critical examination of Ricardo's argument shows, however, that the verdict cannot be sustained.[12] Ricardo was not wrong in any substantive sense and can only be criticised for having changed the timing at which rents are paid by passing from one numerical example (*Works* I, pp. 81–82) to the other one (*Works* I, pp. 82–83). While he at first assumed rents to be paid *post factum*, which conforms to his definition of rent as 'the difference between the produce obtained by the employment of two *equal* quantities of capital and labour' (*Work* I, 71; emphasis added), he then assumed them to be paid *ante factum* (see *Works* I, pp. 82–83), assuming that additional amounts of product of equal size are obtained by increasing amounts of capital. This has understandably irritated readers, but it does not render his analysis 'wrong' or worthless. This can be shown with the help of a simple formalisation.

As regards the first case, assume with Ricardo that *equal* amounts of capital K are employed on n different qualities of land and obtain *decreasing* amounts of product Q_j ($j = 1, 2, \ldots, n$; $Q_1 > Q_2 > \ldots > Q_n$). With rents paid *post factum*, we have

$$(1+r)K + R_j = Q_j \quad (j = 1, 2, \ldots, n)$$

with r as the general rate of profits and R_j as the rent obtained on land of quality j. Since the last portion of capital n (on marginal land) pays no rent, $R_n = 0$, and therefore

$$(1+r)K = Q_n$$
$$r = (Q_n / K) - 1$$
$$R_j = Q_j - Q_n$$

As regards the second case, assume that additional *equal* amounts of product Q are obtained by *increasing* amounts of capital K_j ($j = 1, 2, \ldots, n$; $K_1 < K_2 < \ldots < K_n$). If rents are paid *ante factum*, we have

$$(1+r)(K_j + R_j) = Q \quad (j = 1, 2, \ldots, n)$$

With rent on marginal land being equal to zero, $R_n = 0$, we obtain

$$(1+r)K_n = Q$$
$$r = (Q / K_n) - 1$$
$$R_j = K_j - K_n$$

Confronting the two sets of equations on the one hand with Ricardo's numerical examples on the other shows that the former express precisely what Ricardo does in the latter. There is a remarkable symmetry between differences in outputs produced by the same capital, and differences in capital producing the same output. We may in this context recall Ricardo's statement that when desirous to 'elucidate a principle', he was keen 'to simplify the subject' in terms of illustrations chosen 'at random'.

We may conclude by saying that the substance of Ricardo's argument is perfectly sound and the criticism levelled at it is out of proportion with the venial sin he committed by not informing the reader that he changed the definition of rent as he carried on. It might at most be said that Ricardo was not almost obviously right.[13]

2.6 Exhaustible resources in Ricardo and in more recent economic theory

Ricardo analysed not only renewable natural resources, such as lands of different fertilities, but also exhaustible resources, such as coal or metals. 'Nature, indeed produces them; but it is the labour of man which extracts them from the bowels of the earth, and prepares them for our service' (*Works* I, p. 85). However, one must not expect to find Ricardo's respective analysis in the barely three pages of Chapter III, 'Of the Rent of Mines', in the *Principles*, but rather has to turn to Chapter XXIV, 'Doctrine of Adam Smith Concerning the Rent of Land'.[14] He criticised Smith for confounding profits and rents, which, he insisted, ought to be carefully distinguished, because in the course of the development of a country, and setting aside technical progress, they typically move in *opposite* directions: while the rents of land tend to rise, the rate of profits tends to fall.

Here we are not concerned with Ricardo's criticism of Smith. We rather ask ourselves whether vis-à-vis modern resource economics, which is based on Hotelling's Rule (see Hotelling 1931), Ricardo's analysis is inferior and therefore should be abandoned. This is at least the implication one might draw from the fact that Ricardo's analysis is hardly ever mentioned any longer, as if what was right in it has been absorbed in modern literature, and what was wrong has rightly been jettisoned. However, things are different and vastly more difficult. Ricardo's approach to the problem is not defective and inferior to Hotelling's, the two approaches rather deal with very different worlds contemplated by the theorist and can be integrated into a single analysis.[15]

Let us first be clear about what is meant by the Hotelling Rule. In competitive conditions, and assuming the usual long-period framework of the analysis, all extraction, production, and conservation processes yield a uniform rate of profits. This means that the *in situ* price of a scarce exhaustible resource will rise from one period to another at the profit rate obtaining in the period. With p designating the price of the resource, we thus have

$$p_{t+1} = (1+r_t)\,p_t.$$

Hotelling derived this result within a partial equilibrium framework with an exogenously given and constant rate of interest (profit), in which the following two conditions are met:

i The resource is available in homogeneous quality and in an overall quantity that at any moment of time is known with certainty, and what is known at the beginning of a period is just the amount of the resource inherited from the previous one.
ii In a single period of time the entire amount of the resource can be extracted, that is, there is no capacity constraint limiting the output per unit of time in the extraction industry.

The Hotelling Rule thus contemplates the highly special case of a resource, whose exhaustion is actually foreseeable with certainty.

The situation contemplated by Ricardo (and Smith) is very different. While Ricardo was aware of the principal exhaustibility of certain resources, he did not think that the problem was imminent: first, because 'new and more productive mines may be discovered, in which, with the same labour, more metal may be obtained'; second, because 'Improvements may be made in the implements and machinery used in mining, which may considerably abridge labour'; and third, because 'the facilities of bringing [the resource] to the market may be increased' (*Works* I, p. 86). While these factors tend to reduce the value of the metal, 'the increasing difficulty of obtaining [it], occasioned by the greater depth at which the mine must be worked [etc.]' (ibid.), tend to increase it. Ricardo added: 'By the discovery of America and the rich mines in which it abounds, a very great effect was produced on the natural price of the precious materials' (ibid.).

All things considered, Ricardo felt entitled to approach the problem of exhaustible resources in terms of his theory of differential rent.[16] Setting aside technical progress in exploration, extraction, and other methods, we may for the sake of the argument define Ricardo's approach in terms of the following two assumptions:

i For each exhausted deposit of the resource another one with the same characteristic features will be discovered and the cost of the search in terms of labour and capital will always be the same.
ii The working of each deposit is subject to a capacity constraint that limits the amount of the resource that can be extracted per unit of time.

Since there will generally be deposits of different quality or fertility, each of which is subject to such a constraint, effectual demand will typically be met by working several deposits simultaneously. As in the theory of the rent of land, there will be a marginal, no-rent, deposit worked together with several other, intramarginal deposits that will yield their proprietors differential rents, which are higher the lower are the costs of extraction of one unit of the resource.

In this way, deposits of resources may be dealt with like fixed capital goods, such as machines or other tools of production: whenever one item is worn out a freshly produced one steps in and replaces it (see Kurz and Salvadori 1995, chap. 7). A world that can broadly be characterised in such terms reflects crucial elements of Ricardo's and, more generally, the Classical economists' vision of the issue at hand and is very different from the world contemplated by the Hotelling model. Therefore we do not encounter in the former the concept of royalties, which are a special form of profits – the profits obtained in conservation processes. As regards 'realism', Ricardo's approach may perhaps be said to fare better than the

Hotelling model. Both approaches can be integrated into a single one and combine Ricardo's rent perspective with Hotelling's Rule (see Kurz and Salvadori 2009, 2011).

2.7 On machinery and its effects

We now turn to another Chapter in Ricardo's *Principles*, which had a considerable impact on the subsequent discussion of the problem under consideration and frequently met with a lack of understanding or even severe misunderstanding: the chapter 'On Machinery' added to the third edition of Ricardo's magnum opus.[17] The chapter came as a surprise to his contemporaries, especially McCulloch, because in it Ricardo recanted his previous position according to which any displacement of workers would be swiftly compensated by new employment possibilities, either in the same or in some other industries. He wrote: 'I am convinced, that the substitution of machinery for human labour, is often very injurious to the interests of the class of labourers' (*Works* I, p. 388).

Here we focus attention exclusively on the particular case of *induced innovation*. Whenever new technical knowledge becomes available, cost-minimising producers will have to decide whether or not to adopt the newly available knowledge in terms of new methods of production or new products, such as new machines. It may then turn out that a new method of production or new machine, while it incorporates new technical knowledge, may not be profitable. This is the case when at the real wage rate and prices ruling in the economy at a given place and time, the employment of the new method or machine exhibits extra costs and thus yields its proprietor a lower rate of profit. The new method or machine may, however, be cost-minimising at other levels of the real wage rate and prices of commodities. If such levels happen to be brought about by the endogenous dynamics of the system, the new method of production or machine will be adopted and we face what John R. Hicks (1932) called an 'induced innovation'. The question then is, did Ricardo discuss already the case of induced innovations, and if yes, what did he achieve in this regard?

According to no lesser an authority than Joseph A. Schumpeter, Ricardo nowhere analysed induced innovations. With explicit reference to the machinery chapter, Schumpeter (1954, p. 679, n. 94) contends that Ricardo was unaware of the possibility of machines being introduced 'that are no novelties to producers and, so far as technological knowledge is concerned, could have been introduced but were not introduced before, because it would not have been profitable to do so.' This dictum comes as a surprise, because in Ricardo's chapter it is stated explicitly: 'Machinery and labour are in constant competition and the former can frequently not be employed until labour rises' (*Works* I, p. 395). Hence, there can be little doubt that Ricardo was perfectly aware of the fact that the introduction and diffusion of certain technical novelties (inventions) into the economic system may at first be prevented and then retarded, because the economic environment into which they are born is not conducive to their adoption (innovation). It is only when the environment changes that they will be employed.

Which changes did Ricardo have in mind? He wrote: 'The same cause that raises labour, does not raise the value of machines, and, therefore with every augmentation of capital, a greater proportion of it is employed on machinery' (*Works* I, p. 395). Interpreting this passage, C. E. Ferguson contended: 'one *must* interpret "labour rises" as meaning an increase in the *real* wage rate' (Ferguson 1973, p. 6; emphases added). In his interpretation an increase in the real wage rate would lead to the adoption of a technique that uses less of the factor that has become relatively more expensive, labour, and more of the factor that has become relatively less expensive, machinery. Ferguson interpreted Ricardo's argument as if it concerned a discussion of a choice of technique problem within a static framework. However, there are clear indications that this is not what Ricardo had in mind. He rather referred to a process of development in which capital accumulates and the population grows, but there are no new technical inventions, that is, the 'natural course of things'. In such a dynamic framework the bundle of wage goods constituting the real wage tends to become more expensive relative to machines invented in the past, but not yet introduced. Because of diminishing returns in agriculture the prices of some necessaries, especially corn, will rise relative to commodities produced in the manufacturing sector, such as machines. In order for workers to be able to afford a *given and constant* real wage bundle, *money* wages must increase. This is what Ricardo speaks of when he refers to 'the *same* cause that raises labour, [but] does not raise the value of machines'. In terms of the analytical concept of the w–r relationship, or wage curve: the reference is not to a movement *along* a given curve, but a movement *across* a set of such curves parallel to the abscissa, where each of these curves represents a different quality of land when that land happens to be the marginal (no-rent bearing) quality. This movement reflects the growing scarcity of land, which is accompanied by a rise in the price of corn and thus the price of the real wages bundle relative to the price of a machine that has some time ago been invented. Eventually the change in the relative price under consideration will be such that the machine can profitably be employed. Its employment is thus *induced by price dynamics, given the real wage rate.*

We may illustrate Ricardo's case of induced mechanisation with the help of Figure 2.1. Techniques T_0 and T_3 refer to the w–r relationships belonging to two techniques corresponding to two different stages in the development of the economy in the purely hypothetical case in which the accumulation of capital is carried out without any further improvements in the methods of production. Obviously, T_0 relates to an early stage, T_3 to a later one, in which the no-rent quality of land is of lower fertility than at stage 0. This is reflected, among other things, in a lower rate

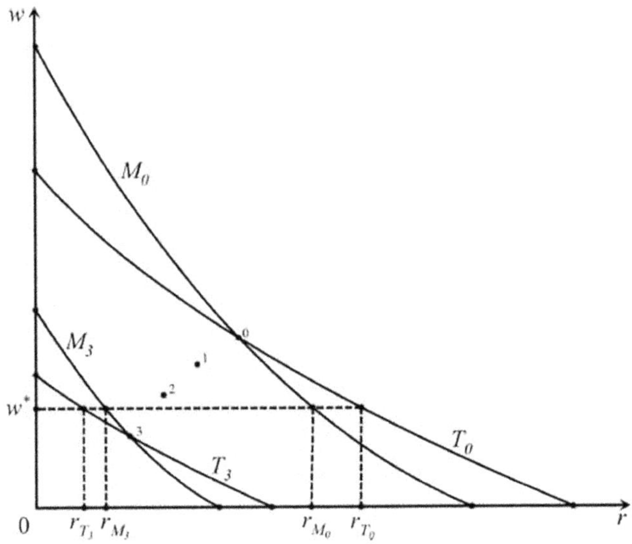

Figure 2.1 Induced mechanisation in Ricardo.

of profits: with a given and constant real wage rate, $w = w^\star$, measured along the ordinate, the rate of profits will fall from $r = r_{T0}$ to $r = r_{T3}$, measured along the abscissa. This fall will be accompanied by a rise in rents on intramarginal lands and in the money wage rate that is just sufficient to counterbalance the corresponding rise in the money prices of wage goods.

If we now take into consideration that at any moment of this process cost-minimising producers will have to ask themselves, whether it would be profitable to shift to a technique employing the machine, the picture changes in the following way. The machine using technique can be represented at any moment of time by a *w*–*r* relationship that is alternative to the technique that does not use it. In Figure 2.1, M_0 is the corresponding wage curve in the initial situation (i.e., when using the machine became an option). However, at the given real wage rate $w^\star$, it was not profitable to adopt the new machine-using method of production and abandon the old one, because whoever would have done so would have incurred extra costs and thus obtained an individual rate of profit lower than the current general rate, r_{T0}. (The inferiority of the new method at the initially prevailing prices (given the real wage rate) is also reflected in a lower level of the general rate of profits associated with M_0 compared with that of T_0: $r_{T0} > r_{M0}$.)

Apparently the new machine will be introduced into the economic system as soon as the 'switch-point' between the *w*–*r* relationships corresponding to the with-machine and the without-machine techniques, M_i and T_i ($i = 0, 1, 2, \ldots$), across the various stages of economic development, crosses the line that is parallel to the abscissa at the level of the given real wage rate w^*. In Figure 2.1 each stage is characterised, in descending order, by a different quality of land that is marginal and different relative prices, and so forth; points 0, 1, 2, and 3 give such switch-points. Through each such point pass two wage curves, one that represents the with-machine system and the other that represents the without-machine system of production. Points 0, 1, and 2 lie above the line and thus correspond to situations in which the machine will not be adopted. However, point 3, the switch-point of techniques M_3 and T_3 lies below the line. In the then prevailing economic conditions, the machine-using technique is superior to its alternative and will be adopted by cost-minimising producers. The general rate of profits in the with-machine situation will be r_{M3}, which is larger than the rate that would be obtained in the without-machine alternative, r_{T3}.

The 'rise in labour' (money wages) is an endogenous mechanism that induces the further mechanisation of production and thus decelerates the falling tendency of the actual rate of profits. It is worth noting that the introduction of improved machinery is accompanied by a reduction in the maximum rate of profits, which obtains at wages that are hypothetically equal to zero. (See the points of intersection of the with-machine w–r relationships with the abscissa.) It deserves to be noted that this type of technical progress Marx thought to dominate the development of capitalist economies: a rise in the 'organic composition of capital' implies a falling maximum rate of profits and in the end, Marx was convinced, also a falling actual rate.[18]

2.8 Foreign trade and comparative advantage

According to Samuelson, Ricardo's theory of comparative advantage is one of the few, if not the only, proposition in economics that is both true and not trivial. That it is not trivial, Samuelson added, 'is attested by the thousands of important and intelligent men who have never been able to grasp the doctrine for themselves or to believe it after it was explained to them' (Samuelson 1969, p. 683). Textbook presentations of the theory are a case in point: they frequently misapprehend or distort Ricardo's argument beyond recognition. This is partly due to the fact that Chapter VII, 'On Foreign Trade', is a hard nut to crack, because in it all major threads of which the fabric of Ricardo's theory is made meet and basically all problems that come to one's mind in the context under consideration are being discussed in quick succession on just a few pages: the causes and effects of foreign trade with respect to production, income distribution, different monetary regimes, the production of specie, technical change, etc.

Here is not the place to discuss the bewildering richness of the chapter or in any detail the gross misunderstandings of it encountered in the literature. I shall rather focus attention on aspects of the problem under

Table 2.1 Ricardo's example in labour terms

Number of men whose labour is required for one year in order to produce a given quantity of	*Cloth*	*Wine*
In Portugal..	90	80
In England	100	120

consideration that are perhaps helpful in clarifying what appears to me to be the gist of Ricardo's argument. I am aware of the fact that what I say in the following differs from other presentations of it, which I consider to be faithful to what Ricardo wrote (and it differs, of course, from the usual textbook presentations of what is called the 'Ricardian model', which distorts his argument beyond recognition).[19]

In the chapter on foreign trade, merchants and money play important roles. In fact, without taking them into account, Ricardo's argument is difficult to understand and will almost inevitably be misinterpreted. Alas, in much of the literature devoted to the principle of comparative advantage both merchants and money are surprisingly entirely absent. This neglect is probably due to the numerical example in terms of which Ricardo illustrates the principle at work (see *Works* I, pp. 135–136). Its assumptions may be tabulated as in Table 2.1.

Ricardo concludes from this that it would be advantageous for England to export cloth in exchange for wine imported from Portugal, and for Portugal to export wine in exchange for cloth from England. Under these circumstances 'England would give the produce of the labour of 100 men, for the produce of the labour of 80' (*Works* I, p. 135).[20] This may easily be misinterpreted as if Ricardo was of the opinion that countries rather than agents (merchants, etc.) trade with one another, and that their direct concern is with quantities of labour (or employment), and not profits and prices. However, as will be seen, what the example illustrates is just the macroeconomic outcome of the micro-behaviour of self-interested agents, with merchants in the front row. In terms of a recently much abused concept we might say that Ricardo cared of course for the micro-foundations of his analysis.

Before we begin with the main argument, a few observations are apposite. Ricardo's argument must be seen against the background of the rest of his analysis in the *Principles.* Without an understanding of this fact it is difficult to come to grips with his trade doctrine. The salient features of the method and the content of Ricardo's general analysis we have discussed in Section 2.3. Here it suffices to recall that Ricardo in a first step typically leaves technical progress out of the picture and assumes that capital accumulates and the population grows vis-à-vis given quantities and qualities of natural resources: only well-known methods of production can be used. In a second step he then every so often investigates how different forms of technical progress, that is, new methods of producing goods, modify the analysis.[21] This method he also applies in the chapter on foreign trade, which exposes readers to a situation that may take them by surprise, but which is perfectly understandable when seen against the background of Ricardo's approach. Setting aside technical progress, more advanced economies are typically characterised by higher (direct and indirect labour) costs of production of agricultural products (on the quality of land that pays no rent); and since these enter as means of subsistence (via the wages of labour) and raw materials into manufactures therefore also by higher (labour) costs of manufactured products. This is reflected in the four numbers of the numerical example above: England, the more developed economy, exhibits higher unit costs (in terms of labour) of both commodities.

Further important (implicit) features of the numerical example are the following. First, production typically needs labour of various skills, capital goods of various kinds, and lands of different qualities. Heterogeneous labours are rendered commensurable in terms of given wage differentials. Capital goods are taken to transmit the labour they embody entirely (circulating capital) or partly (fixed capital) to the product. What matters as regards the domestic value of a given commodity in whose production land is needed is the sum total of labour in its production on that quality of land that pays no rent (later called 'marginal land'). The interpretation of Ricardo's example in much of the textbook literature (and even in scholarly articles) on foreign trade as involving only a single factor of production, homogenous labour, amounts to a travesty of facts.

Second, the two products under consideration, cloth and wine, stand for two types of commodities that perform different roles in the economic system: while cloth is a 'necessary' or wage good, wine is a 'luxury' – the former enters the real wage and thus the production of each and every commodity produced in the economy, whereas the latter does not. The general rate of profits, Ricardo stresses repeatedly, depends only on the conditions of production of wage goods and of commodities that directly or indirectly enter in the production of wage goods. Hence, if due to technical progress in these sectors or due to the opening of trade, wage goods become cheaper in a country, a given and constant *real* wage rate will be reflected in a lower *money* wage rate and a higher general domestic rate of profits. Ricardo explains:

> It has been my endeavour to shew throughout this work, that the rate of profits can never be increased but by a fall in wages, and that there can be no permanent fall of wages but in consequence of a fall [in the price] of the necessaries on which wages are expended. If, therefore, by the extension of foreign trade, or by improvements in machinery, the food and necessaries of the labourer can be brought to market at a reduced price, profits will rise. If, instead of growing our own corn,

> or manufacturing the clothing and other necessaries of the labourer, we discover a new market from which we can supply ourselves with these commodities at a cheaper price, [nominal] wages will fall and profits rise; but if the commodities obtained at a cheaper rate, by the extension of foreign commerce, or by the improvement of machinery, be exclusively the commodities consumed by the rich [e.g. wine], no alteration will take place in the rate of profits. The rate of wages would not be affected, although wine, velvets, silks, and other expensive commodities should fall 50 per cent., and consequently profits would continue unaltered.
>
> (*Works* I, p. 132; see also p. 143)

Ricardo thus sees an analogy between the extension of foreign trade and technical progress as regards their impact on the general rate of profits, given the real wage rate. He concludes: 'Foreign trade … has no tendency to raise the profits of stock, unless the commodities imported be of that description on which the wages of labour are expended' (*Works* I, p. 133).

Third, as has already been indicated, the two commodities differ in the following important respect from one another: while wine is produced in agriculture, which is subject to diminishing returns, cloth is produced in manufacturing, which exhibits constant (or increasing) returns.[22] Since the manufacturing sector uses as inputs commodities (raw materials and means of subsistence) produced in the primary sector (which includes agriculture), the costs per unit of manufactures may nevertheless increase in the course of economic development and international specialisation. This is the case when rising prices of primary products more than balance falling amounts of inputs per unit of output in manufacturing.

Fourth, Ricardo stresses repeatedly that being bound together by 'commercial connexion' does not imply that there will be a tendency towards a uniform rate of profits across all countries involved: 'In one and the same country, profits are, generally speaking, always on the same level; or differ only as the employment of capital may be more or less secure and agreeable. *It is not so between different countries*' (*Works* I, p. 134: emphasis added). While capital can be considered to be freely mobile within a country, this is typically not so between countries. Ricardo traces this back to

> the fancied or real insecurity of capital, when not under the immediate control of its owner, together with the natural disinclination which every man has to quit the country of his birth and connexion, and intrust himself with all his habits fixed, to a strange government and new laws.
>
> (*Works* I, p. 136)

For these reasons 'men of property [are] satisfied with a low rate of profits in their own country, rather than seek a more advantageous employment of their wealth in foreign nations' (*Works* I, p. 137).[23]

Table 2.2 Ricardo's example in currency terms

Price in Reals (Portugal) and Pounds (England) of a given quantity of	*Cloth*	*Wine*
In Portugal (Real)..	90	80
In England (Pound)	100	120

Let us now turn to Ricardo's theory of comparative advantage. The numerical example expresses the basic idea in labour terms, which appears to have distracted the attention away from the mechanism which, according to Ricardo, gives rise to the specialisation indicated. It seems to have escaped the majority of commentators that the first type of agent that enters the stage on the very first page of the chapter on foreign trade is the merchant (see *Works* I, p. 128). He is on the lookout for profitable opportunities, and he is the first beneficiary of foreign trade. We may contemplate with Ricardo two cases, one in which the currencies of the two countries are non-convertible, the other in which money in both consists of gold. In the former case, while there are imports and exports, there are by assumption no money flows between the countries, whereas in the second case there are.

2.8.1 Trade in the case of non-convertible currencies

Assume that Portugal has the Portuguese Real (R) and England the Pound (£), which are non-convertible. Following Ricardo's labour-based approach to value, the money prices of the quantities of cloth and wine in the two countries are proportional to the quantities of labour spent in producing them. Assume for simplicity that the numbers are the same (see Table 2.2).

A stock jobber like Ricardo, versed in seeking out arbitrage opportunities, could easily see the profitable business to merchants involved in this.[24] (In the following we set aside transportation costs.) Take the case of an English merchant. He may buy for 100 £ a given quantity of cloth at home, ship it to Portugal and sell it there for 90 R. With this sum of money he may then buy wine from a Portuguese wine grower and get altogether 90/80 = 9/8 units of wine, where one unit costs 80 R. This quantity of wine he then ships to England and sells it for 9/8•120 £ = 135 £ (or a somewhat lower price). He thus yields a profit of 135 £ – 100 £ = 35 £ (or a little less) or a rate of profit of 35% (or a little less) on an investment of 100 £ over the time it took to export cloth and import wine. Similarly a Portuguese merchant who may buy for 80 R wine, ship it to England, sell it there for 120 £ and buy for this sum 120/100 = 6/5 units of cloth. This quantity of cloth he then ships to Portugal and sells it for 6/5•90 R = 108 R (or a somewhat lower price). He thus yields a profit of 28 Real (or a little less) or a rate of profit of 35% (or a little less) on an investment of 80 R. (It deserves to be noted that both the English and the Portuguese merchant can use one and the same ship to export and to import goods.)

This variant of the gains from trade according to the principle of comparative costs shows that after the opening of trade the first beneficiaries are the merchants: paraphrasing Smith, Ricardo speaks of 'the great profits which are sometimes made by particular merchants in foreign trade' (*Works* I, p. 128) by exploiting given arbitrage opportunities. Consumers will benefit if the domestic prices of imported goods are lowered.

The remarkable fact here is that while goods are exported and imported, the currencies of the two countries do not cross borders. As Ricardo stressed with regard to a slightly different case: 'without the necessity of money passing from either country, the exporters in each country will be paid for their goods' (*Works* I, p. 138).

Investigating the situation contemplated more closely shows that the barter terms of trade of the English merchant differ from that of the Portuguese. The former leaves his country with 1 unit of cloth and returns to it with 9/8 = 1,125 units of wine, whereas the latter leaves his country with 1 unit of wine and returns with 6/5 units of cloth, which implies a rate of transformation of 1 unit of cloth for 0.833… units of wine. The argument thus implies that there is no uniform world market price ratio of the two commodities. In fact there is no world market in the proper sense of the word. There are only domestic markets, which however can be supplied also from abroad.

The above numerical example can obviously refer only to a short-run situation, because as a result of foreign trade Portugal's cloth producers will experience a dwindling and her wine producers a rising effectual demand, whereas in England the reverse holds true. In conditions of free competition, capital (and labour) will at home flow out of disadvantageous and into advantageous sectors. The four numbers do not imply a complete specialisation of Portugal in wine production and of England in cloth production. We refrain from entering into a deeper discussion of the adjustment processes and the patterns of specialisation that might emerge.

2.8.2 Gold as the universal means of exchange

Assume now gold (coins) to be the universal means of exchange and unit of account. The total amount of gold (a producible commodity) in the system (comprising the two countries) is given and fixed. The four numbers are now taken to refer to the gold prices of given quantities of cloth and wine in autarky in Portugal and England. Both commodities are more expensive in England, which again implies profitable business for merchants: goods will be shipped from the country in which they are cheaper (Portugal) to the country in which they are dearer (England). Ships would leave Portugal fully laden, but return to her empty. (We set aside any other goods that might be shipped between England and Portugal.) English producers are bound to stop producing both commodities and Portuguese producers would like to expand production and meet effectual demands in both countries.

Assume that Portugal can do so at constant unit costs. (We thus set aside the market price dynamics that might evolve.) Portugal would then experience a trade surplus and England a trade deficit. This would imply a flow of specie from England to Portugal. The quantity of money in Portugal (England) would increase (decrease) and money prices rise (fall). Foreign trade would thus affect prices and the value of money in the two countries. Ricardo observes:

> But the diminution of money in one country, and its increase in another, do not operate on the price of one commodity only, *but on the prices of all*, and therefore the price of wine and cloth will be both raised in [Portugal], and both lowered in [England].
>
> (*Works* I, pp. 139–140; emphasis added)[25]

This, however, brings about 'such a state of prices as would make it no longer profitable to continue these transactions' (*Works* I, p. 139).

This is indeed the case, as the following consideration shows. Assume for simplicity that prices in each country increase or decrease proportionately, leaving relative (domestic) prices unaffected. If α is the increase per cent of all Portuguese prices and β is the decrease per cent of all English prices, and if p_{PC} (p_{EC}) denotes the initial gold price of cloth in Portugal (England), then the gold price in the two countries would be the same, if

$$(1+\alpha^{\star})p_{PC} = (1-\beta^{\star})p_{EC}$$

This may be considered a break-even point. If prices rose a little more in Portugal or fell a little more in England, the absolute advantage would be reversed: now English cloth would have become less expensive than Portuguese cloth, and the direction of the cloth trade would be redirected from England to Portugal. With regard to the case described by the numerical example, the equation would be fulfilled by all values of α and β satisfying

$$\alpha^{\star} = 1/9 - (10/9)\beta^{\star}$$

As regards wine, its increase in price in Portugal by the same $\alpha^{\star}$ per cent and its decrease in England by the same $\beta^{\star}$ per cent would, on the contrary, not render the two commodities equally expensive in both countries, but would still show an absolute cost advantage of Portugal, since

$$(1+\alpha^{\star})p_{PW} < (1-\beta^{\star})p_{EW}$$

where p_{PW} (p_{EW}) denotes the initial gold price of wine in Portugal (England). English wine would still be a good deal more expensive than Portuguese wine, and Portugal would continue to export and England to import wine. But 'a new distribution of the precious metals', Ricardo emphasises,

> would in some degree have changed [the value of money] in the two countries, it would be lowered in [Portugal] and raised in [England]. Estimated in money, the whole revenue of [England] would be diminished; estimated in the same medium, the whole revenue of [Portugal] would be increased.
>
> (*Works* I, p. 141)

These considerations show that Portugal's (England's) original absolute advantages (disadvantages) in the production of both commodities will not prevail: the specie-flow mechanism will undermine the situation immediately after the opening of trade and will eventually lead to a new pattern of specialisation. The important point to note is this. *The direction of change in absolute cost advantages will bring to the fore the principle of comparative advantage*: as prices rise in Portugal and fall in England, the point will come where English cloth becomes less expensive than Portuguese cloth, while English wine is still more expensive than Portuguese wine. Portugal will thus end up having both a comparative and absolute advantage in the production of wine and England a comparative advantage in the production of cloth, which is reflected in an absolute one in price terms. Assume, for example, that Portuguese prices rise by 10% and English prices drop by 10% compared with the no-trade situation (see Table 2.3). Cloth is now cheaper in England compared with Portugal, but wine is still dearer. The two countries will specialise according to their comparative advantages, which, however, will only become apparent as a consequence of the redistribution of specie between the two countries and the ensuing change in absolute cost advantages due to changes in the price levels in the two countries.

These considerations show that the theory of comparative advantage cannot be told in a way that is faithful to Ricardo, if it leaves out merchants and money. The conventional textbook illustration of the theory involves a gross distortion of Ricardo's doctrine. Ricardo deserves credit for having provided an analytical framework that allows one to discuss the problem of foreign trade in terms of (i) different agents with different

Table 2.3 Specie flow and comparative advantage

Price in ounces of gold of a given quantity of	*Cloth*	*Wine*
In Portugal..	99	88
In England	90	108

interests (producers, merchants, and consumers); (ii) production conceived of as requiring various kinds of labour, capital goods, and lands of different quality; and (iii) money as a necessary medium of exchange. Such a framework, as Ricardo shows, allows also for a discussion of the impact of the scarcity of natural resources and of different forms of technical progress (including progress in the production of the money commodity, bullion) on income distribution, relative prices, and the pattern of specialisation.

2.9 Conclusion

Ricardo variously expressed both his confidence in his theory and at the same time his doubts about being able to express himself convincingly. In a letter to Malthus on 5 October 1816 he stated: 'though I feel strongly the truth of my theory I cannot succeed in stating it clearly' (*Works* VII, p. 71). Ricardo, as is well known, was notorious for his modesty as regards his ability to formulate his ideas in a correct and compelling way. His scepticism had as its deeper reason Ricardo's understanding that there were still numerous open ends in his theory, with new insights contradicting received opinion. Yet, confronted with a 'labyrinth of difficulties', it is truly remarkable how far Ricardo got in his 'most favourite subject' (*Works* VI, p. 263). It is even more remarkable, how often his propositions were misunderstood, misinterpreted, and misstated and criticisms levelled at them, which upon closer scrutiny turn out to be untenable. So much for the alleged contention that the market for economic ideas is a perfect selection mechanism that keeps everything that is correct and useful and sorts out everything that is wrong and useless. Ricardo's works are a treasure trove that still contain ideas that are worth excavating and elaborating.

Acknowledgements

I am grateful to Jérôme Boyer des Roches, Christian Gehrke, Gilbert Faccarello, Neri Salvadori, Bertram Schefold, Yoshinori Shiozawa, Ian Steedman, Katsuyoshi Watarai, Takashi Yagi, and two anonymous referees for most useful comments and suggestions.

Notes

1 On the relationship between the theories of Walras, Wicksell, and Schumpeter, on the one hand, and Ricardo, on the other hand, see Kurz (2000) and Kurz and Salvadori (2002).
2 Marshall's concern with presenting his own theory as a continuation of the objectivist cost-of-production theory of the classical authors, integrated into and amalgamated with the subjectivist marginal-utility theory, made him downplay and even not see fundamental differences between the two.
3 This assessment is foreshadowed in a statement of 1839 by Henry Lord Brougham, who called Ricardo's views often 'abundantly theoretical, sometimes too refined for his audience, occasionally extravagant from his

propensity to follow a right principle into all its consequences, without duly taking into account in practice the condition of things to which he was applying it, as if a mechanician were to construct an engine without taking into consideration the resistance of the air in which it was to work, or the strength and the weight and the friction of the parts of which it was to be made' (*Works* V, p. xxxiii). And in a note in his diary about a dinner at Ricardo's on 12 January 1820, J. L. Mallet speaks of Ricardo's 'entire disregard of experience and practice' (*Works* VIII, p. 152 n. 2).

4 It hardly needs to be stressed that Piero Sraffa's edition of *The Works and Correspondence of David Ricardo* (Ricardo 1951–1973) has improved the Ricardo scholarship considerably by making hitherto unknown papers, correspondence, etc. available to the reader.

5 In the following I draw partially on earlier works I have written alone or together with Christian Gehrke and Neri Salvadori. All remaining misconceptions are, of course, entirely my responsibility.

6 As one commentator remarked, Ricardo 'meets you upon every subject that he has studied with … opinions in the nature of mathematical truths' (*Works* VIII, p. 152 n. 2).

7 While Ricardo typically assumed wages paid *ante factum* (i.e., at the beginning of the uniform period of production), Sraffa assumed wages paid *post factum* (i.e., at its end). However, as can easily be shown this difference does not substantially affect the general argument in the above.

8 Ricardo's basic intuition extended to the cases of fixed capital and scarce land, and also in these respects he can be said to have been on the right scent, deficiencies of his analysis notwithstanding: several of his basic ideas were later given a coherent form by V. K. Dmitriev, Ladislaus von Bortkiewicz, Paul A. Samuelson, Luigi Pasinetti, and especially Piero Sraffa.

9 For the following, see also Kurz (2011).

10 Paul Samuelson once asked Sraffa, whether Ricardo held a labour theory of value. Sraffa is reported to have answered: 'He did and he didn't'. What might at first sight be considered a sibylline response turns out to reflect properly Ricardo's point of view, which, for example, in the third edition of the *Principles* comes to the fore when Ricardo speaks 'of labour as being *the foundation of all value*, and the relative quantity of labour as *almost exclusively* determining the relative value of commodities' (*Works* I, p. 20; emphases added). The following note Sraffa wrote in November 1927 may be read as a comment on Ricardo's statement: 'It is the *whole* process of production that must be called "human labour", and thus causes all product and all values. Marx and Ricardo used "labour" in two different senses: the above, and that of *one* of the factors of production ("hours of labour" or "quantity of labour" has a meaning only in the latter sense). It is by confusing the two senses that they got mixed up and said that value is proportional to quantity of labour (in second sense) whereas they ought to have said that it is due to human labour (in first sense: a non-measurable quantity, or rather not a quantity at all).' (Sraffa Papers D3/12/11: 64; emphases in the original) A confusion of the two senses is widespread in the literature on Ricardo. For example, Mary Morgan recently wrote: 'it is *labour alone that creates value*, and … there is a direct relationship between labour input and value' (Morgan 2012, p. 60; emphasis added). As we have just seen, Ricardo was decidedly *not* of this opinion. However, unable to solve the problem of value and distribution to his own satisfaction, Ricardo clung to the labour embodiment hypothesis; see in this regard the rough draft and unfinished manuscript on *Absolute Value and Exchangeable Value*, written in 1823 shortly before he passed away (see *Works* IV).

11 One should recall however that 'corn' in Ricardo's early reasoning was a term designated to encompass all necessaries, like 'bread' in the Bible (a meaning William Petty took up), and thus represented a bundle of commodities.

12 For the following, see Gehrke et al. (2003).

13 It is not difficult to rectify Ricardo's second numerical example and bring it into line with the first one without affecting the substance of what he says; see Gehrke et al. (2003, p. 296).

14 Ricardo himself deplored his problems with 'the difficult art of composition' (*Works* VII, p. 19). Indeed, as several commentators observed, the structure of the *Principles* leaves much to be desired and reflects the hurry in which it has been put together.

15 For the following, see Kurz and Salvadori (2009, 2011).

16 John Stuart Mill reiterated Ricardo's position, but went a step further. He insisted that the working of exhaustible resources is similar to the working of land (a resource that is taken to be inexhaustible); that in both kinds of activities there are two antagonistic forces at work – diminishing returns and technical progress; and that the potential for technical progress is larger in the mining and other extraction processes than in agriculture (see Mill, 1965, p. 495). But then he even opined that 'the almost inevitable progress of human culture and improvement … *forbids us to consider* [the exhaustion] *as probable*' (p. 496; emphasis added). See in this context also Krautkraemer (1998) on the poor empirical performance of the Hotelling Rule.

17 For the following, see Jeck and Kurz (1983) and Kurz (2010, section 3).

18 For a discussion of Marx's views on the matter and his indebtedness to Ricardo, see Kurz (2010, section 4).

19 The following draws on Kurz (2014). Sraffa (1930) corrected a misinterpretation of Ricardo's famous numerical example by John Stuart Mill. This misinterpretation may be said to have triggered readings of Ricardo that eventually led up to the unfortunate modern textbook interpretation. Ruffin (2002) deserves the credit for having rediscovered Sraffa's correction. However, as Gehrke (2015, in this volume) has shown convincingly, Ruffin had difficulties, in Keynes's words, 'to escape habitual modes of thought and expression'. In interpreting the route via which Ricardo is supposed to have discovered the principle of comparative cost, Ruffin looked at him through the distorting lens of marginalist theory. For a complementary discussion of Ricardo's theory of foreign trade to the one given here, see Faccarello (2015, in this volume) and Maneschi (2015).

20 There is no presumption that cloth and wine are the only commodities produced or consumed in the two countries. However, all other commodities remain in the background in Ricardo's analysis and will also do so here.

21 Some commentators took the first step of his analysis (reflecting his research method) wrongly for a factual statement about the unimportance of technical progress; see most recently Piketty (2014, pp. 5–7). (For a criticism of this view, see the argument in previous sections and Kurz 2010.) The fact is that Ricardo was keen to abstain from speculating about future technical improvements, because no reliable knowledge on them was available. He stressed, however, that 'it is no longer questioned' that improved machinery 'has a decided tendency to raise the real wage of labour' (*Works* IV, p. 35; see also VIII, p. 171), without necessitating a fall in the rate of profits, and that there are no indications that capital accumulation will slow down because of a lack of profits.

22 According to Adam Smith's argument about the social division of labour, which Ricardo accepted, it even exhibits dynamically increasing returns. In Smith the invention of improved machines both results from and propels

forward the division of labour (see WN I.i.8). It is therefore interesting to note that when Ricardo discusses the factors counteracting a fall in the general rate of profits he explicitly refers to 'the improvements in machinery, by the better division and distribution of labour, and by the increasing skill, both in science and art, of the producers' (*Works* I, p. 94).

23 These considerations echo an argument Smith had invoked in *The Wealth of Nations* in order to describe the socially beneficial working of the 'invisible hand'. By investing at home capitalists promote not only their own interest in profits *and* security, but also unconsciously the interest of their home country, by giving employment to their fellow-countrymen (see WN IV.ii.5).

24 This is why I find Ruffin's contention (2005, p. 705) that it took Ricardo a 'great and sustained mental effort' to arrive at the principle of comparative advantage dubious. The textual evidence he puts forward does not support his case; see Gehrke (2015).

25 The passage cited actually refers to the effect of technical progress in one line of production in one of the countries on the pattern of specialisation (*Works* I, pp. 137–140). It has been adapted to the case we are concerned with.

References

Blaug, M., 1997. *Economic theory in retrospect.* 5th ed. Cambridge: Cambridge University Press.

Cannan, E., [1893]1967. *A history of the theories of production and distribution in English political economy from 1776–1848.* London: P. S. King. Reprint 1967, New York: Augustus M. Kelley.

Davis, T., 2002. David Ricardo, financier and empirical economist. *The European Journal of the History of Economic Thought*, 9 (1), 1–16.

Davis, T., 2005. *Ricardo' s macroeconomics: money, trade cycles and growth.* Cambridge: Cambridge University Press.

Faccarello, G., 2015. A calm investigation into Mr Ricardo's principles of international trade. *The European Journal of the History of Economic Thought*, doi: 10.1080/09672567.2015.1086011.

Ferguson, C.E., 1973. The specialization gap: Barton, Ricardo, and Hollander. *History of Political Economy*, 5, 1–13.

Garegnani, P., 1984. Value and distribution in the Classical economists and Marx. *Oxford Economic Papers*, 36, 291–325.

Gehrke, C., 2011. Price of wages: a curious phrase. *In*: R. Ciccone, C. Gehrke, and G. Mongiovi, eds. *Sraffa and modern economics.* Vol. 1. London: Routledge, 405–422.

Gehrke, C., 2015. Ricardo's discovery of comparative advantage revisited: a critique of Ruffin's account. *The European Journal of the History of Economic Thought*, doi: 10.1080/09672567.2015.1074714.

Gehrke, C., Kurz, H.D., and Salvadori, N., 2003. Ricardo on agricultural improvements: a note. *Scottish Journal of Political Economy*, 50 (3), 291–296.

Hicks, J.R., 1932. *The theory of wages.* London: Macmillan.

Hotelling, H., 1931. The economics of exhaustible resources. *Journal of Political Economy*, 39, 137–175.

Jeck, A. and Kurz, H.D., 1983. David Ricardo: Ansichten zur Maschinerie. *In*: H. Hagemann and P. Kalmbach, eds. *Technischer Fortschritt und Arbeitslosigkeit.* Frankfurt am Main: Campus, 38–166.

Jevons, W.S., [1871] 1965. *The theory of political economy*. London: Macmillan. Reprint (1965) New York: Kelley.

Johnson, H.G., 1948. An error in Ricardo's exposition of his theory of rent. *Quarterly Journal of Economics*, 62, 792–793.

Keynes, J.M., 1972. Essays in biography. *In*: A. Robinson and D. Moggridge, eds. *The collected writings of John Maynard Keynes*. Vol. X. London: Macmillan (Referred to as *CW X*), 71–103.

Krautkraemer, J.A., 1998. Non renewable resource scarcity. *Journal of Economic Literature*, 36 (4), 2065–2107.

Kurz, H.D., 2000. Wicksell and the problem of the 'missing' equation. *History of Political Economy*, 32, 765–788.

Kurz, H.D., 2010. Technical progress, capital accumulation and income distribution in Classical economics: Adam Smith, David Ricardo and Karl Marx. *The European Journal of the History of Economic Thought*, 17 (5), 1183–1222.

Kurz, H.D., 2011. On David Ricardo's theory of profits. The laws of distribution are 'not essentially connected with the doctrine of value'. *The History of Economic Thought*, 53 (1), 1–20.

Kurz, H.D., 2014. Comparative advantage: both true and nontrivial. Unpublished manuscript. Graz.

Kurz, H.D. and Salvadori, N., 1995. *Theory of production: a long-period analysis*. Cambridge: Cambridge University Press.

Kurz, H.D. and Salvadori, N., 2002. One theory or two? Walras's critique of Ricardo. *History of political economy*, 34 (2), 365–398.

Kurz, H.D. and Salvadori, N., 2009. Ricardo on exhaustible resources and the Hotelling rule. *In*: A. Ikeo and H.D. Kurz, eds. *The history of economic theory. Festschrift in honour of Takashi Negishi*. London: Routledge, 68–79.

Kurz, H.D. and Salvadori, N., 2011. Exhaustible resources: rents, profits, royalties and prices. *In*: V. Caspari, ed. *The evolution of economic theory. Essays in honour of Bertram Schefold*. London: Routledge, 39–52.

Maneschi, A., 2015. Ricardo's four magic numbers. *In*: H.D. Kurz and N. Salvadori, eds. *The Elgar companion to David Ricardo*. Cheltenham: Edward Elgar, 482–489.

Marshall, A., [1890] 1977. *Principles of economics*. London: Macmillan.

Marx, K., 1954. *Capital*. Vol. I. Moscow: Progress Publishers.

Marx, K., 1959. *Capital*. Vol. III. Moscow: Progress Publishers.

Mill, J.S., 1965. *Principles of political economy with some of their applications to ocial philosophy*. 1st ed. 1848. J.M. Robson, ed. 1965. Toronto: University of Toronto Press.

Morgan, M., 2012. *The world in the model. How economists work and think*. Cambridge: Cambridge University Press.

O'Brien, D., 1975. *The classical economists*. Oxford: Oxford University Press.

Pasinetti, L.L., 2012. Piero Sraffa and the future of economics, *Cambridge Journal of Economics*, 36 (6), 1303–1314.

Piketty, T., 2014. *Capital in the twenty-first century*. Cambridge, MA: Belknap Press.

Ricardo, D., 1951–1973. *The works and correspondence of David Ricardo*. 11 vols. Piero Sraffa, ed. in collaboration with M.H. Dobbs. Cambridge: Cambridge University Press (cited as *Works*, vol. number, page number).

Ruffin, R., 2002. David Ricardo's discovery of comparative advantage. *History of Political Economy*, 34, 727–748.

Ruffin, R., 2005. Debunking a myth: Torrens on comparative advantage. *History of Political Economy*, 37, 711 722.

Samuelson, P.A., 1969. The way of an economist. *In*: Paul Samuelson, ed. *International Economic Relations. Proceedings of the Third Congress of the International Economic Association*. London: Macmillan, 1–11.

Samuelson, P.A., 1977. Correcting the Ricardo error spotted in Harry Johnson's maiden paper. *Quarterly Journal of Economics*, 91, 519–530.

Schumpeter, J.A., 1954. *History of economic analysis*. London: Allen and Unwin.

Smith, A., [1776]1976. An inquiry into the nature and causes of the wealth of nations. *In*: R.H. Campbell and A.S. Skinner, eds. *The Glasgow edition of the works and correspondence of Adam Smith*. two vols. Oxford: Oxford University Press. (In the text quoted as WN, book number, part number, chapter number etc.)

Sraffa, P., 1930. An alleged correction of Ricardo. *Quarterly Journal of Economics*, 44 (3), 539–544.

Sraffa, P., 1951. Introduction. *In:* P. Sraffa and M.H. Dobb, eds. *The works and correspondence of David Ricardo*. Vol. I. Cambridge: Cambridge University Press.

Sraffa, P., 1960. *Production of commodities by means of commodities*. Cambridge: Cambridge University Press.

Walras, L., [1874]1954. *Elements of pure economics*. London: Allen and Unwin [English translation of the definitive edition of Walras (1874) by W. Jaff, e].

Wicksell, K., [1893]1954. *Value, capital, and rent*. London: George Allen & Unwin.

3 Ricardo on machinery

An analysis of Ricardo's examples

Giuseppe Freni and Neri Salvadori

Original paper: Giuseppe Freni and Neri Salvadori (2019) Ricardo on machinery: an analysis of Ricardo's examples, *The European Journal of the History of Economic Thought*, 26(3), 537–553, DOI: 10.1080/09672567.2019.1622756. London: Taylor & Francis Group.

AU: Please check the "first published" citation information is fine in all chapters.

3.1 Introduction

The chapter 'On Machinery' that Ricardo added in the third edition of his *Principles*[1] has attracted the attention of many economists: Whewell (1831), Wicksell ([1923] 1981), Hayek (1931, 1942, 1969), Kaldor (1932), Stigler (1952), Hicks (1969), Hollander (1971), Barkai (1986), Kurz (1984, 2010, see also Jeck and Kurz 1983), Samuelson (1988, 1989, 1994), Morishima (1989, Ch. 8), Davis (1989), Negishi (1990), and Gehrke (2003, 2010), among many others. In many of these contributions the reader can find examples in which substitution of machinery for human labour is injurious to the interests of workers. However, the reader rarely finds a reconstruction of the examples that Ricardo provided in Chapter XXXI of his *Principles* (exceptions are Barkai 1986; Negishi 1990; Gehrke 2010). Rather than seeking to prove that examples can be built which yield the same effects as Ricardo found, this paper aims to prove that *his very examples* can be reconstructed. We will thereby determine a set of assumptions that Ricardo did not state explicitly. Of course we cannot maintain that these are the very assumptions Ricardo had in mind, but certainly they obtain the required result and correspond to other aspects of Ricardo's reasoning that have been detected in the literature.

In other parts of the *Principles* Ricardo in general clarified the role of his examples.

> In all these calculations I have been desirous only to elucidate the principle, and it is scarcely necessary to observe, that my whole basis is assumed at random, and merely for the purpose of exemplification. The results though different in degree, would have been the same in

DOI: 10.4324/9781003138709-4

> principle, however accurately I might have set out in stating the [detailes] .... My object has been to simplify the subject ....
>
> (Ricardo 1951, Works I, pp. 121–122)

In the chapter 'On Machinery' Ricardo considers three examples. One of these, as we will see in Section 3.6, deals with a historical case. In this example employment actually decreased for a while, but new work opportunities were created a little later, albeit not as a consequence of the same process of innovation. This was due to the fact that the economy was growing. To avoid this circumstance and to make his point crystal clear, Ricardo produced his main examples in a circumstance of absence of accumulation.

In Ricardo's canonical framework of analysis, if the growth rate is nought, i.e., the economy is stationary, the profit rate is at its minimum level (i.e., the level at which capitalists have neither an incentive to save nor an incentive to dissave). Since in this framework, with a given wage rate, technical change has the typical property of increasing the rate of profit, an innovation usually triggers a phase of accumulation. Nevertheless, in order to make his point crystal clear, Ricardo assumed that the growth rate and the profit rate are both unchanged after the technical change. However, he failed to explain how this is obtained. We can only speculate. We know that Ricardo was very aware of two special cases in which technical change cannot affect the rate of profit: (i) the case in which the technical change affects neither what land is marginal nor the techniques operated on the marginal land; (ii) the case in which the rate of profit is determined in agriculture and the technical change affects only the technology of manufacture. We will see in Sections 3.2 and 3.5 that Ricardo's examples can be fully understood if these two cases are considered.

To our knowledge, the literature on machinery in Ricardo has never analysed the above aspects of Ricardo's examples.

3.2 Ricardo's main example

Ricardo's chapter 'On Machinery' can be divided into three parts. In the first part, Ricardo outlines the arguments he intends to put forward in the chapter, namely, that 'substitution of machinery for human labour, is often very injurious to the interests of the class of labourers' (Ricardo 1951, Works I: 388). Ricardo states his case very cautiously since he was aware that what he planned to deliver in the chapter was not popular among economists of the time. In fact he himself had held a different opinion in the past: in his *Essay on Profits* he had likened the effects of a low money price of corn to the outcome of improved machinery, 'which it is now no longer questioned, has a decided tendency to raise the real wages of labour' (Ricardo 1951, Works IV, p. 35). In the second part Ricardo produces a numerical example which is designed to illustrate the main argument of the paper. This example will be analysed in this section.

It is helpful to transcribe the whole text with passages numbered for convenient references.

> [1] A capitalist we will suppose employs a capital of the value of 20,000*l.* and that [2] he carries on the joint business of a farmer, and a manufacturer of necessaries. [3] We will further suppose, that 7000*l.* of this capital is invested in fixed capital, viz. in buildings, implements, &c. &c. and that [4] the remaining 13,000*l.* is employed as circulating capital in the support of labour. [5] Let us suppose, too, that profits are 10 per cent., and consequently that the capitalist's capital is every year put into its original state of efficiency, and yields a profit of 2000*l.*
>
> [6] Each year the capitalist begins his operations, by having food and necessaries in his possession of the value of 13,000*l.*, all of which he sells in the course of the year to his own workmen for that sum of money, and, during the same period, he pays them the like amount of money for wages: at the end of the year they replace in his possession food and necessaries of the value of 15,000*l.*, 2000*l.* of which he consumes himself, or disposes of as may best suit his pleasure and gratification. As far as these products are concerned, the gross produce for that year is 15,000*l.*, and the net produce 2000*l.*
>
> [7] Suppose now, that the following year the capitalist employs half his men in constructing a machine, and the other half in producing food and necessaries as usual. During that year he would pay the sum of 13,000*l.* in wages as usual, and would sell food and necessaries to the same amount to his workmen; but what would be the case the following year?
>
> [8] While the machine was being made, only one-half of the usual quantity of food and necessaries would be obtained, and they would be only one half the value of the quantity which was produced before. The machine would be worth 7500*l.*, and the food and necessaries 7500*l.*, and, therefore, the capital of the capitalist would be as great as before; for he would have besides these two values, his fixed capital worth 7000*l.*, making in the whole 20,000*l.* capital, and 2000*l.* profit. [9] After deducting this latter sum for his own expenses, he would have a no greater circulating capital than 5500*l.* with which to carry on his subsequent operations; and, therefore, his means of employing labour, would be reduced in the proportion of 13,000*l.* to 5500*l.*, and, consequently, all the labour which was before employed by 7500*l.*, would become redundant.
>
> [10] The reduced quantity of labour which the capitalist can employ, must, indeed, with the assistance of the machine, and after deductions for its repairs, produce a value equal to 7500*l.*, it must replace

> the circulating capital with a profit of 2000*l.* on the whole capital; but if this be done, if the net income be not diminished, of what importance is it to the capitalist, whether the gross income be of the value of 3000*l.*, of 10,000*l.*, or of 15,000*l.*?
>
> (Ricardo 1951, Works I. pp. 388–389)

Passages 1–6 clearly refer to a long-period position in which the rate of profits is 10%, but the economy is stationary (see in particular passages 5 and 6). Let us call $r_{\min}$ the rate of profits of the stationary economy; hence $r_{\min} = 0.1$. In this economy, only the production of a farmer producing necessary goods is analysed (see passage 2). Let us refer to the commodity produced by the farmer as corn; corn is the necessary good and therefore it is the commodity consumed by workers. Since the capitalist is a farmer, landlords also exist, although payment of rent is not mentioned. One may surmise that rent is paid in corn and subtracted from the product. Production is carried out with land, fixed capital (passage 3), and circulating capital, which consists of wages alone (passage 4), as in Pasinetti's Ricardian model (Pasinetti 1960). Fixed capital is everlasting (passage 5). In modern theory, a long-period described by Ricardo in passages 1–6 can be stated as follows.

There are three processes for producing corn, each with a different quality of land, labour, and fixed capital that is everlasting and one process to produce the fixed capital. The input-output coefficients are represented in Table 3.1. There exist 260 units of land of quality 1; 500 units of land of quality 2; and 20000 units of land of quality 3. The wage rate equals 1 unit of corn. The fixed capital/labour ratio equals 7/13 in all processes. Relative prices can therefore be considered as independent of distribution. In effect Ricardo measures all commodities in sterling without attention to changes in prices as a function of the rate of profits, which is possible only if the labour theory of value holds. For the moment we will assume that corn is the commodity consumed by all classes.

If all qualities of land are cultivated, prices are determined by the Equations

$$(35p_{fc}+65)(1+r)+13\rho_1 = 117.5+35p_{fc}$$
$$(35p_{fc}+65)(1+r)+10\ \rho_2 = 80+35p_{fc}$$

Table 3.1 The input-output patterns of the first example: the pre-innovation technology

Processes	*Fixed capital*	*New machine*	*Labour*	*Land 1*	*Land 2*	*Land 3*	*Corn*	*Fixed capital*	*New machine*
(1)	35		65	13			117.5	35	
(2)	35		65		10		80	35	
(3)	35		65			65	75	35	
(4)	35		65					110	

$$(35p_{fc}+65)(1+r) = 75+35p_{fc}$$
$$(35p_{fc}+65)(1+r) = 110p_{fc}$$

where p_{fc} is the price of fixed capital. The last two equations determine $p_{fc} = 1$ and $r = 0.1$. The first two equations determine $13\rho_1 = 42.5$ and $\rho_2 = 0.5$; where ρ_i is the rent paid for the use of land of quality i. If the capital to be invested is 20000, as in Ricardo's example, then all lands are cultivated, the intensities of operation of the processes are $x_1 = 20$; $x_2 = 50$; $x_4 = 0$; and x_3 is determined by the equation

$$100(x_1 + x_2 + x_3) = 20000;$$

i.e., $x_3 = 200 - 20 - 50 = 130$: Hence we have, as in Ricardo's example, that fixed capital equals 7000, the profit rate is 0.1, but now we have made rents explicit. Employment equals 13000. Since fixed capital is everlasting, the fact that $x_4 = 0$ means that the economy is stationary. Nevertheless process (4) contributes to determining prices.

Let us turn to Ricardo's wording. Passages 7–9 clearly refer to a transition from one long-period position to another. The transition lasts only one year. In this year half of the capital is employed in the production of a machine; the other half is used to produce corn (passage 7). The rate of profits is unchanged, which may be read as meaning that the marginal land does not change. The value of the machine is equal to cost plus profit at the rate of 0.1. This may in turn be read as meaning that production of the machine does not involve the use of land. The value of the corn produced does not involve rents either, but this can be interpreted, as before, in the sense that rent has been deducted and paid in corn (passage 8). At the end of the transition year the capitalist has the new machine, but the amount of corn he/she can use as circulating capital is strongly reduced, even if the quantity of total capital is the same as above. Moreover, with the new machine and the reduced amount of circulating capital the farmer can produce the required amount of corn (passage 9). Passage 10 describes the long-period position resulting from the innovation; the economy is still stationary since the rate of profits is still 0.1. This implies that the marginal land is unchanged and the process of producing corn on it is likewise unchanged. However, the capitalist is *not* indifferent between introducing the new machine or not. If the machine is specific to a quality of land different from the marginal land that is inframarginal after the innovation, then the capitalist recognises, before the introduction, that he can reap an extraprofit, but after the introduction the extraprofit is appropriated by the landlords, since the rate of profits is determined by the technology used on the marginal land. In modern theory the transition period described by Ricardo in passages 7–8 and the long-period position consequent upon the innovation described by Ricardo in passages 9–10 could be stated as follows.

Table 3.2 The input-output patterns of the first example: the innovation technology

Processes	*Fixed capital*	*New machine*	*Labour*	*Land 1*	*Land 2*	*Land 3*	*Corn*	*Fixed capital*	*Fixed capital*
(5)	3500		6500					3500	1
(6)	$\frac{52500}{3}$	1			500		$\frac{18250}{13}+A$	$\frac{52500}{3}$	1

During the transition processes (1), (2), (3), and (5) are used. After the transition period the processes (1), (3), and (6) are used. Processes (5) and (6) are represented in Table 3.2.

It is easily recognised that at the prices prior to innovation process (5) determines the price of the new machine $p_M = 7500$ and process (6) produces extraprofit since $A > 0$:

$$\left(\frac{52500}{13}+p_M\right)1.1+500\rho_2<\frac{18250}{13}+A+\frac{52500}{13}+p_M \Leftrightarrow A>0$$

However, as soon as the innovation is introduced, the rent on land of quality 2 becomes $\rho_2 = (250 + A)/500$ and extraprofit is appropriated by landlords.[2] If the capital to be invested is 20000, as in the example of Ricardo, then all lands are cultivated, the intensities of operation of the processes are $x_1 = 20$; $x_2 = 0$; $x_4 = 0$; $x_5 = 0$; $x_6 = 1$; and x_3 is determined by the equation

$$100(x_1+x_3)+\frac{52500}{3}+p_M=20000$$

that is $x_3 = 840/13$: Hence we have, as in Ricardo's example, the result that fixed capital equals 7000, the profit rate is 0.1, and employment equals 5500.

In the transition year the intensities of operation of the processes are $x_1 = 20$; $x_2 = 50$; $x_4 = 0$; $x_5 = 1$; $x_6 = 0$; and $x_3 = 30$: The intensity of operation x_3 is determined by the equation

$$100(x_1+x_2+x_3+100x_5)=20000.$$

Hence we have, as in Ricardo's example, the following result: fixed capital equals 7000, the profit rate is 0.1, and employment equals 13000.[3]

We have chosen the available amounts of land in such a way that the marginal land is land of quality 3 both in the long-period position consequent upon the innovation and in the transition year. Moreover, in our example the new machine is specific to land of quality 2; of course we could have chosen a numerical example such that it was specific to land of quality 1 or to a land which is supramarginal before the innovation and inframarginal after the innovation. One could wonder whether a similar result could be obtained with intensive rent instead of extensive rent. The answer is that this could happen only by chance.[4] This seems to exclude that Ricardo could have had this case in mind. On the contrary, the case mentioned above corresponds very clearly to cases that Ricardo knew and had used in his reasonings.

3.3 Ricardo's first comments

Despite the fact that Ricardo produced the example in absence of accumulation, in commenting upon his results, without informing the reader, he refers to them as valid also in general, and therefore also when there is accumulation.

> As, however, the power of saving from revenue to add to capital, must depend on the efficiency of the net revenue, to satisfy the wants of the capitalist, it could not fail to follow from the reduction in the price of commodities consequent on the introduction of machinery, that with the same wants he would have increased means of saving, —increased facility of transferring revenue into capital. But with every increase of capital he would employ more labourers; and, therefore, a portion of the people thrown out of work in the first instance, would be subsequently employed; and if the increased production, in consequence of the employment of the machine, was so great as to afford, in the shape of net produce, as great a quantity of food and necessaries as existed before in the form of gross produce, there would be the same ability to employ the whole population, and, therefore, there would not necessarily be any redundancy of people.
>
> (p. 390)

The increased net revenue may increase saving, and therefore capital and the ability to employ workers. In the case of accumulation mechanisation can be subdivided into a sequence of steps; the first step may result in a reduction in employment even if the following steps may lead to reducing such an effect or even to annulling it. The assumption of absence of accumulation implies that the sequence of steps is reduced to a single step. In other words, Ricardo seems to draw a clear distinction between the negative impact of mechanisation and its (eventually positive) longer-term effects.

Ricardo's second comment on the example is highly technical and is related to his change of opinion mentioned in the first part of his chapter. From a technical point of view the novelty of the chapter is as follows:

> In this case, then, although the net produce will not be diminished in value, although its power of purchasing commodities may be greatly

> increased, the gross produce will have fallen from a value of 15,000*l.* to a value of 7500*l.*, and as the power of supporting a population, and employing labour, depends always on the gross produce of a nation, and not on its net produce, there will necessarily be a diminution in the demand for labour, population will become redundant, and the situation of the labouring classes will be that of distress and poverty.
> (pp. 389–390)

Despite the fact that technical change may increase profit plus rent (the net produce) it may at the same time decrease the resources available for employing workers (the gross produce minus the net produce). A new technique is introduced if it generates extraprofit at the prices holding before the innovation. Ricardo thus surmised that rents plus profit must increase whereas previously he was convinced that wages cannot decrease. As a matter of fact, the reswitching debate proved that even if technology is characterised by single production (and therefore land and fixed capital are *not* among the inputs and the outputs) at a given wage rate, the changes consequent upon technical change may include a rise in capital/income ratio. If this is the case and the capital is constant (or slightly increased), then income is reduced; furthermore, since profit increases, the wage bill is decreased and, therefore, employment is reduced. Of course this cannot hold if technology is such that the labour theory of value prevails (see Salvadori and Steedman 1988). Ricardo's examples demonstrate that even in this case employment may be reduced if fixed capital is introduced.

The example shows very clearly that the 'substitution of machinery for human labour' *may be* 'injurious to the interests of the class of labourers'. The fact that a number of strong assumptions are required to bring home the result does not mean that such an event is rare. The assumptions were mainly invoked to isolate the problem and to allow crystal clear recognition of its occurrence. If, for example, the economy had been growing, the effects of the innovation on growth could not have been sterilised. A similar observation can be put forward for the assumption, implicit in Ricardo, that all classes consume only corn. In his analysis of the example Ricardo removes some of these assumptions and we will follow him.

3.4 Landlords' consumption

What happens if we introduce the assumption that landlords, as in Pasinetti's model (Pasinetti 1960), consume an industrial commodity? Let us follow Pasinetti and call this commodity gold, with the assumption that a units of labour produce one unit of gold. Then the price of gold is $p_2 = wa(1 + r) = 1.1a$. In the pre-innovation economy as well as in the transition economy the landlords obtain a total rent $R = 260p_1 + 500p_2 = 850 + 250 = 1100$. As a consequence, the amount of gold produced is $1000/a$ and employment in the gold sector equals 1000. In the post-innovation economy $R = 1100 + A$. Hence the employment in the gold sector is increased by $A/1.1$. Thus if $A \geq 8250$; then total employment is increased in the post-innovation economy.

Ricardo is very aware of the importance of expenditures of different classes:

> Independently of the consideration of the discovery and use of machinery, to which our attention has been just directed, the labouring class have no small interest in the manner in which the net income of the country is expended, although it should, in all cases, be expended for the gratification and enjoyments of those who are fairly entitled to it.
>
> (p. 392)

In particular, Ricardo considers the consumption of the services of 'menial servants' as the most advantageous for the working class (p. 393). Indeed, if consumption of landlords consists only in menial servants, then $A > 7500$ is enough to increase total employment in the post-innovation economy. Ricardo extends his analysis beyond private consumption to public consumption (pp. 393–394). Note that if the industrial commodity consumed by landlords (gold in Pasinetti's terminology) is produced by using labour and fixed capital, then producers of corn can partially move their capital from corn production on land of quality 3 to gold production. This is not possible when landlords consume a commodity produced by labour alone since if producers of corn partially moved their capital from corn production to gold production, then some fixed capital would not be used; accordingly, its price would fall.

3.5 The industry of the innovator

Ricardo argues that unemployment may also be generated by technical change in less specific cases and in particular if the innovation is introduced in an industry not producing corn; as an example, a clothier is mentioned.

> The case which I have supposed, is the most simple that I could select; but it would make no difference in the result, if we supposed that the machinery was applied to the trade of any manufacturer, — that of a clothier, for example, or of a cotton manufacturer.
>
> (pp. 390–391)

The cloth produced by the clothier is a luxury good,[5] consumed by landlords. Ricardo actually considers the cloth as consumed by capitalists as well:

> by whom would the cloth be demanded? By the farmers and the other producers of necessaries, who employed their capitals in producing

> these necessaries as a means of obtaining cloth: they gave corn and necessaries to the clothier for cloth, and he bestowed them on his workmen for the cloth which their work afforded him.
>
> (p. 391)

However, the exposition is easier to follow if only landlords consume cloth. Ricardo does not produce a proper numerical example despite maintaining that the example 'leads us to the same result; the demand for labour would diminish, and the commodities necessary to the support of labour would not be produced in the same abundance'. In the main example (i) in the transition the same amount of labour is employed, but less corn is produced; (ii) after the transition both a lower amount of labour is employed and less corn is produced. The difficulty now consists in the fact that cloth is consumed by landlords and demand by landlords in terms of corn is unchanged, unless rent is reduced, which can happen only if an inframarginal land becomes marginal; therefore if the price of cloth is reduced, demand by landlords in terms of cloth increases. In Ricardo's words, 'It may be said, however, that the demand for cloth would be as great as before' (p. 391). Therefore the production of the new machine can be obtained only by reducing the production of corn and, as a consequence, the amount of labour that can be employed in the post-innovation economy:

> farmers and others, who only produced necessaries as means to an end, could no longer obtain cloth by such an application of their capitals, and, therefore, they would either themselves employ their capitals in producing cloth, or would lend them to others, in order that the commodity really wanted might be furnished; and that for which no one had the means of paying, or for which there was no demand, might cease to be produced.

The input-output patterns of the example may be represented in Table 3.3. Before the introduction of the machine 1100 units of cloth are produced

Table 3.3 The input-output patterns of the second example

Processes	*Fixed capital*	*New machine*	*Labour*	*Land 1*	*Land 2*	*Land 3*	*Cloth*	*Fixed capital*	*New machine*
(7)	35		65				75	35	
(8)	$\frac{4004}{9}$		$\frac{7436}{9}$					$\frac{4004}{9}$	1
(9)	$\frac{8624}{9}$	1	$\frac{7436}{9}$				1100 + B	$\frac{8624}{9}$	1

with process (7) operated at the intensity 44/3 and they are exchanged with the corn received by the landlords for the use of their land:

$$\frac{1540}{3}r+\frac{2860}{3}(1+r)=260p_1+500p_2$$

Thus overall used fixed capital is 22540/3 and overall employed labour is 41860/3.

In the transition period the clothier operates both processes (7) and (8). This is so since if in the transition period the clothier produces only the new machine and then uses it in the following period to produce cloth, then the profit that is obtained in the transition period is not consumed by the clothier and therefore there is a sort of forced saving. It is not clear if Ricardo considered this fact. More precisely the clothier operates process (7) with intensity 88/45 and process (8) with intensity 1. As a consequence the farmer must reduce the production of corn on the marginal land in order to operate process (7) with intensity 572/45 (or to support someone else who does so). Of course we assume that the existing amount of marginal land is such that the reduction in corn production does not affect which quality of land is marginal: otherwise demand for cloth would also be reduced. Intensity of process (3) is reduced by 572/45 units and therefore the total product of corn is 45440/3, and the corn not consumed by capitalists is 13000. This means that in next period the labour that can be employed is 2860/3 units lower. Since the price of the new machine is 2860/3, the overall capital is unchanged.

After the introduction of the new machine, the price of cloth is reduced, the extraprofit (in terms of production prices) vanishes, and the normal rate of profits is determined in agriculture. Nevertheless, the economy has obtained a long-period position since

$$\frac{8624}{9}r+rp_M+\frac{7436}{9}(1+r)=260p_1+500p_2$$

The price of cloth p_2 is determined by the equation

$$\frac{8624}{9}(1+r)+p_M(1+r)+\frac{7436}{9}(1+r)=\frac{8624}{9}+p_M+(1100+B)\,p_2$$

where $B>0$ in order to have an extraprofit at the prices holding before the innovation. Employment in the transition year is obviously unchanged.

At the end of the transition period, cloth can be produced again by the clothier, but the corn produced in the transition period, which is less than that produced before, may be sufficient since after the transition period the clothier requires a lower amount of necessaries for his workmen. There is no doubt as to the conclusion: demand for labour is diminished and the commodities required to support labour are not produced in the same abundance.

In commenting upon the results of the second example Ricardo refers to them as valid in general, hence also when there is accumulation.

As a consequence, the working population could benefit, in the case of accumulation, 'from the stimulus to savings from revenue, which such an abundant net produce will afford' and 'from the low price of all articles of consumption on which their wages will be expended' (p. 392).

3.6 A further example: a historical case

Ricardo considers it appropriate to refer to a historical example: the substitution of the labour performed by horses for human labour.

> There is one other case that should be noticed of the possibility of an increase in the amount of the net revenue of a country, and even of its gross revenue, with a diminution of demand for labour, and that is, when the labour of horses is substituted for that of man. If I employed one hundred men on my farm, and if I found that the food bestowed on fifty of those men, could be diverted to the support of horses, and afford me a greater return of raw produce, after allowing for the interest of the capital which the purchase of the horses would absorb, it would be advantageous to me to substitute the horses for the men, and I should accordingly do so; but this would not be for the interest of the men, and unless the income I obtained, was so much increased as to enable me to employ the men as well as the horses, it is evident that the population would become redundant, and the labourers' condition would sink in the general scale.
>
> (p. 394)

Now Ricardo can take advantage of the historical facts. Here, instead of everlasting fixed capital, we still have fixed capital, but not everlasting, and we have also circulating capital that is not used for the employment of workers: fodder for the horses. Nevertheless the results are similar. But Ricardo knows that in this case employment actually decreased for a while, but new work opportunities were created, although not in agriculture and such opportunities were not a consequence of the substitution of horses for men.

> It is evident he could not, under any circumstances, be employed in agriculture; but if the produce of the land were increased by the substitution of horses for men, he might be employed in manufactures, or as a menial servant.
>
> (pp. 394–395)

This historical example is helpful in order to understand the role of the assumption of the stationary state. It sheds light on the phenomenon which Ricardo sought to analyse: in a growing economy the unemployment created by the introduction of machinery is absorbed by the growth of the economy, and the only adverse effect that can be detected is merely a temporary decline in growth and some unemployment that could be interpreted as frictional. Actually this example also shows that the introduction of the new method could result in unemployment of human labourers even if it increases the gross revenue. This is so since the new method includes circulating capital that is not used for the employment of workers (see Gehrke 2010, section 2).

3.7 'Machinery and labour are in constant competition'

There are two main points that Ricardo emphasises in the conclusion to chapter XXXI. The first concerns the competition between machinery and labour:

> With every increase of capital and population, food will generally rise, on account of its being more difficult to produce. The consequence of a rise of food will be a rise of wages, and every rise of wages will have a tendency to determine the saved capital in a greater proportion than before to the employment of machinery. Machinery and labour are in constant competition, and the former can frequently not be employed until labour rises.
>
> (p. 395)

Ricardo also provides a historical illustration:

> In America and many other countries, where the food of man is easily provided, there is not nearly such great temptation to employ machinery as in England, where food is high, and costs much labour for its production. The same cause that raises labour, does not raise the value of machines, and, therefore, with every augmentation of capital, a greater proportion of it is employed on machinery. The demand for labour will continue to increase with an increase of capital, but not in proportion to its increase; the ratio will necessarily be a diminishing ratio.
>
> (p. 395)

Even in a sentence in which Ricardo presents a condensed expression of his result, he is very cautious: machinery can *frequently* not be employed until labour rises. Ricardo's argument is based on examples: examples may prove that something could happen yet cannot prove that something will necessarily happen. Not all commentators of Ricardo's text have been so cautious. Many neo-classical authors have argued that Ricardo was actually advocating the idea of technical substitution between labour and machinery. However, examples showing the opposite trends are possible:

for instance, it is interesting to recall here a paper by Hagemann and Kurz (1976), in which two techniques are compared – one employs more roundabout capital than the other; nevertheless, there is a switch point in which at a higher wage rate the less roundabout method is chosen.

Ricardo is very clear on the fact that 'The statements which I have made will not, I hope, lead to the inference that machinery should not be encouraged' (p. 395). Ricardo provides two arguments. The first concerns the fact that improved machinery reduces the prices of commodities and therefore incomes estimated in commodities are higher: this increases savings and accumulation and also increases the demand for labour. The other argument concerns the fact that economies are open and therefore if one country discourages the use of machinery whereas others do not, then competition drives production from the country which discourages the use of machinery to the others and demand for labour would be even lower in that country: '[b]y investing part of a capital in improved machinery, there will be a diminution in the progressive demand for labour; by exporting it to another country, the demand will be wholly annihilated' since 'machinery cannot be worked without the assistance of men' (p. 397).

3.8 Concluding remarks

In this paper we analysed the examples provided in Chapter XXXI of Ricardo's *Principles*. We have reconstructed the examples that Ricardo formulated in the chapter in question and we restated them in terms of modern theory of production. The difficulty was to determine assumptions that Ricardo did not state explicitly. Ricardo made some assumptions to ensure that his argument would be crystal clear. Among these are the stationary state and hence the constancy of the rate of profits between the pre-innovation economy and the post-innovation economy. This condition can be easily obtained in two cases: when the innovation concerns a non-basic commodity and when it concerns an agricultural commodity. Yet the innovation changes neither the marginal land nor the technology used on the marginal land. Ricardo was conscious of these two facts and he seems to have used them in his examples. We also saw that Ricardo was cautious and never asserted that machinery necessarily reduces employment of labour. Indeed the reswitching debate provided examples in which there are two switch-points among two techniques, and whereas in one of them at a higher wage rate the more roundabout capital is chosen, in the other the opposite is observed.

Acknowledgments

We wish to thank, without implicating, Christian Gehrke and Heinz D. Kurz for useful talks and comments on previous versions of this paper. We also thank two anonymous referees for their very useful comments.

Notes

1 It is remarkable that Ricardo omitted to integrate the findings of the new chapter into his rent theory; see Gehrke (2015).
2 Note that the growth rate is unchanged also because it is assumed that landlords do not invest part of their income.
3 It may be thought that capital is 20,000 before the innovation, after the innovation, and during transition because the available amount of capital is given. But this is not so: capital is constant over time since the growth rate is nought, and this is so since the rate of profit is at the level of the stationary state.
4 Intensive rent is formalised in modern literature by the use, side by side, of two processes on homogeneous land. In order to obtain that both the rate of profit and the wage rate are unchanged, both processes need to be changed.
5 Some scholars (see for instance Morishima 1989; Gehrke 2010) consider cloth a necessary good consumed by workers. In this case, the whole model should be changed and the economy can be stationary in the post-innovation economy only in a switch-point so that innovation may be introduced or not. Gehrke justifies his opinion on a few references in Ricardo's *Works* (all outside Chapter XXXI of the *Principles*) to 'food and clothing' as the two main components entering into the workers' wage basket. But then he is obliged to contradict explicitly Ricardo's statement that 'demand for cloth would be [after innovation] as great as before' (p. 391). We thank Christian Gehrke for having provided us with an English version of his paper, published in Chinese.

References

Barkai, H. 1986. "Ricardo's Volte-Face on Machinery." *Journal of Political Economy* 94 (3/1): 595–613. doi:10.1086/261391.
Davis, J. B. 1989. "Distribution in Ricardo's Machinery Chapter." *History of Political Economy* 21 (3): 457–480. doi:10.1215/00182702-21-3-457.
Gehrke, C. 2003. "The Ricardo Effect: Its Meaning and Validity." *Economica* 70 (277): 143–158. doi:10.1111/1468-0335.t01-1-00275.
Gehrke, C. 2010. "Ricardo's Chapter 'On Machinery' and the Long-period Method." *Review of History of Economic Thought* 1 (1): 110–129 (in Chinese).
Gehrke, C. 2015. "Fixed Capital in Agriculture: Richard Jones's Critique of Ricardo's Theory of Rent." *Journal of the History of Economic Thought* 37: 411–430. doi:10.1017/S1053837215000243.
Hagemann, H., and H. D. Kurz. 1976. "The Return to the Same Truncation Period and Reswitching of Techniques in Neo-Austrian and More General Models." *Kyklos* 29 (4): 678–708. doi:10.1111/j.1467-6435.1976.tb01995.x.
Hayek, F. A. 1931. *Prices and Production*. London: George Routledge & Sons.
Hayek, F. A. 1942. "The Ricardo Effect." *Economica* 9: 127–152.
Hayek, F. A. 1969. "Three Elucidations of the Ricardo Effect." *Journal of Political Economy* 77: 274–285. doi:10.1086/259514.
Hicks, J. R. 1969. *A Theory of Economic History*. Oxford: OUP.
Hollander, S. 1971. "The Development of Ricardo's Position on Machinery." *History of Political Economy* 3 (1): 105–135. doi:10.1215/00182702-3-1-105.
Jeck, A., and H. D. Kurz. 1983. "David Ricardo: Ansichten zur Maschinerie." In *Technischer Fortschritt und Arbeitslosigkeit*, edited by H. Hagemann and P. Kalmbach, 38–166. Frankfurt am Main: Campus.

Kaldor, N. 1932. "A Case against Technical Progress?" *Economica* 12: 180–196. doi:10.2307/2549267.

Kurz, H. D. 1984. "Ricardo and Lowe on Machinery." *Eastern Economic Journal* 10 (2): 211–229.

Kurz, H. D. 2010. "Technical Progress, Capital Accumulation and Income Distribution in Classical Economics: Adam Smith, David Ricardo and Karl Marx." *European Journal of History of Economic Thought* 17 (5): 1183–1222. doi:10.1080/09672567.2010.522242.

Morishima, M. 1989. *Ricardo's Economics. A General Equilibrium Theory of Distribution and Growth.* Cambridge: Cambridge University Press.

Negishi, T. 1990. "Ricardo and Morishima on Machinery." *Journal of the History of Economic Thought* 12 (2): 146–161. doi:10.1017/S105383720000170X.

Pasinetti, L. L. 1960. "A Mathematical Formulation of the Ricardian System." *Review of Economic Studies* 27: 78–98. doi:10.2307/2296129.

Ricardo, D. 1951 ssq. *The Works and Correspondence of David Ricardo, 11 volumes,* Edited by P. Sraffa in Collaboration with M. H. Dobb. Cambridge: CUP.

Salvadori, N., and I. Steedman. 1988. "No Reswitching? No Switching!" *Cambridge Journal of Economics* 12 (4): 481–486. doi:10.1093/oxfordjournals.cje.a035072.

Samuelson, P. A. 1988. "Mathematical Vindication of Ricardo on Machinery." *Journal of Political Economy* 96 (2): 274–282. doi:10.1086/261536.

Samuelson, P. A. 1989. "Ricardo Was Right!" *Scandinavian Journal of Economics* 91 (1): 47–62. doi:10.2307/3440162.

Samuelson, P. A. 1994. "The Classical Classical Fallacy." *Journal of Economic Literature* 32 (2): 620–639.

Stigler, G. J. 1952. "The Ricardian Theory of Value and Distribution." *Journal of Political Economy* 60 (3): 187–207. doi:10.1086/257208.

Whewell, W. 1831. "Mathematical Exposition of Some of the Leading Doctrines in Mr. Ricardo's 'Principles of Political Economy and Taxation'." In *Transactions of the Cambridge Philosophical Society*, 1–44. Cambridge: University Press.

Wicksell, K. 1981. "Ricardo on Machinery and the Present Unemployment." *Economic Journal* 91: 200–205.

4 Mark Blaug revisited

A rebel with many causes

Neri Salvadori and Rodolfo Signorino

Mark Blaug passed away on 18 November, 2011. To honor his memory, two events were held in March 2012 – a Memorial Conference at the Erasmus Institute for Philosophy and Economics, Rotterdam (NL) and a seminar hosted by the Scottish Centre for Economic Methodology at the University of Glasgow (UK). Marcel Boumans and Matthias Klaes (2013) edited a book that contains a collection of papers given at these two events and includes some further papers submitted by people who were not able to attend the meetings 'at such short notice' (p. 5; all references to isolated pages are to the book edited by Boumans and Klaes 2013). In addition, the book carries a Foreword by Alan Peacock and consists of two parts: Part I has four chapters – written by John Maloney, Ruth Towse, Bruce Caldwell, and Thomas Mayer – devoted to personal appreciations and memoirs of Blaug; Part II has 12 chapters – written by Richard G. Lipsey, David Laidler, Geoffrey M. Hodgson, Jack Vromen, Harro Maas, Roger E. Backhouse, John B. Davis, Marcel Baumans, Andrea Salanti, Victor Ginsburgh, Christian Handke and Erwin Dekker, and D. Wade Hands – that discuss some of Blaug's favorite topics and put forward critical assessments of his specific contributions to the issues at hand. An extensive bibliography of Blaug's publications and online sources ranging through 29 pages rounds off the book. (The interested reader may also refer to Backhouse's 2012 *HOPE* obituary and the 2013 *EJPE – Erasmus Journal for Philosophy and Economics* – winter special issue for further contributions on Blaug's biography and scholarly achievements.) The title of the book is a paraphrase of the title of a paper by Blaug himself (Blaug 2000) on Henry George.

When the book edited by Boumans and Klaes (2013) was published, we were approached by Maria Pia Paganelli, the Book Review Editor of the *Journal of the History of Economic Thought*, to write a review of it. We already had the opportunity to enter into exchanges with Blaug (Blaug 1999, 2002a, 2003a, 2009; Kurz and Salvadori 2002, 2011; Signorino 2003a and 2003b). Unfortunately, these exchanges were unproductive since both Blaug's and our positions did not get any closer. Thus, for us to review a book celebrating Blaug was not 'business as usual'. Yet, we decided to take up the challenge and wrote a review article (Salvadori and Signorino 2015). In this chapter we dare to take up a tougher challenge: by making

DOI: 10.4324/9781003138709-5

use of all the material elaborated at that time and by providing some further arguments, we give a fresh assessment of all these debates. In particular, to clarify Blaug's thought as well as Sraffa's though on the relationship between rational and historical reconstructions we add a new section devoted to the analysis of some of Sraffa's unpublished documents concerning the reconstruction of Classical economics.[1]

4.1 Personal appreciations

No doubt, those who have already gone through Blaug's autobiography (Blaug 1994) will appreciate the chapters in the first part of the book (pp. 11–28) edited by Boumans and Klaes (2013). Conversely, readers of these biographical chapters will be enticed to get acquainted with Blaug (1994). Particularly touching are the personal memoirs by his wife, Ruth Towse, herself a distinguished cultural economist, where we discover not only that Blaug was fond of 'jazzy' titles (p. 14), but also that he produced his works 'as an oyster produces pearls – out of sheer irritation'. This was true 'especially in his later years' (ibid.).

4.2 Mark Blaug's ideas in retrospect

Readers browsing the many and different topics addressed by the authors of the chapters of Part II of Boumans and Klaes (2013) may get a vivid impression of the breadth of Blaug's interests and scholarship, such as his view of the controversial nature of the quantity theory of money, the notion of competition as an evolutionary process and not as an equilibrium end-state, his diagnosis of the unhealthy status of much of contemporary economics, the role and prospects of the history of economic thought sub-discipline within the broader field of economic research, the problematic coexistence of rational and historical reconstructions of past economics, the trade-off between rigour and relevance within contemporary economic theory, the assessment of Sraffian economics, the role of Popper and Lakatos's philosophies of science in the methodological debate in economics, Baumol and Bowen's cost disease, the subsidisation of performing arts, and the economic analysis of cultural policy. Moreover, as a fitting tribute to the friend and the scholar, the authors developed their chapters *as if* they were actually discussing the topic with Blaug and acknowledged that in all likelihood he would have had the last word. A fitting example of this common attitude is Chapter 6 (pp. 31–62) by Richard Lipsey. Lipsey discusses a number of issues within modern economics, many of which were also addressed by Blaug himself. Some of these issues are purely methodological (such as falsifiability, formalism, the debate concerning testing-also-the-assumptions versus testing-only-the-predictions of a given theory); others are more normative-oriented (such as the intuition-based versus the theory-based debate concerning policy advice);

finally, others are strictly theoretical such as the role of the price system, the notion of competition, technological change, risk and uncertainty, growth, Keynesian (old and new) versus New Classical macroeconomics, and so on and so forth.

Blaug was a well-recognised historian and methodologist of economics. Not surprisingly, seven out of 12 chapters of Part II of Boumans and Klaes (2013) are devoted to historiographical and methodological matters and at least four of them are devoted to the topic of rational and historical reconstructions and the (alleged) trade-off between rigour and relevance. In what follows we focus on these items – along the way, we also take the opportunity to sketch some arguments we would have wished to discuss with Mark.

4.3 Rational versus historical reconstructions

Chapter 10, by Harro Maas (pp. 125–145), provides an analysis of the evolution of Blaug's thought concerning the debate on absolutism versus relativism in the writing of the history of economic thought, to make use of Blaug's juvenile dichotomy, or rational versus historical reconstructions, as he preferred to express himself at a later age. At the start of his career as an historian of economic thought, Blaug was a staunch supporter of the absolutist point of view: he claimed that past economics had to be consistently reconstructed *and* evaluated by means of the analytical concepts and vocabulary provided by modern economics. Such a historiographical project was straightforwardly announced in the very opening sentence of the Introduction of *Economic Theory in Retrospect*, a book whose title contains a Manifesto:

> This is a critical study of the theories of the past; it concentrates on the theoretical analysis of leading economists, neglecting their lives, their own intellectual development, their precursors, and their propagators. Criticism implies standards of judgment, and my standards are those of modern economic theory.
>
> (Blaug 1962 [1985], p. 1)

As is well known, in his later contributions Blaug drastically changed his mind on the comparative worth of rational and historical reconstructions of past economics:

> Although I have been guilty myself of the very sin I have just deplored, I have come to the conclusion that the *only* approach to the history of economic thought that respects the unique nature of the subject material, rather than just turning it into grist for the use of modern analytical techniques, is to labor historical reconstructions, however difficult they are.
>
> (Blaug 2001, p. 152, emphasis added)

The 'sin' Blaug refers to is the attempt by

> some historians of economic thought to sell the subject to their departmental colleagues by reducing history of economic thought to the history of economic analysis, and then by dressing up past ideas in modern garb, often in the form of mathematical models that look just like something that might have appeared in the latest issue of the *American Economic Review* or the *Journal of Political Economy.*

The sin has a proper name: 'I call these "rational reconstructions"' (Blaug 2001, p. 150).

How to explain such a radical change of perspective? Alan Peacock remarks in his Foreword (pp. viii–ix) that Blaug the historian of economics was 'not simply hopeful that appreciation of scholarship encourages us in good habits of reasoning' (p. viii): Blaug's aim also was 'to convince us that the knowledge of the history of economic ideas is a necessary element in the training of an economist' though 'he knew that success in his mission was far from guaranteed' (ibid.). Evidence to support Peacock's guess on Blaug's hidden motives when, in his younger years, he endorsed rational over historical reconstructions may easily be found in Blaug's 1994 intellectual autobiography. To explain his early historiographical choice, Blaug pointed to the necessity of selling the commodity labelled history of economic thought to a set of highly reluctant buyers:

> The history of economic thought was a compulsory graduate course in the 1950s but these students were typical American graduate students: they wanted to learn the tools and techniques of modern economics and to hell with such scholarly subjects as economic history and the history of economic thought. I was aware from the moment the course began that I had to sell the history of economics as somehow relevant to these young Turks. No wonder then that I taught the subject by emphasizing the filiation of purely analytical concepts and continually emphasizing the modernity, and sometimes lack of modernity, of the ideas of the past.
>
> (Blaug 1994, p. 18)

As time went by, Blaug became increasingly aware that, though his *Economic Theory in Retrospect* was widely sold and studied, even more than Schumpeter's 1954 classic *History of Economic Analysis* at least by the students and scholars attending the libraries of Harvard and MIT (Chapter 10, p. 127), the sub-discipline of the history of economic thought had fallen more and more outside the canon of the average economist's education (Blaug 2001). The average PhD student in economics, while heavily trained in subjects such as advanced econometrics or mathematics, is offered negligible (if any) training in the history of economic thought. Why? Whig historiography is among the most likely candidates to the role of villain of the story. If dead economists produced wrong ideas, then the study of past economics is inevitably a veritable waste of time. Similarly, if and when dead economists produced right ideas, these ideas are but a primitive and imperfect version of the ideas currently employed by living economists: again, why bother to study them? George Stigler, Blaug's doctoral supervisor, has put the point harshly but effectively:

> The young theorist, working with an increasingly formal, abstract, and systematic corpus of knowledge, will seldom find it necessary to consult even a late-nineteenth-century economist. He will assume, just as the mathematician or chemist assumes, that all that is useful and valid in earlier work is present – in purer and more elegant form – in the modern theory. Indeed, the young economist will increasingly share the view of more advanced formal sciences that the history of the discipline is best left to those underendowed for fully professional work at the modern level.
>
> (Stigler 1969, pp. 217–218)

To rescue the history of economic thought from the charge of being concerned with morbid antiquarianism and to vindicate the scientific status of professional historians of economic thought, the mature Blaug has been led to reconsider his early historiographical views and to downgrade rational reconstructions of past economics. But, how on earth could Blaug possibly persuade his fellow-economists that the study of the history of economic thought contributes (algebraic) value-added to the collective house of economic knowledge, to paraphrase Samuelson (1974)? A brilliant answer to such a question is provided by John Davis. In Chapter 12 (pp. 159–176), he convincingly links Blaug's changing attitude as concerns the relative worth of historical and rational reconstructions with the evolution of his thought on the issue of the growth of knowledge in economics. Davis claims that Blaug

> turned economists' own market theory tools against them in using an economics of scientific knowledge approach to argue that the 'marketplace of ideas' was neither competitive nor efficient in regard to the production of economic knowledge. From this he was able to argue that the way in which economics developed as a science inevitably involved loss of content, thus undermining the steady progress idea associated with the Whig view, and allowing him to define a role for the history of economic thought in advancing scientific knowledge
>
> (p. 160)

Davis's reconstruction of Blaug's mature thought on the issue of rational and historical reconstructions gives us the opportunity to sketch an argument we dare to think Blaug would have judged worth of his attention (if not of his approval). In our view, rational reconstructions may be cleansed of Whig incrustations just thanks to an elaboration of Blaug's 'loss of content' argument: indeed, one of the main shortcomings of Whig historiography is its strong teleological flavor, that is, the (often implicit) belief that the history of science reveals an in-built and, in the long-run, irresistible drive toward progress (Mayr 1990). By contrast, the actual progress of economic knowledge is based on an ongoing process of selection by the ever-changing historical communities of practising economists concerning which lines of inquiry to pursue and develop and which to neglect and abandon. Ultimately, the time and financial/intellectual resources constraints are always binding! At this juncture, the crucial question is: how to effectively rescue from oblivion those pieces of valuable economic analysis which happened to be neglected by the current generation of economists mostly because, for a variety of reasons, they have been neglected, at their turn, by the previous generations of economists? Our answer to this question is that, as the tools of economic analysis continuously develop, the scope for such rescue operations improves. Let us elaborate on this point a little further. As epigraph to his *Logik der Forschung* (1934), Karl Popper, Blaug's favorite philosopher of science, quoted Novalis's dictum 'Hypotheses are nets: only he who casts will catch'. Seen in this light, scientists are a kind of hunters, empirical regularities their target preys and theories their weapons. Some decades later, in an oft-quoted passage, Sir John Hicks adopted a similar point of view on the relationship between facts and theories in the realm of science:

> Our theories, regarded as tools of analysis, are blinkers...Or it may be politer to say that they are rays of light, which illuminate a part of the target, leaving the rest in darkness. As we use them, we avert our eyes from things which may be relevant, in order that we should see more clearly what we do see. It is entirely proper that we should do this, since otherwise we should see very little. But it is obvious that a theory which is to perform this function satisfactorily must be well chosen; otherwise it will illuminate the wrong things.
>
> (Hicks 1976 [1983], pp. 4–5)

Mutatis mutandis, contemporary analytical tools, and concepts may help present-day historians to detect an analytical argument actually existing within the historical texts under scrutiny but which would have likely escaped their attention if they would have not employed (some of) the analytical categories elaborated by later economists. From this perspective, we fully agree with what the young Blaug wrote in the Preface to the first edition of *Economic Theory in Retrospect*:

> Students are often told of the inspiration to be derived from the study of the history of economics. They are not so often reminded of the inspiration which the historian of economic thought derives from a

> study of contemporary economic theory. *In truth, one should no more study modern price theory without knowing Adam Smith than one should read Adam Smith without having learned modern price theory.* There is a mutual interaction between past and present economic thinking for, whether we set it down in so many words or not, the history of economic thought is being rewritten every generation.
>
> (Blaug 1962 [1985], p. vii, emphasis added)

Rational reconstructions of past economics by means of the contemporary one are, by their very nature, speculative *and* selective. The crucial question is whether a given rational reconstruction turns out to be too speculative and selective or even positively misleading, a historical travesty, to make use of one of Blaug's expressions. The danger of 'creating' rather than 'reconstructing' the historical texts cannot be lightly dismissed. Moreover, it cannot be ruled out that basically the same outcomes may be achieved through historical reconstructions in Blaug's sense, that is, 'attempts to give an account of past thinkers' system of thought "in their own terms", that is, in terms these thinkers would have accepted as a correct description of what they had done' (Blaug 1990, p. 28). (Yet, we ought not to forget that Blaug's definition of historical reconstructions, if interpreted *stricto sensu*, involves a counterfactual that cannot be falsified nor, obviously, verified.) To be sure, rational reconstructions of past economics by means of contemporary analytical categories are far from being an unmixed good. Yet, occasionally they may display valuable comparative advantages over other tools of historical inquiry. After all, to kill a bird it takes either a stone or a bow and an arrow or … a precision rifle!

4.4 Blaug versus Sraffa's 1960 book

Chapter 11 (pp. 146–158), by Roger Backhouse, attempts a reconstruction of the evolution of Blaug's views on Sraffa's 1960 book, *Production of Commodities*, and the ensuing, so-called, Sraffian economics and Sraffian interpretation of Classical economics. Backhouse tries to elucidate the reasons why 'to the end of his life, Mark Blaug was *obsessed* with Sraffian economics' (p. 146, emphasis added). Backhouse observes that Blaug's response to Sraffa's 1960 book was 'slow' (p. 147). While there is no mention of *Production of Commodities* in the main text of the first two editions of *Economic Theory in Retrospect*, subsequently Blaug produced an extensive analysis of Sraffa' s contribution in the pamphlet *The Cambridge Revolution: Success and Failure*, published in 1974 and revised in 1975 (though Backhouse refers only to the first edition). This pamphlet is plagued by a number of misunderstandings of Sraffa's slim book, many, but not all, of them corrected in the second edition (see Steedman 1995). In his 2012 Obituary, Backhouse describes Blaug as a scholar who loved to get the big picture but was both impatient with details and happy to be controversial

(Backhouse 2012, p. 569). Similarly, Boumans and Klaes recollect in their introduction (pp. 1–8) that Blaug 'was not only a 'voracious' reader, but [he] also "wrote faster than God could read"' (p. 2) and, as a consequence, he 'was impatient about minor details' (p. 4) and even he 'was prepared to exaggerate when this was necessary to make a point effectively' (ibid.). One of these obvious mistakes is also referred to by Backhouse (though he forgets to inform his readers that it is actually an overstatement, to say the least) and concerns the idea that the overriding, if not exclusive, aim of Sraffa's book was to solve a technical problem (the invariable measure of value) Ricardo unsuccessfully wrestled with till his untimely death. If this had actually been Sraffa's basic aim, the wide interest that Sraffa's 1960 book aroused would hardly be understandable. On the contrary, the Standard commodity, i.e., what is considered to be the solution to the aforementioned problem, is an argument that could entirely be dispensed with and replaced by the Perron-Frobenius Theorem. Indeed, the proofs concerning the Standard commodity in *Production of Commodities* are substantially proofs of parts of that theorem, a theorem that Sraffa did not know and that his 'mathematical friends' never mentioned to him – see Kurz and Salvadori (1993, 2000).

Backhouse analyses Blaug's attitude towards the Sraffian interpretation of Ricardo to reach a conjectural interpretation of Blaug's 'obsession' in truly Freudian terms: 'he was still trying to defend his rejection of Marxist theory, for if the Sraffians were right, there might be more to the "surplus" approach than he had admitted' (p. 157). Be that what it may, Blaug's steadily growing hostility towards Sraffa's contribution is a kind of corollary, or inevitable byproduct, of his entrenched belief that the work done by Sraffa and the so-called Sraffians ultimately turns out to be but a *species* of a larger *genus*, that of general equilibrium theory (see Blaug 2002b, 2009).

4.5 Rigour versus relevance

A fruitful starting point is what he labelled as the formalist revolution of the 1950s. According to Blaug, such a formalist turn entailed for economic science a trade-off between rigour and relevance: for Blaug, empirical relevance has been sacrificed on the altar of formal rigour and, as a consequence, manifold currents of the economic literature have been transformed into an apparently endless collection of intellectual games played for their own sake (Blaug 2002c, 2003b; see also Chapter 8, pp. 78–97, by Geoffrey Hodgson on Blaug's diagnosis of current economics as a 'sick' discipline). Blaug's hostility towards 'empty formalism' or 'armchair theorizing' led him to pass (mostly negative) judgments on a great number of contemporary research topics: not only general equilibrium theory and Sraffian economics, but also welfare economics, Coasian economics, game theory, mechanism design theory, new classical macroeconomics, and real business cycle theory, to mention just a few. Taking Blaug's 2009 analysis of contemporary economics at face value, one is led to conclude that for Blaug only social choice theory and its crown jewel, Arrow's impossibility theorem, pass both tests, that of formal rigour and that of empirical relevance. In particular, game theory was a red rag to him – as noted by Jack Vromen (Chapter 9, pp. 98–124), Blaug considered evolutionary economics 'as one of the most hopeful and fruitful developments in economics' (p. 98). Yet, he had serious misgivings as concerns evolutionary game-theoretic analyses: Vromen explains Blaug's dismissive attitude by his 'dislike of game theory *tout court*', a dislike 'clearly related to his scathing critique of the dominance of "ugly" formalism in mainstream economics' (ibid.).

Indeed, the very notion underlying Blaug's critical assessment of contemporary economics, i.e., there exists in economics a broad spectrum between two rival goals labelled rigour and relevance, is controversial. To take an example from outside economics: practising physicists do not consider mathematical physics, theoretical physics, and experimental physics as rival disciplines ranging from the most rigorous to the most relevant. Rather, they consider them as complementary disciplines, each with its own canon of rigour *and* relevance. Hence, regardless of one's own personal sympathy with Blaug's indictment of formalism in contemporary economics, the fact remains, as noted by Andrea Salanti (Chapter 14, pp. 191–207), that

> it is not enough to point out the irrelevance of any theory with no empirical sound implications or at least potentially falsifiable consequences, because it would be all too easy for opponents to raise objections about Popperian falsificationism, mainly on the basis that a strict application of such criteria either would lead us to discard a too huge amount of current economic theory, or would leave unanswered the question of the multiplicity of theoretical approaches in economics embedded in so many different strand of heterodoxy.
>
> (p. 202)

Similarly, Marcel Boumans (Chapter 13, pp. 177–190) acknowledges that 'to say that a theory should be falsifiable is simply too vague to understand different practices' (p. 188). Boumans's chapter is indeed a polite and friendly criticism of Blaug's view that 'relevance means having empirical content and being capable of answering any practical question, whereas rigor is taken as a synonym of irrelevance, associated with empty formalism' (p. 177).

4.6 Rational versus historical reconstructions: a view from Sraffa Archive[2]

We regret that Blaug's 1999 and 2009 harsh criticism of Sraffian historiography is based on published contributions only. Blaug never took the opportunity to confront his views with Sraffa's unpublished papers kept at the Wren Library of Trinity College, Cambridge. *Inter alia*, these manuscripts provide quite a few interesting materials for scholars interested in developing a rational reconstruction of Sraffa's research program in those crucial years, the late 1920s, when he was engaged in a two-pronged intellectual effort, to elaborate an original economic theory and to propose an interpretation of Classical economics different from that then dominant one, i.e., the Marshallian one. Here we make use of this documental evidence to sketch what we hope may be considered as an illuminating historical reconstruction in Blaug's sense of the expression, i.e., an attempt to recover the ideas of a past thinker, Sraffa, in terms that he would have recognised as a more or less faithful description of what he had set out to do. In particular, we refer to the folder D3/12/4 dated November 1927 and entitled 'Notes, essentially preparations for Lectures 1928–31'. In what follows we focus on two documents. The first document is entitled 'Principio' [Inception *NS&RS*]:

> I shall begin by giving a short "estratto" [extract *NS&RS*] of what I believe is the essence of the classical theories of value, i.e. of those which include W. Petty, Cantillon, Physiocrats, A. Smith, Ricardo + Marx. This is not the theory of anyone of them, but an extract of what I think is common to them. I state it of course not in their own words, but in modern terminology and it will be useful when we proceed to examine their theories to understand their portata [reach *NS&RS*] from the point of view of our present inquiry. It will be a sort of "frame", a machine, into which to fit their own statements in a homogeneous pattern, so as to be able to find what is common in them and what is the difference with the later theories. Then I shall go over these theories very cursorily, dealing with them not at all exhaustively but examining only those points which are relevant to my present purpose.
> (D3/12/4: 12.recto)

In this document Sraffa made clear two points. First, Sraffa acknowledged that (i) he is focusing on a well-defined subset of Classical economics, i.e., the theory of value and distribution; (ii) within such subset, he is selecting and isolating only the analytical elements common to the Classical authors under scrutiny; (iii) his historiographical inquiry is functional to the development of his own analytical contribution. Blaug dubbed Sraffian historiography as 'an amazingly narrow interpretation that omits some of the most exciting and indeed fruitful elements of the classical authors' (Blaug 1999, p. 215). If violation of the requirement to tell the whole truth implies saying a falsehood, the above passage shows that Sraffa's one was a 'strategic falsehood'.[3]

Second, Sraffa pointed out that he is going to build his 'frame' by means of what appears to be a four-step strategy: the first step is the isolation of a few analytical elements of Classical economics; the second step is the fitting of the isolated analytical elements of Classical economics into a consistent and homogeneous theory; the third step is the translation of Classical language into modern one; the fourth and final step is the comparison between the reconstructed Classical theory and the subsequent neo-classical theory. Blaug wrote that the Sraffian interpretation of Classical economics requires that

> We assume that perfect truth is found in *Production of Commodities,* and then we read backward, finding Sraffa in much of Ricardo and Max, although much less in Smith and Mill, and forget about almost everything else in classical economics because it will not fit the Procrustean bed of the interpretation (ibid.).

The above passage shows that no *a priori* assumption of perfect truth is required or involved in the Sraffian interpretation of Classical economics. If by 'perfect truth' Blaug meant 'the whole truth and nothing but the truth', Sraffa was perfectly aware that he was violating the 'whole truth' requirement; but he thought that such violation was, so to speak, the analytical price to pay for the sake of a meaningful comparison between two different analytical objects, the Classical and the neo-classical theory of value and distribution.[4]

The second document we discuss is entitled 'Metaphysics' (D3/12/4:14 recto – 17 recto). In this document we locate the rational foundation for the four-step strategy underlying Sraffa's historiography we have outlined above. Sraffa claims that 'The relations between things obviously do'nt [*sic*] exist, they are merely a creation of our minds' (D3/12/4:14.verso). Hence, an analysis of the mechanisms through which human minds create theories to understand reality cannot be ignored. Economists living in different historical periods have produced their theories by means of different frames and have expressed them in different terminologies. These differences may prove a formidable barrier to comprehension. In the words of Sraffa, 'It is terrific to contemplate the abysmal gulf of incomprehension that has opened itself between us and the classical economists' (D3/12/4:14. recto). For Sraffa, though the Classical economists 'said things which were perfectly true even according to our standards of truth' and 'expressed them very clearly in terse and unambiguous language'; modern economists are unable to 'understand a word or what they said' (ibid.). Sraffa's explanation for this lack of understanding is the role played by what Sraffa calls 'metaphysics' present within the theories, models, arguments, etc. set forth by economists living in different historical periods.

> [B]y metaphysics here I mean, I suppose, the emotions that are associated with our terminology and frames (schemi mentali) [mental patterns *NS&RS*] - that is, what is absolutely necessary to make the theory living (lebendig [alive *NS&RS*]) capable of assimilation and at

> all intelligible. If this is true, it is an exceptional example of how far a difference in metaphysics can make to us absolutely unintelligible an otherwise perfectly sound theory … If this is true it also shows … how little our metaphysics affect the truth of our conclusions, and how the same truths can be expressed in two widely divergent forms. Our metaphysics is in fact embodied in our technique; the danger lies in this, that when we have succeeded in thoroughly mastering a technique, we are very liable to be mastered by her.
>
> (D3/12/4:15.recto)

> Still more terrific. In the middle of the 19th century a man succeeds, either by accident or by superhuman effort, in getting again hold of the classical theory: he improves it, and draws its practical consequences from it.
>
> (D3/12/4:17.recto)[5]

For Sraffa the word 'metaphysics' does not concern an alleged property of the object of study, its existence or non-existence, but rather a property of the epistemic structure, 'schemi mentali' by the economist/observer. From our perspective, the main implication of Sraffa's thesis is that modern neo-classical economists can understand reality as well as the theory produced by past economists only through their mental schemes, analytical techniques, and language to which they are accustomed. Accordingly, their assessment is conditioned by their mental schemes, they are mastered by their technique. We dare to claim that no less than a 'superhuman effort', to make use of Sraffa's own expression, is required to free oneself from her own mental schemes to adopt the mental schemes of past economists.

The understanding of Classical theory of value and distribution therefore passes through a change of metaphysics and a translation of language. As the famous Neapolitan gesture by Sraffa demonstrated to an astonished Wittgenstein, different people play different *linguistic games*. In the absence of such a translation, neo-classical economists are led to understand in the only way that their mental schemes, their analytical technique, and their language allow them to understand theories elaborated within a radically different mental scheme, analytical technique, and language.

To resume a distinction dear to Blaug between historical reconstruction and rational reconstruction Sraffa has consciously chosen to elaborate a rational reconstruction and a language translation of a well-defined portion of Classical economics because he thought that any attempt to propose a historical reconstruction of the totality of classical theory would be doomed to failure, to misunderstanding, precisely because of the problems of metaphysics (in the sense of Sraffa) highlighted above. The Marshallian interpretation of Ricardo is the most eloquent example of the fact that without a prior rational reconstruction of Ricardo's economics the historical reconstruction may result in Whig historiography, i.e., the attempt to show the superiority of present doctrines over past ones. Our main contention is that Blaug's thesis, rational reconstructions are isomorphic to Whig historiography, turns out to border with the opposite of truth: historical reconstructions when they are conducted in the absence of a full awareness of the different metaphysics are very likely to generate Whig results.

4.7 Conclusion

Blaug was a fierce combatant and relished intellectual disputes. He changed his mind several times, but he never tried to hide this fact. He liked frank discussions of his hits and misses and we venture to say that he would have enjoyed discussing the arguments developed in this chapter (as well as in the book edited by Boumans and Klaes 2013). Blaug championed arguments that are starkly different from ours. In particular, we have tried to explain why Sraffa's historiography should be acquitted from any charge of Whiggism. By contrast, Sraffa's manuscripts show that Sraffa had a sophisticated metatheory as concerns the elaboration of historical accounts of past economics. His historiographical work exemplifies that, as Lakatos put it, though 'the history of science is always richer than its rational reconstruction', yet 'the most important problems of external history are defined by internal history' (Lakatos 1971, p. 105).

Notes

1 Sraffa's manuscripts are kept at the Wren Library of the Trinity College (Cambridge, UK). Interested readers may freely consult Sraffa Archive online at https://janus.lib.cam.ac.uk/db/node.xsp?id=EAD%2FGBR%2F0016%2FSRAFFA.
2 The content of this section was not included in Salvadori and Signorino (2015).
3 We use this expression in Mäki's sense. According to Mäki, 'idealizations are not just false, but deliberately so, associated with *an awareness of their falsity.* Their falsehood is obvious, and it is accepted for a purpose. Idealizations are strategic falsehoods, deliberately employed by modelers to achieve their goals' (Mäki 2020, p. 218, Mäki's emphasis).
4 On the distinction between 'the whole truth' and 'nothing but the truth' see Mäki (1992, pp. 341–342), who *inter alia,* clarifies how an isolative theory inevitably violates several kinds of truth.
5 Kurz (2021, p. 186) claims that for Sraffa the man who succeeded to get again hold of Classical economics was Marx. Though Sraffa did not explicitly mention the name of Marx in the paragraph quoted in the text, we fully agree with this interpretation. Kurz (2021) provides a comparison between Pareto and Sraffa on the issue of the role played by 'metaphysics' within economics.

References

Backhouse, Roger E. (2012). Mark Blaug, 1927–2011. *History of Political Economy,* 44 (4), pp. 567–582.

Blaug, M. (1962 [1985]). *Economic Theory in Retrospect.* 4th edition. Cambridge: Cambridge University Press.

Blaug, M. (1974 [1975]). *The Cambridge Revolution, Success or Failure? A Critical Analysis of Cambridge Theories of Value and Distribution*. 2nd edition. London: Institute of Economic Affairs.

Blaug, M. (1990). On the Historiography of Economics. *Journal of the History of Economic Thought*, 12 (1), pp. 27–37.

Blaug, M. (1994). Not Only an Economist –Autobiographical Reflections of a Historian of Economic Thought. *The American Economist*, 38 (2), pp. 12–27.

Blaug, M. (1999). Misunderstanding Classical Economics: The Sraffian Interpretation of the Surplus Approach. *History of Political Economy*, 31 (2), pp. 213–236.

Blaug, M. (2000). Henry George: Rebel with a Cause. *The European Journal of the History of Economic Thought*, 7 (2), pp. 270–288.

Blaug, M. (2001). No History of Ideas, Please, We're Economists. *Journal of Economic Perspectives*, 15 (1), pp. 145–164.

Blaug, M. (2002a). Kurz and Salvadori on the Sraffian Interpretation of the Surplus Approach. *History of Political Economy*, 34 (1), pp. 237–240.

Blaug, M. (2002b). Is there Really Progress in Economics?, in S. Boehm, C. Gehrke, Heinz D. Kurz and R. Sturn (eds). *Is There Progress in Economics? Knowledge, Truth and the History of Economic Thought*. Cheltenham, UK and Northampton, MA. Edward Elgar, pp. 21–41.

Blaug, M. (2002c). Ugly Currents in Modern Economics, in Mäki, U. (ed.). *Fact and Fiction in Economics: Models, Realism, and Social Construction*. Cambridge: Cambridge University Press, pp. 35–56.

Blaug, M. (2003a). Rational vs Historical Reconstruction: A Counter-Note on Signorino's Note on Blaug. *The European Journal of the History of Economic Thought*, 10 (4), pp. 607–608.

Blaug, M. (2003b). The Formalist Revolution of the 1950s. *Journal of the History of Economic Thought*, 25 (2), pp. 145–156.

Blaug, M. (2009). The Trade-Off between Rigor and Relevance: Sraffian Economics as a Case in Point. *History of Political Economy*, 41 (2), pp. 219–247.

Boumans, M. and M. Klaes (eds) (2013). *Mark Blaug: Rebel with Many Causes*. Cheltenham, UK and Northampton, MA: Edward Elgar, pp. ix + 302.

Hicks, John R. (1976 [1983]). "Revolutions" in Economics, Reprinted in *Classics and Moderns*, Vol. III of *Collected Essays in Economic Theory*. Cambridge, MA: Harvard University Press.

Kurz, Heinz D. (2021). 'Superhuman efforts' and the Theory of Value and Distribution. Sraffa on Pareto, in Deepankar Basu and Debarshi Das (eds). *Conflict, Demand and Economic Development: Essays in Honour of Amit Bhaduri*, London: Routledge India, pp. 171–190.

Kurz, Heinz D. and N. Salvadori (1993). The 'Standard Commodity' and Ricardo's Search for an 'invariable measure of value', in M. Baranzini and G. C. Harcourt (eds). *The Dynamics of the Wealth of Nations. Growth, Distribution and Structural Change*, London: Macmillan.

Kurz, Heinz D. and N. Salvadori (2000). Sraffa and the Mathematicians: Frank Ramsey and Alister Watson, in T. Cozzi and R. Marchionatti (eds). *Piero Sraffa's Political Economy. A Centenary Estimate*, London and New York: Routledge.

Kurz, Heinz D. and N. Salvadori (2002). Mark Blaug on the "Sraffian Interpretation of the Surplus Approach". *History of Political Economy*, 34 (1), pp. 225–236.

Kurz, Heinz D. and N. Salvadori (2011). In Favor of Rigor and Relevance: A Reply to Mark Blaug. *History of Political Economy*, 43 (2), pp. 607–616.

Lakatos, I. (1971). History of Science and its Rational Reconstructions. *Boston Studies in the Philosophy of Science*, VIII, pp. 91–136.

Mäki, U. (1992). On the Method of Isolation in Economics, in Idealization IV: Intelligibility in Science, edited by Craig Dilworth. *Poznan Studies in the Philosophy of the Sciences and the Humanities*, 26, pp. 316–351.

Mäki, U. (2020). Puzzled by Idealizations and Understanding their Functions. *Philosophy of the Social Sciences*, 50(3), pp. 215–237.

Mayr, E. (1990). When is Historiography Whiggish? *Journal of the History of Ideas*, 51 (2), pp. 301–309.

Salvadori, N. and R. Signorino (2015). Review of '*Mark Blaug: Rebel with Many Causes*' edited by Marcel Boumans and Matthias Klaes, Cheltenham, UK and Northampton, MA, USA: Edward Elgar, 2013. *Journal of the History of Economic Thought*, 37 (4), pp. 615–623.

Samuelson, Paul A. (1974). Rejoinder: Merlin Unclothed, a Final Word. *Journal of Economic Literature*, 12 (1), pp. 75–77.

Signorino, R. (2003a). Rational vs Historical Reconstructions. A Note on Blaug. *The European Journal of the History of Economic Thought*, 10 (2), pp. 329–338.

Signorino, R. (2003b). A Rejoinder. *The European Journal of the History of Economic Thought*, 10 (4), pp. 609–610.

Steedman, I. (1995). Sraffian Economics and the Capital Controversy, in F. Moseley (ed). *Heterodox Economic Theories: True or False?* Aldershot: Edward Elgar, pp. 1–45.

Stigler, George J. (1969). Does Economics have a Useful Past? *History of Political Economy*, 1 (2), pp. 217–230.

II

On Sraffa's contribution

5 The construction of long-run market supply curves

Some notes on Sraffa's critique of partial equilibrium analyses

Giuseppe Freni and Neri Salvadori[1]

Original paper: Giuseppe Freni and Neri Salvadori (2013) The construction of the long-run market supply curves: Some notes on Sraffa's critique of partial equilibrium analysis in Enrico Sergio Levrero, Antonella Palumbo, Antonella Stirati (eds), *Sraffa and the Reconstruction of Economic Theory: Volume Three. Sraffa's Legacy: Interpretations and Historical Perspectives*, 189–216. Basingstoke: Palgrave Macmillan.

5.1 Introduction

The 1925 Italian paper by Piero Sraffa, 'On the relations between cost and quantity produced', originally published in *Annali di Economia* as 'Sulle relazioni fra costo e quantità prodotta', proposes a thorough and devastating criticism of Marshallian economics based on the method of partial equilibrium analysis of competitive prices. Just five years later Sraffa has no hesitation in concluding his contribution to the 1930 *Economic Journal* Symposium on Increasing Returns and the Representative Firm with the advice that Marshall's theory 'should be discarded' (Sraffa 1930, p. 93). Note that Sraffa will never reconsider this issue, at least in published contributions, with the notable exception of a very brief hint in the Preface of his 1960 book, *Production of Commodities by Means of Commodities*.

Sraffa's Italian paper has been the object of converse interpretations, also because of the 1926 *Economic Journal* paper, 'The laws of returns under competitive conditions'. Joan Robinson (1933) claims that Sraffa in 1926 has introduced the basic elements for the imperfect competition revolution, then blossomed in the early 1930s. (See also Shackle 1967.) Roncaglia (1978, 1983, 1991, 1998), among other interpreters, maintains that imperfect competition was but an ephemeral detour from the main stream of Sraffa's research program: the paper of 1925 would rather constitute the prelude to a radical criticism of the neo-classical theoretical approach, a criticism fully developed in *Production of Commodities*.

DOI: 10.4324/9781003138709-7

Mongiovi (1996) contends that Sraffa genuinely saw imperfect competition as a way to rescue Marshallian theory from practical irrelevance even if, by 1927, he saw there was another way: to ditch Marshall and to go back to the classicals.

Moreover, the true nature of Sraffa's 1925 critique of Marshallian economics is still an open issue. Is it a purely logical criticism, that is, a criticism aimed at detecting some *non sequitur* within the formal skeleton of Marshallian economics, or, on the contrary, is it first and foremost an empirical criticism of the Marshallian explanation of the actual working of real world competitive markets? More recently, some authors (see, for instance, Signorino 2000 and 2001) argue that both logical and empirical elements are tightly intertwined in Sraffa's mid 1920s critique of Marshall: Sraffa attempts at reconstructing in a logically consistent way the Marshallian partial equilibrium model of competitive markets in order to carefully identify the boundaries of its theoretical domain, that is, the empirical situations which are logically feasible within that model. In other words, the question addressed by Sraffa was the following: what potentially observable facts concerning the industrial sectors of a given economy may be consistently analysed by means of the Marshallian partial equilibrium competitive model, *once all the various assumptions necessary to make that model logically consistent have been explicitly stated and their implications carefully spelled out and evaluated*? According to such an interpretation, Sraffa demonstrates that Marshall's theoretical model, once reconstructed in a logically consistent way, is endowed with a theoretical domain much narrower than the average Marshallian economist of the mid 1920s was inclined to grant. That is the basic reason why the Marshallian boxes on returns to scale stay stubbornly empty, as reported by Clapham (1922).

Such an interpretation allows to explain the evolution of Sraffa's thought from his early contributions to the work of the 1960 book with no need of any regret or turning point in the evolution of his thought. It allows also to establish a link with the analyses proposed by other authors (notably, Samuelson 1971) unaware of the fact that they have been following basically Sraffa's same analytical path, though from a different theoretical standpoint. In fact, the analytical arguments employed by Sraffa (1925) to show how narrow is the theoretical domain of Marshall's partial equilibrium method turn out to be almost indistinguishable from those used by Samuelson (1971) to prove the existence of specific cases in which that method actually holds: see Freni (2001). (Samuelson 1991 partially acknowledged this point.)

Though the debate on Sraffa (1925) has been extensive, a rational reconstruction of Sraffa (1925) that makes use of the tools of modern theory of production to achieve an immediate didactical purpose is still lacking. Such a reconstruction appears particularly needed today since almost all microeconomics textbooks portray the Marshallian partial equilibrium model of competitive markets as the benchmark model. Moreover, the same textbooks, either do not mention at all Sraffa's criticism, a criticism – it is worth stressing – that has never been refuted, or devote to it just a brief footnote or a special appendix as if it were a *curiosum* of which only the most pedantic students could be interested in (as an example considers Kreps 1990, Section 3 of Chapter VIII, where Sraffa is not even mentioned as the author of the criticism).

The structure of the chapter is the following. In Section 5.2 we present our interpretation of Sraffa (1925) as a preliminary to the following sections. Since the aim of this paper is not that of textually justifying such an interpretation (readers interested in a detailed exegetical analysis of the Sraffian text may usefully consult the above mentioned references), we felt free to proceed by making reference to the standard description of the partial equilibrium theory generally found in contemporary textbooks. On two points only we differentiate our exposition. Contemporary textbooks seldom try to explain the genesis of variable returns to scale. On the contrary, one of the aims pursued by Sraffa was to clarify that decreasing returns to scale are generated by the presence of primary factors available in a limited amount while increasing returns to scale are generated by the presence of external scale economies (in the 1925 paper Sraffa is quite clear about the classical roots of this distinction). Even if passed over in silence, these two statements have never been disputed. Therefore, in the analyses and in the examples that we provide here decreasing and increasing returns to scale are generated exactly in that way. Yet, we have chosen to employ the usual U-shaped average cost curves, which require the presence of indivisible constant costs (or quasi-constant). A greater loyalty to the Sraffian text would have required an exposition in terms of firms' average and marginal costs curves that are initially constant and then increasing.

In Sections 5.3 and 5.4 of this chapter we reformulate the criticism of Sraffa (1925) concerning the construction of the market supply curves used in partial equilibrium analyses, with the help of examples, also numerical ones, and by making use of the analytical tools elaborated by the modern theory of production. Section 5.3 is devoted to decreasing returns and Section 5.4 to increasing returns to scale. In each of these two sections we employ two sets of examples. The first set of each section is numerical and employs a discrete technology, analogous to that used by Sraffa (1960) whereas the second set employs a continuous technology of the type routinely used in textbooks: the production function known as Cobb-Douglas. The former example of every set shows the logical necessity of a further assumption (neither mentioned by Marshall, nor by contemporary textbooks authors) to give a precise meaning to the market supply curves used in partial equilibrium analyses. The latter example of the set shows that, thanks to this assumption, the difficulty is eliminated. In each section, the additional necessary assumption is the same in both sets and the two additional assumptions mentioned here are, obviously, those highlighted by Sraffa (1925).

In none of the examples in Sections 5.3 and 5.4 do we make use of means of production which are themselves produced. This is so because, as it was shown by Steedman (1988, see also Freni 2001), in the 1925 paper, Sraffa does not treat capital theory, contrary to what he did in the 1960 book. Both in 1925 and in 1960 Sraffa considered sectoral interdependencies of a technological nature, but these are two very different species of the same genus. The type of sectoral interdependence considered by Sraffa (1960) has its origin in the fact that in the production of a given commodity other commodities are required, and these commodities are themselves produced. By contrast, the type of sectoral interdependence considered by Sraffa (1925) is a consequence of the fact that, apart from constant returns to scale industries, commodities are produced either by technologies which employ the same primary inputs (in the decreasing returns case) or by means of technologies characterised by external economies (in the increasing returns case). Finally, in Section 5.5 we draw some conclusions.

5.2 Preliminaries

In this section we propose our interpretation of Sraffa (1925) in a synthetic form. Sraffa focuses on the construction of market supply curves within the Marshallian partial equilibrium model. Sraffa (1998 [1925], p. 356) makes clear that:

> the aim [of the theory] is to arrive at a general and organic conception of the supply curve, such that ultimately this curve is symmetrical to the corresponding demand curve for each commodity.

In a footnote in the Introduction Sraffa (1998 [1925], p. 324, footnote 4) warns his readers 'once and for all that throughout this essay we are always dealing with long periods'.

Accordingly, Sraffa is not interested simply in the construction of the long-run market supply curve of a given commodity; but also, and particularly, in the coordination of that curve with the corresponding demand curve. Sraffa reminds his readers that Marshall's theory is a symmetrical theory of value in which demand conditions (subjective elements) and supply conditions (objective elements) carry equal theoretical weight in the determination of the competitive equilibrium price of a given commodity. The lengthy and meticulous analysis of the nature of decreasing, increasing, and constant returns to scale provided by Sraffa (1925, sections II–IV) as well as their theoretical representation is specifically targeted to verify the extent and the limits of such a symmetry in the realm of the theory of competitive value. Sraffa (1998 [1925], pp. 325–326) writes:

> The importance of the laws of variation of cost in relation to the determination of the price of single commodities has appeared only in

> consequence of the «fundamental symmetry of the general relations in which demand and supply stand to value». [...] Such symmetry depends on the non-proportionality of the total cost of production to the quantity produced. If the cost of production of every unit of the commodity under consideration did not vary with variations in the quantity produced the symmetry would be broken; the price would be determined exclusively by the expenses of production and demand would be unable to have any influence on it at all.

Up to now we have dealt with the analytical content of Marshall's theory. As concerns methodology, Marshall adopted partial equilibrium analysis. Partial equilibrium analysis requires that the interdependencies between the various markets of final goods of a given economy are, so to speak, frozen in the *ceteris paribus* clause: partial equilibrium theorists analyse a single market of a final good at a time and assume that (i) prices and quantities determined in all other markets of final goods are given and that (ii) changes in the price or the quantity produced in the market under scrutiny do not have any discernible impact on the prices and the quantities produced in the other markets of final goods. Partial equilibrium theorists look for first approximation results, by assuming that these assumptions hold at least for small variations in the data. Such a methodology imposes strong constraints on the theorists who want to use it in a formally correct way. In the words of Sraffa (1998 [1925], pp. 358–359):

> (1) the supply curve must be independent, both of the corresponding demand curve, and also of the supply curves of all the other commodities; (2) the supply curve is valid only for slight variations in the quantity produced, and, if we depart too far from the initial equilibrium position, it may become necessary to construct an entirely new curve, since a large variation would, in general, be incompatible with the condition *ceteris paribus*.

On the contrary, Sraffa maintains that the above-mentioned assumptions cannot hold *even* for *small variations*, because the same forces that are responsible for an appreciable change in a given market are responsible also for a change of the *same order of magnitude* in other markets, unless theorists are willing to introduce some additional assumptions. But theorists tempted to resort to this exit strategy from the logical cul-de-sac highlighted by Sraffa should be aware of the fact that such a choice has a very unpleasant consequence: a drastic reduction of the theoretical domain of their model.

Having clarified the aim of Sraffa's criticism, let us try to clarify its content. We accomplish this task with reference to the way in which the equilibrium of a single market is depicted in contemporary textbooks, though, as noted above, we pay greater attention to the genesis of variable returns to scale.

Let us consider Figure 5.1. In the diagram on the LHS the long-period average and marginal cost curves of the unique type of incumbent firms are given (if there were more than one type, however, the average cost curve of every type would have the same minimum). In the diagram on the RHS the equilibrium of a single market with constant returns to scale is analysed. The straight line *SS* represents the market long-run supply curve. The long-run market equilibrium price is $p^\star$ irrespective of the quantity demanded. In the case of a shift of the market demand curve from curve *DD* to the curve *D′D′* the long-run market equilibrium is broken and we enter into the domain of the short-run adjustments:[2]

1. Market price increases along the short-run market supply curve *ss* which is obtained by summing up horizontally the relevant parts of the marginal cost curves of the incumbent firms in that moment of time.
2. The increment of the short-run market equilibrium price involves the formation of extra-profits for the incumbent firms (represented by a rectangle that has for its basis the produced amount and for its height the distance between the marginal cost and the average cost at that produced amount). This fact creates an entry incentive for firms outside the market.
3. The entry of new firms in the market shifts the market supply curve rightwards from *ss* to *s′s′*. This process goes on until the short-run market equilibrium price stays above $p^\star$.
4. When the short-run market equilibrium price catches up to $p^\star$ again the extra-profits are zero and therefore the entry incentive for outside firms vanishes. The market under scrutiny has finally reached a new long-run equilibrium position.

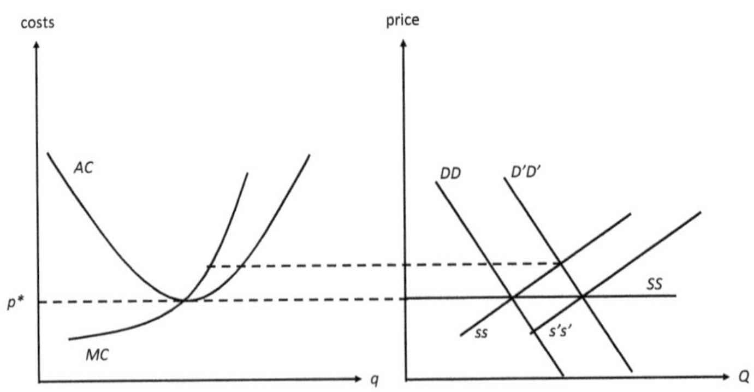

Figure 5.1 Firm and industry equilibria in Marshallian analysis: constant returns.

Curve *SS* of the diagram to the RHS in Figure 5.1 has exactly the same ordinate of the minimum average cost represented in the diagram on the left: in correspondence to that price there are no positive or negative extraprofits. In a market with constant returns to scale the long-run equilibrium price is determined by the minimal average cost of production. Demand conditions (and alongside with them all subjective elements, like consumers' preferences) simply play no role.

Let us now consider Figure 5.2. The difference between Figure 5.1 and Figure 5.2 consists in the fact that in Figure 5.2 two types of firms are assumed to exist. The minimum of the average cost curve of firms of type 1 is lower than that of firms of type 2, but in order to produce firms of type 1 require the use of a non-reproducible natural resource. This implies that only a given number N_1 of firms of type 1 can enter into the market; moreover N_1 firms of type 1 that produce the quantity corresponding to the minimum of the average cost curve can produce no more than the amount Q_{1m}. What happens if demand is larger than Q_{1m}? Initially, firms of type 1 can increase their production but at a higher cost: market price goes up along the corresponding short-run supply curve. In this range the short-run supply curve coincides with the long-run one since no other firm can enter the market. In fact, in order to enter the market an external firm needs the non-reproducible natural resource that is already totally employed by the incumbent firms (obviously, these could be bought and sold, but without any increment in the overall number of incumbent firms). When, however, the amount produced and sold in the market reaches the level Q_{1M}, the marginal cost of firms of type 1 coincides with the marginal (and average) cost of firms of type 2. Hence, if total production is larger than Q_{1M}, firms of type 2 can enter the market. Firms of type 1 cannot increase the amount produced by each of them,

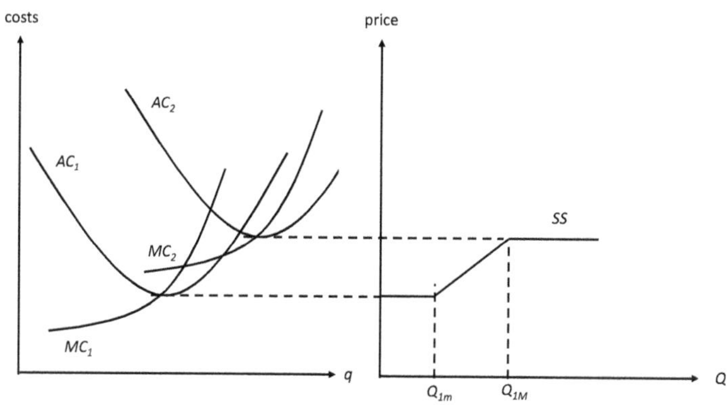

Figure 5.2 Firm and industry equilibria in Marshallian analysis: decreasing returns.

because this increase could be obtained only at a marginal cost larger than that paid by firms of type 2. Consequently the supply curve has three ranges: in the first one and in the third one it is constant (but at different levels), in the intermediate one it is positively sloped.

We need to be more precise on one point. In the diagram on the LHS of Figure 5.2 the average cost curve depicted does not include the rent of the non-reproducible natural resource. If we insert this cost, then the curve AC_1 jumps up to the right in such a way that its minimum is at the same level of the minimum of curve AC_2 and is along the marginal cost curve MC_1, which, instead is unchanged since the cost for the payment of the rent has the character of a fixed cost for the firm – on this point see Viner (1931, pp. 30–32).

The argument developed above can be generalised in various directions. A first generalisation is the following. Let us assume that in a given market there are many types of firms; each type is characterised by the use of a non-reproducible natural resource: the supply curve will be such as to have a substantially positively sloped with horizontal small ranges of negligible amount. In these conditions, a movement of the demand curve, and therefore a variation in the consumers' preferences, has a direct bearing on the determination of market equilibrium price not only in the short-run, but also in the long-run.

Another generalisation is the following. We take into consideration the existence of a quantity threshold in the market. If the overall amount produced exceeds the threshold, firms can introduce an appropriate division of labour among firms and therefore they can make use of a technology characterised by smaller average (and marginal) costs. An example of this kind is represented in Figure 5.3: firms have at their disposal technology 1 if the overall amount produced is smaller than Q_1; but they have at their disposal technology 2 in the opposite case. In this scenario, the supply curve SS is a step curve with two horizontal ranges in which the

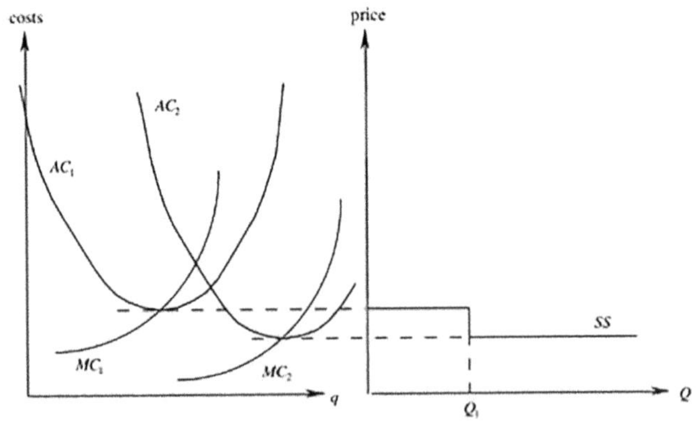

Figure 5.3 Firm and industry equilibria in Marshallian analysis: increasing returns.

latter range is lower than the former. Obviously, the introduction of many thresholds of this type can lead to a supply curve which is substantially negatively sloped, with horizontal ranges of small or negligible size.

Let us go back to the content of Sraffa's criticism of Marshall. In our view, it concerns the search for the conditions for the above arguments to hold. For Sraffa, the Marshallian model, once reconstructed in a logically consistent way, needs the introduction of additional assumptions which inevitably makes the domain of Marshall's theory much narrower and, therefore, drastically reduce the set of empirical phenomena covered by that model.

When the question is considered in this light, the content of Sraffa's critique can be summarised as an answer to a question that both mid-1920s Marshallian economists and contemporary textbook authors did not and do not tackle: is the theoretical domain that can legitimately be investigated by means of the Marshallian approach sufficiently large to cover empirically significant cases of non-constant returns to scale? Or, rather, would it not be wiser to restrict the use of the partial equilibrium methodology to the analysis of the constant returns to scale case?

5.3 Diminishing returns

This section contains two sets of examples that clarify the point raised by Sraffa as regards the diminishing returns to scale case. In the first set we assume that there are only four processes to produce two goods, apples and pears. These four processes produce apples and pears using land and labour. Assume that there is leisure time and that the increase in production of apples or pears, or both, results in a reduction of leisure time at the same wage rate. This set contains two examples. In the first one land is a homogeneous factor of production, that is, there is a single quality of land which can be used for the production both of apples and pears. In the second example, on the contrary, there are two distinct qualities of land, one to produce apples and one to produce pears. Thus, each quality of land is sector-specific. Only in this latter case, that is in the case of sector-specific factors of production, may theorists construct two independent market supply curves, as prescribed by partial equilibrium theory, while in the former case this is not possible. These two examples should clarify the logic underlying the following statement (Sraffa 1998 [1925], p. 359):

> [The hypotheses of increasing costs] are satisfied only in those exceptional cases where the totality of a factor is used in the production of a single commodity. But, in general, each factor is used by a number of industries that produce different commodities, and in this case only a supply curve of the totality of those commodities is possible, based on the assumption that the group of industries that have a common factor can be regarded as one single industry.

And yet:

> The substance of the argument rests on the fact that the increase in production of a commodity leads to an increase in the cost both of the commodity itself, and of the other commodities of the group. The variations belong to the same order of magnitude, and therefore are to be regarded as being of equal importance. Either we take into account these variations for industries of the group, and we must pass from the consideration of the particular equilibrium of a commodity to that of general equilibrium; or else those variations in all industries are ignored, and the commodity must be considered as produced under constant costs. What is inadmissible is that the equal effects of a single cause are at the same time considered to be negligible in one case, and of fundamental importance in the other. However, it is necessary to accept this absurdity if one wishes to give a general, and not an anomalous character, to the supply curve of a product under conditions of increasing costs. (p. 360)

In the former example, the four processes are represented as in Table 5.1 and it is assumed that there are 300 units of land. Furthermore, we assume, for the sake of simplicity, that landlords have no alternative use for their land. Hence the reservation price of land is zero. Wages and rents are paid *post factum*.

Let labour be the *numeraire*. If process (*i*) is activated and process (*i*) refers to the production of apples ($i = 1, 3$), then the following equation must be satisfied

$$t_i q + l_i = p_a$$

where q is the rate of rent and p_a is the price of a unit of apples, both measured in terms of labour. Similarly, if process (*i*) refers to the production of pears ($i = 2, 4$), then the following equation must be satisfied

$$t_i q + l_i p_p$$

where p_p is the price of one unit of pear in terms of labour. Let us call A the amount of apples produced and P the amount of pears produced.

Table 5.1 Processes: decreasing returns and homogeneous land

Processes	*Land*	*Labour*		*Apples*	*Pears*
(1)	2	5	→	1	—
(2)	3	6	→	—	1
(3)	1	10	→	1	—
(4)	2	15	→	—	1

If land is not scarce, competition among landlords requires that rent is zero (and equal to the reservation price). In these circumstances $p_a = 5$ and $p_p = 6$, otherwise a profit could be achieved by operating processes (5.1) or (5.2). Moreover

$$2A + 3P \leq 300 \tag{5.1}$$

otherwise the production of apples and pears would use more land than is available. If inequality (5.1) is not satisfied, but the inequality

$$A + 2P \leq 300 \tag{5.2}$$

is, then either process (5.3) or process (5.4), or both, are operated. Suppose that the processes (5.1), (5.2), and (5.4) are operated. Then

$$\begin{aligned} 2q + 5 &= p_a \\ 3q + 6 &= p_p \\ 2q + 15 &= p_p. \end{aligned}$$

Consequently, $q = 9$, $p_a = 23$, and $p_p = 33$. But at these prices producers may obtain a profit by operating process (5.3) since

$$q + 10 = 19 < 23 = p_a.$$

Thus, processes (5.1), (5.2), and (5.4) cannot be operated together since there is process (5.3). If, on the contrary, processes (5.1), (5.2), and (5.3) are operated together, then

$$\begin{aligned} 2q + 5 &= p_a \\ 3q + 6 &= p_p \\ q + 10 &= p_a \end{aligned}$$

Consequently, $q = 5$, $p_a = 15$, $p_p = 21$, and producers cannot make a profit by operating process (5.4) since

$$2q + 15 = 25 > 21 = p_p$$

These prices can be realised only if landlords' competition does not annihilate rent, that is, only if land is fully cultivated. Let A_1 be the amount of apples produced with process (5.1) and let A_3 be the amount of apples produced with process (5.3), then the constraint

$$2A_1 + 3P + A_3 = 300$$

must hold. This equation, together with the obvious constraints

$$\begin{aligned} &A_3 = A - A_1 \\ &0 \leq A_1 \leq A, \end{aligned}$$

implies that processes (5.1), (5.2), and (5.3) can be operated together if and only if.

$$300 - A \leq A + 3P \leq 300 \tag{5.3}$$

Finally, if

$$A + 3P > 300,$$

but inequality (5.2) is satisfied, then both processes (5.3) and (5.4) must be operated. The same procedure used above shows that then process (5.1) cannot be operated, otherwise a profit would be gained by operating process (5.2). The operation of processes (5.2), (5.3), and (5.4) determines the prices $q = 9$, $p_a = 19$, e $p_p = 33$. Furthermore, these processes can be activated together only if

$$300 - P \leq A + 2P \leq 300.$$

The results achieved above are summarised in Figure 5.4. There are three areas in the space (A, P), whose borders are obtained by the inequalities (5.2) and (5.3). In each area we have a pair of prices for apples and pears: (5, 6), (15, 21), and (19, 33). On the segment that separates the first two areas only processes (5.1) and (5.2) are activated, but land is fully utilised, hence

$$0 \leq q \leq 5$$

since if $q > 5$ a profit can be realised by operating process (5.3). On the same segment we have that

$$p_a = 5 + 2q$$
$$p_p = 6 + 3q.$$

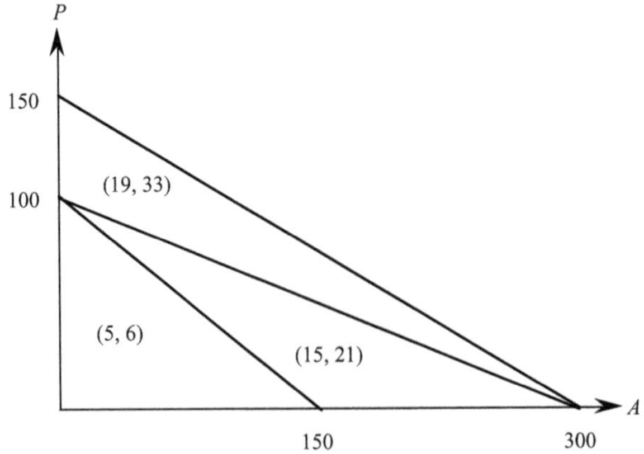

Figure 5.4 Partition of equilibria: decreasing returns and homogeneous land.

On the segment that separates the second and the third area only processes (5.2) and (5.3) are operated, land is fully utilised and

$$5 \leq q \leq 9,$$

for if $q < 5$ producers would obtain a profit by operating process (5.1) and if $q > 9$ producers would obtain a profit by operating process (5.4). On the same segment we have that

$$p_a = 10 + q$$
$$p_p = 6 + 3q.$$

From Figure 5.4 we immediately get that given the amount of apples (pears), we can build a relationship between the quantity of produced pears (apples) and its price, but in building this curve we cannot keep constant the price of apples (pears): whenever the price of one commodity changes, the price of the other changes too: both price changes are due to the variation in the rent of a common factor, land.

As Sraffa had clearly indicated, if each industry technology displays diminishing returns to scale since it is the only user of a sector-specific factor, then a partial equilibrium supply curve for each industry can be built. The result is crystal-clear if we suppose that there are two kinds of land and that the known processes to produce apples and pears are those of Table 5.2. From the table we easily see that land 1 is specific to the production of apples and land 2 is specific to the production of pears. Furthermore, we assume the existence of 300 units of land of quality 1 and 300 units of land of quality 2.

Similarly to the way we built Figure 5.4, we can build Figure 5.5. In this case, however, the price of pears is either 6 or 33, depending on whether the amount of pears produced is less or greater than 100, quite independently of the produced amount and price of apples. Similarly, the price of apples is either 5 or 15, depending on whether the amount of apples produced is less than or greater than 150, quite independently of the produced amount and price of pears. In fact, if the amount of apples (pears) produced is less than 150 (100), only process (5.1) (process (5.2))

Table 5.2 Processes: decreasing returns and sector-specific lands

Processes	*Land 1*	*Land 2*	*Labour*		*Apples*	*Pears*
(1)	2	—	5	→	1	—
(2)	—	3	6	→	—	1
(3)	1	—	10	→	1	—
(4)	—	2	15	→	—	1

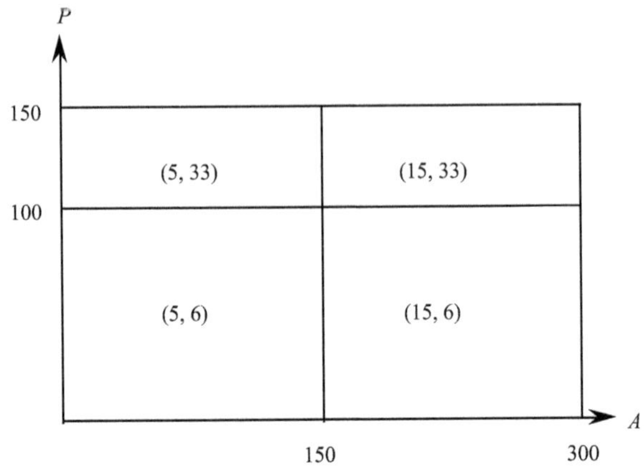

Figure 5.5 Partition of equilibria: decreasing returns and sector-specific lands.

is operated. On the contrary, if the amount of apples (pears) produced is greater than 150 (100), process (5.1) (process (5.2)) alone would require more land 1 (land 2) than that available and then it will be operated jointly with process (5.3) (process (5.4)), the most expensive in terms of labour, but less expensive in terms of land of quality 1 (land of quality 2). The rate of rent on the land of quality 1 (land of quality 2) will be determined by the condition that the two processes (5.1) and (5.3) (processes (5.2) and (5.4)) have the same costs.

The above remarks conclude the analysis of our examples with discrete technologies. The second set of examples we wish to analyse is characterised by the fact that the conditions of production of apples and pears may be represented by two Cobb-Douglas production functions. As in the previous set of examples, apples and pears are produced using labour and land. We assume again that there is leisure time and that the increase in production of apples or pears, or both, results in a reduction of leisure time at the same wage rate. Also this set contains two examples. In the first, land is of a single quality, that is it is not sector-specific and thus may be used both for the production of apples and pears. In the second, on the contrary, there are two distinct qualities of land, one to produce apples and a different one to produce pears. Only in this latter case, that is in case of sector-specific factors, may theorists construct two independent market supply curves, while in the first case this is not possible. These two examples, therefore, lead exactly to the same conclusion as the previous set of examples.

Assume that the production functions of apples and pears are, respectively,

$$Y_a = AL_a^{\alpha}T_a^{1-\alpha} \tag{5.4}$$

$$Y_p = BL_p^{\beta}T_p^{1-\beta} \tag{5.5}$$

and that the amount of existing land is T. From the condition of full utilisation of land, we get

$$T_a + T_p = T. \tag{5.6}$$

Furthermore, profits maximisation by means of independent producers implies

$$\alpha A L_a^{\alpha-1} T_a^{1-\alpha} p_a = 1 \tag{5.7}$$
$$(1-\alpha) A L_a^{\alpha} T_a^{-\alpha} p_a = \rho \tag{5.8}$$
$$\beta B L_p^{\beta-1} T_p^{1-\beta} p_p = 1 \tag{5.9}$$
$$(1-\beta) B L_p^{\beta} T_p^{-\beta} p_p = \rho, \tag{5.10}$$

where p_a is the price of one unit of apples in terms of one unit of labour, p_p is the price of one unit of pears in terms of one unit of labour, ρ is the rate of rent in terms of one unit of labour. By obvious manipulation of the equations (5.4), (5.7), and (5.8), we obtain the equations

$$L_a = \alpha Y_a p_a \tag{5.11}$$
$$\rho T_a = (1-\alpha) Y_a p_a \tag{5.12}$$
$$A(\alpha Y_a p_a)^{\alpha} \left[\frac{(1-\alpha) Y_a p_a}{\rho} \right]^{1-\alpha} = Y_a .$$

The last equation can be written more usefully

$$p_a = C\rho^{1-\alpha} \tag{5.13}$$

where

$$C = \frac{1}{A\alpha^{\alpha}(1-\alpha)^{1-\alpha}}.$$

Similarly, from equations (5.5), (5.9), and (5.10), we obtain

$$L_p = \beta Y_p p_p \tag{5.14}$$
$$\rho T_p = (1-\beta) Y_p p_p \tag{5.15}$$
$$p_p = D\rho^{1-\beta} \tag{5.16}$$

where

$$D = \frac{1}{B\beta^{\beta}(1-\beta)^{1-\beta}}.$$

From equations (5.6), (5.12), (5.13), (5.15), and (5.16) we obtain

$$\rho T = (1-\alpha) C Y_a \rho^{1-\alpha} + (1-\beta) D Y_p \rho^{1-\beta}$$

that is

$$T=(1-\alpha)CY_a\rho^{-\alpha}+(1-\beta)DY_p\rho^{-\beta}. \tag{5.17}$$

It is immediately recognised that for each pair (Y_a, Y_p), with $Y_a>0$ and $Y_p>0$, the function

$$\varphi(\rho, Y_a, Y_p)=(1-\alpha)CY_a\rho^{-\alpha}+(1-\beta)DY_p\rho^{-\beta}$$

is decreasing and

$$\lim_{\rho\to 0}\varphi(\rho, Y_a, Y_p)=+\infty, \lim_{\rho\to+\infty}\varphi(\rho, Y_a, Y_p)=0,$$

for which for each pair (Y_a, Y_p), with $Y_a>0$ and $Y_p>0$, the equation (5.17) has one and only one solution, see Figure 5.6. This remark allows to define the function

$$\rho=\Phi(Y_a, Y_p). \tag{5.18}$$

Furthermore, it is easily noted that

$$\frac{\partial\varphi(\rho, Y_a, Y_p)}{\partial Y_a}>0, \frac{\partial\varphi(\rho, Y_a, Y_p)}{\partial Y_p}>0;$$

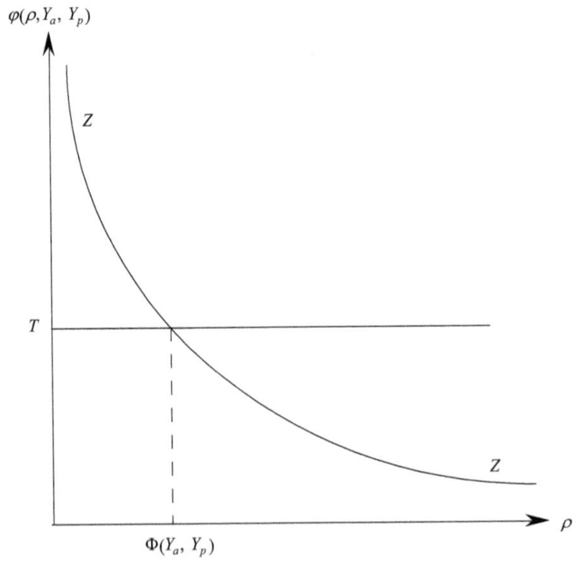

Figure 5.6 Equation (5.17) has one and only one solution.

for which an increase in Y_a (or an increase in Y_p) moves upwards the curve ZZ of Figure 5.6, and then raises the value of ρ that satisfies equation (5.17). Accordingly

$$\frac{\partial\Phi(Y_a, Y_p)}{\partial Y_a} > 0, \quad \frac{\partial\Phi(Y_a, Y_p)}{\partial Y_p} > 0.$$

Finally, from equations (5.13), (5.16), and (5.18) we obtain

$$p_a = C\left[\Phi(Y_a,\ Y_p)\right]^{1-\alpha}$$
$$p_p = D\left[\Phi(Y_a,\ Y_p)\right]^{1-\beta}$$

So, for a given Y_p, p_a is an increasing function of Y_a, but, as in the former example of the first set, we cannot keep p_p constant: whenever the price of a commodity changes, the price of the other commodity changes too: both price changes are due to the variation of the rent of the common factor, land.

To confirm Sraffa's conclusion (if each industry technology displays diminishing returns to scale being the only user of a specific factor, then a partial equilibrium supply curve for each industry can be built) suppose there are two kinds of land available in the amounts T_1 and T_2, for which equation (5.6) is replaced by equations

$$T_a = T_1 \tag{5.19}$$
$$T_p = T_2. \tag{5.20}$$

Also, since there are two qualities of land there are also two rent rates for which equations (5.12) and (5.15) are replaced by equations

$$\rho_1 T_a = (1-\alpha) Y_a p_a \tag{5.21}$$
$$\rho_2 T_p = (1-\beta) Y_p p_p. \tag{5.22}$$

Therefore, from equations (5.4), (5.11), (5.19), and (5.21) we obtain

$$A(\alpha Y_a p_a)^{\alpha} T_1^{1-\alpha} = Y_a$$

from which we obtain

$$p_a = \frac{Y_a^{\frac{1-\alpha}{\alpha}}}{A^{\frac{1}{\alpha}} \alpha T_1^{\frac{1-\alpha}{\alpha}}}. \tag{5.23}$$

Similarly, from equations (5.5), (5.14), (5.20), and (5.22) we obtain

$$p_p = \frac{Y_p^{\frac{1-\beta}{\beta}}}{B^{\frac{1}{\beta}} \beta T_2^{\frac{1-\beta}{\beta}}}. \tag{5.24}$$

Each of the supply curves (5.23) and (5.24) is totally independent from the price and the produced quantity of the other goods, that, therefore, can be kept constant.

5.4 Increasing returns

In this section we provide two sets of examples that clarify the point raised by Sraffa as concerns the increasing returns to scale case. Sraffa acknowledges that Marshall had already recognised that economies of scale internal to the individual firm are incompatible with competitive markets:

> The cases in which productivity grows as a consequence of variations in the size of the single firm cannot be accommodated in the theory of price determination in a regime of free competition, since it is clear that, if a firm can decrease its costs without limit by increasing production, it would continue to reduce the selling price until it had acquired the whole market. We would then have abandoned the hypothesis of competition.
>
> (Sraffa 1998 [1925], pp. 344–345)

It follows that increasing returns to scale are compatible with perfect competition only if their genesis is related to the presence of economies external to individual firms:

> The external economies constitute a link that unites the conditions of production of the individual firms in the industry. The cost of production of each firm is not determined solely by the quantity that it produces itself, but also, at the same time, by the quantity produced by all the other firms. In studying the individual equilibrium, three variables must therefore be considered: cost, quantity produced by the single firm, and quantity produced by the industry as a whole.
>
> (Sraffa1998 [1925], p. 347)

But individual firms do not take into consideration these external effects in making their own maximising decisions:

> The hypothesis of free competition fixes the limits between which the theory of decreasing costs based on external economies is applicable. It implies that, by considering «an industry» as the set of firms that produce a given commodity, each firm must be so small relative to the industry, that the influence of a variation in the quantity produced by the firm on the market price can be taken as negligible.
>
> (Sraffa 1998 [1925], p. 347)

But this is not enough. The only scale economies compatible with the partial equilibrium methodology and thus with the *ceteris paribus* clause must be of a very particular type: sector-specific scale economies, that is, economies internal to the industry under scrutiny. To put it briefly, competitive markets are incompatible with firms' internal scale economies, partial equilibrium methodology is incompatible with industry external economies (or non-sector-specific scale economies). The Marshallian mountain of decreasing costs has brought forth the mouse of scale economies external to individual firms and internal to a given industry:

> It is necessary that the advantages of increased production in the industry considered should not have repercussions in any way on the other industries. The economies of large scale production must be «external» from the point of view of the individual firms, but «internal» from the point of view of the industry. It is a question of seeing within what limits it is reasonable to suppose, on the one hand, a close interdependence among firms in an industry, and, on the other hand, an absolute independence of the same firms from producers of other commodities. If we investigate what these external economies really consist of, we find that very few of them possess such a qualification. The most important ones, if indeed they do derive in part from the development of a single industry, are generally to the advantage of all the industries found in the district in which the development is taking place. This is especially true for those basic external economies «which result from general progress of industrial environment», and for those deriving from the development of means of communication and transport.
>
> (Sraffa 1998 [1925], p. 362)

In the first set of examples we present we assume that the processes represented in Table 5.2 are always available, regardless of the quantity produced. There are, however, thresholds and when these thresholds are exceeded other processes are available. In the former example, these thresholds are relative to the total amount of labour used in the production of apples and pears, while in the latter, these thresholds are relative to the amount of labour employed in the production of apples as regards the processes used in the production of apples and the amount of labour employed in the production of pears as regards the processes used in the production of pears. We show that in the latter case, a market supply curve independent from the price and the quantity produced of the other commodity can be built, while the same may not hold in the former example.

In the first example we assume that in addition to the processes of Table 5.2, always available, the processes of Table 5.3 and Table 5.4 are available too. Processes of Table 5.3 are available when the total amount of labour employed is greater than or equal to 600 units, whereas the processes of Table 5.4 are available when the amount of labour employed is greater than or equal to 900 units. In addition we assume the existence of 300 units of land of quality 1 and 300 units of land of quality 2.

It may be easily demonstrated that when all processes (5.1)–(5.9) are available, producers use only the processes (5.8) and (5.9) and therefore prices are $p_a = 2$, $p_p = 4$. But processes (5.8) and (5.9) are available only if

$$2A + 4P \geq 900. \tag{5.25}$$

It may be easily demonstrated also that when only processes (5.1)–(5.7) are available, apples are produced only with process (5.5) and pears are produced either with process (5.6), if the total quantity of pears produced is less than 150, or with both processes (5.6) and (5.7), if the total amount of pears produced is larger than 150. But the three processes (5.5), (5.6), and (5.7) are available only if

$$4A + 5P \geq 600. \tag{5.26}$$

Then in the portion of the plane in which the inequality (5.26) is satisfied and (5.25) is not, $p_a = 4$, $p_p = 5$ if $P \leq 150$, and $p_p = 24$ if $P \geq 150$.

Finally, if the available processes are processes (5.1)–(5.4) and process (5.7) and inequality (5.26) is not met, apples are produced only with process (5.1) and pears are produced with process (5.2) if the amount of total pears produced is less than 100 or with both processes (5.2) and (5.7) if the amount of total pears produced is greater than 100. Note that when the amount of apples produced is larger than 100, process (5.7) is available. So when inequality (5.26) is not satisfied, $p_a = 5$ and either $p_p = 6$, if $P \leq 100$, or $p_p = 15$, if $P \geq 100$.

The results obtained are summarised in Figure 5.7, where the triangle without display of prices is too small to contain the pair (5, 15). From Figure 5.7 we see immediately that given the amount of a commodity

Table 5.3 Further processes available when labour employed is greater than or equal to 600 units

Processes	*Land 1*	*Land 2*	*Labour*		*Apples*	*Pears*
(5)	1	—	4	→	1	—
(6)	—	2	5	→	—	1
(7)	—	1	12	→	—	1

Table 5.4 Further processes available when labour employed is greater than or equal to 900 units

Processes	*Land 1*	*Land 2*	*Labour*		*Apples*	*Pears*
(8)	1	—	2	→	1	—
(9)	—	1	4	→	—	1

whenever the price of a commodity changes because of increasing returns to scale the price of the other commodity also changes, since both prices change as a consequence of the same externality. Hence given the amount of a commodity we can build a relationship between the quantity produced of the other commodity and its price, but in building this curve we cannot keep constant the price of the commodity whose amount is given when the price of the other commodity decreases due to increasing returns to scale. (Note that we can keep locally constant the price of apples when the price of pears increases due to the diminishing returns to scale that this example contemplates.)

A similar example, but with economies external to firms and internal to industries is easily obtained by assuming that process (5.5) (process (5.8)) is available when the labour employed in the production of apples is greater than or equal to 300 (450) units and processes (5.6) and (5.7) are available (process (5.9) is available) when the labour employed in the production of pears is greater than or equal to 300 (500) units. In this case it is possible to consider as given the price and quantity produced of a commodity when the price and quantity produced of the other good is changed. Simple calculations in fact show that the prices which are to be determined are those represented in Figure 5.8.

In the second set of examples we use the production functions (5.4) and (5.5), but we assume that the coefficients A and B are functions of the

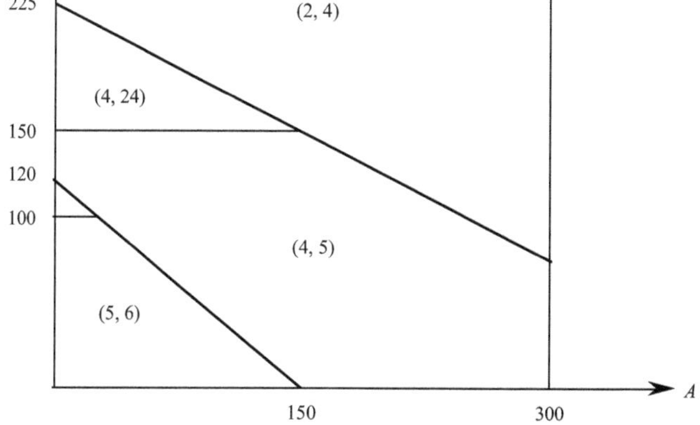

Figure 5.7 Partition of equilibria: increasing returns and industry external economies.

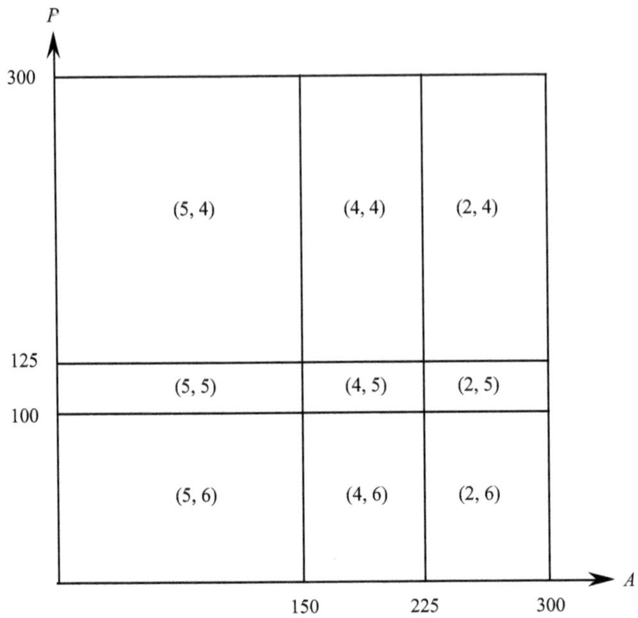

Figure 5.8 Partition of equilibria: increasing returns and sector-specific scale economies.

amount of labour used on average in the two sectors, $\bar{L}_a$ and $\bar{L}_p$. Furthermore we assume that the two types of land are sector-specific (equations (5.19) and (5.20)) and, to simplify the notation, we put $T_1 = 1$ and $T_2 = 1$.

In the first example we have

$$A = \bar{L}_a^{\gamma}\bar{L}_p^{1-\gamma}$$
$$B = \bar{L}_a^{1-\delta}\bar{L}_p^{\delta},$$

and then

$$Y_a = \bar{L}_a^{\gamma}\bar{L}_p^{1-\gamma}L_a^{\alpha} \tag{5.27}$$
$$Y_p = \bar{L}_a^{1-\delta}\bar{L}_p^{\delta}L_p^{\beta}. \tag{5.28}$$

Since each firm considers $\bar{L}_a$ and $\bar{L}_p$ as given, the conditions for profit maximisation are still given by equations (5.7)–(5.10). In particular, the following conditions, which correspond to equations (5.7) and (5.9), hold

$$\alpha\bar{L}_a^{\gamma}\bar{L}_p^{1-\gamma}L_a^{\alpha-1}p_a = 1 \tag{5.29}$$
$$\beta\bar{L}_a^{1-\delta}\bar{L}_p^{\delta}L_p^{\beta-1}p_p = 1 \tag{5.30}$$

In equilibrium, however, the quantities that firms consider as given are equal to the actual sizes and, therefore, $\bar{L}_a = L_a$ and $\bar{L}_p = L_p$. The replacement of these equilibrium conditions in equations (5.27)–(5.30) then leads to the following system

$$Y_a = L_p^{1-\gamma} L_a^{\alpha+\gamma} \tag{5.31}$$

$$Y_p = L_a^{1-\delta} L_p^{\beta+\delta} \tag{5.32}$$

$$\alpha Y_a p_a = L_a \tag{5.33}$$

$$\beta Y_p p_p = L_p. \tag{5.34}$$

Define $\Delta = (\alpha+\gamma)(\beta+\delta)-(1-\delta)(1-\gamma)$ and assume that the parameters satisfy the following inequalities: $0<\gamma<1$, $\gamma+\alpha>1$, $0<\delta<1$, $\delta+\beta>1$, $\Delta>\beta+\delta$ and $\Delta>\gamma+\alpha$. It may be easily seen that from the equations (5.31) and (5.32) we obtain

$$L_a = \frac{Y_a^{\frac{\delta+\beta}{\Delta}}}{Y_p^{\frac{1-\gamma}{\Delta}}}, \quad L_p = \frac{Y_p^{\frac{\alpha+\gamma}{\Delta}}}{Y_a^{\frac{1-\delta}{\Delta}}},$$

which inserted in equations (5.33) and (5.34) give us the equilibrium prices as a function of quantity

$$p_a = \frac{Y_a^{\frac{\delta+\beta}{\Delta}-1}}{\alpha Y_p^{\frac{1-\gamma}{\Delta}}} \tag{5.35}$$

$$p_p = \frac{Y_p^{\frac{\alpha+\gamma}{\Delta}-1}}{\beta Y_a^{\frac{1-\delta}{\Delta}}}. \tag{5.36}$$

Under the conditions postulated, given the amount of a commodity, we can construct an inverse relation between the quantity produced of the other commodity and its price, but in building this curve we cannot keep constant the price of the commodity whose amount is given. In fact this price decreases because of the same externality that makes the relationship between quantity produced and price of the other commodity decreasing.

Of course, the economies external to firms are also internal to industries if and only if $\gamma=1$ and $\delta=1$. Under these conditions, the denominators of the right members of equations (5.35) and (5.36) reduce to a constant and supply curves of the two goods become, therefore, perfectly independent.

5.5 Concluding remarks

In this chapter we have made use of the analytical tools provided by the contemporary theory of production to confirm the analytical results achieved by Sraffa in his 1925 Italian paper. The analysis of long-run equilibria of economies in which firms operate in a regime of free competition can account for non-constant returns to scale and make use of the partial equilibrium methodology if and only if two additional assumptions are postulated: (i) scarce resources responsible for diminishing returns to scale are sector-specific and (ii) external economies responsible for increasing returns to scale are sector-specific, that is, external to the firms active in a given industry and internal to the industry under scrutiny. These two additional assumptions drastically reduce the theoretical domain of the Marshallian partial equilibrium model of competitive prices. Therefore, our analysis confirms Sraffa's final verdict on Marshall's theory: '[it] cannot be interpreted in a way which makes it logically self-consistent and, at the same time, reconciles it with the facts it sets out to explain' (Sraffa 1930, p. 93).

Notes

1 We wish to thank, without implicating, Antonio D'Agata, Heinz D. Kurz, Gary Mongiovi, Alessandro Roncaglia, and Rodolfo Signorino for their careful reading and detailed comments on an earlier version of this Chapter. Usual disclaimer applies. A previous version of this paper appeared in Italian in *Tra Economia e Società*, edited by A. D'Agata, E. Giardina, and E. Sciacca, Milan: Giuffrè, 2006.

2 If curve $D'D'$ were to the left of curve DD a symmetrical argument applies: incumbent firms make losses instead of extraprofits in the short run and, as a consequence, some of them will exit from the market in the long-run; the curve $s's'$ would be to the left of curve ss.

References

Clapham, J.H. (1922). Of Empty Economic Boxes. *The Economic Journal*, vol. 32, pp. 305–314.

Freni, G. (2001). Sraffa's Early Contribution to Competitive Price Theory. *The European Journal of the History of Economic Thought*, vol. 8, pp. 363–390.

Kreps, D. M. (1990). *A Course in Microeconomic Theory* (Hemel Hempstead: Harvester Wheatsheaf).

Mongiovi, G. (1996). Sraffa's Critique of Marshall: A Reassessment. *Cambridge Journal of Economics*, vol. 20, pp. 207–224.

Robinson, J.V. (1933). *The Economics of Imperfect Competition* (London: Macmillan).

Roncaglia, A. (1978). *Sraffa and the Theory of Prices* (Chichester: Wiley & Sons).

Roncaglia, A. (1983). Piero Sraffa and the Reconstruction of Political Economy. *Banca Nazionale del Lavoro Quarterly Review*, vol. 36, pp. 337–350.

Roncaglia, A. (1991). Sraffa's 1925 article and Marshall's Theory. *Quaderni di Storia dell'Economia Politica*, vol. 9, pp. 373–397.

Roncaglia, A. (1998). Sraffa, Piero, as an Interpreter of the Classical Economists, in H. D. Kurz and N. Salvadori (eds), *The Elgar Companion to Classical Economics* (Cheltenham: Edward Elgar), vol. II, pp. 399–404.

Samuelson, P. A. (1971). An Exact Hume-Ricardo-Marshall Model of International Trade. *Journal of International Economics*, vol. 1, pp. 1–18. Reprinted in R. C. Merton (ed.), *The Collected Scientific Papers of Paul A. Samuelson*, Vol. III, 1972 (Cambridge, MA: The MIT Press), pp. 356–373.

Samuelson, P. A. (1991). Sraffa's Other Leg. *Economic Journal*, vol. 101, pp. 570–574. Reprinted in J. Murray (ed.), *The Collected Scientific Papers of Paul A. Samuelson*, Vol. VI, 2011 (Cambridge, MA: The MIT Press), pp. 312–316.

Shackle, G. L. S. (1967). *The Years of High Theory: Invention and Tradition in Economic Thought 1926–1939* (Cambridge: Cambridge University Press).

Signorino, R. (2000). Method and Analysis in Piero Sraffa's 1925 Critique of Marshallian Economics. *The European Journal of the History of Economic Thought*, vol. 7, pp. 569–594. Reprinted in Heinz D. Kurz and Neri Salvadori (eds) *The Legacy of Piero Sraffa*. Volume I. (Cheltenham, UK and Northampton, MA: Edward Elgar), 2003, pp. 241–266.

Signorino, R. (2001). An Appraisal of Piero Sraffa's 'The Laws of Returns under Competitive Conditions'. *The European Journal of the History of Economic Thought*, vol. 8, pp. 230–250. Reprinted in Heinz D. Kurz and Neri Salvadori (eds) *The Legacy of Piero Sraffa*. Volume I. (Cheltenham, UK and Northampton, MA: Edward Elgar), 2003, pp. 267–287.

Sraffa, P. (1925). Sulle relazioni fra costo e quantità prodotta. *Annali di Economia*, vol. 2, pp. 277–328.

Sraffa, P. (1926). The Laws of Returns under Competitive Conditions. *The Economic Journal*, vol. 36, pp. 535–550. Reprinted in H.D. Kurz and N. Salvadori, *The Legacy of Piero Sraffa*, Vol. I, pp. 44–59 (Cheltenam: Edward Elgar), 2003.

Sraffa, P. (1930). A Criticism. A Rejoinder. *The Economic Journal*, vol. 40, pp. 89–93.

Sraffa, P. (1960). *Production of Commodities by Means of Commodities. Prelude to a Critique of Economic Theory* (Cambridge: Cambridge University Press).

Sraffa, P. (1998 [1925]). On the Relations between Cost and Quantity Produced, in L.L. Pasinetti (ed.) *Italian Economic Papers*, Vol. III, pp. 323–363; translation of Sraffa (1925). Reprinted in H.D. Kurz and N. Salvadori, (eds) *The Legacy of Piero Sraffa*, Vol. I, pp. 3–43 (Cheltenam: Edward Elgar), 2003.

Steedman, I. (1988). Sraffian Interdependence and Partial Equilibrium Analysis. *Cambridge Journal of Economics*, vol. 12, pp. 85–95.

Viner, J. (1931). Cost Curves and Supply Curves. *Zeitschrift für Nationalökonomie*, vol. 3, pp. 23–46.

6 Classical economics after Sraffa[1]

Heinz D. Kurz and Neri Salvadori

Original paper: Heinz D. Kurz and Neri Salvadori (2015) Classical Economics after Sraffa, *Cahiers d'économie politique / Papers in Political Economy*, 69, 45–72.

6.1 Introduction

It can hardly be disputed that the edition of *The Works and Correspondence of David Ricardo* and especially Piero Sraffa's Introduction in Volume I, containing Ricardo's *Principles* (Sraffa, 1951), together with Sraffa's *Production of Commodities by Means of Commodities* (Sraffa, 1960), had a major impact on the way in which the Classical economists, especially Ricardo, are seen today. Sraffa's contributions cast new light on the centrepiece of Classical economics – the theory of value and distribution. The latter forms the foundation of all other economic analysis of the Classical authors, such as, for example, the problems of capital accumulation and economic development, of foreign trade and of taxation.

In this chapter, we focus attention on this centrepiece and adopt Sraffa's view as to the 'standpoint ... of the old classical economists from Adam Smith to Ricardo'. According to him, their (and also his) 'investigation is concerned exclusively with such properties of an economic system as do not depend on changes in the scale of production or in the proportion of "factors"' (Sraffa, 1960, p. v). Profits (and rents) are explained in terms of the surplus product left after all used-up means of production and real wages have been deducted from gross outputs and a uniform rate of profits obtains in conditions of free competition. The concept of 'Classical economics' under consideration is defined in *analytical*, not in *chronological* terms. It focuses attention on authors who advocated a *surplus approach* to the theory of value and distribution. The widespread chronological definition, which also subsumes under Classical economics contributions from, for example, Thomas Robert Malthus or Jean-Baptiste Say, is therefore of little help, because it patches over crucial differences in the various authors' respective theories.

While Sraffa's edition and new interpretation was at first received with great enthusiasm and was approved of by scholars from different intellectual

DOI: 10.4324/9781003138709-8

camps,[2] things soon changed when it was gradually understood that it undermined not only the received view of the Classical authors, but also, and more importantly, the view that modern marginalist or neoclassical economics, in whatever form, was the legitimate heir of the Classicals. The use of terms such as 'neo'-classical, 'new' classical, etc. bear witness to the apparent desire of the advocates of the analyses under consideration to present their contributions as continuing the tradition that the Classical economists had established.[3] By putting forward a new and sharp definition of the essence of the Classical approach to the theory of value and distribution, Sraffa provided a criterion that allowed one to discriminate between legitimate and spurious uses of the term 'Classical'. Still more importantly, it allowed one to embark on the challenging task of excavating and then developing what had been 'submerged and forgotten since the advent of the "marginal" method' (Sraffa, 1960, p. v).

This was indeed badly needed, since thick layers of interpretation, conceiving of the Classical authors as marginalist economists 'waiting to be born' (Samuelson, 1978, p. 1415), stood in the way of a thorough reception of Sraffa's new view. Attempts to ward off his re-interpretation abounded. The picture became blurred again and split the profession into three groups: those who accepted and elaborated on Sraffa's interpretation; those who were keen to defend the received marginalist interpretation of Ricardo, as it had forcefully been advocated by Alfred Marshall; and those who criticised Sraffa without necessarily embracing the marginalist view of the world and of the Classical economists. The first group included, among others, Krishna Bharadwaj, Pierangelo Garegnani, Luigi Pasinetti, Bertram Schefold, and Ian Steedman; the second group Paul Samuelson, John Hicks, and Samuel Hollander; and the third group Mark Blaug.[4]

In his hitherto unpublished papers, Sraffa maintained that the study of the varied history of the theory of value and distribution was the truly important thing, not least because this history ran parallel with major economic and socio-political developments. He intended to write the history of the subject, but was prevented from doing so because of the difficulties he encountered with regard to the Ricardo edition (see Gehrke and Kurz, 2002) and the analytical obstacles he had to overcome, frequently with the help of his 'mathematical friends', in elaborating on the reformulation and rectification of the Classical theory of value and distribution. His unpublished papers contain a huge amount of material, and critical comments on it, designed to be used in such a history. They also contain the elements on the basis of which we can reconstruct how Sraffa arrived at his 'equations of production' and the inspiration he received from the writings of the Classical authors. As such, they can be expected to lead to a renewed interest in the characteristic features of the Classical theory of value and distribution and a re-assessment of the difference between it and marginalist theory. This chapter will focus attention on the material under consideration as it is available in Sraffa's papers, which can deepen our understanding of Sraffa's published work and his view of the genuine significance of the Classical theory and its fundamental difference from the marginalist one.

The composition of the chapter is as follows. Section 6.2 summarises the situation as regards the interpretation of the Classical economists at the beginning of the twentieth century. Section 6.3 summarises the essence of Sraffa's understanding of the Classical 'standpoint' as it comes to the fore in his unpublished writings. Section 6.4 deals with the labour theory of value, which according to many interpreters is an indispensable part of the Classical theory of value and distribution, whereas Sraffa was of the opinion that it involved a 'corruption' of it (see, for example, Sraffa Papers D3/12/4: 2(1)). Section 6.5 provides a short summary account of contributions to various fields in economics rooted in a reformulated and rectified Classical theory after Sraffa; the fields mentioned include the treatment of fixed capital, capital utilisation, renewable and exhaustible natural resources, foreign trade, economic growth, and taxation. Section 6.6 summarises the criticism of marginalist theory. Section 6.7 concludes.

We have individually, together, or jointly with other authors written on various different aspects of the issues here under consideration. In the present chapter we will draw on our earlier work, large parts of which are conveniently available in Kurz and Salvadori (1998, 2003, 2007, 2015); see also Kurz (1998, 2002, 2003, 2006, 2011, 2012, 2013).

6.2 The conventional view

In the first half of the twentieth century there was a fairly wide consensus as to the nature of the Classical economists' contribution to political economy, especially to the theory of value and distribution, and its relation to marginal economics, which already had or was about to become the mainstream in large parts of the profession at around the turn of the nineteenth century. This position was well expressed by Alfred Marshall in his *Principles of Economics* (1890). He portrayed Adam Smith, David Ricardo, and other authors he dubbed 'Classical' as precursors of his own theory of demand and supply. The Classicals, he argued, were possessed of a fairly well-developed theory of production and thus supply, but lacked an equally developed theory of demand. Classical theory, which had provided us with the concept of marginal productivity in the theory of intensive diminishing returns, could easily be reconciled with modern theory, based on the concept of marginal utility. A judicious combination and amalgamation of the two, as he, Marshall, had elaborated, was considered to accomplish the task and bring to fruition the seed the Classical economists had sown. Marshall thus disagreed strongly with William Stanley Jevons, who in his *Theory of Political Economy* (1871) had contended that the Classical analysis was entirely useless. Jevons deplored what he called 'the mazy and preposterous' assumptions underlying the doctrine of the 'Ricardian school' and advocated its abandonment rather than its further development and completion.

There were, of course, still scholars who neither thought that the legacy of the Classicals was worthless nor that it could easily be absorbed into marginalist theory. They felt that the Classicals had developed a theory of value and distribution that was fundamentally different from marginalist theory and that the former's shortcomings did not reflect deficiencies beyond remedy, as Jevons and his followers had contended. Interestingly, amongst those keeping the Classical flag flying in various countries there was almost unanimous agreement that a defining characteristic of the Classical approach to the theory of value and distribution was the labour theory of value.[5] In fact, Classical and especially Ricardo's economics came close to being erroneously identified with the labour theory of value. It was then only natural to consider Marx's labour-value-based reasoning as a straightforward confirmation of the Classical tradition, although Marx ([1867] 1954) himself had given *Capital* the subtitle *A Critique of Political Economy*, meaning, of course, first and foremost the political economy of Smith, Ricardo, James Mill, Torrens, etc.

This elicits two remarks. First, with the benefit of hindsight one might say that both supporters and critics of Classical theory, as well as those who saw a continuity between the 'innovators' – that is, the marginalists – and the Classicals, got it wrong. In particular, the idea that the labour theory of value (interpreted as meaning that labour is the only source of value) is an integral part of the Classical theory and that the latter stood or fell with it, on the one hand, and the idea that in the marginalist theory there was no room for it whatsoever, on the other, cannot be sustained. Scrutiny shows that despite their insistence on the original novelty of their approaches, authors such as Jevons, Eugen von Böhm-Bawerk, and John Bates Clark were – ironically – all convinced that in conditions of free competition relative prices in long-run equilibrium equal relative labour values.[6] What they essentially disputed was the causality invoked by the Classical authors, which leads from cost of production in terms of amounts of labour to normal prices. As against this they insisted that the natural starting point is the needy individual and its estimation of goods. The choices of individuals are then said to bring about a situation in which relative marginal utilities with respect to the various goods are equal to relative prices, which in turn are equal to the relative quantities of labour needed directly and indirectly in their production.

Second, as is well known, Marx distinguished between what he called 'classical political economy' and 'vulgar economics'. By the latter he meant an economic analysis that fails to analyse the inner relations and contradictions of bourgeois society, but deals only with its surface and is essentially apologetic. Yet his main criticism concerned propositions of the Classical economists, and especially of Smith and Ricardo, whom he took seriously and from whom he learned a great deal. This appears to have (mis)led many commentators into thinking that Marx's analysis did not constitute an attempt at developing classical political economy by shedding its weaknesses and elaborating on its strengths (as Marx saw them), but was a fundamental break away from it. This view is based on a fundamental misunderstanding, which, alas, still shapes the perception of many Marxists, of the relationship between Marx and his precursors.

When in the above we referred to the benefit of hindsight, we had of course in mind the situation subsequent to Piero Sraffa's 'Introduction' in Volume I of the Ricardo edition (1951), and even more so to his 1960 book. Sraffa's interpretation of the Classical economists as advocates of a 'surplus' approach to the theory of value and distribution not only totally changed today's scholars' perspective on authors such as Smith and Ricardo, it also attributed to this approach a genuine significance that is fundamentally different from the marginalist one. After Sraffa the situation was completely different from what it was before. This does not mean that there were no other authors who had anticipated elements of Sraffa's interpretation of the Classicals (such as, for example, Ladislaus von Bortkiewicz) or who had insisted on striking differences between the marginalist and the Classical approaches (such as, for example, the young Joseph A. Schumpeter). It means that only Sraffa managed to fundamentally alter the perception of the analytical core of Classical economic theory, of how it compares to the marginalist one, and of how insights derived from the former lead to a criticism of the latter.

6.3 Sraffa: Classical economics – a 'science of things'

We now turn to Sraffa's reconstruction of the Classical approach to the theory of value and distribution, followed by his rectification of it, which overcomes the deficiencies of the version that was handed down from Smith via Ricardo and Marx to later authors. Put briefly, the Classical economists and Marx were unable to develop a coherent, logically unassailable theory of value and distribution, because the analytical tools at their disposal were not up to the complexity of their highly sophisticated and empirically rich concepts: production conceived of as a circular flow generating a surplus product, where inputs are advanced at the beginning of the production period and consist of heterogeneous commodities. The mismatch between tools and concepts landed these authors in an impasse, with which they tried to cope as best as they could. The result of this impasse was the labour theory of value. Whereas Smith and Ricardo insisted that it held exactly true in explaining relative prices in exceptional circumstances only, and Ricardo opined that it could be seen as an approximation to a correct theory of value and distribution, of which he was not possessed, Marx contended that the 'law of value' was true with regard to the aggregate of all commodities: in terms of labour-value-based reasoning both the general rate of profits of the system as a whole and the prices of production of commodities corresponding to this rate could be ascertained. This was the origin of the (infamous) problem of the 'transformation' of values in prices.

According to Sraffa, the labour theory of value involved a 'corruption' of the Classical approach to the theory of value and distribution. For example, in a note entitled 'Degeneration of cost and value', probably written in November 1927, Sraffa insisted: 'A. Smith & Ricardo & Marx indeed began to corrupt the old idea of cost, from food to labour. But their notion was still near enough to be in many cases equivalent' (Sraffa's Papers D3/12/4: 2(1)). In what sense did the labour theory of value involve a corruption of Classical theory? In the following we summarise in desperate brevity (to use one of Schumpeter's favourite phrases) how Sraffa arrived at this characterisation in the period extending from the second half of 1927 to 1931, and what it meant. The reader interested in a more thorough account of the chronology of Sraffa's early re-constructive and critical work is asked to consult some of our earlier works on the matter; see, in particular, Kurz and Salvadori (2004, 2005a, 2005b), Gehrke and Kurz (2006), and Kurz (2012).

Sraffa was extremely well read in Alfred Marshall's *Principles* and for some time thought that *this* was economics, *tout court*.[7] He was critical of Marshall's analysis (see Sraffa 1925, 1926), but felt that any attempt at improving upon the state of the art in the field had to start from Marshall. He rejected Marshall's concept of 'real costs', which involved subjectivist elements such as disutility, abstinence, waiting, and the like. For a short while Sraffa even contemplated the possibility of purging Marshall's analysis of its subjectivist elements and tried to conceive of demand and supply schedules in purely objectivist terms. However, he soon realised that this did not lead him anywhere. At around the same time he delved deeper and deeper into the analyses of the Classical economists. He had been clear at an early time that their analyses differed in important respects from those of the later marginalists, but it was far from clear to him wherein precisely the difference consisted. He now grasped that a characteristic feature of their theory of value was that it was based on what he called 'physical real cost', or 'physical cost' for short: the value of a commodity reflected the amounts of commodities – raw materials, means of production and means of subsistence in the support of workers – that had of necessity to be 'destroyed' in the production of the commodity under consideration. Production involved destruction, and value had to do with the amounts of commodities so destroyed.

Sraffa encountered numerous expressions in the writings of the Classical authors of the physical real cost approach and noted them in his papers. The most remarkable ones are perhaps the following two – one by William Petty, the other by James Mill. Petty (1986) advocated a 'physician's outlook' on economic matters; Sraffa cited approvingly Petty's 1676 decision

> to express my self in terms of *Number, Weight*, or *Measure* ... and to consider only such Cases, as have visible Foundations in Nature, leaving those that depend upon the mutable Minds, Opinions, Appetites, and Passions of particular Men, to the Consideration of others.
>
> (Sraffa's Papers, D3/12/4: 3)

Petty's statement is particularly interesting, because it confronts the physical real cost point of view with an early expression of the subjectivist point of view. James Mill (1826, p. 165) on the other hand had put forward the following remarkable proposition: 'The agents of production are the commodities themselves ... They are the food of the labourer, the tools and the machines with which he works, and the raw materials which he works upon.' Reflecting these statements, in a document composed in December 1927, Sraffa called Classical economics explicitly a 'science of things' (Sraffa's Papers D3/12/61: 2) as opposed to Marshall's economics, which was a science of motives.[8]

But how could one ascertain the values of commodities in terms of physical real costs? In order to determine the value of commodity U one had to know the values of commodities X, Y, Z ... used up in its production. In short, it appeared as if one was trapped in circular reasoning, explaining (and determining) the values of commodities in terms of the values of commodities. So how did the Classical economists (and Marx) try to get out of the trap? They sought to reduce all commodities to an 'ultimate measure of value' and render them commensurable in terms of it. Thus William Petty suggested to use a 'loaf of bread' (or also 'corn') – representing workers' bundle of means of subsistence – as an ultimate measure of value: 'bread' was needed directly and indirectly in the production of all commodities, because in all productions workers had to be employed and fed. Similarly, Smith used 'corn' as a generic term including all means of subsistence of workers (see Smith 1976 *WN* I.xi.e.29); Ricardo followed him in this regard.

In Sraffa's early manuscripts we also encounter attempts to reduce commodities to some ultimate measure of value. However, Sraffa did so by starting from systems of simultaneous equations. He quickly discovered that several commodities could serve as an ultimate measure of value: in the case of a system without a surplus product, all commodities produced are 'necessaries', that is, they are indispensable in each and every line of production. Hence each and every commodity enters into the production of each and every commodity. Here things are relatively simple and each type of reduction must result in the same exchange ratios between commodities. In systems with a surplus, distributed in the form of wages or profits, things are not so. While the reduction of wages appears to cause no problem, to which ultimate measure of value ought profits to be reduced? And would all reduction series lead to the same exchange ratios between commodities?

As is well known, the Classical authors eventually took labour as the common measure of value, since labour was considered an indispensable input in the production of all commodities. According to Sraffa this involved the said corruption. Relative prices, Sraffa had convinced himself in late 1927, could be ascertained without falling into circular reasoning by formulating and then solving a system of simultaneous production equations. This was the tool the Classical economists would have needed in order to formulate their surplus approach to the theory of value and distribution in a consistent way and to avoid the pitfalls into which they had fallen.

Beginning in November 1927, Sraffa developed square systems of equations (dealing with single production) in which no more is produced of the different commodities than is consumed productively, that is, systems *without a surplus product*. This is what he called his 'first equations'. He swiftly moved on, in the late 1920s, to investigate *systems with a surplus product*, without and with durable instruments of production (fixed capital) and given and constant real wages in his 'second equations', followed by an investigation of the impact of a variation in real wages on the 'rate of interest', the notion he used at the time, and relative prices in his 'third equations'. This led him to analyse the mathematical properties of the following systems of equations (we take gross output quantities of the various quantities as defining one unit of the respective output).

Without a surplus product:

$$\mathbf{p} = \mathbf{A}^{+}\mathbf{p} \tag{6.1}$$

Here $\mathbf{p}$ is the price vector and $\mathbf{A}^{+}$ is the input matrix (per unit of output) of the means of production-cum-means of subsistence in the support of workers productively consumed during the annual cycle of production (known also as the 'augmented' matrix, which takes account of the fact that in the Classical perspective wages belong to the capital advanced at the beginning of the production period).

With a surplus product:

$$\mathbf{p} = (1 + R)\mathbf{A}^{++}\mathbf{p} \tag{6.2}$$

Here R is the general rate of profits and $\mathbf{A}^{++}$ is the production matrix corresponding to the new situation. (With wages at some socio-historical subsistence level reflected in matrix $\mathbf{A}^{++}$, R gives the rate of return in the prevailing socio-technical conditions.)

When Sraffa discussed the impact of a change (rise) in real wages on the rate of profits and relative prices, he at first followed Ricardo, who had contemplated a hypothetical redistribution that is proportional to the surplus product in the initial situation. If the entire surplus product goes hypothetically to workers, we are back to a system like (6.1) with $\mathbf{A}^{++}$ in the place of $\mathbf{A}^{+}$.

We need not dwell here on the long journey Sraffa undertook before arriving at his 1960 book, a journey that was twice interrupted for several years (basically between 1931–1942 and 1946–1956) because the Ricardo edition required all his attention and energy. Here it suffices to draw attention to a passage in Whitehead (1926), which Sraffa annotated and which paraphrases the essence of what he was doing in the late 1920s. Whitehead had remarked on the success of science since the seventeenth century: 'Science was becoming, and has remained, primarily *quantitative. Search for measurable elements among your phenomena, and then search for relations between these measures of physical quantities*' (Whitehead 1926, pp. 63–64, emphasis added).

We now discuss briefly why, according to Sraffa, the labour theory of value was not an indispensable part of the Classical approach to the theory of value and distribution, but rather reflected a weakness of their analyses. Had they been possessed of a coherent theory of value and distribution with regard to a system in which heterogeneous commodities are produced by the self-same commodities, they would not have had to have recourse to an assumption that was admittedly not fully true (Ricardo), but served as a device not to be 'stopped by the word price', as Ricardo once put it (*Works*, IV, p. 348).

6.4 The labour theory of value vs. the *value theory of labour*

Once Paul Samuelson asked Sraffa whether Ricardo held a labour theory of value. Sraffa is reported to have answered: 'He did and he didn't'. What might at first sight be considered a sibylline response turns out to properly reflect Ricardo's point of view, which, for example, in the third edition of the *Principles* comes to the fore when Ricardo speaks 'of labour as being *the foundation of all value*, and the relative quantity of labour as *almost exclusively* determining the relative value of commodities' (Ricardo *Works* I, p. 20; emphases added). The following note which Sraffa wrote in November 1927 may be read as a comment on Ricardo's statement and puts the issue under consideration into sharp relief:

> It is the *whole* process of production that must be called "human labour", and thus causes all product and all values. Marx and Ricardo used "labour" in two different senses: the above, and that of *one* of the factors of production ("hours of labour" or "quantity of labour" has a meaning only in the latter sense). It is by confusing the two senses that they got mixed up and said that value is proportional to quantity of labour (in second sense) whereas they ought to have said that it is due to human labour (in first sense: a non measurable quantity, or rather not a quantity at all).
>
> (Sraffa's Papers D3/12/11: 64; emphases in the original)

Ricardo considered labour as the 'foundation' of all value, 'a non measurable quantity, or rather not a quantity at all' in the words of Sraffa, and he felt entitled to *approximate* value in terms of labour values.[9] Sraffa illustrated the confusing of the two senses with respect to Robert Torrens's approach to the problem:

> Torrens knew that the (absolute) value of the product is determined by (in fact, is) the amount of things that have been destroyed for its production. But he did not see his way through without finding a "common measure" of them: he probably felt a repulsion to, or thought that it could not be done, *to sum together quantities of heterogeneous things measured in different units. This was of course fatal: he started to find something common in them, upon which to base his measurement: the labour theory was ready at hand ... The result was of course absurd.*
>
> (Sraffa's Papers D3/12/5: 26)

The statement that the result was 'absurd' applies to a system with a surplus, whereas with regard to systems without a surplus it can be shown that the price vector in equation (6.1) is proportional to the vector of labour values appropriately constructed (see Kurz and Salvadori, 2009). Sraffa apparently was not aware of this when he developed and discussed his 'first equations'. The reason is obvious: there is no need to talk of labour – all that matters are physical real costs of production. Labour values therefore are of no importance in the analysis, they are at best secondary magnitudes (we return to this question below). The labour theory of value, Sraffa concluded at the time, involved a 'corruption' of the tradition established by Petty and the physiocrats, who are said to have had the right concept of 'cost'. In this context it is worth mentioning that in a document of some 50 pages composed in the summer of 1929, Sraffa explained in detail why he then thought that labour was *not* a 'quantity' that could be taken as a datum in value theory (see also the reflection of his argument in D3/12/13: 2, and Kurz and Salvadori, 2009 and 2012). He expounded that his objection to the approach in terms of labour quantities 'è basata sulla veduta essenzialmente fisiocratica, che il *valore* sia una quantità intrinseca degli oggetti, quasi una *qualità fisica o chimica*' (Sraffa's Papers D3/12/12: 7, emphases added).[10] The physical interpretation is neatly corroborated by a document entitled 'Physical Costs & Value', contained in a folder 'Nov. [1927]', which reads:

> When I say that the value of a product is "determined" by the physical volume of commodities used up in its production, it should *not* be understood that it is determined by the value of those commodities. This would be a vicious circle, because the value of the product is equal to the value of the factors *plus* the surplus produced.

> What I say is simply that the numerical proportions between amount of factors and amount of product *is*, by definition, the absolute value of the product.
>
> (Sraffa's Papers D3/12/11: 101; emphases in the original, "not" is underlined twice in the original)

And in a document contained in the same folder, he also talked of 'physical value' (Sraffa's Papers D3/12/11: 75).

Some people seem to think that labour values are something natural and simple. However, they are typically not (see Kurz and Salvadori, 2009). Here there is no need to enter into a discussion of the difficulties involved. We rather ask ourselves where labour values are supposed to come from. If in the production of one unit of commodity U certain amounts of commodities X, Y, Z,... are consumed productively, then in order to be able to ascertain the labour value of U, one would have to know already the labour values of X, Y, Z, ... As Sraffa stressed, determining values by means of values involves 'a vicious circle' – values ought to be determined in terms of magnitudes that are not themselves values.[11] In a system with a circular flow of commodities and a surplus product, labour values can be ascertained by solving a special system of simultaneous equations, namely the one in which the rate of profits is equal to zero – values are then shown to depend exclusively on the methods of production and productive consumption actually in use. Hence labour values reflect but a very special constellation of the sharing out of the product among workers and capitalists. To emphasise this fact, in the early 1940s Sraffa coined the term 'Value Theory of Labour' (see Sraffa's Papers D3/12/44: 3 and D3/12/46: 24): values are proportional to labour quantities if and only if there are no profits (setting aside the exceedingly special case of uniform input proportions across all industries of the economy).

Only in the case Ricardo contemplated, in which production processes start with 'unassisted labour', can labour values be ascertained in an easy and straightforward manner by adding up labour quantities from the beginning of the time-staggered labour process until its end. Marx objected to this conceptualisation of production as a unidirectional or linear process of finite duration that there is no stage in the production process of developed economies that does not involve some 'constant capital', that is, produced means of production. The implication of this is, of course, that labour values can only be ascertained by solving a system of simultaneous equations – they are nothing else than production prices corresponding to a particular distribution of income ($r = 0$).

Finally we remark briefly on the 'transformation problem'. As Sraffa's interpretation of the Classical authors shows, if the Classical physical real cost approach is developed coherently, it simply does not face this problem. *In Classical economics there is no transformation problem.* This does not mean that one cannot in certain cases get from labour values to prices of production in a logically consistent way. It only means that the latter can be determined totally independently of the former, which are therefore redundant in the analysis (Steedman, 1977). Interestingly, in non-trivial cases in which one can go from labour values to prices of production, the use of Sraffa's Standard commodity is required (see Kurz and Salvadori, 2009). In this perspective the labour theory of value (interpreted as meaning that labour is the only source of value) is not an indispensable building block of Classical economics. Wrongly attributing to the Classical authors such a theory had the effect of rendering their whole analysis vulnerable to criticism and was responsible for its premature abandonment.

6.5 Applying the Classical approach

The impact of *Production of Commodities by Means of Commodities* was enormous. Roncaglia (1978 [1975]) includes an appendix with a list of publications on Sraffa's book published up to the mid-1970s. It includes hundreds of items. The first section of the appendix draws attention to a large number of reviews of the book and mathematical formulations of various parts of it, and the numerous interpretations put forward in relation to the received thought of Classical economists, Marx, and some neoclassical economists. More recently, Bellino (2008) has discussed 35 reviews of the book in some detail. In the second section of his bibliography Roncaglia lists works concerning particular aspects of Sraffa's book. Here we find several papers concerning the Standard commodity (its interpretation, its role within the book, its relationship with Ricardo's 'invariable measure of value', and with the so-called 'transformation problem' of labour values in prices of production in Marx), joint production, fixed capital, and land. We devoted a whole paper to the Standard commodity (Kurz and Salvadori, 1993) and will not discuss it here. For a more recent survey of the literature on Sraffa, see Aspromourgos (2004).

While the problem of single production was investigated swiftly after the publication of Sraffa's book, the problems of joint production, fixed capital, and land needed a great deal more time, and some were in fact investigated only after 1978. A summary account is apposite; see also the book edited by Salvadori and Steedman (1990), which includes the relevant literature up to the late 1980s. A common aspect concerning Sraffa's treatment of these issues concerns the fact that the number of processes involved may be equal to the number of commodities. The question is not trivial especially in the case of joint production, but Sraffa indicated the solution to it. The problem left was whether the number of processes involved *needs* to be equal to the number of commodities. Schefold (1978a, 1978b) and Bidard (1986), among others, proved that in some cases the answer is positive, but in some others it is not. This result led to the abandonment of the treatment of the problem in terms of equations (Sraffa) and to its treatment in terms of inequalities (von Neumann). However, in the cases in which joint production is not pure and is related only to the presence of fixed capital and/or land, the system is 'square', to use the expression coined in the literature to indicate that the number of processes involved is equal to the number of commodities produced.

In Appendix D Sraffa explains how the method of treating what is left of fixed capital at the end of the year as a kind of joint product is foreshadowed in some Classical economists. We devoted an entire paper to this issue (Kurz and Salvadori, 2005a) and will not discuss it here. In Chapter X Sraffa presents his analysis of fixed capital, but he limits it to the case in which only one machine is used, the efficiency of this machine is constant, and the machine is not transferable between sectors. The subsequent literature has almost completely generalised the issue. Roncaglia (1971) analysed the case in which machines are jointly utilised and their efficiency is constant. (He did not investigate the transferability of machines, but on the basis of the assumptions he employed there would be no problem in doing so.) Schefold (1971, 1978c) investigated the case in which the efficiency is not constant and machines are not jointly used and not transferable. Salvadori (1988, 1999) studied both the case in which efficiency is not constant and machines are jointly used and not transferable and the case in which efficiency is not constant and machines are not jointly used and transferable, provided that efficiency paths are independent of the sector in which the machines are used. Huang (2015) provided an analysis in which efficiency, while not constant, is subject to some restrictions, and machines are used jointly and are transferable. In all these analyses it is confirmed that prices do not depend on output proportions but only on income distribution, except for the case in which machines are jointly used; in this case the growth rate plays a role in the choice of techniques and therefore prices are determined once *both* the rate of profit (or the wage rate) and the growth rate are known.

In Chapter XI Sraffa presents his analysis of land. Actually Sraffa (1960, p. 74) refers to 'Natural resources which are used in production, such as land and mineral deposits'. However, we know from the correction of the proofs of his book that at the last minute he dropped parts of a section devoted to what he in his preparatory notes had called 'wasting assets' (see Kurz and Salvadori, 2001a, pp. 290–293). Sraffa considers extensive and intensive rent when a single agricultural commodity exists. The problem of multiple agricultural products is mentioned, but not dealt with. The analysis of extensive rent is limited to the case in which the rate of rent with regard to one quality of land is equal to zero, with no closer consideration of the quality of land to which this applies. Once again Sraffa is mainly concerned with the issue of the equality of the number of processes involved and the number of commodities the prices of which have to be ascertained, given the gross amounts of the different products that have to be produced. Sraffa's analysis of intensive rent is limited to two issues: the existence of two processes to produce the agricultural commodity, which guarantees squareness (§87), and the connection between this analysis and a process of 'intensive' diminishing returns (§88). Quadrio-Curzio (1967, 1980), Montani (1972, 1975), Kurz (1978), and Salvadori (1986) provided detailed accounts of extensive and intensive rent.

The case of scarce natural resources such as land(s) makes it abundantly clear that relative prices and income distribution cannot be ascertained independently of the gross output levels of the different commodities to be produced (a fact that should have already been clear given Sraffa's warnings that constant returns to scale are not assumed in his book). In the case of intensive diminishing returns a rent will emerge if the land under consideration is scarce, which is typically reflected in the coexistence of two methods of production by means of which the land is utilised. It has also been confirmed that 'fertility' (in the sense of unit costs of production) is not an intrinsic property of lands, but depends on the rate of profits. (Sraffa had clarified this as early as in Sraffa, 1925). Abraham-Frois and Berrebi (1980, chap 4) and Saucier (1981, chap X) have shown the possibility of external differential rent by operating one process producing corn and two processes producing an industrial commodity that need corn in different amounts per unit of output; Saucier (1981, p. 234) has called this variety of rent 'external differential rent'. Bidard (2011) has shown that similar results may obtain when more than one agricultural product exists. It has been confirmed that if the quantities in effectual demand are independent of prices, then the system is square, but it does not need to be so if they are not.

All these analyses of land have been carried out on the assumption that the economy is in a self-replacing state, that is, it is stationary. In case output quantities change over time, the scarcity of land(s) changes over time as well and prices, the rates of rent, and the competitive rate of profits (or, alternatively, the real wage rate) cannot remain constant. A similar problem arises when natural resources other than land – which Ricardo took to be possessed of 'original and indestructible powers' (*Works*, I, p. 67) – are taken into account, which Sraffa did not do in any depth. The reference is to exhaustible resources, such as oil or minerals. These have been investigated starting from a Classical-Sraffian framework of analysis. In another paper (Kurz and Salvadori, 2015, chap. 16) we reviewed the whole debate, starting from what can be found on this issue in Sraffa's papers, followed by an analysis of the seminal paper by Parrinello (1983), and the subsequent debate, including an extensive analysis of Ricardo's views on mines.

In Appendix A Sraffa explains how from the economic system one can extract a 'smaller self-replacing system the net product of which consists of only one kind of commodity'; this can be done for each and every commodity. Sraffa calls such a miniature system a 'sub-system'. The basic idea underlying the construction can be traced far back in the literature and is to be found, for example, in Marx and also in Ricardo. It is also known as a vertically integrated system. Its characteristic feature is that it needs only labour and natural resources as inputs from the outside because all capital goods are reproduced within the integrated industry. Pasinetti (1988, 1989) elaborated the concept further and formalised it.

Sraffa's book also provided the basis for a reformulation of the pure theory of international trade, paying special attention to the fact that capital consists of heterogeneous produced means of production. A start was again made by Parrinello (1970), followed by several contributions by Steedman, Metcalfe and Steedman, and Mainwaring, who showed that several of the traditional trade theorems, derived within the Heckscher-Ohlin-Samuelson trade model, do not carry over to a framework with a positive rate of profits and heterogeneous capital goods; see in particular the collection of essays in Steedman (1979b). Attention was also paid to the analysis of the small open economy, the world economy (see Steedman, 1979a), and taxation (see for instance Metcalfe and Steedman, 1971).

Production of Commodities was also an important tool in investigating issues in the history of economic analysis. The list of contributions and themes is too huge to be covered here; we illustrate the kind of findings in this literature in terms of three cases. As a matter of fact the price system studied by Sraffa (1960) can be found *in nuce* in many authors including Marshall and Walras, but also Marx and, obviously, Ricardo. Steedman (1977) scrutinised Marx's labour-value-based reasoning with the help of Sraffa (1960), and showed that it cannot generally be sustained. In a paper devoted to Walras's 'Refutation of the English Theory' in the *Elements* we refuted Walras's criticism of Ricardo. We also showed that the Sraffa type of price system is contained in Walras's construction and showed that the Classical theory of value and distribution is fundamentally different from Walras's neoclassical one (see Kurz and Salvadori, 2002). In some other papers we have related the most prominent models of the New Growth Theory (NGT) literature to the Classical tradition of economic thought (see, for example, Kurz and Salvadori, 1998, chap 4). In a very precise sense the NGT can be said to involve a *return* to modes of thought and the method of analysis characteristic of the Classical authors. In terms of method, the NGT is *long-period* theory, advocated by Adam Smith and developed by David Ricardo. In terms of content, many of the models of the NGT dispense with the traditional neoclassical determination of the rate of profit in terms of the supply of and demand for 'capital'. Indeed the profit rate is determined by technology because it is assumed that there is a technology producing 'labour'. In order to render this fact acceptable to a twentieth-century audience, the factor has been given new names and enters the stage either as 'human capital' or 'knowledge'. The readers of *Production of Commodities* may immediately recall that when at the beginning of chapter II (§§ 4–5) wages are regarded as entering the system 'on the same footing as the fuel for the engines or the feed for the cattle' (Sraffa, 1960, p. 9), the profit rate and the prices are determined by technology alone. On the contrary, when workers get a part of the surplus, the quantity of labour employed in each industry has to be represented explicitly, and the profit rate and the prices can be determined only if an extra equation determining income distribution is introduced into the analysis. The additional equation generally used by advocates of neoclassical analysis is the equality between the demand and the supply of 'capital', which requires the homogeneity of this factor. But no extra equation is required in the NGT since, as in Ricardo and in §§ 4–5 of Sraffa's book, there is a technology producing 'labour'.

6.6 A critique of marginalist theory

The subtitle of *Production of Commodities* is 'Prelude to a critique of economic theory', the reference being to 'the marginal theory of value and distribution' (Sraffa, 1960, p. vi). Indeed, for a long time after the publication of Sraffa's book the emphasis was almost exclusively on the explicit or implicit criticism of that theory contained in the book in the so-called Cambridge controversies on the theory of capital. Here we need not dwell on it; for summary accounts, see Harcourt, 1972; Kurz and Salvadori, 1995, chap 14; Garegnani, 2012; Petri, 2015. It suffices to draw the reader's attention to a book by Opocher and Steedman (2015) on *Full Industry Equilibrium* in which they chart out the implications of a rigorously long-period point of view for the supply side in conventional microeconomic theory. They show in particular that there is generally no presumption that the demand for a factor changes inversely with the factor price, as is commonly assumed in this kind of analysis. This has far-reaching implications for the theory and implies that much of what economists conventionally take to be unobtrusive facts are not uncontroversial at all.

6.7 Concluding remarks

After the publication of the Ricardo edition and Sraffa's 1960 book, the perception and understanding of the Classical economists' approach to the theory of value and distribution changed markedly. Sraffa deserves the credit for having freed that approach from thick layers of misinterpretation and for having shown that it had been abandoned – 'submerged and forgotten' – prematurely. In particular, the Classical approach was not flawed beyond remedy, as Sraffa's reformulation and elaboration of it demonstrated. What is more, the Classical approach turned out not only to be rich in content and now available in a logically consistent form, it also provided a perspective or standpoint from which major deficiencies of marginalist theory could be seen, which up until then had passed unnoticed. Apparently, the development of economics does not follow a path shaped by a perfect selection mechanism that abandons anything that is erroneous and weak and keeps everything that is true and useful. After Sraffa, economics is no longer what it was.

Notes

1 Paper given at the conference 'What have we learnt on Classical economics since Sraffa?', Université Paris Ouest Nanterre, 16–17 October 2014. We are grateful to the participants of the conference for useful discussions following the presentation of our paper. We should also like to express our gratitude to two anonymous referees and Ghislain Deleplace for their valuable comments and suggestions. It hardly needs to be said that the responsibility for the views expressed in this paper is entirely ours.

2 See, for example, the numerous reviews of Sraffa's edition of Ricardo's works and correspondence, written by economists representing various intellectual orientations in economics.

3 A little more than a decade ago, Robert Lucas (2004) expressed this view in the following way: 'I think of all progress in economic thinking, in the kind of basic core of economic theory, as developing entirely as learning how to do what Hume and Smith and Ricardo wanted to do, only better'. However, it is not clear which elements in Lucas's writings are supposed to reflect the influence of the Classical economists. For example, the assumption of a single 'representative agent' is totally alien to the Classical authors, who stressed power and information asymmetries in society and distinguished between different social classes, whose interests, as Adam Smith (1976) insisted (*WN* I.xi.p), are by no means the same; see also Kurz (2015).

4 The culminating point of the attempted 'counter-revolution' was arguably Samuelson (1978), to which Garegnani (2007) replied; see also the debate between the two in Kurz (2013).

5 For evidence with respect to the German-speaking world, see Kurz (1995). German authors who can be mentioned in this context include Heinrich Dietzel, Franz Oppenheimer, and Emil Lederer.

6 Jevons (1871, p. 182), for example, wrote: 'thus we have proved that commodities will exchange in any market at the ratio of the quantities produced by the same quantity of labour'. See also Kurz (1995).

7 Sraffa's working copy of Marshall (1920 [1890]) is studded with annotations, criticisms, and remarks.

8 In a paper titled 'A Plea for Pure Theory', William Cunningham (1892) had already confronted the different views of Petty and Marshall. Sometime in the period from May to July 1928, Sraffa probably excerpted and commented on the following lines from it: '"Prof. Marshall describes economics as the science of *measurable motives* (Present Position, p. 31). This ... seems to me to be the very gist of the difference in treatment" C. is opposed to this and agrees with W. Petty. He wants to deal with "external phenomena" "laying a solid foundation of fact." "But when we start from motives, we lose all this advantage. What actually weighs with a man and determines him in any course of conduct, is not a thing we can observe ... Motives are not obvious and we are likely to be mistaken about them"' (Sraffa's Papers D3/12/9: 18).

9 A confusion of the two senses is widespread in the literature on Ricardo. For example, Mary Morgan recently wrote: 'it is *labour alone that creates value*, and ... there is a direct relationship between labour input and value' (Morgan, 2012, p. 60; emphasis added). As we have just seen, Ricardo was *not* of this opinion.

10 English translation: 'is based on the essentially physiocratic point of view that value is a quantity that is intrinsic to the objects, almost a physical or chemical quality'.

11 As he stressed in a document presumably written in the second half of 1929, echoing a dictum by Petty, relative prices and income distribution had to be

ascertained exclusively in terms of 'quantities [that] have an objective, independent existence at every or some instants of the natural (i.e., not interfered with by the experimenter) process of production and distribution; they can therefore be measured physically, with the ordinary instruments of measuring number, weight, time, etc.' (Sraffa's Papers D3/12/13: 2).

References

Abraham-Frois, G. and Berrebi, E. (1980). *Rentes, rareté, surprofits*, Paris: Economica.

Aspromourgos, T. (2004). "Sraffian Research Programmes and Unorthodox Economics", *Review of Political Economy*, 16(2), pp. 179–206.

Bellino, E. (2008). "Book Reviews on *Production of Commodities by Means of Commodities*", in G. Chiodi and L. Ditta (eds), *Sraffa or an Alternative Economics*, New York: Palgrave Macmillan, pp. 23–41.

Bidard, Ch. (1986). "Is Von Neumann Square?", *Zeitschrift für Nationalökonomie*, 46, pp. 401–419.

Bidard, Ch. (2011). "Extensive Rent and Multiple Equilibria", in N. Salvadori and Ch. Gehrke (eds) *Keynes, Sraffa and the Criticism of Neoclassical Theory*, London, Routledge, pp. 201–213.

Cunningham, W. (1892). "A Plea for Pure Theory", *Economic Review*, 2, pp. 25–41.

Garegnani, P. (2007). "Professor Samuelson on Sraffa and the Classical Economists", *European Journal of the History of Economic Thought*, 14, pp. 181–242.

Garegnani, P. (2012). "On the Present State of the Capital Controversies", *Cambridge Journal of Economics*, 36(6), pp. 1417–1432.

Gehrke, C. and Kurz, H. D. (2002). "Keynes and Sraffa's "difficulties with J.H. Hollander": A Note on the History of the RES Edition of *The Works and Correspondence of David Ricardo*", *European Journal of the History of Economic Thought*, 9(4), pp. 644–671; reprinted pp. 93–119 in Kurz, H. D. and Salvadori, N. (2007), *Interpreting Classical Economics: Studies in Long-period Analysis*, London: Routledge

Gehrke, C. and Kurz, H. D. (2006). "Sraffa on von Bortkiewicz: Reconstructing the Classical Theory of Value and Distribution", *History of Political Economy*, 38(1), pp. 91–149.

Harcourt, G. C. (1972). *Some Cambridge Controversies in the Theory of Capital*, Cambridge: Cambridge University Press.

Huang, B. (2015). "A Fixed Capital Model with Transferable and Jointly Utilized Machines in the Sraffa Framework", *Metroeconomica*, 66, to appear (doi: 10.1111/meca.12076).

Jevons, W. S. (1871). *The Theory of Political Economy*. London: Macmillan.

Kurz, H. D. (1978). "Rent Theory in a Multisectoral Model", *Oxford Economic Papers*, 30, pp. 16–37.

Kurz, H. D. (1995). "Marginalism, Classicism and Socialism in German-speaking Countries, 1871–1932", in I. Steedman (ed.), *Socialism and Marginalism in Economics 1870–1930*, London and New York: Routledge, pp. 7–86.

Kurz, H. D. (1998). "Against the Current: Sraffa's Unpublished Manuscripts and the History of Economic Thought", *European Journal of the History of Economic Thought*, 5(3): 437–451; reprinted pp. 652–656 in Kurz, H. and Salvadori, N. (eds) 2003, *The Legacy of Piero Sraffa*, vol. II, Cheltenham: Edward Elgar Publishing.

Kurz, H. D. (2002). "Sraffa's Contributions to Economics: Some Notes on his Unpublished Papers", pp. 177–196 in Nisticó, S. and Tosato, D. (eds), *Competing Economic Theories: Essays in Memory of Giovanni Caravale*, London: Routledge.

Kurz, H. D. (2003). "The Surplus Interpretation of the Classical Economists", pp. 167–183 in Samuels, W., Biddle, J. and Davis, J. (eds), *The Blackwell Companion to the History of Economic Thought*, Oxford: Blackwell.

Kurz, H. D. (2006). "The Agents of Production are the Commodities Themselves: On the Classical Theory of Production, Distribution and Value", *Structural Change and Economic Dynamics*, 17: 1–26; reprinted pp. 131–158 in Kurz, H. D. and Salvadori, N. (2007), *Interpreting Classical Economics: Studies in Long-period Analysis*, London, Routledge.

Kurz, H. D. (2011). "On David Ricardo's Theory of Profits: The Laws of Distribution Are "Not Essentially Connected with the Doctrine of Value"", *History of Economic Thought*, 53(1), pp. 1–20.

Kurz, H. D. (2012). "Don't Treat Too Ill My Piero! Interpreting Sraffa's Papers", *Cambridge Journal of Economics*, 36, pp. 1535–1569; reprinted in this volume.

Kurz, H. D. (ed.) (2013). *The Theory of Value and Distribution in Economics. Discussions between Pierangelo Garegnani and Paul Samuelson*, London and New York: Routledge.

Kurz, H. D. (2015). "Adam Smith on Markets, Competition and Violations of Natural Liberty", *Cambridge Journal of Economics*, 40(2), pp. 615–638; reprinted in this volume.

Kurz, H. D. and Salvadori, N. (1993). "The "standard commodity" and Ricardo's Search for an "Invariable Measure of Value"", pp. 95–123 in Baranzini, M. and Harcourt, G. C. (eds), *The Dynamics of the Wealth of Nations: Growth, Distribution and Structural Change—Essays in Honour of Luigi Pasinetti*, London, Macmillan; reprinted pp. 123–147 in Kurz, and Salvadori, 1998.

Kurz, H. D. and Salvadori, N. (1995). *Theory of Production: A Long-period Analysis*, Cambridge: Cambridge University Press.

Kurz, H. D. and Salvadori, N. (1998). *Understanding 'Classical' Economics: Studies in Long-period Theory*, London: Routledge.

Kurz, H. D. and Salvadori, N. (2001a). "Sraffa and the Mathematicians: Frank Ramsey and Alister Watson", pp. 187–216 in Cozzi, T. and Marchionatti, R. (eds), *Piero Sraffa's Political Economy: A Centenary Estimate*, London, Routledge; reprinted pp. 187–216 in Kurz, H. and Salvadori, N. (2003), *Classical Economics and Modern Theory: Studies in Long Period Analysis*, London: Routledge.

Kurz, H. D. and Salvadori, N. (2001b). "Classical Economics and the Problem of Exhaustible Resources", *Metroeconomica*, 52(3), pp. 282–296; reprinted pp. 259–271 in Kurz, H. and Salvadori, N. (2003), *Classical Economics and Modern Theory: Studies in Long Period Analysis*, London: Routledge.

Kurz, H. D. and Salvadori, N. (2002). "One Theory or Two? Walras's Critique of Ricardo", *History of Political Economy*, 34(2), pp. 365–398; reprinted pp. 52–78 in Kurz, H. and Salvadori, N. (2007), Interpreting *Classical Economics: Studies in Long Period Analysis*, London: Routledge

Kurz, H. D. and Salvadori, N. (2003). "*Classical Economics and Modern Theory: Studies in Long Period Analysis*, London: Routledge.

Kurz, H. D. and Salvadori, N. (2004). "Man from the Moon: on Sraffa's Objectivism", *Économies et Sociétés*, 35: 1545–1557; reprinted pp. 120–130 in Kurz,

H. D. and Salvadori, N. (2007), *Interpreting Classical Economics: Studies in Long-period Analysis*, London: Routledge.
Kurz, H. D. and Salvadori, N. (2005a). "Removing an 'insuperable obstacle' in the Way of an Objectivist Analysis: Sraffa's Attempts at Fixed Capital", *European Journal of the History of Economic Thought*, vol. 12, no. 3, 493–523; reprinted pp. 119–149 in Kurz, H. D., Pasinetti, L. L. and Salvadori, N. (eds) 2008. *Piero Sraffa: The Man and the Scholar—Exploring his Unpublished Papers*, London: Routledge.
Kurz, H. D. and Salvadori, N. (2005b). "Representing the Production and Circulation of Commodities in Material Terms: On Sraffa's Objectivism", *Review of Political Economy*, vol. 17, no. 3, 69–97; reprinted pp. 249–277 in Kurz, H. D., Pasinetti, L. L. and Salvadori, N. (eds) 2008. *Piero Sraffa: The Man and the Scholar—Exploring his Unpublished Papers*, London: Routledge.
Kurz, H. D. and Salvadori, N. (2007). *Interpreting Classical Economics: Studies in Long-period Analysis*, London: Routledge.
Kurz, H. D. and Salvadori, N. (2009). "Sraffa and the Labour Theory of Value: A Few Observations", pp. 187–213 in Vint, J., Metcalfe, J. S., Kurz, H. D., Salvadori, N. and Samuelson, P. A. (eds), *Economic Theory and Economic Thought: Festschrift in Honour of Ian Steedman*, London: Routledge.
Kurz, H. D. and Salvadori, N. (2012). "On the 'vexata questio of Value': Ricardo, Marx and Sraffa", Chapter 12 in Taylor, L., Rezai, A. and Michl, T. (eds), *Analytical Insights and Social Fairness: Economic Essays in the Spirit of Duncan K. Foley*, London: Routledge.
Kurz, H. D. and Salvadori, N. (2015). *Revisiting Classical Economics. Studies in Long-Period Analysis*, London: Routledge.
Lucas, R. E. (2004). "My Keynesian Education", in M. de Vroey and K. Hoover (eds), *The IS-LM Model: Its Rise, Fall and Strange Persistence.* Annual Supplement to Vol. 36 of *History of Political Economy*, Durham, NC: Duke University Press.
Marshall, A. (1920). *Principles of Economics*, 1st edn 1890, 8th edn 1920. Reprint, reset, London: Macmillan, 1977.
Marx, K. (1954). *Capital*, vol. I, Moscow: Progress Publishers. English translation of *Das Kapital*, vol. I, Hamburg (1867): Meissner.
Metcalfe, J. S., Steedman, I. (1971). "Some Effects of Taxation in a Linear Model of Production", *The Manchester School*, 39, pp. 171–85.
Mill, J. (1826). *Elements of Political Economy*, 3rd edn, London: Henry G. Bohn.
Montani, G. (1972). "La teoria ricardiana della rendita", *L'Industria*, 3–4, pp. 221–243.
Montani, G. (1975). "Scarce Natural Resources and Income Distribution", *Metroeconomica*, 27, pp. 68–101.
Morgan, M. (2012). *The World in the Model. How Economists Work and Think*, Cambridge: Cambridge University Press.
Opocher, A. and Steedman, I. (2015). *Full Industry Equilibrium*, Cambridge: Cambridge University Press.
Pasinetti, L.L. (1988). "Growing Subsystems, Vertically Hyperintegrated Sectors and the Labour Theory of Value", *Cambridge Journal of Economics*, 12(1), pp. 125–134.
Pasinetti, L.L. (1989). "Growing Subsystems and Vertically Hyper-Integrated Sectors: A Note of Clarification", *Cambridge Journal of Economics*, 13(3), pp. 479–480.

Parrinello, S. (1970). "Introduzione ad una teoria neoricardiana del commercio internazionale", *Studi Economici*, 25, pp. 267–321.

Parrinello, S. (1983). "Exhaustible Natural Resources and the Classical Method of Long-Period Equilibrium", in Kregel (1983), pp. 186–199.

Petri, F. (2015). "Capital Theory", in G. Faccarello and Heinz D. Kurz (eds), *Handbook of the History of Economic Analysis, Vol. III*, Cheltenham: Edward Elgar, forthcoming.

Petty, W. (1986). *The Economic Writings of Sir William Petty*, edited by C.H. Hull, vols. I and II, Cambridge 1899: Cambridge University Press. Reprinted in one volume, New York: Kelley.

Quadrio-Curzio, A. (1967). *Rendita e distribuzione in un modello economico plurisettoriale*, Milano: Giuffrè.

Quadrio-Curzio, A. (1980). "Rent, Income Distribution, and Orders of Efficiency and Rentability", in Pasinetti (1980), pp. 218–240; reprinted in Quadrio Curzio (1990), pp. 21–47.

Ricardo, D. (1951–1973). *The Works and Correspondence of David Ricardo*, 11 vols, edited by P. Sraffa with the collaboration of M. H. Dobb, Cambridge, UK: Cambridge University Press.

Roncaglia, A. (1971). "Il capitale fisso in uno schema di produzione circolare", *Studi Economici*, 26, pp. 232–245. English translation in Roncaglia (1978).

Roncaglia, A. (1978). *Sraffa and the Theory of Prices*, New York: Wiley.

Salvadori, N. (1986). "Land and Choice of Techniques within the Sraffa Framework", *Australian Economic Papers*, (25), pp. 94–105.

Salvadori, N. (1988). "Fixed Capital Within the Sraffa Framework", *Zeitschrift für Nationalökonomie*, (48), pp. 1–17.

Salvadori, N. (1999). "Transferable Machines with Uniform Efficiency Paths", in Mongiovi G. and Petri F. (eds), *Value, Distribution and Capital*, London and New York: Routledge, pp. 297–313.

Salvadori, N. and Steedman, I. (eds) (1990). *Joint Production of Commodities*, Aldershot: Edward Elgar.

Samuelson, P. A. (1978). "The Canonical Classical Model of Political Economy", *Journal of Economic Literature* 16(4), pp. 1415–1434.

Saucier, P. (1981). *Le choix des techniques en situation de limitations de ressources*, Ph.D. thesis, Université de Paris-II, mimeo.

Schefold, B. (1971). *Mr. Sraffa on Joint Production*, Ph.D. thesis, University of Basle, mimeo.

Schefold, B. (1978a). "Fixed Capital as a Joint Product", *Jahrbücher für Nationalökonomie und Statistik*, 192, pp. 415–439.

Schefold, B. (1978b). "Multiple Product Techniques with Properties of Single Product Systems", *Zeitschrift für Nationalökonomie*, 38, pp. 29–53.

Schefold, B. (1978c). "On Counting Equations", *Zeitschrift für Nationalökonomie*, 38, pp. 253–285.

Smith, A. (1976). *An Inquiry into the Nature and Causes of the Wealth of Nations*, two vols, in Campbell, R. H. and Skinner, A. S. (eds), *The Glasgow Edition of the Works and Correspondence of Adam Smith*, Oxford: Oxford University Press.

Sraffa, P. (1925). "Sulle relazioni fra costo e quantità prodotta", *Annali di Economia*, **2**, pp. 277–328. English translation in Pasinetti, Luigi L. (ed.) *Italian Economic Papers*, Bologna: Il Mulino, 1998, pp. 323–363. Reprinted in Kurz, H. D. and Salvadori, N. (eds) *The Legacy of Sraffa*, Vol. 1, Cheltenham: Elgar, pp. 3–43.

Sraffa, P. (1926). "The Laws of Returns under Competitive Conditions", *Economic Journal*, 36, pp. 535–550.
Sraffa, P. (1951). "Introduction", in Ricardo (1951 ssq.), *Works* I, pp. xiii–lxii.
Sraffa, P. (1960). *Production of Commodities by Means of Commodities*, Cambridge: Cambridge University Press.
Steedman, I. (1977). *Marx after Sraffa*, London: New Left Books.
Steedman, I. (1979a). *Trade Amongst Growing Economies*, Cambridge: Cambridge University Press.
Steedman, I. (ed.) (1979b). *Fundamental Issues in Trade Theory*, London: Macmillan.
Whitehead, A.N. (1926). *Science and the Modern World, Lowell Lectures 1925*, Cambridge: Cambridge University Press.

7 On the 'photograph' interpretation of Piero Sraffa's production equations

A view from the Sraffa archive

Heinz D. Kurz and Neri Salvadori[1]

Original paper: Heinz D. Kurz and Neri Salvadori (2018) On the 'photograph' interpretation of Piero Sraffa's production equations: A view from the Sraffa archive in Marcella Corsi, Jan Kregel, Carlo D'Ippoliti (eds), *Classical Economics Today: Essays in Honor of Alessandro Roncaglia*, 113–128. London: Anthem Press.

7.1 Introduction

Alessandro Roncaglia in his book *Sraffa e la teoria dei prezzi* (1975), an English version of which was published as *Sraffa and the Theory of Prices* (1978), put forward the view that Sraffa's systems of price equations are best interpreted in terms of a 'photograph' taken of the economic system at a given moment of time or, rather, a snapshot of a cycle of production of the system. He wrote,

> The determination of prices was studied at a given moment of time, given the prevailing technology. [...] In other words, the classical economists' analysis of prices examined the situation of a given economic system at a given moment in time, much like a photograph of the system at an instant in time.

He added,

> In this way all the economic variables which were not the object of analysis could be considered as given. Theoretical investigation could concentrate attention on the "virtual" movement of specific variables and on the relations between these variables as if they were being considered "isolated in a vacuum." In the case of *Production of Commodities by Means of Commodities* the choice of variables to be analysed has fallen on the relations that exist between prices of production and the distributive variables, the wage rate and the rate of profits.
>
> (Roncaglia 1978, p. 21)[2]

DOI: 10.4324/9781003138709-9

This short contribution revolves around the metaphor of 'photograph' and its possible meaning(s) in Sraffa's preparatory papers leading up to his 1960 book and the book itself. We proceed in the following way. We ask, first, whether, and if so, when Sraffa came across the metaphor in the literature and used it himself (Section 7.2). Next we draw the attention to another, but closely related, metaphor Sraffa used: 'the man from the moon', and its possible relation to Ricardo's activities in Parliament (Section 7.3). Then we discuss a statement by Maffeo Pantaleoni in one of his books that Sraffa annotated. His annotations throw some light on the materialist or objectivist approach Sraffa was keen to develop in the late 1920s and at the beginning of the 1930s (Section 7.4). Then we reflect upon the relationship between Sraffa's analysis in his 1960 book and what he called 'the standpoint [...] of the old classical economists from Adam Smith to Ricardo' (Sraffa, 1960, p. v) in the theory of value and distribution (Section 7.5). The metaphor of the photograph reappears in Sraffa's correspondence with a German student in 1968, and its meaning there is precisely the one implied by Sraffa's characterisation of the Classical as opposed to the marginalist approach in the theory of value and distribution. The way Roncaglia uses it is similar (Section 7.6). The paper concludes with a few final observations (Section 7.7).

7.2 Sraffa and the metaphor of 'Photograph'

In Sraffa's hitherto unpublished manuscripts and notes and in his annotations in books and papers, kept at Trinity College Library, Cambridge, the term 'photograph' appears a couple of times in different contexts. We do not know whether Roncaglia came across the term when he and John Eatwell took stock of Sraffa's papers in the 1970s, before Sraffa appointed Pierangelo Garegnani as his literary executor, who with the help of Krishna Bharadwaj produced the first catalogue of Sraffa's papers.[3] Here we provide, first, a reference to the term photograph in a book by Cunynghame that Sraffa had read and annotated. Next, we turn to his preparatory notes for his 1960 book, which he began to compose as early as November 1927, but had to interrupt beginning in 1930 because of his appointment to the editorship of Ricardo's works and correspondence by the Royal Economic Society. He resumed the work on what he called 'my book' in 1942, but had to interrupt it once more after the discovery of Ricardo's correspondence with James Mill, and finally was able to put together the book from his old notes from 1955 to 1958. Finally, we will consider the use of the metaphor in Sraffa's correspondence.

7.2.1 An annotation in one of Sraffa's books

The term photograph is probably first mentioned in the context of Sraffa's critical scrutiny of marginalist or demand and supply theory, with the focus on market equilibrium. In 1904, Henry Cunynghame had published *A Geometrical Political Economy, Being an Elementary Treatise on the Method of Explaining Some of the Theories of Pure Economic Science by Means of Diagrams*. The book is in Sraffa's library (item 2243) and is annotated by him. There is reason to presume that Sraffa read it at an early time. In his treatise, Cunynghame stresses right at the beginning,

> All the curves mentioned in this book are intended to be applicable to *states of equilibrium*, reached after temporary oscillations have ceased; or rather, since all things are in a state of perpetual flux, as *instantaneous photographs* taken at times *when the market conditions are normal*.
>
> (1904, p. 3; second emphasis added)

In the margin of this passage, Sraffa put a straight line. By straight lines he typically signalled the relevance of a passage from the point of view of his own studies at the time or approval of the proposition contained in it. The important thing to note here is that the photograph under consideration has been taken at the right moment, that is, when the economic system is in a 'state of equilibrium' or, somewhat less stringent, when 'market conditions are normal'. As anyone who has ever used a camera to catch a moment or a particular situation knows, the art consists in pushing the trigger button at the 'right moment'. Missing it gives a picture that does not catch in full what the photographer was interested in showing and in the extreme nothing of interest at all. Obviously, 'hitting the moment' presupposes that the photographer already has an idea of the object to be caught and seeks to catch it when it materialises. Cunynghame's wording makes it very clear that the trigger button of the camera must not be pressed arbitrarily, that is, at any time, but precisely when equilibrium or normal market conditions obtain. Since they will hardly ever be realised in actual fact, it should also be clear that the photograph cannot be taken to capture the realised state of markets in an actual economy, but refers to an idealised state, one that is hypothetically in equilibrium or exhibits normal market conditions. In Marshallian partial equilibrium theory, the point of reference is the intersection between a demand and a supply function, as Cunynghame stresses. The photograph thus conveys the image the photographer has in his mind of a very particular situation in the market. It does not portray reality as it is, but as the photographer thinks it is, focusing attention on the magnitudes in terms of which certain phenomena (relative prices and income distribution) can be explained.

Cunynghame (1904, p. 3) then asks whether there is a difference between a Marshallian short and a long-period analysis and opines, 'It does not seems to me, nor do I understand Professor Marshall to say (see *Principles of Economics*, bk. 5, chap. 4, p. 416, 1890 ed.), that there is any fundamental difference between short-period and long-period curves'.

Interestingly, there is also a straight line along this passage in Sraffa's copy of the book. What did Sraffa wish to express by annotating the passage in this way at the time when he annotated it? We cannot know for sure, but will put forward some considerations that might perhaps contain a clue to grasping what he probably had in mind. However, we will postpone this discussion and first turn to documents from Sraffa's unpublished papers.

7.2.2 *Sraffa's unpublished papers*

7.2.2.1 *Difference vs. change*

In a manuscript of several pages entitled 'Difference vs. Change', contained in a folder with the title 'After 1927', which can safely be assumed to have been written in the first period of his constructive work (1927–1930), Sraffa made an attempt to clear up what he considered to be a fundamental confusion in the theory of value. Immediately below the document's title he added: '(simultaneous) (succession in time)', the former bracketed term obviously relating to 'Difference' and the latter to 'Change'. He wrote,

> The general confusion in all theories of value (except Marx probably) must be explained by the failure to distinguish between two entirely distinct types of questions and the universal attempt of solving them both by one single theory.
>
> The two questions are:
>
> 1 What determines the [*difference* in the?] values at which various commodities are exchanged in a given market on a given instant?
> 2 What determines the *changes* in the values of commodities at different times? (e.g. of *one* commodity)
>
> (Sraffa Papers, D3/12/7: 115; Sraffa's underlining is italicised here)[4]

Sraffa, after some deliberation, concluded, 'The first problem gives rise to a geometrical theory, the second to a mechanical one' (Sraffa Papers, D3/12/7: 117). With regard to the first problem/theory he adds that 'Its object is, as it were, the *photograph* of a market place' and that it

> must be solved by the theory of value. The second, I think, can only be solved by the theory of industrial fluctuations. All the old confusion between cause and measure of value is connected with the mixing up of the two questions.
>
> (Ibid.; emphasis added)

Against the background of this distinction he then argued that Marshall's theory 'can only be understood as an attempt to solve the first question in terms of the second' (ibid.). What about Marx's theory? Sraffa observed that Marx wanted to tackle both problems in terms of a single theory by focusing attention on what is common to all commodities. Marx asked, first, if today coal exchanges for boots at a given ratio, 'what is the common element, the substance which enters in equal quantity in the two things, hidden behind the widely different appearances?' He asked, secondly, if a year ago the exchange rate was different, 'what is the difference, hidden behind the identical appearance of these two pairs of boots, which makes them different in exchange?' Sraffa then added,

> this way of putting the distinction is confusing. If the 'common substance' is drawn in for the first case, it is clear that as it explains the equality in the first case, it will explain the difference in the second. Besides the making of the first a matter of equality and of the second a matter of difference, is a purely verbal trick [...].
>
> (Sraffa Papers, D3/12/7: 118)

What to make of this? First, the metaphor of photograph is again invoked with regard to markets and the relative prices solving the corresponding equations. The theory has to capture the constellation of forces responsible for the observed prices, and the picture shot is supposed to expose them. As regards the search for a 'common substance', Marx's (in)famous *tertium comparationes*, the question is, of course, what it is and what its properties are, whether it is unique, whether it can be known independently of solving the equations of production, whether it remains the same when time goes by and so on. As regards intertemporal (and also interspatial) comparisons, there seems to be no presumption that there is a common substance 'embodied' in commodities produced at different times, the 'substance', if any, is rather bound to change over time.

In this document the metaphor of a photograph appears to be invoked as an alternative to that of a motion picture: a single photograph can highlight elements one might easily lose sight of when confronted with a quick sequence of snapshots as in a film, but the dynamical aspects can, at least partially, be lost.

7.2.2.2 *Working capital*

In a note entitled 'Working capital', stemming from November 1927, Sraffa reflected upon a lecture by Keynes he had attended, in which Keynes had argued that 'Circulating capital is exceedingly small'. After some deliberation Sraffa concluded that 'W[orking] Capital is exceedingly small because it is the photograph of what exists at any one moment, not of what has been spent during the period'. Hence the metaphor of the photograph is misleading in the present context or, rather, it provides only very limited information that can easily be misread. If the whole picture of the social process of production is taken into account, firms turn out to have a huge working capital. Sraffa explains,

> Nobody holds stocks. What matters is to have ready command over stocks, to be able to rely with certainty upon possibility of procuring it. But this is *money*. Firms have an enormous working capital because they have money. This *is* capital [...].
>
> (Sraffa Papers, D3/12/11: 37; emphasis in the original)

Sraffa here refers to the distinction between stocks and flows. Clearly, a photograph can only depict stocks, but as Sraffa's eventual treatment of fixed capital using the joint-products method shows, stocks may be represented as a sequence of flows and actually this representation is much more useful. Once again the question is asked how much a single photograph can show or explain compared to a motion picture, but in the present context a photograph is clearly inferior, because it may provide a distorted picture of reality.

7.2.2.3 Time, labour, value

Finally we turn to a manuscript of three pages dated 'Oct. 1929', in which Sraffa discusses anew what a theory of value has to accomplish (Sraffa Papers, D3/12/13: 1(1–3)). At the time when he wrote it he had already elaborated the method of reduction of prices to dated quantities of labour and felt that the Böhm-Bawerkian concept of 'period of production' could be employed as an alternative to his equations. We transcribe the manuscript in full.

Sraffa introduces the issue in the following way:

> The real question is:
>
> Given the situation of an / (number of) / industry / (completely integrated vertically) / *at one instant* (i.e. given all physical, chemical, etc. connotations[5] and measurements of the situation, but excluded all economic connotations, especially values, utilities, productivities, etc.), and assuming all men exactly alike to one another (both for wages they receive, and value they add to the product) is it possible to deduce the value of its product per unit of time?
>
> Or, is the above possible, given the same data for, *not* an instant, bur for *a period of time*, such that all the different operations should be performed within it? (more exactly: such a proportion of them that the defect should be smaller than any assigned proportion.) (This would be, roughly, a year in agriculture; but one day, or perhaps one hour in case of continuous shifts, in the motor industry).
>
> (Sraffa Papers, D3/12/13: 1(1); here words underlined once are italicised and words underlined twice are underlined and italicised.)

He goes on:

> As regards labour, the answer is simple enough: so far as it is concerned, value will be proportional to the number of workers employed.
>
> It is with capital that difficulties arise: for, while for labour we have defined a measure by assuming all workmen to be equal, we have no such measure for capital: *it is composed of heterogeneous objects*, which cannot be measured, "qua" capital, by number or weight, etc.
>
> (Ibid.)

How to deal with this problem?

> Suppose the above difficulty is overcome by measuring capital as accumulated labour; i.e. adopting the *second* question [sic! The reference ought to be to equation, meaning the approach in terms of periods of production rather than simultaneous equations], and assuming that all the various acts of labour are performed within a period of production, and that their order of succession is known.
>
> Thus, "time" is part of our assumptions, i.e. they are not instantaneous: but it is a peculiar time, or perhaps only a part of time. It admits only of cyclical change, i.e. it is a sort of circular time: changes take place, but only recurrent changes, which periodically lead back to the original position: no permanent, or "true," change is allowed.
>
> With these assumptions we can go as far as the second equations [i.e. with a surplus], and also introduce rent (to some extent: but we must assume knowledge of wages (*or* of rate of interest). To dispense with the last knowledge, we must pass to the "marginal" analysis: and this involves knowledge (and possibility) of possible changes—different from anything that actually occurs, in the course of the "steady process." How can this difficulty be overcome?

Sraffa continues:

> Clearly, we must reduce *all* the data to things that actually happen, excluding inexistent possibilities. Only such things are measurable, and can enter the theory as "knowns," or "constants"; and, in reality, only really happening things can be real causes and determine effects.
>
> (Sraffa Papers, D/12/13: 1(2))[6]
>
> This notion of time is important: it really substitutes "instantaneous photographs" as opposed to ordinary time. It is only a part of ordinary time, it has only some of its connotations: it includes events, / also different events, / but not change of events. It enables us to compare two simultaneous, but not instantaneous, events—just as if they were "things."

> It is, in effect, equivalent to the physicist's *dt* (as understood by Russell (Outline of Phil. [1927], p. 122)[7]—a time in which effects follow causes, but so closely that there is no room either for dispersion or for entering of foreign influences: *dt* does this by differentiation (making the time so short as actually to leave no room for change in circumstances: the cause & effect are perfectly contiguous—nothing is in between)—our "time" does this by "assuming" away all changes, (i.e. "coeteris paribus"? no: by positing the problem in the form of finding the conditions of repetition indefinitely, or even once)
>
> This conception of time enables us to take into account, not only *stocks* (as the instantaneous view does) but also steady or cyclical *flows* (which that does not), while still using the geometrical model.
>
> (Sraffa Papers, D3/12/13: 1(3); italics added)

Once again photograph and motion picture are contrasted, but now, with reference to a repetitive or self-replacing process, an appropriately redefined concept of the former is considered to capture adequately the case under consideration. The kind of photograph Sraffa speaks of cannot be arbitrary, and, strictly speaking, it cannot be a one-shot snapshot but rather a picture (or sequence of pictures) that contains all the necessary information concerning an entire period of the production of commodities by means of commodities. It conforms to Roncaglia's snapshot of a cycle of production of the system.

7.3 Another metaphor: the 'Man from the Moon'

Interestingly, Sraffa also employed another metaphor as a shorthand to describe the same thing: the 'man from the moon'. The note in which he used it was composed presumably towards the end of the early period of his work, that is, in 1929 or 1930. He characterised his first and second equations (in ink) in the following way:

> The significance of the equations is simply this: that if a man fell from the moon on the earth, and noted the amount of things consumed in each factory and the amount produced by each factory during a year, he could deduce at which values the commodities must be sold, if the rate of interest must be uniform and the process of production repeated. In short, the equations show that the conditions of exchange are entirely determined by the conditions of production.
>
> (Sraffa Papers, D3/12/7: 87)

This note is interesting for several reasons. First, while it does not refer to a photograph, it contemplates on what an impartial observer, coming from another planet, would see on earth and what he could infer with regard to relative prices and the rate of interest. He would see physical quantities of things (inputs) being transformed into other things (outputs). A photograph would have the task to show these quantities. It would not show the rate of interest and relative prices: these would rather be the result of the impartial observer's mental work, seeking to find a system of relative prices that support the distribution of the social surplus in terms of a uniform rate of interest across all productive activities. This condition is superimposed on what could be seen in a photograph and reflects particular social institutions or 'rules of the game', such as free competition. From this it follows that the photograph metaphor is of limited use only because it is unable to capture the essence of the problem at hand: the observer's projection of given social conditions onto a given physical scheme of production and establishing the implications that follow from them (interest rate, prices).

Second, presumably in 1942 when Sraffa resumed his constructive work and reread his old notes, he added (in pencil) 'Man from the Moon' and also put two straight lines along the passage in the margin. These additions evoke two remarks. First, characterising the situation under consideration with reference to the man from the moon echoes an event that took place in British Parliament on the occasion of a debate on agricultural distress on 30 May 1820. In the debate Ricardo is reported to have said that, 'because he consulted the interests of the whole community, he would oppose the corn-laws' (Ricardo, *Works* V, p. 49). A Mr. Brougham, the Member for Winchelsea, who supported the agriculturalists' motion in favour of additional protective measures, qualified Ricardo's argument as if it came from a man that 'had dropped from another planet' and lived in an 'Utopian world' (Ricardo, *Works* V, p. 56).[8] The reference to the 'man from the moon' may thus be seen as a metaphor designed to indicate the need to take a detached point of view, to see things as they are and not through the tinted glass of some particular interest group. What was badly needed was an objectivist perspective rooted in indubitable facts, such as the productive transformation of things, i.e., commodities, and not a partisan outlook on matters.[9]

Third, and closely related to what has just been said, one has to stay away from existing explanations of income distribution and relative prices and make a fresh start. The man from the moon was by definition in the lucky position of being unaffected by received doctrines (marginalist theory or the labour theory of value) and could seek a new solution to an old problem. This solution, Sraffa implied, the man from the moon could easily find because of his unprejudiced point of view – he is in fact taken to see at a glance what some economists do not see at all and others see only vaguely, namely, that the rate of interest and relative prices follow from the given conditions of production. Economic theory may be a formidable tool that allows us to grasp aspects of a complex subject matter, but it may also mislead or bedazzle us.

The metaphor of the man from the moon can be seen as a development of the metaphor of the photograph. In our interpretation both are steps in Sraffa's search for a nonsubjectivist, objectivist explanation of relative prices and income distribution, which was at the heart of Sraffa's research program. We have put forward ample evidence from Sraffa's papers in support of this interpretation and refrain from repeating ourselves here. The interested reader is asked to consult Kurz and Salvadori (2004, 2005), Gehrke and Kurz (2006), Salvadori and Signorino (2007), and Kurz (2012). We rather reflect upon the issues at hand around an annotation in one of Sraffa's books we have not mentioned up until now that provides a welcome foil for our discussion.

7.4 Interpreting Sraffa's approach vis-à-vis a statement by Pantaleoni

We now turn to Sraffa's annotations in the second edition of Maffeo Pantaleoni's *Principii di economia pura*, published in 1894 (see Sraffa's Library, item 2302), a book he was familiar with and had read at an early time of his career as an economist.[10] Pantaleoni writes,

> La ragione quindi per fermarsi soltanto sulla utilità delle cose come una funzione della loro quantità, e non altresì sulla loro utilità come una funzione dei nostri bisogni, o una funzione delle loro proprietà fisico-chimiche, *sta esclusivamente nella maggior fecondità di questo concetto.*
> (1894, pp. 99–100; emphasis added)[11]

Sraffa puts two straight lines in the margin of this passage, signalling it to be very important. The question is why? We know that from an early time onwards he doubted the alleged 'superior fecundity' of marginal utility theory that Pantaleoni extolled. What were the reasons the latter gave in support of it, and could they be sustained in Sraffa's view?

When singling out marginal utility theory as the best option available to economists, Pantaleoni had to show that alternative approaches to the theory of value and distribution were untenable or at any rate inferior. Sraffa was especially interested to hear what Pantaleoni had to say against attempts to see the values of commodities as rooted in the 'physical-chemical properties' of commodities. Why did Pantaleoni think that the values of commodities, that is, 'things' (*cose*), could not be explained in this way? Pantaleoni saw such approaches as carrying over John Dalton's atomic theory straight away to the sphere of economics. However, Pantaleoni was convinced that this was not possible. Dalton's atomic theory is based on two laws: (i) the law of the conservation of mass and (ii) the law of definite proportions or constant composition: in any given chemical compound, the elements are always combined in the same proportion by mass. Are commodities not just embodiments of well-specified amounts of various things, elements, or atoms 'productively consumed' when produced? The analogy with chemical compounds is indeed close at hand. Water, for example, is both a chemical compound and typically also a commodity and can be represented by $2H_2O = 2H_2 + 2O$. It is always 'produced' in the same way by combining elements H and O in a given composition. If this analogy was to extend to all commodities, then all commodities could be conceived of in terms of the elements constituting them.

Pantaleoni disputed the second of the two laws, the law of constant composition, because in economics one and the same commodity can typically be produced not only in one way, but in different ways involving different proportions of the physical-chemical elements out of which the commodity is made. This follows from two facts. First, producers are commonly faced with a choice amongst a set of alternative methods of production to produce the same commodity, which is known as the choice of technique problem. Second, even if there would be only a single method available, workers who operate the method could be fed, clothed, and housed in different ways, again implying that the object they produce may be conceived as exhibiting, or 'embodying', different physical-chemical compositions.

These observations are obviously correct and must not be ignored. They speak against the possibility of carrying atomic theory over to economics in a straightforward manner, and Sraffa was perfectly aware of this. But did this mean that the physical cost approach to the theory of value and distribution had to be entirely abandoned in favor of marginal utility theory, as Pantaleoni concluded, or could it serve as the starting point of a theory that could be given a coherent form and was possessed of a great fecundity? And what can be said about the coherence, or otherwise, of the marginalist theory of value and distribution? Was it really possessed of a superior fecundity, as Pantaleoni opined?

Here we cannot provide detailed answers to the two questions raised. We ask the reader to consult some works of ours in which we dealt with them in greater detail (see Kurz, 2012, 2016; Kurz and Salvadori, 2005; Salvadori and Signorino, 2007). It suffices to point out the following. First, in case Dalton's atomic theory could directly serve as the foundation of the theory of value, the distinction between short and long period would collapse, because natural laws hold at any moment of time and the production of any commodity would always consist in the transformation of well-specified amounts of energy and mass into a new form of energy and mass.[12] Photographs taken at any instant of time of this process would always show the same picture. This explains perhaps why in the early phase of his constructive work Sraffa vacillated as to the importance of the distinction between long- and short-period.[13]

Second, in November 1927 Sraffa began to elaborate his 'first' equations relating to an economic system without a surplus, that is, a system in which no more is produced of the different commodities than is consumed productively (means of sustenance of workers and means of production).

In a document entitled 'Physical Costs & Value', contained in a folder 'Nov. [1927]', he noted as regards the values determined in terms of his simultaneous equations:

> When I say that the value of a product is "determined" by the *physical volume of commodities used up in its production*, it should *not* be understood that it is determined by the value of those commodities. This would be a vicious circle, because the value of the product is equal to the value of the factors [...].
>
> What I say is simply that the numerical proportions between amount of factors and amount of product *is*, by definition, the absolute value of the product.
>
> (Sraffa Papers, D3/12/11: 101, first emphasis added, "not" is underlined twice in the original)

And in a document contained in the same folder, he also talked of 'physical value' (Sraffa Papers, D3/12/11: 75).

Sraffa also made it clear that the physical cost approach to the theory of value was not his discovery or invention, but was anticipated in earlier works. What he, Sraffa, did was simply to provide a consistent formulation of the approach (followed by its extension to systems with a surplus, without and with fixed capital, joint production proper, and scarce natural resources). The physical cost approach, he surmised, was foreshadowed, for example, in the just price doctrine of the canonists, but it essentially derived from the '*veduta essentialmente fisiocratica, che il valore sia una quantità intrinseca degli oggetti, quasi una qualità fisica o chimica*', as he put it in a document composed in the summer of 1929 (Sraffa Papers, D3/12/12: 7).[14] He was on the lookout of traces of the physical cost approach in the Classical authors and encountered many. The perhaps most remarkable statement in this regard he came across was contained in the third edition of James Mill's *Elements of Political Economy*, in which Mill stated, 'The agents of production are the commodities themselves [...] They are the food of the labourer, the tools and the machines with which he works, and the raw materials which he works upon' (Mill 1826, 165). In summer 1929, Sraffa stated explicitly that he was keen to elaborate an 'atomic analysis' (Sraffa Papers, D3/12/13: 16(9)), and in August 1931, in a critical retrospect, he characterised his previous analytical efforts as having been concerned with developing 'an entirely objective point of view', which is 'the natural science point of view' (D3/12/7: 161(3)).[15]

Before we proceed, the following deserves to be stressed. In terms of his first equations Sraffa was able to show convincingly that Pantaleoni's rejection of an approach based on the physical-chemical properties of things (i.e., commodities) was not well grounded. In the case of the no surplus economy, which is the realm of pure necessity, this approach was the only one capable of explaining 'necessary prices', that is, those prices that allow the self-replacement of the system. The question then was whether the approach could also be successfully carried over to the with-surplus case, and for a while Sraffa appears to have been convinced that it could. This was possible, he thought, by extending the realm of necessity to include it. He felt that this could be accomplished by distinguishing between *natural costs*, on the one hand, and *necessary social costs*, on the other, which implied interpreting the surplus (profits) as a necessary social cost levied upon workers by the capitalist society. Extending the 'natural science point of view', Sraffa insisted, implied that 'We shall have to adopt *that definition which makes the scale of absolute values identical with what it was when there was no surplus*' (Sraffa Papers, D3/12/6: 14; emphasis added). In this way the logic applying to values in the case of production for subsistence was taken to apply also to the with-surplus case. This necessitated reducing the surplus – i.e., an 'effect' for which there had to be 'sufficient cause', as Sraffa wrote in Sraffa Papers, D3/12/7: 161 – to some 'cost' or other. Interest, Sraffa at the time insisted, reflects some objective necessity, rooted in some objective 'social' as opposed to 'natural' obstacles that have to be overcome: '*Interest appears thus as the necessary means of overcoming an obstacle to production*. It is a *social necessity* as distinguished from the material necessity of, say, putting coal into a locomotive that it may do its work' (Sraffa Papers, D3/12/18: 11; emphases added).[16]

If this extension of the natural science point of view was admissible, a purely physical cost of production approach to the theory of value would have been possible. Alas, it was not as Sraffa found out towards the end of the first period of his constructive work. Here we need not dwell on the reasons that prompted Sraffa to abandon the undiluted natural science point of view he at first had endorsed; see, therefore, Kurz (2012, pp. 1546–1551). It suffices to mention that he saw very clearly that with a choice of technique and flexible consumption patterns of workers the Law of definite proportions could not be carried over to economics and the problem of income distribution could not be reduced to one of necessary cost.[17]

7.5 *Production of commodities by means of commodities*

We now turn to Sraffa's 1960 book, the upshot of his earlier efforts. In the book we do not encounter the metaphors 'photograph' and 'man from the moon', but it becomes abundantly clear what the equations mean and that they are designed to reformulate in a logically consistent way the approach to the theory of value and distribution of the Classical economists. Sraffa in fact states explicitly in the preface of the book that the 'standpoint' he takes 'is that of the old classical economists from Adam Smith to Ricardo, which has been submerged and forgotten since the advent of the "marginal" method' (Sraffa, 1960, p. v). And he also specifies very clearly how in his view the 'method' of the Classical authors differs from that of the marginalists: in the former

> No changes in output and (at any rate in Parts I and II) no changes in the proportions in which different means of production are used by an industry are considered, *so that no question arises as to the variation or constancy of returns.* (Ibid. emphasis added)

He adds, 'The investigation is concerned exclusively with such properties of an economic system as do not depend on changes in the scale of production or in the proportions of "factors"' (ibid.). In other words, the Classical economists investigated a *given system of production*, that is, they were keen to establish its properties as regards the distribution of income and relative prices. This method, Sraffa maintained, was in marked contrast to the marginalist method:

> The marginalist approach requires attention to be focused on change, for without change either in the scale of an industry or in the "proportions of the factors of production" there can be neither marginal product nor marginal cost. In a system in which, day after day, production continued unchanged in those respects, the marginal product of a factor (or alternatively the marginal cost of a product) would not merely be hard to find – it just would not be there to be found.
> (Ibid.)

This is a warning to his readers: marginal products and marginal costs are analytical objects, not observable ones. In fact, even in a stationary state the observer could calculate the marginal product of a factor or the marginal cost of a commodity, provided that infinitesimal changes *were* (counterfactually) assumed; but obviously no observer can experience them. Things are different with respect to what Wicksteed called 'spurious' margins. Sraffa explained, 'The most familiar case is that of the product of the "marginal land" in agriculture, when lands of different qualities are cultivated side by side' (ibid.). In this case two different objects are envisaged by the observer and the difference between them defines the increments implicit in the concept of margin. This concept of margin was actually introduced by the Classical economists. Sraffa reminds us, 'P. H. Wicksteed, the purist of marginal theory, [...] condemns such a use of the term "marginal" as a source of "dire confusion"' (ibid., pp. v–vi).

The production equations Sraffa then discusses in chapters 1 and 2 of the book are actually variants of those he had elaborated in the late 1920s. Sraffa describes technology by listing industries, where each industry is considered as fully described by the list of inputs it employs and the list of outputs it produces. Where do these data come from? Sraffa (1960) is silent about this. However, many remarks from the unpublished manuscripts (among them those mentioned in the above) clarify that these data are supposed to have been directly observed, as it is the case with the man from the moon. As regards the prices he determines for given real wages (conceived as an inventory of commodities), he stressed explicitly that 'such classical terms as "necessary price," "natural price" or "price of production" would meet the case' (ibid., p. 9). In the with-surplus case these prices involve a uniform rate of profits on the value of the capital goods advanced in each industry of the economy. When Sraffa in chapter 12 of his book discusses the choice of technique problem, he starts from the premise that the choice 'will be exclusively grounded on cheapness' (ibid., p. 83). The prices are seen to be the outcome of the cost-minimising behavior of producers: 'At any given level of the general rate of profits, the method that produces at a lower price is of course the most profitable of the two for a producer who builds a new plant' (ibid., p. 81).

Finally, we draw the attention to Sraffa's correspondence after the publication of his book. Interestingly, the 'photograph' metaphor reappears in it once and confirms the meaning we discussed in the above: its purpose is to draw the attention to the Classical approach, which is fundamentally different from the marginalist one, and to emphasise its objectivist character revolving around the concept of physical costs and its development.

7.6 Sraffa's correspondence

In February 1968, Sraffa received a letter from a German student, Rüdiger Soltwedel, asking him about the meaning and purpose of his equations, which were a riddle to him, having been educated in the marginalist mode of thinking. In Sraffa's reply dated 1 March 1968, the metaphor of photograph is used again:

> As regards your own interpretation, I must say frankly that you have gone astray the moment you speak of "equilibrium" or of "elasticity of factor supply": all the quantities considered are what can be observed by taking a photograph. There are no rates of change, etc. This point of view was that of the classical economists (e.g. Ricardo), whereas supply & demand curves were introduced in the middle of the 19th century. Economists are now obsessed with them and cannot think without them. My chapter V, which gives you such a headache, could be understood as an attempt to solve a problem set by Ricardo, and which I described in my Introduction (sections IV & V) of Vol. I of the *Works of Ricardo*, 1951.
>
> (Sraffa Papers, C 294: 2)

In this letter the metaphor of the photograph is used precisely in the sense expounded in the preface of Sraffa's 1960 book when specifying the difference between the Classical and the marginalist approach to the theory of value and distribution. The Classical economists from Smith to Ricardo explained the rate of profits (the real wage rate) and relative prices in terms of a given system of production in use and a given real wage rate (a given rate of profits). The sense also conforms to the one given by Roncaglia: we do have on the one hand a set of given facts (*explanans*) and on the other a set of magnitudes (wage rate, rate of profits, relative prices) whose relationships are to be determined (*explanandum*). These relationships define the 'mathematical properties' (Sraffa, 1960, p. 23) of the system of production under consideration and thus how a change in one variable (e.g., the wage rate) implies corresponding changes in the other variables (the rate of profits, prices).[18]

7.7 Concluding remarks

In this paper we scrutinise the metaphor of 'photograph' and the related one of 'man from the moon' in Sraffa's papers leading up to his 1960 book, in his annotations in his books, and in his correspondence. We show that the main purpose of the first metaphor was to emphasise the most important distinguishing feature of the Classical approach to the theory of value and distribution as compared with the marginalist one. While the former analyses a given system of production with regard to its properties concerning income distribution and relative prices, the latter confronts the given system with an imagined adjacent system, as is reflected in concepts such as marginal productivity and marginal cost. The metaphor of the photograph was meant to express the focus on a given system and the absence of changes in outputs and factor input proportions. The metaphor of the man from the moon was meant to express the data from which the Classical theory of value and distribution starts its reasoning, which differ markedly from the marginalist data: given quantities of commodities as inputs (including means of subsistence of workers), on the one hand, and outputs, on the other. 'Natural prices' or 'prices of production' are fully determined in terms of these givens. In this context it is perhaps interesting to point out that up until the final stage of preparing his manuscript for print, Sraffa tinkered with the idea of giving the book the title 'Production of Commodities by Commodities'. This is fully in accordance with the man from the moon metaphor and expresses well the objectivist nature of the analysis. We touch upon the relationship between Sraffa's analysis and 'a purely natural science point of view' by commenting on a statement in a book by Pantaleoni that Sraffa had annotated. Finally we show that Roncaglia's use of the metaphor of photograph is in the spirit Sraffa had intended.

Notes

1 We are grateful to Christian Gehrke, Bertram Schefold, and Alex Thomas for valuable comments on an earlier draft of this paper.
2 Roncaglia reiterated these statements in Roncaglia (2009).

3 The catalogue now typically used is the one elaborated by Jonathan Smith, archivist of Trinity College Library; see http://www.trin.cam.ac.uk/SRAFFA. In the following all references to Sraffa's papers are to it and the labelling convention it uses.

4 He inserted a note written in all probability in the same period, which reads: 'Perhaps the two questions are better enunciated thus: (1) differences in value of two commodities at one time (2) changes in value of one commodity at two times (value in terms of commodities in general: whence Ricardo's troubles for finding an "unchanging measure of value," which in the first question is not involved).'

5 In the margin he adds: 'including wages, or not?'

6 When Sraffa at the beginning of the 1940s discovered that Bortkiewicz (1906, pp. 970–971) had enunciated essentially the same principle, he henceforth spoke of Bortkiewicz's 'dictum'; see Gehrke and Kurz (2006, pp. 115–118).

7 The reference is obviously to Russell (1927).

8 He reiterated this characterisation on 7 March 1821; see Ricardo (*Works* V, p. 85).

9 As Sraffa put it in a note written 'After 1927' (and probably in 1930, after Sraffa had been appointed to the editorship of Ricardo's works and correspondence), 'we are looking for the objective ground of value, and not for what the producers or their accountants, or the economists regard as sensible' (Sraffa Papers, D3/12/7: 27). This specification of the aim of his investigation is to be found in the context of a critical discussion of the labour theory of value.

10 When Pantaleoni died in 1924, Sraffa published an obituary in *The Economic Journal* signed as P. S. (Sraffa, 1924), in which he called him 'the prince' of economics in Italy – a characterisation with ambivalent meanings, including a reference to the prince in Machiavelli's treatise *Il Principe.* Pantaleoni had contributed an important essay on the role of power in economics and on the relationship between the strong and the weak (Pantaleoni, 1898). He was a towering figure in Italian economics around the turn of the century. A propagator of Marshallian economics in Italy and a staunch advocate of markets and competition, he towards the end of his life leaned towards fascism.

11 English translation: 'Therefore the reason to focus attention only on the utility of things as a function of their consumption, and not also on their utility as a function of our needs and wants or a function of their physico-chemical properties, *rests exclusively with the greater fecundity of this concept.*'

12 We here ignore that possibility that some fractions of the amounts of inputs will not enter in full the output, but get dissipated into the environment.

13 This is just another example reflecting Sraffa's vivid interest in whether and what the natural sciences had to offer to the economist who sought to elaborate an objectivist or materialist approach to the problem of value and distribution. If Dalton's atomic theory could be applied in a straightforward manner to economics, which according to Sraffa it could not, the commodity composition of each and every 'thing' would be knowable and fixed, and production at any point in time would *always* reflect this composition. A sequence of instants, that is, a period whatever its length, would not give a different picture of chemical compounds. It would always be true, for example, that $2H_2 + 2O$ would give $2H_2O$. In this case the distinction between short and long run would not add anything to our understanding. However, in economics things are different precisely because an economy that gravitates towards a cost-minimising long-period position typically changes the way in which commodities are being produced and thus the commodity composition of inputs that enter them. This is so, because in the short period the methods of production actually employed are typically not fully adjusted to the other data of the Classical approach to value and distribution (real wages and gross output levels).

14 English translation of the Italian phrase: 'essentially physiocratic point of view that value is a quantity that is intrinsic to the objects, almost a physical or chemical quality.'

15 In Sraffa (1960, p. 3) we will eventually read that the values solving the first equations 'spring directly from the methods of production'; in his papers he also used the (Ricardian) term 'absolute values' with regard to the case under consideration.

16 It deserves mention that this idea was still present when in the summer of 1942, Sraffa, after having read his old notes, resumed his constructive work and jotted down a list of topics (regarding the planned contents of the book he was to write). It contains, among other things: '2) With profits—everything a necessity' (D3/12/15).

17 For a discussion of the steps Sraffa took as a consequence of this, see Kurz and Salvadori (2005), Gehrke and Kurz (2006), and Kurz (2012).

18 Interestingly enough, the uniqueness of the Standard commodity is here related only to its role as an invariable measure of value, but this is suggested as a way to understand the latter, that is, a way to relate it to a practical consideration and not to the abstract tool that is used to prove many of the propositions in the first part of the book.

References

Bortkiewicz, L. v. (1906). Der Kardinalfehler der Böhm-Bawerkschen Zinstheorie, *Schmollers Jahrbuch* 30: 943–972.

Cunynghame, H. 1904. *A Geometrical Political Economy: Being an Elementary Treatise.* Oxford: Clarendon Press.

Gehrke, C., and H. D. Kurz. 2006. "Sraffa on von Bortkiewicz: Reconstructing the Classical Theory of Value and Distribution." *History of Political Economy* 38, no. 1: 91–149; reprinted in H. D. Kurz and N. Salvadori (2015) *Revisiting Classical Economics: Studies in Long-Period, Analysis*, 142–192, London: Routledge.

Kurz, H. D. 2012. "Don't Treat Too Ill my Piero! Interpreting Sraffa's Papers." *Cambridge Journal of Economics* 36, no. 6: 1535–1569.

Kurz, H. D. 2016. *Economic Thought: A Brief History.* New York: Columbia University Press.

Kurz, H. D., and N. Salvadori, N. 2004. "Man from the Moon: On Sraffa's Objectivism." *Économies et Sociétés* 35: 1545–1557; reprinted in H. D. Kurz and N. Salvadori (2007) *Interpreting Classical Economics: Studies in Long-period Analysis*, 120–130. London: Routledge.

———. 2005. "Representing the Production and Circulation of Commodities in Material Terms: On Sraffa's Objectivism." *Review of Political Economy* 17, no. 3: 413–441; reprinted in H. D. Kurz, L. L. Pasinetti, and N. Salvadori (2008) *Piero Sraffa: The Man and the Scholar*, 249–277. London: Routledge.

Marshall, A. 1890. *Principles of Economics.* London: Macmillan.

Mill, J. 1826. *Elements of Political Economy*, 2nd ed. London: Henry G. Bohn.

Pantaleoni, M. 1894. *Principi di economia pura*, 2nd ed. Florence: Barbera.

———. 1898. "An Attempt to Analyse the Concepts of 'strong and weak' in their Economic Connection." *Economic Journal* 8, no. 30: 183–205.

Ricardo, D. (1951 ssq.). *The Works and Correspondence of David Ricardo*, 11 volumes, edited by P. Sraffa with the collaboration of M.H. Dobb, Cambridge: Cambridge University Press. In the text referred to as *Works*, volume number and page number.

Roncaglia, A. 1975. *Sraffa e la teoria dei prezzi*. Bari: Laterza. (English edition: *Sraffa and the Theory of Prices*. Chichester: John Wiley, 1978).

———. 2009. *Piero Sraffa*. London: Palgrave Macmillan.

Russell, Bertrand. 1927. *An Outline of Philosophy*. London: George Allen and Unwin.

Salvadori, N., and R. Signorino. 2007. "Piero Sraffa: Economic Reality, the Economist and Economic Theory: An Interpretation." *Journal of Economic Methodology* 14, no. 2: 187–209; reprinted in H. D. Kurz and N. Salvadori (2015), *Revisiting Classical Economics: Studies in Long-period Analysis*, 70–92. Abingdon: Routledge.

Sraffa, P. 1924. "Maffeo Pantaleoni." *The Economic Journal* 34, no. 136: 648–653.

———. 1960. *Production of Commodities by Means of Commodities. Prelude to a Critique of Economic Theory*. Cambridge: Cambridge University Press.

III

Production of commodities by means of commodities in its making

8 Sraffa's constructive and interpretive work, and Marx

Christian Gehrke and Heinz D. Kurz

Original paper: Christian Gehrke & Heinz D. Kurz (2018) Sraffa's Constructive and Interpretive Work, and Marx, *Review of Political Economy*, 30:3, 428–442, DOI: 10.1080/09538259.2018.1442783. London: Taylor & Francis Group.

8.1 Introduction

The publication of Sraffa's *Production of Commodities by Means of Commodities* (1960) has been a landmark in the appraisal of Marx's contribution to economic theory. Sraffa demonstrated that relative prices and the rate of profits are fully determined in terms of the technical conditions of production and the real wage rate; that is, the objective data underlying the approach of the Classical economists and Marx. Labour values are derived magnitudes providing no additional information, and are therefore redundant.

With the opening of Sraffa's papers in the Wren Library at Trinity College, Cambridge, it has become possible to study in detail the development of his interpretive and constructive work culminating in the *Production of Commodities by Means of Commodities*. The picture that emerges from Sraffa's papers with regard to the relationship of his own work to Marx's contribution to economic theory turns out to be both clear and straightforward *and* more complicated than might have been expected. Sraffa clearly regarded Marx as: (i) an author who had rediscovered the surplus approach to the theory of value and distribution, had reconstructed its analytical structure and historical development, and had sought to elaborate on it; and (ii) an economic theorist firmly rooted in the surplus approach tradition who had made important *analytical* contributions to its further development, thus carrying it beyond the state in which it had been left by Ricardo. At the same time, however, the picture is also more complicated, because at the beginning of his interpretive and constructive work, which can be dated to the second half of 1927, Sraffa considered it necessary to put Marx's and Ricardo's labour-based approach to the theory of value and distribution to one side, and to work out his systems of equations by elaborating on the *physical real cost* approach which he had encountered in their precursors, in particular William Petty and the French Physiocrats.

DOI: 10.4324/9781003138709-11

During the entire first period of his constructive work, which extended roughly from the second half of 1927 to the end of 1931, Sraffa completely eschewed Marx's labour-based reasoning and concepts, and for quite some time, in fact well into 1929, he was convinced that 'labour' must not enter as a quantity at all into his (Sraffa's) production equations. It is only at the beginning of the 1940s, and then more intensively during the second period of his constructive work, extending mainly from 1942 to 1946, that one encounters clear expressions of a change in Sraffa's critical attitude towards the labour theory of value and in his critical assessment of the usefulness of Marx's labour-based concepts. The reason for this was that he saw that Marx had re-captured the circularity aspect of social production (which had to some extent got lost in Smith and Ricardo), and had been struggling with problems similar to those he himself was addressing, and how Marx had tried to cope with them in terms of his labour-based reasoning.

In our reading, Sraffa's appreciation of Marx's achievements developed in close relation to his own constructive work, and was undergoing considerable change over time.[1] Hence, in the following sections of this article we provide a brief reconstruction of the development of Sraffa's thought, with particular emphasis on its relation to his appraisal of Marx's contributions.[2]

8.2 Physical real cost and simultaneous equations

Sraffa's work on the reconstruction and modern reformulation of the Classical approach to the theory of value and distribution emanated from notes that he composed in the summer of 1927 in preparation for his 'Lectures on Advanced Theory of Value', which he was supposed to give at the University of Cambridge beginning in October (but which were then postponed for a year and held from 1928 to 1931). As early as the end of 1927, Sraffa, in one of his notes, referred to '*mia teoria* [my theory]' and the '*libro* [book]' he intended to write (D3/12/11: 55). Sraffa's papers show that the years from 1927 to 1931 were the period in which he laid the foundations of his book. It was then that he saw the distinctive character of 'the standpoint of the old classical economists' (Sraffa, 1960, p. v) in the theory of value and distribution and it became clear to him that it was not just an early and somewhat crude version of Marshall's theory.[3]

Sraffa was impressed by the Classical authors' explanation of all incomes other than wages in strictly *objective* terms on the basis of the social surplus product that obtains after all means of production and all means of subsistence in support of workers have been deducted from given outputs. According to Sraffa, this method had found a particularly clear expression in a passage in Petty's *Political Arithmetick* in which Petty advocated the '"physician's" outlook', which implied expressing himself exclusively

> in Terms of *Number, Weight* or *Measure*; to use only arguments of Sense, and to consider only such Causes, as have visible Foundations

in Nature; leaving those that depend upon the mutable Minds, Opinions, Appetites, and Passions of particular Men, to the Consideration of others.

([1899] 1986, Vol. I, p. 244; quoted by Sraffa in D3/12/4: 3, original emphasis)

Petty's *physicalist* or *natural science* point of view, which explicitly eschews subjectivist notions, Sraffa also encountered in other Classical authors. Even more physicalist in character is Mill's (1826, p. 165) dictum: 'The agents of production are the commodities themselves ... They are the food of the labourer, the tools and machines with which he works, and the raw materials which he works upon'. Sraffa in the early period fully endorsed the *objectivist* methodology advocated by Petty, which he regarded also to be in accordance with the methodological imperatives of modern science, as can be seen from his annotations in and excerpts from contemporary books on modern physics by Planck, Heisenberg, and others.[4]

Against Marshall's concept of 'real cost', which referred to magnitudes that are not directly observable and not measurable, Sraffa therefore put that of *physical real cost* (see the evidence collected in folder D3/12/42, pp. 33–56).[5] Marshall had conceived of the 'real cost' of a commodity as 'the exertions of all the different kinds of labour that are directly and indirectly involved in making it; together with the abstinences or rather the waitings required for saving the capital used in making it' ([1890] 1977, p. 282). While Petty and the Physiocrats focused on the commodities actually consumed or 'destroyed' in the production of some other commodities, that is, on *physical amounts of things*, the notion of 'real cost' introduced by Marshall invoked disutility, pain, and abstinence experienced by agents, that is, *psychic elements*. Sraffa firmly rejected Marshall's subjectivist notion of 'real cost' and stressed: 'The sort of "costs" which determines values is the collection of material things used up in production' (D3/12/7: 106). As to labour, Sraffa sided with Petty, who had insisted that what matters are the means of subsistence in support of the workers or, for short, 'bread' or 'food' – not labour.[6]

From November 1927 Sraffa began to elaborate his equations of production, first for a system without a surplus ('first equations'), then for one with a surplus ('second equations'). For example, in a document composed in the winter of 1927 to 1928, Sraffa stated:

No surplus –

$$\left.\begin{array}{l} A = a_1 + b_1 + c_1 \\ B = a_2 + b_2 + c_2 \\ C = a_3 + b_3 + c_3 \end{array}\right\} \text{where } \begin{array}{l} A = \sum a \\[2ex] B = \sum b \\[2ex] C = \sum c \end{array}$$

> These are homogeneous linear equations. They have infinite sets of solutions, but the solutions of each set are proportional. These proportions are univoche [unique].
>
> These proportions we call ratios of Absolute values. They are purely numerical relations between the *things* A, B ... They are not necessarily the ratios, in which exchange will actually take place in any community in which the quantities of things respectively used in production (i.e. consumed) and produced satisfy those equations: such actual ratios of exchange are also conditioned by such things as legal institutions, etc. which vary in different organisations of society and which are 'arbitrary', i.e. irrelevant, from our present point of view.
>
> (D3/12/5: 2, emphasis added)

Sraffa apparently interpreted these equalities in two ways. First, he saw them as the tabulation of production processes with A, B, and C as gross outputs of three commodities and a_i, b_i, and c_i as the amounts of the three commodities used up in the production of the respective gross outputs (i = 1, 2, 3). Second, he appears to have interpreted them as equations, although there are no unknowns for which a unique solution (except for a proportionality factor) could be found. Yet, in the following months he wrote down systems of his first equations in which he explicitly used two letters for each quantity, one expressing the amount of units of the commodity and the other its value (or price) (see, for example, the system of equations in D3/12/6: 18). As Sraffa stressed, the important result of his inquiry was that relative prices are fully determined by solving a set of simultaneous equations in which only objective data describing the social production process mattered as proximate determinants.

Sraffa swiftly also saw that, in the case of his first equations, it was possible to 'reduce' the value of a commodity to the amounts of some other commodity needed directly and indirectly in its production (see D3/12/7: 30–31). Therefore, the exchange ratios of any two commodities may be conceived as reflecting the relative amounts of any one of the commodities in the system used up, directly and indirectly, in the production of one unit of the two commodities under consideration. It thus became obvious to him that, once the problem was approached from a rigorous physical real cost point of view, the notion of a 'common measure' loses much of the appeal it had in the earlier authors, including Marx.

From the end of November 1927 Sraffa also wrote down equations with a surplus, in which $A \geq \Sigma a$, $B \geq \Sigma b$, $C \geq \Sigma c$, and at least one inequality is a strong one. These he called his 'second equations', which can be seen as a direct extension of the 'first equations':

$$v_a A = (v_a a_1 + v_b b_1 + c_1) r$$
$$v_b B = (v_a a_2 + v_b b_2 + c_2) r$$
$$C = (v_a a_3 + v_b b_3 + c_3) r$$

Here, v_j is the value of commodity j (j = a, b), commodity c serving as standard of value ($v_c = 1$), and r is the interest factor (1 + interest rate).[7]

When Sraffa showed this equation system to Frank Ramsey, his mathematical friend reformulated the system of homogeneous linear equations by first putting it into its canonical form and then by setting the determinant of the coefficients equal to zero in order to obtain a non-trivial solution. This was sufficient for him to see that there are solutions for the v_i's and r for any number of equations; that is, processes and therefore commodities. Hence relative prices and the (competitive, that is, uniform) rate of interest (or profits) can be determined exclusively in terms of physical data.[8]

8.3 Sraffa's critical stance towards the labour theory of value

From scrutinising the contributions of the earlier Classical authors, most notably Petty, Cantillon, and Quesnay, Sraffa concluded that the adoption of the labour theory of value by the later writers had involved a 'corruption' of the surplus approach. In a note entitled 'Degeneration of cost and value', probably written in November 1927, he insisted: 'A. Smith and Ricardo and Marx indeed began to corrupt the old idea of cost—, from food to labour. But their notion was still near enough to be in many cases equivalent' (D3/12/4: 2(1)). He expounded:

> The fatal error of Smith, Ricardo, Marx has been to regard 'labour' as a quantity, to be measured in hours or in kilowatts of human energy, and thus commensurate to value. … All trouble seems to have been caused by small initial errors, which have cumulated in deductions (e.g. food of worker = quantity of labour, is *nearly* true). Petty had foreseen the possibility of being misunderstood.
>
> (D3/12/11: 36; similarly D3/12/4: 4)

In this early phase, which extended well into 1929, Sraffa was strictly opposed to employing the concept of labour as a 'quantity' in his equations. In an illuminating document stemming from November 1927, he insisted:

> It is the *whole* process of production that must be called 'human labour', and thus causes all product and all value. Marx and Ricardo used 'labour' in two different senses: the above, and that of *one* of the factors of production ('hours of labour' or 'quantity of labour' has a meaning only in the latter sense). It is by confusing the two senses that they got mixed up and said that value is proportional to quantity of labour (in second sense) whereas they ought to have said that it is due to *human labour* (in first sense: *a non measurable quantity, or rather not a quantity at all*).[9]
>
> (D3/12/11: 64; emphasis added)

Sraffa's critical stance at the beginning of his constructive work towards using the concept of labour in the second sense is documented in several notes and manuscripts composed in the late 1920s, and in annotations in his books.

According to Sraffa, Petty and the Physiocrats not only had the right notion of cost; they also advocated a view of production that was congenial to modern industrial societies. They envisaged production as a *circular flow* rather than, as is the case in the 'Austrian' view of production, prominently advocated by Eugen von Böhm-Bawerk, as a one-way avenue leading from the services of original factors of production via a *finite* number of stages to consumption goods. However, as Sraffa noted, when 'commodities are produced by commodities ... the idea that the process of production has a beginning and an end [must be replaced] with that that it is a circular one—an idea first introduced by the Tableau économique' (D3/12/7: 2). Sraffa paid tribute to François Quesnay's ingenious analytical expression of the circular flow idea in terms of his *Tableau Économique* by equating his equations with it (see D3/12/16: 7).[10]

Why, then, had the Classical economists and Marx failed to elaborate a consistent theory of value and distribution on the basis of (i) production viewed as a *circular flow* and (ii) the twin concepts of *physical real costs* and *social surplus*? In Sraffa's view, the main reason derived from a mismatch between the analytical concepts and the (mathematical) tools at their disposal. More specifically, as Sraffa had demonstrated with his first and second equations, the tool needed to bring to fruition both conceptual elements (i) and (ii) were *simultaneous equations* and the knowledge of what their properties are and how to solve them. As Sraffa stressed in a document written in all probability in late 1927 or early 1928, the role of physical real costs in determining value is 'seen only in general equilibrium' (D3/12/42: 46).[11] The indispensable tool – simultaneous equations – alas, was not at the disposal of the Classical authors and Marx, who therefore tried to solve the problems in a roundabout way, typically by first identifying some 'ultimate measure of value' by means of which heterogeneous commodities were meant to be rendered homogeneous. Several authors, including Smith, Ricardo, and Marx, had taken 'labour' to be the sought standard and therefore arrived at some version of the labour theory of value. However, the route via labour values was not really a way out of the impasse: commodities are produced by means of commodities and therefore the quantities of labour embodied in them cannot be determined, except in special cases, other than from simultaneous equations.[12]

8.3.1 Tertium comparationis

Sraffa variously contemplated the problem of the 'common third' – that is, the problem of whether qualitatively different commodities could be said to represent equal or different quantities of the same substance – by discussing the statement in a famous fragment of Heraclitus, quoted by Marx in Volume I of *Capital* (see Marx 1954, p. 107 n.), whose English translation reads: 'All things are exchanged for fire, and fire for all things, as goods for gold and gold for goods'. In a note written in the Lent term of 1928, Sraffa suggested that 'electricity' might be substituted for 'fire' as the 'common third' or 'substance'.[13] A possible explanation for this suggestion is that, in modern times, electricity is an input in each and every commodity and that, in particular circumstances, there may be exchange ratios of commodities that are proportional to the relative overall amounts of electricity 'embodied' in the various commodities. Or perhaps Sraffa's reference to 'electricity' derived from his reading of some contemporary books on modern physics. Max Planck, in *The Universe in the Light of Modern Physics*, stated:

> If we compare the old theory with the new, we find that the process of tracing back all qualitative distinctions to quantitative distinctions has been advanced very considerably ... According to the modern view, there are no more than two ultimate substances, namely positive and negative *electricity*.
>
> (1931, p. 16, emphasis added)

Interestingly, in his personal copy of the book Sraffa had annotated these statements.

8.3.2 Doing away with 'human energy'

Another objection to the labour theory of value may also be related to Sraffa's reading of books devoted to the natural sciences and methodological issues. For example, he had carefully studied and annotated Poincaré's *La Science et l'Hypothèse* (1902), especially the chapter 'Énergie et Thermodynamique', and from these and annotations in other books we may infer that he believed economists must not ignore the laws of physics, chemistry, and biology.[14] According to Sraffa, this request spoke in favour of the physical real cost approach and against the labour-based approach:

> The difference between the 'physical real costs' and the Ricardo–Marxian theory of 'labour costs' is that the first does, and the latter does not, include in them the natural resources that are used up in the course of production (such as coal, iron, exaustion [sic] of land) [Air, water, etc. are not used up: as there is an unlimited supply, no subtraction can be made from ∞.] *This [is] fundamental because it does away with 'human energy' and such metaphysical things.*[15]
>
> (D3/12/42: 33, emphasis added)

8.3.3 A 'purely mystical conception'

Closely related to the above is Sraffa's opposition to the view typically held by advocates of the labour theory of value, according to which the wage labour of human beings must be singled out, to the exclusion of other kinds of labour, when dealing with the problem of value. As Sraffa noted, this view was not restricted to such authors as Ricardo and Marx, but was encountered also in Edgeworth or Marshall (see D3/12/42: 36). In fact, a 'key note' of Marshall's *Principles* was 'that free human beings are not brought up to their work on the same principles as a machine, a horse, or a slave' ([1890] 1977, p. 504). Sraffa objected in a note composed between May and July 1928:

> There appears to be no objective difference between the labour of a wage earner and that of a slave; of a slave and of a horse; of a horse and of a machine; … *It is a purely mystical conception that attributes to human labour a special gift of determining value.* Does the capitalist entrepreneur, who is the real 'subject' of valuation and exchange, make a great difference whether he employs men or animals? Does the slave owner?
>
> (D3/12/9: 89, emphasis added)

Sraffa's argument echoes an observation by McCulloch that had been criticised by Marx in the *Histoire* (1925, Vol. VII, pp. 22, 24). Sraffa did not agree with the criticism. In his own index of the volume, he stressed: 'Sbagliata critica c.[ontra] McCulloch [Mistaken criticism of McCulloch] 22, 24'. He also noted: 'Smith appelle un boef [sic] un ouvrier productif [Smith calls an ox a productive worker] 23', which Sraffa considered to be the correct view (and a remnant of the earlier physical real cost approach in Smith's *Wealth*).

8.3.4 The 'historical' labour theory of value

Sraffa also reconsidered the view, which had been put forward by several authors, including Smith, McCulloch, Torrens, and Engels, that the labour theory of value holds in primitive societies. At the end of the 1920s he consulted contemporary contributions to economic history, anthropology, and ethnology and annotated, inter alia, passages dealing with the historical interpretation of the theory. In Bücher (1910), Sraffa read that 'labour among primitive peoples is something very ill-defined' (see D3/129: 50); in Eldridge (1923, pp. 21, 22, 42) that 'in India waiting is a rule'; that 'time is immaterial where price is concerned'; and that 'not labour-saving but material-saving devices of modern industry have the greatest vogue in China' (see D3/12/10: 18). He also excerpted from Firth (1929) and noted that Hoyt (1926) provides 'striking examples' of a 'failure to accord value to time and labour even when exchange is well-developed'

(D3/12/9: 42). All this confirmed Sraffa's view that what mattered for the determination of commodity values were physical real costs.

8.4 Sraffa's 'third equations': the concept of wages as a share

On the basis of his first and second equations, Sraffa had shown that if the physical real cost approach of the Classical authors is developed coherently there is no such problem as the 'transformation' of values into prices of production, with which Marx had struggled in vain. This does not mean that one cannot get, in certain cases, from labour values to production prices in a logically consistent way. It only means that the latter can be determined entirely independently of the former, which are therefore redundant in the analysis (see Steedman 1977). Interestingly, in non-trivial cases in which one can go from labour values to prices of production, the use of Sraffa's Standard commodity is required. However, before we can discuss this, we must first take note of some further steps in the development of Sraffa's constructive work.

While in his first and second equations Sraffa assumed wages to be given as an inventory of commodities, he shortly afterwards began to investigate, for a given system of production, how a hypothetical change in wages affected the rate of profits and relative prices. In this regard, he once again followed Ricardo, who had also investigated the implications of the workers' participation in the sharing out of the surplus product, and had thus arrived at his fundamental proposition on distribution, according to which the rate of profits is inversely related to 'proportional' wages, that is, to the *share* of wages in the social product. Adopting Ricardo's share concept of wages forced Sraffa not only to dispense with the concept of given real (i.e., commodity) wages, but also to reconsider his earlier view that there is no good reason for attributing a specific role to 'human labour', because there was 'no objective difference' between the labour of a slave, a horse, a worker, or a machine.

Sraffa now pointed out that, while the amount of fodder given to a horse, for instance, is decided by its owner exclusively on grounds of economy, the level of wages paid to workers is the outcome of a bargaining process between capitalists and workers. In a manuscript written in 1942, Sraffa (D3/12/16: 18) expounded that in his first and second equations 'the food and sustenance of the workers [are] treated … on the same footing as that of horses'. Significantly, he added: 'Men however (and in this they are distinguished from horses) kick'. This implied that wage labour could no longer be treated on a par with other kinds of labour in terms of the physical real costs it involved, but had to be taken explicitly into account. Since wages were typically paid to workers in relation to the work performed, Sraffa eventually convinced himself that human labour had to be treated as a measurable quantity. While soundings of doubt concerning his earlier view can be traced back to the summer of 1929 (see in particular his notebook D3/12/12), it was only from 1931 onward that he began to assume that wages were paid in relation to the labour performed and we encounter equations in which the labour employed in industry i, L_i, is explicitly given (see D3/12/7: 166, 159(1)).

Sraffa at first does not appear to have been aware that with wages absorbing the entire surplus product relative prices can be shown to be proportional to the relative quantities of labour embodied in the various commodities, provided relative wage rates are taken to reduce different kinds of concrete labour to some kind of simple or social labour. Labour values thus simply reflect a very special constellation of the sharing out of the surplus product among workers and capitalists. To emphasise this fact, Sraffa in the early 1940s coined the term 'value theory of labour' (see D3/12/44: 3). Labour values, far from being simply observable, require the solution of a system of simultaneous equations, which in addition must be associated with a particular distributional constellation.

With workers participating in the sharing out of the surplus, another Classical concept lost much of its former appeal: that of *ante factum* payment of wages, which implied reckoning wages as belonging to the capital advanced at the beginning of the (uniform) period of production. Ricardo and Marx had retained this assumption, but it sat uncomfortably with the rest of their analyses. While Sraffa at first followed them, towards the end of 1943, after careful deliberation,[16] he decided to take wages to be entirely paid out of the product. This prompted him to reconsider the Classical distinction between 'necessaries' and 'luxuries' and to elaborate the more technical distinction between 'basic' and 'non-basic' products.

When (re-)reading some of Marx's works in the early 1940s, Sraffa found that the latter had spotted a serious flaw in Ricardo's argument (see, in particular, Marx [1861–1863] 1989, pp. 226–227, 419). Marx approved of Ricardo's new concept of proportional wages and had translated it into his own concept of 'rate of surplus value', S/V, with S as the labour value of the (net) social surplus (profits) and V as the social variable capital, that is, wages. Ricardo had assumed that his fundamental proposition on distribution applied not only to a given system of production in use but also to technologically changing systems. Against this, Marx had objected that Ricardo had erroneously identified the rate of profits with the rate of surplus value and had thus overlooked a second determinant of the former: the technical conditions of production as they are reflected in the 'organic composition of capital' of the system as a whole.

Ricardo's blunder was due to the simplifying assumption he typically entertained in much of his observations on the wage–profit relationship; namely, that capital consists entirely of, or can be resolved entirely into, wages. (The implication of this assumption is that, when wages vanish, the rate of profits goes to infinity.) Yet in a circular system of production this is not the case: however far back one carries the reduction of prices to dated quantities of labour and thus wages, there is always a commodity residue left. For this reason, there is a *finite* maximum rate of profits corresponding to zero wages. Therefore the rate of profits can fall or rise even if proportional wages remain constant (and remain constant even if proportional wages change). This becomes clear when we turn to Marx's expression for the rate of profits[17]:

$$r = \frac{S}{C+V} = \frac{S/L}{C/L+V/L} = \frac{1\text{-V/L}}{1/R+V/L} = \frac{R(1-w)}{1+Rw} \tag{8.1}$$

with *C* as the labour value of constant capital, *L* as the amount of living labour expended during the year, *w* as the share of wages (*V/L*, or the rate of surplus value, $(1-w)w^{-1}$), and *R* as the inverse of the organic composition of capital (*C/L*). Obviously, the general rate of profits depends on two magnitudes instead of only one: *R* and *w*. In Marx's conceptualisation, *(L/C)* = *R* gives the maximum rate of profits that corresponds to zero wages and thus an infinite rate of surplus value. If, in the course of economic development, the maximum rate of profits happens to fall, and proportional wages remain constant, the actual rate of profits is bound to fall. Differentiating *r* partially with respect to *R*, we get

$$\frac{\partial r}{\partial R} = \frac{1-w}{(1+Rw)^2} > 0.$$

In a manuscript written in 1943, Sraffa criticised von Bortkiewicz (1906–1907), who had objected to Marx's 'law of the tendency of the rate of profits to fall' (LTRPF), pointing out, inter alia, that von Bortkiewicz had followed Ricardo in assuming unidirectional or linear production processes, and had thereby missed the importance of the maximum rate of profits.[18] This does not mean, however, that Sraffa fully endorsed Marx's argument or considered the LTRPF to be generally valid. It had not escaped his attention that Marx's statement of the law was marred by some inconsistencies,[19] and that Marx had himself drawn attention to various counter-acting tendencies that could extenuate or even reverse the fall of the rate of profits. Interestingly, annotations in his working copy of Volume III of *Capital* indicate that Sraffa appears to have entertained doubts about the exposition of the LTRPF being true to the original, and he even seems to have made attempts to study Marx's original manuscripts at the International Institute of Social History in Amsterdam in order to compare them with the text published by Engels after Marx's death. As the *MEGA*² edition shows[20] Engels's editorial interventions and additions indeed made the statement of the law appear more firm and definitive than seems justified in view of Marx's original texts.[21] Focusing attention on the case of a *given* system of production in use, Sraffa in his book credited Marx with having seen that, in a circular flow framework, the maximum rate of profits (corresponding to zero wages) is finite, not infinite (Sraffa, 1960, p. 94).

8.4.1 From the 'hypothesis' to the Standard commodity

When in the late 1920s Sraffa began to study the dependence of the rate of profit on wages, he had to face the problem that, with a change in wages, relative prices also change. The existence of these price changes made it difficult to ascertain how a given change in wages affected the *rate* of profits, which relates to the part of the surplus product going to capital owners. In a document composed in the first half of 1931, Sraffa contemplated the special case in which a change in distribution has no impact on the value of the social capital (or aggregate of the means of production employed) relative to that of the social product (or the totality of the goods produced):

> It may be said that the value of total capital in terms of total goods produced cannot vary [as a consequence of a variation of wages and a contrary variation of profits], since the goods are composed in exactly the same proportions as the capitals which have produced them.
>
> (D3/12/7: 157(3))

Sraffa was clear that the proposition was 'false', but surmised that it 'may contain an element of truth' (ibid.). When he came back to the issue in November 1943, he clarified that his proposition was based on the 'statistical compensation of large numbers' (D3/12/35: 28) and henceforth called it 'My Hypothesis' or simply 'Hypothesis'. As Sraffa saw at the beginning of the 1940s, it was precisely this hypothesis that was also underlying Marx's labour-based concept of a given organic composition of capital for the system as a whole that can be ascertained independently of the distribution of the product. However, at that time he had already convinced himself that the 'element of truth' referred to resided neither in the statistical compensation of large numbers nor in the labour-based evaluation of social product and social capital. It was clear to him also that no actual economic system could ever be expected to strictly satisfy the 'hypothesis'. Sraffa therefore explored the possibility of constructing an artificial system that did so. This artificial system had to possess all the properties of that part of the actual system out of which it was constructed (that is, the set of 'basic equations') and at the same time offer a straightforward expression of one of these properties: the inverse relation between the actual rate of profits and the share of wages.

This Sraffa accomplished in January 1944 in terms of the Standard system and Standard commodity in a set of notes he interestingly titled 'Hypothesis' (see D3/12/36: 61–85). The upshot of the argument developed with the help of these concepts was the establishment of a simple linear relationship between the rate of profits, r, and proportional wages, w,

$$r = R(1-w) \tag{8.2}$$

where now R is the *standard ratio* or *maximum rate of profits* and w is the share of wages in the net income of the Standard system. Equation (8.2) may be said to incorporate what is sound in Equation (8.1) and at the same time overcome its deficiencies.

While Sraffa had started to develop his production equations in the late 1920s, assuming wages to be paid *post factum*, by eschewing Marx's labour-based constructions, he later realised that the latter had not only re-captured the circular flow conception of social production of Petty and the Physiocrats, but had also operated with a variant of the 'Hypothesis', and had come close to working out a correct solution. This is, we believe, the main reason for Sraffa's appreciation of Marx's achievements. In fact, Sraffa went so far as to maintain that 'M. [Marx] knew all this' (D3/12/36: 67 (verso)). This interpretation is confirmed by numerous documents written in the mid-1940s and late 1950s, and others following the publication of Sraffa's 1960 book. Thus in some notes that he drafted in 1961 for a reply to Stephen Bodington, who had reviewed his book under the *nom de plume* 'John Eaton',[22] Sraffa stated:

> If we want to follow in Marx's footsteps and pass from values to prices of production and from rate of surplus value to rate of profits, the Standard system is a necessary adjunct: for that passage implies going through certain averages and if these are calculated without weights (or with the weights of the real system), a result which is only approximately numerically correct is obtained. If an exact result is wanted the proportions of the St.[andard] Syst.[em] of eq[uation]'s q's must be applied as weights. ... This is not stated explicitly in the book, but is implied.
>
> (D3/12/111: 118)

Sraffa then composed a set of notes entitled 'Risposta a Eaton [Reply to Eaton]' (D3/12/111: 127–130), in which he showed how the general rate of profits can be an exact weighted average of the different industries' rates of profit, calculated for the different industries on the basis of the labour values of the products, by using the Standard system's proportions as weights.[23] In connection with his reply to Eaton, Sraffa also composed a note in which he spelt out his reading of Marx's 'value hypothesis', which renders his above exclamation that 'M. [Marx] knew all this' intelligible. He insisted:

> The propositions of M. [Marx] are based on the assumption that the comp.[osition] of any large aggr.[egate] of commodities, e.g. wages, profits, const.[ant] cap.[ital], consists of a random selection, so that the ratio between the aggr.[egate] values (rate of s.[urplus] v.[alue], rate of p.[rofit]) is approx.[imately] the same whether measured at 'values' or

> at the p.[rices] of prod.[uction] corresp.[onding] to any rate of s.[urplus] v.[alue]
>
> This is obviously true, and one could leave it at that, if it were not for the tiresome objector, who relies on hypothetical deviations ... It is clear that M[arx]'s proportions are not intended to deal with such deviations. They are based on the assumption (justified in general) that the aggregates are of some average composition.
>
> (D3/12/111: 141)

In order to be *exactly* true, the proportions would have to be those of the Standard commodity. In Sraffa's reading, this is indeed what Marx had in mind. To the above he added: 'i.e. Marx *assumes* that wages and profits consist *approximately* of quantities of st.[andard] com[modity]' (D3/12/111: 141, original emphasis), and put two straight lines in the margin. Sraffa interprets Marx here as assuming that the properties of the actual economic system come close to those of the Standard system and that therefore profits and wages reflect, approximately, quantities of the Standard commodity.

8.5 Concluding remarks

When, in 1927 at the latest, Sraffa first realised the existence of a distinctive Classical approach to the theory of value and distribution, he composed a note in which he praised Marx for having previously got hold of this approach again, for having reconstructed its development from Petty and Boisguilbert through to Torrens and Ricardo, and for exploring further its potential by divesting it of the 'vulgar' reformulations associated with authors like J.-B. Say, N. Senior, and J. S. Mill:

> Still more terrific. In the middle of the 19th century a man succeeds, either by accident or by superhuman effort, in getting again hold of the classical theory: he improves it, and draws its practical consequences from it.
>
> (D3/12/4: 17)

However, Sraffa was convinced that the right notion of cost, that of *physical real cost*, from which Petty and the Physiocrats had correctly started, had been 'corrupted' by the adoption of the labour theory of value. In Sraffa's view, it was therefore necessary to jettison Marx's labour-based approach and the concepts associated with it, and to make a fresh start by combining the modern tool of systems of simultaneous equations with the Classical concepts of physical real cost and the circular flow view of production. Sraffa showed in terms of his 'second equations' that the general rate of profits and relative prices are fully determined by the objective data from which he started. Labour value magnitudes, being themselves merely derivatives of the given physical conditions, have no role to play in this determination and are at best superfluous.

The evidence laid out especially from the first period of Sraffa's reconstructive and interpretive work documents his critical attitude towards the labour theory of value and his advocacy of the concept of physical real cost. However, when towards the end of the first period Sraffa began to discuss systems with a surplus and workers' participation in the sharing out of the surplus, he convinced himself that quantities of labour had to be included in the objective data from which the rate of profits and relative prices were to be determined.

In the second period of his constructive work, which extended mainly from 1942 to 1946, Sraffa then explored systematically the relationship of his own concepts and findings with those of Marx. He found that Marx had spotted a serious flaw in Ricardo's fundamental proposition concerning income distribution: in some parts of his analysis Ricardo had for simplicity taken social capital to consist only of wages, or to be reducible to wages in a finite number of steps, and so he had overlooked that, with a circular flow concept of production, the rate of profits depends not only on proportional wages (that is, the share of wages) but also on the technical conditions of production. Sraffa credited Marx with having recaptured the circular flow aspect of social production; with having discovered that in these conditions the maximum rate of profits is finite; and with having specified its magnitude as the inverse of the organic composition of capital as a whole. The latter was seen to be independent of income distribution. The idea of the ratio of the value of the social product to the social capital to be invariant to changes in income distribution had been invoked by Sraffa as early as 1931. This invariance condition, Sraffa soon realised, was not satisfied by any actual system, but could be generated by using a special construction. This was the device of the Standard system elaborated by Sraffa in January 1943.

Acknowledgments

We are grateful to three anonymous referees of this journal for their most helpful comments and suggestions, and to Neri Salvadori for allowing us to draw on some previous work that was carried out jointly with him by one or both of us. The usual caveats apply.

Disclosure statement

No potential conflict of interest was reported by the authors.

Notes

1 This implies also that we do not share the interpretations of Marx's role in the development of Sraffa's thought suggested by De Vivo (2003) and Gilibert (2003), according to whom Marx's schemes of simple reproduction in Volume II of *Capital* 'were the source of Sraffa's equations' (De Vivo 2003, p. 57). These interpretations have been shown to be lacking in textual evidence, and to be contradicted by what Sraffa actually wrote, in Kurz (2015) and Kurz

and Salvadori (2015). The following summary account of the development of Sraffa's thought draws heavily on some of our earlier work, alone or together or in collaboration with Neri Salvadori; in particular on Kurz (2006), Gehrke and Kurz (2006), and Kurz and Salvadori (2009), as well as on Kurz and Salvadori (2001, 2005).

2 With the publication in the *MEGA*^{2} edition of the manuscripts that Marx composed for Volumes II and III of *Capital* it has become possible to study in detail the textual differences between Marx's original manuscripts and Engels' edition. While this will not be a main object in this chapter's discussion, we shall take the opportunity to point out some instances in which Engels presented Marx's argument in a modified if not distorted way.

3 See Garegnani (2005).

4 For more details, see Kurz and Salvadori (2005).

5 To distance himself from Marshall, Sraffa coined the term 'physical real cost', but later switched to 'physical cost'.

6 While Sraffa associated the physical real cost approach with Petty and his notion of 'the days food of an adult Man, at a Medium', he also pointed out that it was the latter notion which led to the adoption of labour as a common measure of value by the Classical economists and Marx. In an undated document he noted, under the heading 'Physical real cost':

> This theory coincides with the labour theory of cost. In effect, we cannot measure, for lack of common unit, goods which are in the cost: but ultimately, if we go back enough, all goods come to labour, and if we want to go behind labour, we find the goods commanded by labourers: if we want to measure them, the only unit is "quantity of goods necessary to support a labourer for one day". This is roughly constant, and therefore we can take "an hour of ordinary labour" as unit.
>
> (D3/12/42: 56)

7 It deserves to be noted that, in his early work on '*mia teoria* [my theory]', Sraffa used marginalist concepts such as 'factor of production' (see D3/12/11: 64) or 'interest rate' and not Marxian ones. It was only in the early 1940s, after he had resumed his constructive work and thus long after he had laid the groundwork for his own analytical construction, that he began to use Marxian concepts such as 'reproduction' or 'organic composition of capital'. This provides further evidence in support of the view that he developed his ideas not by starting from Marx, but from Marshall and the marginalists, whose theory he wished to refute.

8 For a discussion of the collaboration between Ramsey and Sraffa, see Kurz and Salvadori (2001).

9 In this context, it should be noted that in his copy of the French edition of Marx's *Theorien über den Mehrwert* – the eight volumes of the *Histoire des doctrines économiques* (Marx 1924–1925) – which he read in the summer of 1927, Sraffa noted carefully all passages in which Marx distanced himself explicitly from an approach that proceeds exclusively in terms of commodities or 'use values'. Right at the beginning of the *Histoire* Marx took issue with Petty, who had singled out food, not labour, as the measure of value. In the margin, Sraffa placed a wrinkled line along the passage in which Marx contended that any such physical input '*n'est pas la mesure immanente des valeurs*' (1924–1925, Vol. I, p. 3 fn). On the flyleaf at the end of Volume VI we find in Sraffa's own index the entry, 'Marx against physical costs 122' (Marx 1924–1925, Vol. VI).

10 At this time Sraffa did not relate his equations to Marx's schemes of reproduction in Volume II of *Capital*. Only in the early 1940s did he note the family resemblance between Marx's schemes of simple reproduction and his 'first equations'; see Kurz (2015).

11 On 11 January 1928, there is in Sraffa's Cambridge Pocket Diary a reference to page 288 of Volume II of Vilfredo Pareto's *Les systèmes socialistes* (1902), where he stresses the necessity of determining (relative) prices in terms of simultaneous equations and criticises the older economists, who did not have this tool at their disposal, for trying to simplify matters by taking a sufficiently large number of the variables under consideration as known magnitudes.
12 As Sraffa noticed in the second period of his constructive work, in special circumstances the quantity of labour embodied can be seen at a glance. This is the case in Marx's scheme of simple reproduction, for example, where the quantity of labour employed in both departments – department I producing means of production and department II means of consumption – is equal to the labour value of the net product consisting only of consumption goods. Marx's scheme can be said to foreshadow the concept of 'subsystem' or 'vertically integrated sector'; see Sraffa (1960, Appendix A) and Pasinetti (1973).
13 See document (D3/12/10: 24).
14 For more details, see Kurz and Salvadori (2005).
15 Sraffa, in fact, thought to be able to cover not only renewable natural resources, such as lands of unchanging qualities, but also exhaustible resources, such as mineral ores and oil deposits. For a long time he intended to treat both kinds of resource in his 1960 book, although at the proof stage he dropped the corresponding passage.
16 For a detailed discussion of Sraffa's vacillation with regard to the adoption of a gross wage concept, see Gehrke (2015).
17 As Marx explicitly pointed out, the definition of 'profit' and 'rate of profit' he used in this context refers to the *total* surplus value and thus includes all three components into which surplus value is being transformed: 'industrial profit', interest, and ground-rent. For a more detailed discussion of this point and its relevance for Marx's critique of Ricardo's explanation of the falling rate of profit, see Gehrke (2012, pp. 58–63) and Kurz (2015, pp. 93–95).
18 For a more detailed account, see Gehrke and Kurz (2006).
19 Sraffa noted, for instance, the problem of the incompatibility of a constant real wage rate with a constant rate of surplus value when the productivity of labour is changing.
20 See, in particular, Marx ([1863–1867] 2012).
21 For a more detailed account, see Kurz (2013).
22 See Eaton (1960).
23 The point was then established, with some slight differences, also in the secondary literature; see Meek (1961).

References

(Books in Sraffa's library at Trinity College, Cambridge, are indicated by "SL" followed by the catalogue number.)

Bortkiewicz, L. von. 1906/1907. 'Wertrechnung und Preisrechnung im Marxschen System.' *Archiv für Sozialwissenschaft und Sozialpolitik*, in three parts: 23: 1–50, 25 (1907): 10–51 and 445–488. English translation of parts II and III as Bortkiewicz, L. 1952. 'Value and Price in the Marxian System.' *International Economic Papers* 2: 5–60.

Bücher, K. 1910. *Industrial Evolution*. New York: Burt Franklin.

De Vivo, G. 2003. 'Sraffa's Path to *Production of Commodities by Means of Commodities*: An Interpretation.' *Contributions to Political Economy* 22: 1–25.

Eaton, J. 1960. 'Il Modello di Sraffa e la Teoria del Valore-lavoro.' *Societa* 5: 711–734. English translation in E. Bellino. 2006. "Banfi, Eaton, Dobb and Johnson

Review Sraffa's Production of Commodities." *Storia del Pensiero Economico* 2: 182–200.

Eldridge, F. R. 1923. *Oriental Trade Methods.* New York: D. Appleton and Company.

Firth, R. W. 1929. *Primitive Economics of the New Zealand Maori.* With a Preface by R. H. Tawney. London: George Routledge. (SL 1020)

Garegnani, P. 2005. 'On a Turning Point in Sraffa's Theoretical and Interpretative Position in the Late 1920s.' *The European Journal of the History of Economic Thought* 12 (3): 453–492.

Gehrke, C. 2012. 'Marx's Critique of Ricardo's Theory of Rent: A Reassessment.' In *Classical Political Economy and Modern Theory. Essays in Honour of Heinz D. Kurz*, edited by C. Gehrke, N. Salvadori, I. Steedman, and R. Sturn, 51–84. London: Routledge.

Gehrke, C. 2015. 'Subsistence-cum-surplus Wages Versus Gross Wages: A Note.' In *Economic Theory and its History. Essays in Honour of Neri Salvadori*, edited by G. Freni, H. D. Kurz, A. M. Lavezzi, and R. Signorino, 219–232. London: Routledge.

Gehrke, C., and H. D. Kurz. 2006. 'Sraffa on von Bortkiewicz: Reconstructing the Classical Theory of Value and Distribution.' *History of Political Economy* 38 (1): 91–149.

Gilibert, G. 2003. 'The Equations Unveiled: Sraffa's Price Equations in the Making.' *Contributions to Political Economy* 22: 27–40.

Hoyt, E. E. 1926. *Primitive Trade. Its Psychology and Economics.* London: Kegan Paul, Trench, Trubner & Co.

Kurz, H. D. 2006. 'The Agents of Production are the Commodities Themselves. On the Classical Theory of Production, Distribution and Value.' *Structural Change and Economic Dynamics* 17 (1): 1–26.

Kurz, H. D. 2013. 'Das Problem der nichtintendierten Konsequenzen. Zur Politischen Ökonomie von Karl Marx.' In *Marx-Engels Jahrbuch 2012/13.* Berlin: Akademie Verlag.

Kurz, H. D. 2015. 'Sraffa's Equations Unveiled? A Comment on Gilbert.' In *Revisiting Classical Economics: Studies in Long-Period Analysis*, edited by H. D. Kurz, and N. Salvadori, 70–92. London: Routledge.

Kurz, H. D., and N. Salvadori. 2001. 'Sraffa and the Mathematicians: Frank Ramsey and Alister Watson.' In *Piero Sraffa's Political Economy: A Centenary Estimate*, edited by T. Cozzi, and R. Marchionatti, 254–284. London: Routledge.

Kurz, H. D., and N. Salvadori. 2005. 'Representing the Production and Circulation of Commodities in Material Terms: On Sraffa's Objectivism.' *Review of Political Economy* 17 (3): 413–441.

Kurz, H. D., and N. Salvadori. 2009. 'Sraffa and the Labour Theory of Value: A Few Observations.' In *Economic Theory and Economic Thought: Festschrift in Honour of Ian Steedman*, edited by J. Vint, J. S. Metcalfe, H. D. Kurz, N. Salvadori, and P. A. Samuelson, 187–213. London: Routledge. Kurz, H. D., and N. Salvadori. 2015. 'On the Beginnings of Sraffa's Path to *Production of Commodities by Means of Commodities*: A Comment on De Vivo.' In *Revisiting Classical Economics: Studies in Long-Period Analysis*, edited by H. D. Kurz, and N. Salvadori, 226–244. London: Routledge.

Marshall, A. [1890] 1977. *Principles of Economics.* Reprint of the 8th Edition (1920). London: Macmillan.

Marx, K. [1861–1863] 1989. *Economic Manuscript of 1861–63. A Contribution to the Critique of Political Economy ["Theories of Surplus Value"].* Vol. 31 of *Karl Marx, Frederick Engels: Collected Works.* New York: International Publishers.

Marx, K. [1863–1867] 2012. *Ökonomische Manuskripte 1863–1867, Teil 2 (Manuskript 1863/65 zum 3. Buch des „Kapital").* In *MEGA II 4.2. Das „Kapital" und Vorarbeiten.* 2nd ed. (first edition 1993). Berlin: Akademie Verlag.

Marx, K. [1867] 1954. *Capital*, Vol. I. Moscow: Progress Publishers. English translation of *Das Kapital*, Vol. I, Hamburg 1867: Meissner.

Marx, K. 1924–1925. *Oeuvres Complètes de Karl Marx. Histoire des Doctrines Économiques.* Translated by J. Molitor. Eight volumes. Paris: Alfred Costes. (SL 3699)

Meek, R. 1961. 'Mr Sraffa's Rehabilitation of Classical Economics.' *Scottish Journal of Political Economy* 8: 119–136.

Mill, J. 1826. *Elements of Political Economy.* 3rd ed. (First edition 1821). London: Baldwin, Cradock, and Joy. (SL 1363)

Pareto, V. 1902. *Les Systèmes Socialistes.* 2 vols. Paris: V. Giard & E. Brière. (SL 1774)

Pasinetti, L. L. 1973. 'The Notion of Vertical Integration in Economic Analysis.' *Metroeconomica* 25: 1–29.

Petty, W. [1899] 1986. *The Economic Writings of Sir William Petty*, edited by C. H. Hull. Vols I and II, originally published in 1899. Cambridge: Cambridge University Press. (SL 1587). Reprinted in one volume 1986. New York: A. M. Kelley.

Planck, M. 1931. *The Universe in the Light of Modern Physics.* London: George Allen & Unwin. (SL 3622)

Poincaré, J. H. 1902. *La Science e l'Hypothese.* Paris: Ernest Flammarion. (SL 3137)

Sraffa, P. 1960. *Production of Commodities by Means of Commodities.* Cambridge: Cambridge University Press.

Steedman, I. 1977. *Marx after Sraffa.* London: Verso.

9 Don't treat too ill my Piero!

Interpreting Sraffa's papers

Heinz D. Kurz[*]

Original paper: Heinz D. Kurz (2012) Don't treat too ill my Piero! Interpreting Sraffa's papers, *Cambridge Journal of Economics*, 36:6, 1535–1569, DOI: https://doi.org/10.1093/cje/bes065. Oxford: Oxford University Press, on behalf of the Cambridge Political Economy Society.

> In economic theory the conclusions are sometimes less interesting than the route by which they are reached.
>
> Sraffa Papers, C 26[1]

9.1 Introduction

When John Maynard Keynes wrote his essay in biography on Thomas Robert Malthus, he asked Piero Sraffa, who at the time was working on the edition of the works and correspondence of David Ricardo, whether he could use the material Sraffa had collected and which included Ricardo's exchange with Malthus. In his letter to Keynes of 23 December 1932, Sraffa most willingly granted Keynes permission to use as much of the material as he wished, but added: 'don't treat too ill my David!' He was aware that Keynes estimated Malthus a great deal higher than Ricardo, an estimation Sraffa did not share.

Sraffa is no more immune to misinterpretation today than Ricardo was then. Having been invited by the organisers of the workshop on 'New Perspectives on Sraffa's Work', held at Queens' College, Cambridge, in July 2010, to comment on the papers published in this Special Issue devoted to Sraffa, who in my view is one of the greatest economists and deepest thinkers of the twentieth century, my first reaction was that this is an impossible task. However, as the remaining general editor, because Pierangelo Garegnani is no longer with us, I was glad to be able to comment, especially as I felt there are some misinterpretations, some of which

* The author is grateful to Christian Gehrke, Geoff Harcourt, Nerio Naldi, Neri Salvadori, Bertram Schefold, and Ian Steedman for valuable comments and the editors of *CJE*, especially Stephanie Blankenburg and Stephen Pratten, for useful suggestions on an earlier draft of this paper.

DOI: 10.4324/9781003138709-12

are serious. I do not claim, of course, to be possessed of a knowledge and understanding of Sraffa's writings that is beyond doubt – I do not claim to know the 'truth and nothing but the truth'. That would be a ridiculous claim vis-à-vis an author who is known for the depth and breadth of his knowledge, his sharpness, originality, profundity, and seriousness – 'one of the most remarkably clear minds of the twentieth century', as Pasinetti (Pasinetti, 2012a, p. 1304) calls him. Only someone who measured up to his intellectual status would perhaps be entitled to make such a claim, but probably wouldn't. Whilst I admit not to know the full truth, listening to the authors of the papers given at the workshop and then reading the papers accepted for publication in this Special Issue since May 2012 convinced me that some of the propositions contained therein are misleading and cannot be sustained.

This is what I could accomplish in the time given to me. Obviously, I had to limit my comments to just a few of the papers and I could not develop my argument with the care and circumspection the problems dealt with would deserve.

For obvious reasons I focus attention on the papers concerned with reconstructing or commenting on Sraffa's intellectual development that led up to the publication of his 1960 book, i.e., the papers by Bellofiore, Davis, Pasinetti, Porta, Scazzieri, and Sinha. Surprisingly, the analytically more demanding problems Sraffa had to master – i.e., fixed capital, scarce natural resources, and universal joint production – play hardly any role in the papers under consideration, an exception being Pasinetti's. This is odd because Sraffa was very clear that the fecundity of the 'standpoint … of the old classical economists from Adam Smith to Ricardo' (1960, p. v) he had adopted depended crucially on whether it was capable of tackling satisfactorily these important real-world problems. Elaborating a consistent theory that covered the cases mentioned caused him a lot of headaches, forced him to reorient his work several times, greatly helped in this regard by his 'mathematical friends', especially Abram S. Besicovitch, and retarded the completion of his book. Yet these problems receive little attention in the papers discussed here. Another surprising fact is that in these papers, again with the exception of Pasinetti's, the criticism of the marginalist theory, which was so important to Sraffa, is given short shrift. This is strange, because from an early time onwards Sraffa scrutinised critically not only Marshall's partial equilibrium theory, but also the Austrian and American variants of marginalism, i.e., the theories of Eugen von Böhm-Bawerk and John Bates Clark, Knut Wicksell's attempt at integrating the temporal Austrian and the Walrasian approaches and Vilfredo Pareto's general equilibrium theory, to mention but the most important ones. The critical part of Sraffa's research programme is taken up essentially only in the late Pierangelo Garegnani's contribution (Garegnani, 2012)[2] and then, mostly implicitly, in a number of what may be called applied economics papers, which discuss contemporary economic problems, especially the recent financial turmoil, from a non-marginalist perspective (viz. Barba and De Vivo, 2012, Panico et al., 2012; Pasinetti, 2012b; Wilkinson, 2012). These papers demonstrate impressively the relevance of Sraffa's and Keynes's ideas for an understanding of recent historical events. I learned a great deal from them, but it is beyond the scope of my comment to embark upon them.

Since I agree with the main thrust of Luigi Pasinetti's thoughtful perspective on Sraffa's work, I deal with the few and fairly minor elements in which my view differs from his as my argument proceeds. I am also in agreement with what Jonathan Smith (2012) says in his contribution and take this opportunity to express anew my sincere gratitude to him, the director, David McKitterick, and the staff of the Wren Library for effective support over many years. Jonathan Smith's catalogue of Sraffa's papers has been of invaluable help in the editorial project. Nerio Naldi (2012) has unearthed new important facts concerning Sraffa's life, career, and relationships and ought to be thanked for not allowing even the most miniscule piece of information to go undetected. Keynes had famously called Sraffa 'the man from whom nothing is hid'. Had he only been given the chance to know Nerio!

The composition of the comment is the following. Section 9.2 sets the stage in terms of formulating criteria that ought to be followed when interpreting an author. Unfortunately, not all the authors appear to respect these criteria, which is responsible for some serious misinterpretations. This is shown in Section 9.3, which contains a first round of general comments on the papers under discussion. Section 9.4 then provides a summary account of the early development of Sraffa's interpretive and (re-)constructive work. This provides the needed background against which the papers under consideration will be discussed. The argument is interspersed with critical comments on particular propositions put forward in the latter. The following shorter sections then comment briefly on the main messages of the papers, one by one. I begin with Davis (Section 9.5), followed by Scazzieri (Section 9.6), Porta (Section 9.7), Bellofiore (Section 9.8), and Sinha (Section 9.9). Section 9.10 contains some concluding remarks.

As already indicated, I have decided not to go into any assessment on the positive contributions on Sraffa, which are numerous in many papers presented at the Conference, and which I leave to the readers themselves to evaluate. Instead, following the remark by Sraffa to Keynes, given in the title of this comment, I concentrate on dispelling the many misunderstandings that might arise from some of the papers.

9.2 On the danger of misinterpretation

The dangers of misinterpretation have been vividly described in the literature. For example, in Ernst Bernheim's *Lehrbuch der historischen Methode* we read that if one's interpretation is not 'constrained by methodical discipline', the enterprise is in danger of degenerating into an exercise of safeguarding one's preconceived opinions and prejudices:

> One then hears and reads from the sources what in the sense of an already assumed position one has hoped and expected to hear and read in them; one closes one's apprehension entirely or partially with regard to those data that contradict the preliminarily elaborated opinion or that request its revision.
>
> (Bernheim, 1894, pp. 468–469, my translation)

Any serious reconstruction has to be subjected to 'methodical discipline'. This involves, first, scrutinising the interpretation suggested against the pieces of evidence put forward in its support in order to find out whether there is indeed the alleged correspondence between the two. It involves, second, confronting the reconstruction with the complementary set of material in order to see whether it is contradicted by it and involves an illusion due to the selected material on which it is based.

In his *Studies in Words*, C. S. Lewis describes vividly the danger of misinterpreting:

> The highly intelligent and sensitive reader will, without knowledge, be most in danger of [committing errors]. His mind bubbles over with possible meanings. He has ready to hand un-thought-of metaphors, highly individual shades of feeling, subtle associations, ambiguities – every manner of semantic gymnastics – which he can attribute to the author. Hence the difficulty of 'making sense' out of a strange phrase will seldom be for him insuperable. Where the duller reader simply does not understand, he misunderstands – triumphantly, brilliantly. *But it is not enough to make sense. We want to find the sense the author intended.*
>
> (Lewis, 1960, pp. 4–5, emphasis added)

Indeed, the only thing that matters in our case is to find *the sense Sraffa intended*. It hardly needs to be mentioned that this is an extremely difficult task, not least because Sraffa's views on particular problems changed considerably over time. However, some precautions can and ought to be taken in order not to misunderstand and misinterpret all too easily, brilliantly or otherwise.

It is interesting to note that a passage from Antonio Gramsci's Prison Notebooks (Gramsci, 1948) touches directly upon these questions. Gramsci wrote it presumably shortly before he learned about Sraffa's appointment to the editorship of Ricardo's works. It relates to the problem of reconstructing Marx's thought. It is not unlikely that problems of interpretation had been discussed between Sraffa and Gramsci before the latter's imprisonment, that is to say between 1924 and 1926, when they spent long hours in intense conversation. The note reads:

> *Question of method.* If one wants to study the birth of a conception of the world that has never been exposed systematically by its founder (and whose essential coherence is not to be established in each single manuscript or set of manuscripts, but in the entire development of the multifaceted (vario) intellectual work in which the elements of the conception are implicit) *it is necessary first to make a philologically meticulous work, carried out with a maximum of scrupulousness as to exactness, of scientific honesty, of intellectual loyalty, of the absence of any preconception and apriorism or position taken.* It is necessary, first of all, to reconstruct the intellectual process of development of the given thinker in order to identify the elements that became stable and 'permanent', that is those that have been assumed as his proper thoughts, different from and superior to the 'material' previously studied, which served as a stimulus; only these elements are essential moments of the process of development.[3,4]

The first edition of Gramsci's Prison Notebooks is in Sraffa's library in Cambridge (see item 3979) and it is annotated. In the margin of the paragraph quoted, Sraffa added a straight line, whereas in the margin of the emphasised passage (which in the book is underlined by Sraffa) there are two straight lines. Sraffa's own editorial work has rightly been praised for its philological meticulousness, its maximum scrupulousness as to exactness, its scientific honesty, its intellectual loyalty, and the absence of any preconceptions and apriorisms or position taken. It has also rightly been praised for Sraffa's identification of elements in Ricardo's thought, which in the course of time became stable and permanent, i.e., especially his reconstruction of the development of Ricardo's theory of value and distribution (see Pasinetti, 2012a, pp. 1310–1311).[5]

Compared with the Ricardo editorial project, the Sraffa project is incomparably more difficult. Sraffa published very little during his lifetime, but he wrote a lot. There are several thousand pages in his unpublished papers that contain preparatory notes, explorations of specific ideas, elaborations of particular points, alternative approaches to a problem, early drafts of sections, and whole chapters, etc., which eventually culminated in the publication of *Production of Commodities by Means of Commodities* (1960). His respective work extended over a long period of time, from the mid-1920s to 1959, interrupted twice, each time for an entire decade or more, because the edition of Ricardo's works and correspondence absorbed all his energy (see Ricardo, 1951–1973 and also n. 28 below). Sraffa was a most attentive student of the old and contemporary economics literature, but his intellectual curiosities and interests went far beyond it, including especially recent developments in the natural sciences, especially physics, chemistry, and biology, and in philosophy. His studies and manuscripts reflect impressively his comprehensive intellectual concerns and the numerous and diverse sources he tapped. In private conversation, Sraffa is reported to have called his notes and papers an 'iceberg', the tip of which is his published work. Hence, what is needed is an investigation of that iceberg – the materialisation of the inspirations he derived from many different sources, of the process of his intellectual development and of the progress of his analytical work. The papers ought to be studied together with the sources he explicitly refers to in them, many of which are to be found in his library: his books and other pieces of literature, several of which are annotated and contain indexes prepared by Sraffa himself on the flyleaves at the end of the items or on their inside back covers. The annotations and the indexes of his books frequently exhibit a complex age structure. They were apparently composed at different times, reflecting Sraffa's progressing analytical preoccupations, which in turn are echoed in his notes and manuscripts. On the basis of his handwriting, which changed over time, and of echoes in his notes and papers, his annotations, and entries in his indexes can often, with a reasonable degree of confidence, be ascribed to one of the three main periods of his constructive work (broadly, 1927–1931, 1941–1945 and 1955–1959) and in some cases even to particular years within those periods. Then there are Sraffa's diaries, which contain useful hints as to which problems he was working on when, which literature he consulted and with whom he discussed the problems with which he was concerned. Then there is Sraffa's correspondence and exchange of notes with other scholars (most notably his 'mathematical friends', especially Besicovitch) and observations by others on the progress of Sraffa's work (especially Keynes in the early period). Lastly, there is circumstantial evidence of various kinds that may be taken into account, but ought to be treated with caution and circumspection.

Hence, in order to avoid as far as possible the pitfalls of misunderstanding and misinterpreting, which are particularly numerous in the case of Sraffa, a first and obvious precaution is to take into account all the information at our disposal. Yet, given the sheer mass and complexity of the material at hand, this does not do away with the necessity of proceeding in terms of working hypotheses, or 'speculations', as to how the material might reasonably be interpreted. As soon as one feels entitled to put forward such a working hypothesis, and has collected the documents which, after careful scrutiny, philological and other, appear to support it, one ought to go over the material once again explicitly on the lookout for documents that *contradict* the hypothesis. Since, as has already been mentioned, Sraffa tried out many ideas and concepts, some of which he kept while others he abandoned, documents can be set aside that reflect ideas or concepts jettisoned by him: they can safely be assumed not to have contributed to what became 'stable and permanent' in Sraffa's analysis. (This does not mean that they are unimportant, because, as Sraffa stressed in his papers, it is via committing errors and correcting them that man learns.) However, if there are documents that are neither compatible with the interpretation suggested nor can be put to one side on the grounds just mentioned, one has to face the fact that one's working hypothesis is either entirely or partly wrong and therefore has to be abandoned or amended.

This brings me to a first set of observations on the papers under consideration.

9.3 First comments on the papers

My criticism of some of the contributors to this discussion, especially Porta and Sinha and to a lesser extent Bellofiore, is that they do not follow the established standards in exegetical work. The desire to make sense is quite natural, and to be quick (or original) in this regard might be regarded as a sign of high intelligence and sensitivity. This is not bad in itself, provided it respects the standards mentioned. I remember when I was first exposed to Sraffa's papers in the mid-1990s. I felt lost in a dark ocean of thoughts, desperately seeking to get ground under my feet by taking any piece of information I could relate to. When Sraffa's papers were first opened to the public, a presumably widely held expectation or preconceived view was that Sraffa's production equations (1960) could be traced back to Marx's schemes of reproduction. I at any rate began to study the papers with this view in mind, after having been invited by the late Pierangelo Garegnani to join the editorial team. In order to steady myself in that ocean I collected anything that supported this (and other) preconceived view(s) of mine. I built little heaps of notes and documents, designed as small islands sticking out from the sea of darkness on which I was on safe ground, or so I thought. Yet the more I entered into the complex material and the more I gradually began to understand its architecture and contents, the clearer it became to me that the view, plausible as it looked at first sight, could not be sustained. Christian Gehrke and Neri Salvadori with whom I collaborated closely over many years, in and out of Cambridge, had reached the same conclusion. We published individually or in teams of two a number of papers in which this was argued in some detail (for references, see below).

Some other scholars, such as Giancarlo De Vivo (2003) and Giorgio Gilibert (2003), had in the meantime published or were just about to publish papers in which they supported with different degrees of confidence, definiteness, and circumspection the view that Sraffa had directly started from Marx. Apparently they had built their own little heaps of notes and documents and felt to be more or less on solid ground to risk an interpretation of the origin of Sraffa's early constructive work and especially his systems of equations. This was fair enough. Alas, when seeing the evidence put forward in support of them, I was not convinced. When I talked to

Pierangelo Garegnani about this he received my view with great reservation, if not disbelief. At the time he was of the opinion that especially Gilibert's reconstruction had much in its favour. I sat down and composed a document in which I showed that the evidence that was meant to support the case actually did not and sent it to Pierangelo. After having read the piece and having gone through the material again himself in preparation of his 'turning point' paper, he apparently changed his opinion and abandoned the previously held view (see, as a reflection of this, Garegnani, 2005, pp. 487-488, n. 30).

I report these events because the Marxian legacy in Sraffa's work appears to be still a big issue, as the papers under discussion in this comment show. To be very clear, I have never seen any compelling evidence in support of the hypothesis that the systems of equations Sraffa began to elaborate from 1927 onwards derived from Marx's schemes of reproduction in Volume II of *Capital* or from his treatment of the so-called 'transformation problem' in Volume III. This does not mean in the least that Marx was unimportant to Sraffa. There are numerous references to Marx in the papers belonging to the first (re-)constructive period of Sraffa's works, as there are numerous references to many other authors, especially Marshall, Ricardo, Smith, and Pareto. But there are no signs that Marx's theory of value and distribution was the basis from which Sraffa started. It is essentially only in the second period, i.e., in the 1940s, that all of a sudden Sraffa begins to develop his argument against the background of and frequently in direct confrontation with Marx's theory, using Marxian terms such as 'organic composition of capital', 'rate of surplus value', etc. It is in this period that Sraffa sees how close Marx had come within a strictly circular flow framework of production to a correct solution of some of the problems he, Sraffa, was concerned with. Among other things, Marx had to be credited with the discovery that the maximum rate of profits was finite, not infinite; a fact Bortkiewicz had lost sight of with his 'Austrian' conceptualisation of production in his criticism of Marx.

These and related matters have been expounded in detail, especially in Kurz (1998, 2002, 2003, 2006), Gehrke and Kurz (2002, 2006), and Kurz and Salvadori (2004, 2005a, 2005b, 2009), but apparently to little avail.

In the following section I turn to a discussion of Sraffa's rediscovery and elaboration of the 'standpoint of the old classical economists' in the theory of value and distribution. For the sake of brevity I will have to proceed in terms of apodictic statements, focusing attention on what became stable and permanent and setting aside many of the ideas Sraffa first adopted, but then abandoned because they did not lead him anywhere.

Two remarks are apposite before I begin the main argument. First, the story to be told is all about continuity and change in Sraffa's thinking. Whoever has taken at least a casual look at Sraffa's papers cannot have missed the fact that there are many small and a few large turning points in his analytical work. The reader is repeatedly confronted with expressions of despair when avenues Sraffa followed turned out to be dead ends. His papers reveal a scholar who was at least as critical towards his own work as towards the works of others. He accused himself of having committed 'blunders', 'stupidities', and 'errors' and exclaimed, for example, '*disastro del modello*' (D3/12/20: 50), when after months of hard work he found out that the approach chosen was flawed. Research is an open-ended process and typically one cannot know beforehand where one's thoughts will lead. Even if he started with certain 'visions' (Schumpeter) or preconceptions, there is no reason to presume that someone like Sraffa, who took nothing for granted and questioned everything, would slavishly stick to them. Sraffa repeatedly stressed that it would be naïve to assume that there are no broader philosophical concerns behind economic theories and that politics plays no role in the genesis of such theories. While Sraffa's political leanings inspired his intellectual work, they did not overwhelm it. He would not allow ideological affinities to blur his logic. His unpublished papers document his honesty, ruthless self-criticism, and love of truth. He had candour and courage and followed his reasoning where it led him, not just where the preconception, with which he may have started, wanted it to go.

There remains, however, the astounding fact that despite all the leaps and bounds and turning points and changes in Sraffa's intellectual development, his work is characterised by a remarkable continuity (see also Pasinetti, 2012a, p. 1312). What is the reason for this? The short answer given here is that Sraffa, when confronted with an economic theory, quickly developed an intuition as to whether it can be sustained or not, and what its strengths and weaknesses were. In this regard, his impeccable logic and his concern with whether the theory was able to explain the facts it purported to explain played an important role. He thus swiftly detected flaws and shortcomings in the theory (as in the case of Marshall or Hayek) and formed an opinion about whether these can be remedied or not. His meticulous critical scrutiny of the theoretical proposition under consideration then typically confirmed his intuition. This applied both to propositions he found in the literature and to propositions he had elaborated himself. In short, Sraffa never followed wrong avenues for a long time. His thoughts, one might perhaps say in retrospect, oscillated around a path, and never deviated from it very much, that was bound to lead to a coherent restatement of the Classical approach to the theory of value and distribution. It may be reasonably speculated that had his (re-)constructive work not been interrupted, he might have been able to elaborate the set of analytical propositions contained in his 1960 book by the late 1930s or early 1940s.

9.4 Classical economics: a *science of things*

Let me now summarise in 'desperate brevity' (to use Schumpeter's expression) Sraffa's concept of the Classical approach to the theory of value and distribution.

9.4.1 Physical real costs

In the 1920s, Sraffa convinced himself that there was a fundamental difference between Marshall's theory, then the main representative of the marginalist approach, and that of some earlier authors. He had encountered William Petty's plea for the 'physician's outlook' on economic problems and cited approvingly the latter's 1676 choice 'to express my self in terms of *Number*, *Weight*, or *Measure* ... and to consider only such Cases, as have visible Foundations in Nature, leaving those that depend upon the mutable Minds, Opinions, Appetites, and Passions of particular Men, to the Consideration of others' (D3/12/4: 3). He also came across James Mill's remarkable proposition: 'The agents of production are the commodities themselves ... They are the food of the labourer, the tools and the machines with which he works, and the raw materials which he works upon' (Mill, 1826, p. 165). These and similar statements led him to confront Marshall's concept of 'real cost' of production (including disutility, abstinence, or waiting as costs) with that of material or 'physical real cost', i.e., the amounts of various commodities (means of production and means of subsistence of workers) that have necessarily to be 'destroyed', or 'consumed productively', given the system of production in use. In a document composed in December 1927, Sraffa called Classical economics explicitly a 'science of things' (D3/12/61: 2) as opposed to Marshall's economics, which was a science of motives.[6]

But how could the values of commodities be ascertained on the basis of physical real costs? This led Sraffa to develop, beginning in November 1927, first, square systems of equations (dealing with single production) in which no more is produced of the different commodities than is used up productively, i.e., systems without a surplus product.[7] This is what he called his 'first equations'. He swiftly moved on, in the late 1920s, to investigate systems with a surplus product, without and with durable instruments of production and given and constant real wages in his 'second equations', followed by an investigation of the impact of a variation in real wages on the rate of interest and relative prices in his 'third equations'.

9.4.2 Sraffa's equations

This is not the place to discuss the various steps Sraffa made here or his collaboration with Frank Ramsey over the solvability of his systems of equations (see Kurz and Salvadori, 2001; Gehrke and Kurz, 2006). I shall, rather, argue that there is no compelling evidence that Sraffa started from Marx's schemes of reproduction or from his labour theory of value. This has been most strongly advocated by Gilibert (2003). I take the liberty of briefly discussing parts of his paper for two reasons. First, it is referred to in some of the contributions to this Special Issue and has repeatedly been cited in the wider literature as containing a demonstration of the

Marxian origin of Sraffa's equations.[8] Second, Gilibert puts forward some evidence, which deserves to be scrutinised carefully because, if interpreted correctly, it explains, I surmise, why Sraffa called Classical economics a *science of things*. The scope of the following argument thus transcends a narrow criticism of certain propositions of Gilibert and is directly pertinent to an assessment of the papers in this Special Issue. Let me add that I find other versions of the claim that Sraffa's equations have a Marxian origin similarly unconvincing, but due to space constraints cannot enter into a discussion of them here.

Gilibert interpreted Sraffa's following system with three equations, dated winter 1927 (D3/12/5: 2), as a reflection of Marx's (three-sector) scheme of simple reproduction.[9] I reproduce the document in full and italicise parts of it:

> No surplus –
>
> $$\left.\begin{aligned} A &= a_1 + b_1 + c_1 \\ B &= a_2 + b_2 + c_2 \\ C &= a_3 + b_3 + c_3 \end{aligned}\right\} \text{ where } \begin{aligned} A &= \sum a \\ B &= \sum b \\ C &= \sum c \end{aligned}$$
>
> These are homogeneous linear equations. They have infinite sets of solutions, but the solutions of each set are proportional. These proportions are univoche {unique}.
>
> These proportions we call ratios of Absolute values. They are purely numerical relations between the *things* A, B … They are not necessarily the ratios, in which exchange will actually take place in any community in which *the quantities of things respectively used in production (i.e. consumed) and produced* satisfy those equations: such actual ratios of exchange are also conditioned by such things as legal institutions, etc. which vary in different organisations of society and which are 'arbitrary', i.e. irrelevant, from our present point of view.
>
> (D3/12/5: 2, emphasis added)

Interpreting these equations, Gilibert insisted:

> In fact, these 'equations' *make sense only* if we interpret them as a simple algebraic transcription (with letters substituted by numbers) of a Marxian scheme with three industries (simple reproduction is attested by the Σ conditions), and without surplus.
>
> *The quantities summed are homogeneous, all being measured in money terms.*
>
> (Gilibert, 2003, p. 32, emphases added)

Before I comment on his reasoning, let me first recall how in his 1960 book Sraffa tabulated the conditions of production of an industry. We find, for example, on the first page of the main text of his book the expression:

280 qr. wheat + 12 t. iron → 400 qr. wheat.

(Sraffa, 1960, p. 3)

What is the difference between this expression and any one of those in document D3/12/5: 2 above? Here it suffices to note that from a purely formal point of view Sraffa employs in both expressions the algebraic sign '+', whereas in the former compared with the latter he uses the symbol '→' instead of the algebraic sign '='. Now, the meaning of Sraffa's 1960 tabulation of production processes has generally been considered as crystal clear, and as far as I know nobody has ever seriously objected that by using the algebraic sign '+' Sraffa is guilty of having committed the trivial error of summing up heterogeneous quantities.

The uncertainty as to the meaning of the expressions in the note of winter 1927 therefore appears to have a great deal to do with Sraffa's use of the equality sign and his speaking, in fact, of equations. However, if his abstract expressions were simply read as tabulations of productive operations, giving the physical amount of the output of a process on one side of the equality sign and the physical amounts of the different things used up in the course of its production on the other, then some of the uncertainty would effectively be removed. Yet are we entitled to read the above expressions in the way suggested? Gilibert implicitly says 'no', because in his view the above expressions 'make sense only' if all quantities involved are interpreted as 'being measured in money terms'. This dictum comes as a surprise in view of the text Sraffa appended to his system, which, unfortunately, Gilibert quotes only in part (2003, p. 33). In that text the reference is explicitly to 'the *things A, B* ...'. Still more explicitly – yet, alas, not quoted by Gilibert – the reference is to '*the quantities of things respectively used in production (i.e. consumed) and produced*'.[10] Not only did Sraffa not say that he had conceptualised his above expressions in terms of quantities measured in money terms, he actually said something very different, namely that the magnitudes under consideration were 'quantities of things'.

Sraffa, as is evidenced by several of his papers (see Sections 9.4.3 and 9.4.4), was particularly afraid of 'small errors' because they have a tendency to grow into big ones. (Small errors, one might add, are less easy to discover and therefore have a potential of hidden effectiveness.)

I now turn to some pieces of evidence from Sraffa's papers and library, which contradict the interpretation that the starting point of Sraffa's theory was Marx. I restrict my attention to a single area of evidence; other areas are mentioned in Kurz (2003, 2006) and Gehrke and Kurz (2006).

The area under consideration is the relationship of Sraffa's work to the sciences. Let me just remark that in the 1920s, *systems of equations* were widely employed not only in the sciences but also in economics, and Sraffa referred to several of them in his notes and papers and also in his annotations in books. He had meticulously studied, in particular, Vilfredo Pareto's general equilibrium theory, which was formulated in terms of simultaneous equations, and the latter's criticism of cost-of-production and labour theories of value. An important question, therefore, is in which regard are Sraffa's systems of equations different from those he encountered in the economics literature?

9.4.3 Sraffa and the sciences

Scholars studying Sraffa's papers will have come across what can safely be considered the companion document of the one just discussed (D3/12/11: 87).[11] It is entitled 'Value without Surplus' and is contained in a folder dated by Sraffa 'end of November, 1927'. There is reason to presume that it pre-dates the document used by Gilibert (D3/12/5: 2). It is apposite to reproduce it in full:

$$\begin{array}{ccccc} A = & a_1 & + b_1 & + c_1 \\ B = & a_2 & + b_2 & + c_2 \\ C = & a_3 & + b_3 & + c_3 \\ \hline & \parallel & \parallel & \parallel \\ & A & B & C \end{array}$$

Questo è un *determinante*. Inoltre, le somme verticali sono uguali alle somme orizzontali.

> Vedere se a questo determinante è possibile applicare il metodo di Volterra (Chini, p. 35) per trovare il numero dei 'componenti indipendenti' del sistema. Questo forse servirebbe: a) quando non tutti i beni entrassero come fattori di ciascuno. b) quando ci sia surplus, cioè considerando i vari surpluses come merci diverse (supponendo cioè che appena sorge il surplus, si continua a produrre la stessa quantità di 'grano' di prima, e le risorse residue vengon tutte dedicate a produrre gioielli e altre cose 'improduttive') (D3/12/11: 87).[12]

The reference is to a book by Mineo Chini entitled *Corso speciale di matematiche con numerosi applicazioni ad uso principalmente dei chimici e dei naturalisti* (1923, 6th edn).[13] The book is in Sraffa's library and is annotated. In the above document Sraffa draws attention explicitly to page 35 of that book. On this page he annotated a passage dealing with substances of determinate chemical composition and systems of such substances. This discussion is immediately followed by Chini's investigation of the solutions of the corresponding linear systems (ibid., pp. 36 et seq.), which is also annotated by Sraffa. The passage reads:

Quando si abbia un certo numero di sostanze di determinata composizione chimica, ciascuna delle quali possa prendersi in quantità arbitraria, è chiaro che i vari corpi semplici che entrano a far parte di un tale sistema non sempre potranno a loro volta prefissarsi tutti in quantità arbitraria, ma in generale sarà possibile ciò soltanto per un certo numero di essi. Le quantità (masse) dei rimanenti elementi resteranno invece pienamente determinate da quelle prestabilite per i primi; i quali vengono perciò detti i *componenti independenti* del sistema. {The underlinings are by Sraffa and there is an arrow pointing from the last underlined item to the last but one; in the margin of the passage Sraffa put two straight lines. The text runs on:} Per ottenere il numero di questi componenti (del quale si fa uso per es. quando si voglia applicare ad un complesso eterogeneo la cosidetta *regola delle fasi*), il prof. Volterra, in una delle sue pubblicazioni (*Atti della R. Accademia dei Lincei* – Seduta del 22 novembre 1903), ha indicato il metodo sequente. (Chini, p. 35, original emphases; subsequently Chini expounds Volterra's method)[14, 15]

What to make of this? A few observations must suffice.

9.4.4 The natural science point of view: no effect without a sufficient cause

First, it is worth emphasising that right at the beginning of his work on the 'equations', in November 1927, Sraffa consulted a book on mathematics, and, perhaps significantly, not a book on pure mathematics, but one on mathematics for chemists and natural scientists. This is fully in accordance with a fact that until now appears to have largely escaped the attention of many commentators on Sraffa: his vivid interest in contemporary developments in the natural sciences and his attempt to develop an approach in economics in full recognition of these developments. He was particularly fascinated by quantum physics and thermodynamics. This met with his materialist and objectivist orientation. He studied meticulously such authors as Heinrich Hertz, Jules Henri Poincaré, Alfred N. Whitehead, and A. S. Eddington.[16] He excerpted, for example, the following passage on the physicist Werner Heisenberg from an essay on 'the quantum theory' by H. S. Allen published in *Nature* in 1928: 'Heisenberg put forward the demand that only such quantities as are observable should be represented in the mathematical formulation of *atomic theory* … This led to the development of the matrix mechanics, every term in a matrix corresponding to something which is, at least ideally, observable' (Allen, 1928, p. 891, emphasis added; cited in D1/9: 13).[17] In summer 1929, Sraffa stated explicitly that he was keen to elaborate an 'atomic analysis' (D3/12/13: 16 (9)); and in August 1931, in a critical retrospect, he characterised his previous analytical efforts as having been concerned with developing 'an entirely objective point of view', which is 'the natural science point of view' (D3/12/7:161 (3)). This view implied that

> we must start by assuming *that for every effect there must be sufficient cause, that the causes are identical with their effects, & that there can be nothing in the effect which was not in the causes: in our case, there can be no product for which there has not been an equivalent cost, and all costs (= expenses) must be necessary to produce it.*
>
> (D3/12/7: 161 (3), emphasis added)

Sraffa saw this kind of view foreshadowed in the writings of such authors as Petty, the physiocrats and Anonymous (1821).

Second, in view of what has just been said, and more particularly in view of Sraffa's reference to Chini (1923) above, there is reason to think that Sraffa wrote his above 'first equations' as chemists do since Lavoisier, who in the late eighteenth century presented chemical reactions first as a balance sheet and then as an algebraic equation, with the name of a substance expressing the equality of constituents and compound, e.g. '$2H_2O = 2H_2 + O_2$'.[18] From a perspective revolving around the concept of balancing, the analogy between a product that obtains as the result of the 'destruction' of necessary quantities of means of production and means of subsistence, on the one hand, and a chemical reaction conceived of as a balance of the weights of inputs and outputs, on the other, is close at hand. In both cases the balance expresses conservation of mass/energy. Seen in this way, there appears to be nothing 'cryptic or obscure' about Sraffa's first equations, as Gilibert maintains. This is indirectly confirmed by Sraffa's text of D3/12/11: 87. He stresses (see Section 9.4.3) that into the quantities of the substances – which he calls 'beni' or 'merci' (i.e., goods or commodities) – on the LHS of the equality sign 'enter' the quantities of the substances – which he calls 'beni' or 'fattori' (i.e., goods or factors) – on the RHS of the equality sign.[19] Hence there can be hardly any doubt that in the identical production schemas contained in the twin documents, D3/12/11: 87 and D3/12/5: 2, the reference is *directly* to physical quantities of goods, or commodities, or factors, and *not* to quantities in terms of money or labour.

Third, and closely connected with what has just been said, an expression of the type '$2H_2O = 2H_2 + O_2$' may even be regarded as a proper algebraic equation when interpreted as follows: 'the mass of two molecules of water is equal to the mass of two molecules of hydrogen plus the mass of one molecule of oxygen'. In this interpretation, H_2O is not just a symbol for water, but has a quantitative aspect: it is the mass of a molecule of water. Similarly, an expression of the type '$11A = 3A + 9B$' (D3/12/11: 17) could be interpreted both as a tabulation of a production process (and in this case it is not an algebraic equation) and as an algebraic equation saying: 'The value of 11 units of *A* equals the sum of the value of 3 units of *A* and 9 units of *B*'. Obviously, in this interpretation *A* and *B* assume the true meaning of prices, but a system of such algebraic equations is *non-contradictory* only in the case in which there is no surplus, as Sraffa kept stressing (see, e.g., D3/12/6: 16 and D3/12/2: 32–35). Lastly, it deserves mention that more recently chemists use two symbols: '=' (or '↔') when the reaction is reversible, and '→' when it is not. Since single processes of production are irreversible, one might wonder whether it is for this reason that in his book Sraffa switched to the latter symbol.[20]

9.4.5 'Physical value'

Fourth, we have seen that Sraffa characterised his own approach as belonging to the tradition established by Petty and the physiocrats, who are said to have had the right concept of 'cost'. In this context it is worth mentioning that in a document of some 50 pages composed in the summer of 1929, Sraffa explained in detail why he then thought that labour was *not* a 'quantity' that could be taken as a datum in value theory (see also the reflection of his argument in D3/12/13: 2) and Kurz and Salvadori (2009)). He expounded that his objection to the approach in terms of labour quantities

> è basata sulla veduta essenzialmente fisiocratica, che il *valore* sia una quantità intrinseca degli oggetti, quasi una *qualità fisica o chimica*.
>
> (D3/12/12: 7, emphases added)[21]

This characterisation is fully in accordance with the evidence laid out here. The physical interpretation is neatly corroborated by a document entitled 'Physical Costs & Value', contained in a folder 'Nov. [1927]', which reads:

> When I say that the value of a product is 'determined' by the *physical volume of commodities used up in its production*, it should *not* be understood that it is determined by the value of those commodities. This would be a vicious circle, because the value of the product is equal to the value of the factors *plus* the surplus produced.
>
> What I say is simply that the numerical proportions between amount of factors and amount of product *is*, by definition, the absolute value of the product.
>
> (D3/12/11: 101, first emphasis added, 'not' is underlined twice in the original)

And in a document contained in the same folder, he also talked of 'physical value' (D3/12/11: 75).

9.4.6 The realm of necessity extended to the with-surplus case: the problem of 'withdrawing'

Fifth, the text of D3/12/11: 87 above also 'unveils', if we may use Gilibert's term, another important and closely related aspect of Sraffa's early work. In the late 1920s he was keen to stay analytically within the realm of *necessities*. The latter obtains in an unadulterated way in the no-surplus or 'natural' economy and is reflected in the first equations. The no-surplus case, Sraffa insisted, 'would exhibit the true absolute costs' (D3/12/6: 11) of the different commodities and, employing a term Ricardo used, their corresponding 'absolute values'. Interestingly, when using the term 'physical value' of products, he insisted that it '*is* equal to what has been consumed' (D3/12/1: 5; see also D3/12/10: 54). He showed that the sought-after ratios, or (relative) values, are uniquely determined by the socio-technical conditions of production and can be ascertained by solving a set of linear homogeneous production equations.[22]

Yet what about the with-surplus case? The 'natural science point of view' Sraffa had assumed implied that 'We shall have to adopt *that definition which makes the scale of absolute values identical with what it was when there was no surplus*' (D3/12/6: 14, emphasis added). In this way the logic applying to values in the case of production for subsistence was taken to carry over to the with-surplus case. This necessitated reducing the surplus, or interest (the term he employed at the time) – i.e., an 'effect' for which there had to be 'sufficient cause' – to some 'cost' or other.[23] Interest, Sraffa insisted, reflects some objective necessity, rooted in some objective 'social' as opposed to 'natural' obstacles that have to be overcome:

> *Interest appears thus as the necessary means of overcoming an obstacle to production*. It is a *social necessity* as distinguished from the material necessity of, say, putting coal into a locomotive that it may do its work.
> (D3/12/18: 11, emphases added; see also ibid.: 3–6)[24]

The upshot of this 'natural science point of view' is contained in a number of documents dealing with the concept of 'withdrawing'. Income distribution reflects the 'scramble for the surplus' (Sraffa Papers D3/12/11: 83). As the context in which Sraffa uses this expression makes clear, the reference is to Adam Smith's discussion of the 'dispute' over the distribution of income between 'workmen' and 'masters' in chapter VIII of book I of *The Wealth of Nations* (Smith, 1976, WN I.viii). There, Smith also states: 'In the long-run the workman may be as necessary to his master as the master to him, but the necessity is not so immediate [in the short run]' (Smith, 1976, WN I.viii.12). This idea is developed by Anonymous (1821) and recurs in Sraffa in the late 1920s. How much must each party receive in order not to *withdraw* its productive resource? The question raised here asks, in modern terms, what is the reservation price of each resource?

Workers have to be paid, as Smith stressed, a real wage that allows their 'race' to reproduce itself, a hypothesis Sraffa adopted. Due to a (postulated) lack of alternatives to the use of their land, landowners have to be paid a zero rent if their land is not scarce. Lastly, capitalists: interest has to be paid, Sraffa argued, in order to prevent capitalists from 'withdrawing' their circulating capital (including the wear and tear of fixed capital), thus thwarting the 'self-replacement' of the economy.[25] This is why in his early with-surplus equations he applies interest only to the circulating part of capital, but not to the fixed part, which has perplexed readers (see Kurz and Salvadori (2005a)). Correspondingly, Sraffa at the time conceived of the surplus product as the physical input into an artificial industry producing 'luxuries' or 'gioielli e altre cose "improduttive"' (as we read in the above document see Section 9.4.3) for capitalists (see also D3/12/8: 29). By construction, luxuries were meant to satisfy the condition mentioned in (a) above: 'quando non tutti i beni entrassero come fattori di ciascuno'. These artificial goods are 'unproductive' in the sense that, while produced, they are not themselves employed in production. They serve only a single purpose: they are the incentive needed to make capitalists refrain from withdrawing their circulating capital. These goods are thus envisaged to perform with regard to capital what workers' means of subsistence perform with regard to labour: the payment of the former is a *social*, that of the latter a *natural* necessity for production to go on unhampered.

As Sraffa noted in the document of August 1931 referred to in Section 9.4.4, in this way the surplus was made to 'disappear' or 'melt away' (D3/12/7: 161 (3)). His 'where there is an effect there must be sufficient cause' point of view is confirmed by a document from winter 1927–1928. In it Sraffa concluded with respect to the new equations he had elaborated: 'These absolute values *with* surplus are no more what is necessary to *enable* to produce *A*, but what is necessary to *induce* to produce *A*' (D3/12/6: 10). By introducing an artificial (composite) commodity hypothetically produced by means of the surplus product of the actual system as an input, Sraffa sought to assimilate the with-surplus case to the no-surplus one. By tucking away the surplus in an artificial industry, the resulting equations would be rendered non-contradictory and solvable in the conventional way, just like his first equations. And at the same time he was able to solve the problem of income distribution in an objective way in terms of the relative strengths of the parties involved. Or so he thought.[26]

As Whitehead had remarked on the success of science since the seventeenth century:

> Science was becoming, and has remained, primarily quantitative. *Search for measurable elements among your phenomena, and then search for relations between these measures of physical quantities.*
>
> (Whitehead, 1926, pp. 63–64, emphasis added; annotated by Sraffa)

This Sraffa had done. I conclude by remarking that in his work on his first systems of equations I did not spot a single atom emanating from Marx's schemes of reproduction. Labour values played no role in all this. Claims to the contrary are without foundation. Sraffa's repeated reproach that the labour theory of value in Smith, Ricardo and Marx involved a 'corruption' of the correct concept of cost was no 'passing mood', as Porta (2012, p. 1377, fn 40) contends. The issue at hand was not a question of being in one mood or another, but of solving an intricate analytical problem. As a matter of fact, Sraffa was not clear at first how the solutions to his systems of equations related to labour values, because 'labour' (as opposed to the remuneration of workers in terms of a bundle of subsistence goods, Petty's 'bread') was not a quantity he felt should be considered at all. It was basically only in the 1940s that he investigated the relationship between the two.

9.4.7 *What about Euler's theorem?*

But was the way in which Sraffa tried to overcome the problem of self-contradiction of his systems of equations in the with-surplus case convincing? Sraffa quickly saw that it was not. Why should the claims of the different parties to the product in terms of their power to threaten society by withdrawing their productive resources just exhaust the product, neither more nor less? No compelling reason could be given in support of the 'incentives' Sraffa had invoked to generate precisely this result. And was he not thereby just putting forward a conception that shared a problem with marginal productivity theory, which he felt was wrong (but could not yet show conclusively that it was)? Sraffa saw himself confronted with an imputation problem parallel to the one marginalist authors had encountered: is the sum of claims to the social product expressed by workers, capitalists and landlords in terms of marginal productivities of the factors of production exactly equal to the product, or not? Knut Wicksell and Philip Wicksteed had made clear that only in conditions of constant returns to scale is the answer 'yes'. It is no surprise, then, that in this context Sraffa in a couple of notes referred to Euler's theorem. But can constant returns to scale be assumed in a 'Classical' world characterised by a deepening division of labour and the dynamically increasing returns to scale that come with it, as Adam Smith had insisted, recently supported by Allyn Young?

To cut a long story short, after some careful deliberation Sraffa abandoned the approach he had followed – clearly also some sort of 'turning point' in his analysis – and in August 1931 drafted a paper entitled 'Surplus Product' (D2/12/7: 161), which Neri Salvadori and I have discussed in detail (Kurz and Salvadori, 2004, 2005b) and on which John Davis presents further reflections in his stimulating contribution to this Special Issue.[27] This document may be considered to mark Sraffa's 'breakthrough' to the sort of analysis we then encounter in his 1960 book, in which the system moves with one degree of freedom regarding income distribution. I shall not dwell on this here, but hasten on to some further elements in Sraffa's thought that are of great importance for a proper understanding of what he did and why, and why some interpretations contained in this Special Issue cannot be sustained.

9.4.8 The question asked of the theory of value

By mid-1931, Sraffa was optimistic he had finally found a way out of the impasse into which his 'natural science point of view' had led him in systems with a surplus product: he thought he had found the right equations. The problem of the distribution of the surplus could not be decided by means of these, but had to be decided with reference to forces 'outside' them. Depending on these forces, wages would be higher or lower and the rate of interest correspondingly lower or higher, a result Sraffa had already established in 1928 with reference to Ricardo's famous proposition that proportional wages and the rate of profit are inversely related to one another. In a document contained in a folder that gives 'May–July 1928, May 1932' as the times in which the notes were drafted, Sraffa provides a definition of what the theory of value is to accomplish:

> The question asked of the theory of value is the following: Given (from experience) the prices of all commodities … find a set of conditions that will make these prices appear to be necessary. This means, given the unknowns, find the equations (i.e. the constants) … But this is the general question, the problem of finding the theory of value: when it is solved, once and for all, the particular questions asked are the reverse, i.e. given the constant equations, *if the value of one of the constants is varied, how are the resultant prices determined*? But of course this is only a matter of calculation.
>
> (D3/12/9: 65, emphasis added)

Given the equations of production, varying one element of the data or 'constants' (e.g., methods of production, or real wage rate, or gross output levels) allows one to trace its impact on the unknowns (relative prices, the other distributive variables). The discussion of such changes in some data and their impact on the unknowns permeates Sraffa's reconstructive work and also his 1960 book. There Sraffa discusses, inter alia, the impact of different levels of wages on the rate of profits and relative prices (especially in chapter III), or the impact of technical change in basic as opposed to non-basic industries on income distribution and relative prices (1960, pp. 7–8), or the impact of a change in output vis-à-vis extensive and intensive diminishing returns in agriculture (1960, chapter X).

The following observations are apposite at this point.

9.4.9 An important breakthrough

The first one concerns the contention that Sraffa's focus on elaborating his systems of equations implied a 'drastic' restriction of 'the horizon of his research programme' (Pasinetti, 2001, p. 145). This is certainly true in the sense that Sraffa had to cut down on what Pasinetti aptly called Sraffa's 'impossibly grand research programme' at the beginning of his research. The task of working out a correct theory of value turned out to be vastly more difficult than Sraffa had at first thought and absorbed much of his energy, which he could have devoted to other tasks.[28] Porta (2012, p. 1359) is right in attributing to Salvadori and me the claim that Sraffa was driven by 'a quest for absolute rigour'. But his was not a vain exercise motivated by ideological concerns that lacked economic relevance. As Ricardo had insisted, following in the footsteps of Adam Smith (see Kurz and Sturn, 2012), a correct theory of value was an indispensable prerequisite for a theory of capital accumulation, technical progress, and economic growth. As Poincaré famously put it: 'il y'a des problèmes qu'on se pose et des problèmes qui se posent'. The problem Sraffa had put to himself, i.e., reconstructing the Classical theory of value and distribution, in fact entailed a host of further problems that were put to him. It would probably not be an exaggeration to say that what from one perspective looks like a drastic restriction of Sraffa's original research programme, from another perspective involves a considerable extension of it. The scientific community ought to be grateful to Sraffa that he did not give in to the difficulties he encountered, but eventually mastered the task in spite of all the toil and trouble this involved and the moments of despair he experienced.

Elaborating a coherent theory of value of Classical orientation represents, as Pasinetti stressed (2012a, p. 1307), 'a remarkable achievement'. First, it provided, as Sraffa's papers show, the sought basis from which one may discuss major Classical themes, such as the law of the tendency of the rate of profits to fall or the impact of certain taxes on distribution and prices. Second, in addition to this positive task it allows one to tackle the negative one of refuting the marginalist theory of value and distribution. There are a great many documents in Sraffa's papers in which he applies his equations to a criticism of the received variants of this theory. It is also doubtful that the Cambridge controversies in the theory of capital would have taken place without his 'Prelude to a Critique'. Lastly, Pasinetti (2001, p. 149) is correct in pointing out that Sraffa failed to accomplish a task he considered of great importance: that of providing a history of the theory of cost, value, surplus, and its distribution. Sraffa did indeed not succeed in bringing to fruition the critical and the historical parts of his huge research programme in terms of fully worked out chapters of his projected book or separately published treatises. But as the papers show impressively, and the edition of them will hopefully confirm, there is a tremendous amount of material related to these two tasks. I wonder whether the fact that Sraffa accepted the idea of getting his papers published posthumously indicates that he wished the public to have access to the previously hidden part of the iceberg and especially to what it contained in a preliminary form with respect to the two tasks mentioned.

9.4.10 Counterfactuals

Triggered by a paper by Sen (2003), there has been some debate about whether or not Sraffa was opposed to counterfactual reasoning. Sinha in his contribution to the present issue contends boldly that Sraffa 'consistently refrains from counterfactual reasoning' (Sinha, 2012, p. 1335). Following this logic, Sraffa is said to have conceived of his prices as those *actually* ruling in the market. If this was so, then how could Sraffa centre his argument on the concept of a *single* price for each commodity and *uniform* rates of profit both within and across all industries?

More seriously, as we have seen in the above, the contention that Sraffa consistently refrained from counterfactual reasoning is simply false. Of what interest could an economics without any such reasoning possibly be? However, Sraffa did feel that invoking counterfactuals was something that ought to be done with utmost care and circumspection. For good reasons he abhorred the kind of counterfactual reasoning employed by the marginalist authors, because he was convinced that it led us onto treacherous ground. He asked, in particular, what is the meaning of an infinitesimal increase in the 'quantity of capital' in a world in which there are several capital goods? It has no meaning at all unless we are in the fancy world of a 'wheat' economy in which wheat is the only produced means of production.

This brings me to the related issue concerning the role of the 'wheat' or 'corn model' in Sraffa's reconstruction of the Classical approach to the theory of value and distribution and then of the Standard commodity, problems that play an important role in the papers under consideration.

9.4.11 The 'corn model' and the Standard system

The time and energy devoted to discussion of the corn model is, in my view, totally out of proportion to its importance. In Porta (2012, p. 1337, fn 40), the corn model is even elevated to 'the signal instance of pure and unambiguous quantity measurement, which suits Sraffa's needs perfectly well'. What are these needs? They are, supposedly, to interpret Ricardo in a straightforward Marxian manner. The clue Sraffa is said to have received from Marx, who in the *Theories of Surplus Value* argued that the physiocrats saw surplus in agriculture and not in industry because in agriculture workers produce and consume the same thing, which is not so in industry. Sraffa is then said to have made 'generous use' of it, 'without ever mentioning Marx, except in the unpublished manuscripts

[!]' (Porta, 2012, p. 1377, fn 40; the reference is to D3/12/11: 100). Porta appears to have forgotten that earlier in his paper (Porta, 2012, p. 1363) he draws attention to Section 1 of Appendix D, 'References to the Literature', where Sraffa (1960, p. 93) refers explicitly to Marx's above interpretation of the physiocrats.

Porta contends that the respective passage in Marx was for Sraffa some sort of Archimedean point from which he could see how to satisfy his need to reinterpret Ricardo in the sought-after manner (see also Porta, 2012, pp. 1361–1362). Sraffa's concept of the Standard system, we are told, was simply a continuation of this endeavour, being 'itself the direct product of the Marxian idea that in agriculture the creation of surplus value emerges as most evident and less objectionable' (Porta, 2012, p. 1363). To this he adds: 'Sraffa's standard commodity is a specific point coherent with his Marxian research programme. Sraffa advanced a possible solution to the Marxian problem of finding a composite commodity taking the place of the physiocratic produce' (ibid.).

This elicits the following remarks. First, the idea that the 'country', i.e., agriculture, is capable of self-reproduction, whereas in the 'town', i.e., in industry, 'there neither is nor can be any reproduction of substances', is, of course, already to be found in Smith (1976, WN III.i.1). The reason for this is 'the great and essential difference which nature has established between corn and almost every other sort of goods', the former being needed in the production of all commodities, while the latter are not (WN IV.v.a.23). Smith uses 'corn' here as a generic term including all means of subsistence of workers (see WN I.xi.e.29), just as Petty before him (1986, p. 89) (and Ricardo after him).[29] Sraffa therefore called Smith's absorption of physiocratic ideas into his own system aptly 'agrocentric'. Second, the irony is that in the *Tableau économique* it is not the case that agriculture can reproduce itself independently of industry, because it receives means of production (ploughs, etc.) from the latter. Therefore, Marx's characterisation involves an abstraction, which applies more to Smith than to the physiocrats.

Third, and most important, Sraffa was from the beginning of his constructive work concerned with elaborating a general theory of value and therefore not much interested in special cases, which, suggestive as they may be, had already been left behind in the writings of some of the Classical authors. He was particularly intrigued by Ricardo's conjecture that 'the great questions of Rent, Wages, and Profits … *are not essentially connected with the doctrine of value*' (Ricardo, *Works* vol. VIII, p. 194, emphasis added).[30] This point of view is reflected in all three editions of the *Principles* in terms of a numerical example, which satisfies the homogeneity condition between *aggregate* output and *aggregate* capital (see Ricardo, *Works* vol. I, pp. 50, 64–66). In the example there are three commodities, all of which enter the real wage rate and thus count as 'necessaries' or capital goods needed in the production of the three commodities themselves.

The three commodities are hats, coats and corn. Ricardo assumes that of 100 units produced of each commodity, both workers and landlords are paid 25 (or 22) units. Profits consist accordingly of 50 (or 56) units of each commodity. If capital consists only of the real wages bill, an assumption Ricardo employs in much of his reasoning on profits, the rate of profits can be ascertained independently of values and amounts to (50/25) = 2 [or (56/22) = (28/11)]. Here we have a case, to paraphrase Porta, of 'pure and unambiguous quantity measurement, which suits Ricardo's needs perfectly well'– more than a century before Sraffa allegedly tried to read into Ricardo Marx's corn model interpretation of the physiocrats!

What is more, the Standard commodity was certainly *not* Sraffa's 'possible solution to the Marxian problem of finding a composite commodity taking the place of the physiocratic produce', as Porta contends (Porta, 2012, p. 1363). Working out some of Ricardo's problems within his own analytical framework, such as the impact of a change in wages on the rate of profits and relative prices in what Sraffa called his 'third equations', he at one point entertained an idea echoing Ricardo's example above. In a document dated February 1931, he wrote: 'it may be said that the value of total capital in terms of total goods produced cannot vary {consequent upon a change in the interest rate}, since the goods are composed exactly in the same proportions as the capitals which have produced them'. He added that this proposition is of course 'false, but may contain an element of truth' (D3/12/7: 157(3)). Twelve years later, in November 1943, he stressed that this proposition was based on the assumption of a 'statistical compensation of large numbers' (D3/12/35: 28), and then the proposition recurred under the name 'My Hypothesis' or simply 'Hypothesis', before Sraffa succeeded in elaborating the Standard commodity in early 1944. The Standard system, Sraffa emphasised, provides 'tangible evidence of the rate of profits as a non-price phenomenon' (D3/12/43: 4), confirming the correctness of Ricardo's conjecture above.

To conclude, it should be stressed that Marx lacked any understanding of Ricardo's search for an 'invariable measure of value'.[31] Since Marx was convinced that he had succeeded in elaborating a correct theory of prices of production and of profits based on labour values, an idea he felt was present in Ricardo, the latter's concern struck him as a regression. Therefore to him the proper invariable measure, which, however, was of no interest whatsoever, was an 'average commodity' built of *all* the commodities produced in the economic system and taken with the *actual* quantities produced (see Kurz and Salvadori, 2012). Sraffa was clear that Marx's theory was not fully correct. As he wrote in reaction to a review of his 1960 book:

> if we want to follow in Marx's footsteps and pass from values to prices of production and from rate of surplus value to rate of profits, the Standard System is a necessary adjunct: for that passage implies going

> through certain averages and if these are calculated without weights (or with the weights of the real system), a result which is only approximately numerically correct is obtained. If an *exact* result is wanted the proportions of the St. Syst. of eq's q's {the multipliers applied to the actual system's industries} must be applied as weights. – This is not stated explicitly in the book, but is implied.
>
> (D3/12/111: 118)

The ground is now prepared to discuss the main propositions contained in the papers under consideration one by one. I begin with John Davis's piece on the kind of objectivism Sraffa advocated from mid-1931 onwards. Next I deal briefly with Roberto Scazzieri's claim that Sraffa pursued a Smithian research programme. Then I turn to Pier-Luigi Porta's rather different claim that Sraffa's Marxist agenda overwhelmed his research. It follows a discussion of Riccardo Bellofiore's Marxist fundamentalism. I conclude with some comments on Ajit Sinha's 'new' interpretation of Sraffa.

9.5 Modern materialism and 'supervenience physicalism'

On the basis of the material from Sraffa's papers presented and the interpretation provided in Kurz (2003) and Kurz and Salvadori (2004, 2005b), John Davis puts forward the idea that around mid-1931 Sraffa 'reoriented and also deepened his philosophical view' and anticipated a position that in the last third of the twentieth century became known as 'supervenience physicalism'. According to Donald Davidson (1970), a main advocate of this orientation in philosophy, supervenience is a relation of dependence between two things that excludes their identification. Its characteristic feature, in Davis's words, is that

> Mental events (or states) … are not identified with physical events (or states), and therefore cannot be reduced to them, but they nonetheless depend or supervene upon them … [T]his supervenience relation … provides a means of giving primacy to the physical without adopting the implausible reductionist idea that mental states just are physical states.
>
> (Davis, 2012, p. 1346)

The object-based conception of physicalism under consideration is not tied to a particular state of the natural sciences and especially physics, Davis argues, it is rather 'essentially an expression of methodological or scientific naturalism, the general view that science advances through empirical investigation of nature' (ibid.). Applied to economics, one can say that 'all economic facts are determined by and depend on physical facts, but that the economic is nonetheless not reducible to the physical' (ibid., n. 11).

Since my knowledge of this branch of philosophy is very limited, I cannot fully judge Davis's claim, but according to my reading of Sraffa's works, as it is also reflected in Section 9.4 above, his post-1931 papers may indeed be characterised in the way Davis does. In the following I draw the reader's attention to a document stemming from 1942, the time when Marx's writings became a focal point of Sraffa's work, which may have a bearing on the issue at hand: Sraffa's reflections upon Karl Marx's thesis number X on Feuerbach. In it Sraffa rejects the vulgar view that mental states can be reduced to, or are nothing but, physical states.

9.5.1 'Das Sein bestimmt das Bewußtsein'

When Sraffa resumed his constructive work in early 1942, we find among his notes a discussion of Marx's proposition in *Die deutsche Ideologie*: 'Das Sein bestimmt das Bewußtsein' or, in the 1938 English translation of the book (Marx, 1938a), 'Being determines consciousness'. In a note in Italian dated 20 February 1942, Sraffa wrote:

> When one says that being determines consciousness, one does not mean to assert a (causal) relation between two universals. This would make no sense, because a causal relation can rule only between particulars: to state a relation between universals means that this relation always holds good between pairs of particulars which compose the pair of universals – but not between the two members of this universal pair itself.
>
> Moreover, the relation of determination is a special form of the relation of causality: this must be a correspondence (for example, a similarity) between two members of the relation, such that one can assert a specific law, which allows one to recognize/identify the cause, given the effect (or viceversa); not an abstract causality which in each particular case can only be known a posteriori (for example the 'causes' of an unforeseen and perhaps even unforeseeable event [chance, accident].
>
> Thus, between a mode of production and the ideology, which corresponds to it, there is a relation of determination, a similarity. But when the ideology becomes a cause of change in the mode of production, there is no similarity whatsoever between the old ideology and the new mode of production – it is an abstract cause, but one cannot say that it determines it (? it is a 'causa essendi', but not a 'causa cognoscendi').

On 26 May 1942, he added the following exemplification:

> An example of this relation of determination is the relation between bodies and their shadows. The body determines the shadow in the same sense in which being determines consciousness: and there is no

> reciprocity. But then the shadow is also a material object and can itself be the cause of other things, for example a tree casts a shadow, and this causes a mushroom to grow. However there is a determination, a similarity, between the tree and its shadow, which does not obtain between that shadow and the mushroom: in this latter case there is, rather, a 'similarity' or relation between shadow and mushroom – but not between *this* shadow and the mushroom, but between shadows in general, any shadow. Furthermore, Marx says (in *German Ideology*, Eng. tr. p. 14) about ideologies (morals, religions etc.) and the corresponding forms of consciousness: 'They have no history, no development; but men, developing their material production and their material intercourse, alter, along with this their real existence, their thinking & the products of their thinking. Life is not determined by consciousness, but consciousness by life.'[32]
>
> The same, identically, is valid with regard to bodies and their shadows: the former have their own movement and their own history – the shadows only reproduce the movement and history of the former.
>
> (D3/12/42: 21–22) (My translation; it was kindly improved by Ian Steedman)[33]

Can Sraffa's interpretation of Marx be considered reflecting supervenience physicalism? I wonder what John Davis thinks about this.

9.5.2 The 'scramble for the surplus'

A few propositions contained in Davis's paper I find difficult to accept. Most importantly, his interpretation of some statements in Sraffa's note entitled 'Surplus Product', which is central to our discussion here, I consider unfounded. Davis cites the following passage from it: 'When we have defined our "economic field", there are still outside causes which operate in it; and its effects go beyond the boundary … The surplus may be the effect of the outside causes; and the effects of the distribution of the surplus may lie outside' (D3/12/7: 161 (3-5); see Davis, 2012, p. 1348). He maintains, correctly I think, that from this follows that 'the "economic field"' – that is, Sraffa's equations – cannot be regarded as a fully 'closed system', and that an analysis of those 'outside causes' (and effects) had to be elaborated in another part of the theory in order to complement the 'economic field' (ibid., p. 1349). Davis adds:

> Given his objectivist characterisation of the 'economic field' and his rejection of subjectivist thinking regarding commodity values, it seems that these 'outside causes' *need to be somehow explained in subjectivist terms.*
>
> (Ibid., emphasis added)

And later in his paper he contends that Sraffa's

> case is that of economies that produce a surplus where distribution, *which is not determined objectively* as are the values of commodities in terms of physical real cost, nonetheless comes to play a role in the determination of commodity values.
>
> (Davis, 2012, p. 1353, emphasis added)

The passages cited from Sraffa's note provide no basis to attribute to him the view that the determination of income distribution is to be explained 'in subjectivist terms'. Numerous statements in his published and unpublished work make it clear that he was not of this opinion. The problem Sraffa hit upon in his note was rather that a purely 'natural science point of view' had landed him in a dead end, as we saw in Section 9.4 above. This does not mean that his concern with an objectivist approach had to give way to a subjectivist one, as Davis seems to imply. Income distribution reflects the 'scramble for the surplus', Sraffa insisted. And like Adam Smith before him he referred to institutional and policy factors affecting distribution; viz. in his papers and in Sraffa (1960, p. 33), the emphasis on the impact of 'the level of the money rates of interest' on the general rate of profits. Sraffa, as I read him, was clear that a purely objectivist analysis was not possible, but he was keen to stay aloof from subjectivist considerations in his reasoning as much as possible. His 1960 book shows how far he could get in this regard. He was convinced that the history of economic analysis has provided compelling evidence that subjectivist concepts such as, for example, the concept of 'abstinence' in the theory of interest often served an ideological purpose and contaminated the analysis.

Lastly, while Sraffa was clear that it is not possible to exclude all references to 'inducements' from economic explanations, he felt that important inducements are *systemic*. When Adam Smith insisted that 'universal competition … *forces* every body to have recourse to [good management] for the sake of self-defence' (1976, WN I.xi.b.5, emphasis added) and Marx spoke of the 'coercive law of competition', they implied that the economic system imposes upon agents certain behaviours that have to be adopted in the interest of their survival as carriers of certain economic roles. Thus, competitive conditions enforce cost-minimising behaviour on the part of producers. When in part III of his book, 'Switch in Methods of Production', Sraffa deals with the choice of technique problem, he refers to the 'producer', who will decide the choice in terms of the 'cheapness' of the methods available to him.[34] The producer is forced to do so, we might add, because of competition and on the assumption that he wishes to survive in the competitive struggle as a producer.

9.6 'Horizontal' versus 'vertical prices'

I agree with Scazzieri that '[t]he work on the intellectual sources of *PCC* is work on the analytical structure of that book' (Scazzieri, 2012, p. 1317). I also agree with him that Sraffa paid attention 'to Smith's attempts to identify the material foundation of a "commercial society"' (ibid., p. 1320). But he appears to exaggerate when he calls Smith's theory 'the backbone of *PCC*' and that '*PCC* can be considered to be a product of the political economy programme associated with Smith' (ibid., p. 1316). He then advocates the distinction between a theory dedicated to an economic system 'independent of institutional premises' (Scazzieri, 2012, p. 1316) and a theory that takes into account such premises. He opines that such a distinction is implied in Sraffa's work and then argues that it can be brought to the fore by distinguishing between a 'horizontal' and a 'vertical' structure of value.

In Sraffa there is indeed such a distinction and it relates to the hypothetical realm of pure natural necessity, i.e., the no-surplus economy, in which institutions are taken to play no significant role, on the one hand, and the with-surplus economy, in which institutions help to decide in particular the distribution of the surplus, on the other. As equations (1) and (2) of Scazzieri's paper show, he starts instead from a with-surplus economy and focuses attention on the usual Sraffa price system in matrix notation, on the one hand, $\mathbf{p} = \mathbf{a}_{[n]}w + \mathbf{pA}(1 + \pi)$, and the vertically integrated representation of the price system, on the other, $\mathbf{p} = \mathbf{v} + \mathbf{pH}\pi$ (where he now implicitly assumes labour commanded prices; it would have been good, had a new symbol for the price vector been used). He adds: 'Horizontal and vertical prices, while mutually compatible, draw attention to different properties of the economic system' (Scazzieri, 2012, pp. 1318–1319).

I was struck by their characterisation as being 'mutually compatible' with one another because they are two different ways of saying the *same* thing (see Kurz and Salvadori, 1995, ch. 6). But Scazzieri appears to imply that this is not the case. He contends that they 'clearly belong to two different levels of an explanation' (Scazzieri, 2012, p. 1320). Starting from the vertical representation and reducing prices to sums of profit rate-weighted quantities of labour, which leads to his equation (3), he maintains that 'different institutional set-ups would encourage different weighting criteria'. For example, 'a decreasing weights economy … would take the attitude that "bygones are bygones", and pricing would primarily be based on the consideration of direct labour needed in the finishing stages of the production process' (ibid., p. 1319). I find this puzzling. First, the reduction carried out is not a reduction in *historical* time. It is rather an analytical device to clarify the role of compound interest in the determination of relative prices. All products are produced *simultaneously*, and the methods of production envisaged are exclusively the current ones and not past ones. Second, the profit-rate weights at stake cannot be arbitrarily given: a constraint binding changes in the distributive variables – the real wage rate, but now presumably n different rates of profit – still applies. There corresponds, then, a modified horizontal price equation, à la equation (1), with differential rates of profit r_j ($j = 1, 2, \ldots, n$), to a vertical reduction equation *to be derived from the former*: they express (and explain) the *same* thing in different forms. They would only differ, if with the same technique represented by $(\mathbf{A}, \mathbf{a}_{[n]})$ or $(\mathbf{H}, \mathbf{v})$, where $\mathbf{H} = \mathbf{A}(\mathbf{I} - \mathbf{A})^{-1}$ and $\mathbf{v} = \mathbf{a}_{[n]}(\mathbf{I} - \mathbf{A})^{-1}$, were associated two different distributions of income depending on which price structure is looked at. But this is not a case of changing the perspective on a *given* system, but a case of *changing the system* that is looked at.

9.7 Sraffa – 'a magnificent stage director'?

Porta has not followed the maxims exposited in Section 9.2 above as regards the problem of finding the sense Sraffa intended. Indeed, he mocks those who attempt to reconstruct meticulously the path along which Sraffa arrived at his results: 'With the exception of Pasinetti, all these contributions are based on a painstakingly oversubtle, decontextualised, philological analysis of Sraffa's own words—which is one of the curses [!] of the Sraffian literature' (Porta, 2012, p. 1360). He adds: 'This is a case where little is resolved by splitting hairs in textual analysis' (ibid.). More importantly, he insists: 'Only a fool [!] would take him [Sraffa] at face value' (ibid., p. 1373). I do, for the most part, take Sraffa at face value. What follows? Porta, in contrast, does not take Sraffa at his word, but pretends to know what is hidden 'behind the curtain' of 'Sraffa's notes and jottings' (ibid., p. 1379): his 'character and personality' (ibid., p. 1357). This is to be unmasked, thereby providing 'new perspectives on Sraffa's thought' (ibid., p. 1365, fn 18). To him, 'Sraffa was always a magnificent stage director, with a great sense of theatre' (ibid., p. 1370), mostly acting '*behind the scenes*', where his 'ambition was *much greater*' (ibid., p. 1371) and driven by '*his own desired ability*', inspired by Marshall, to transform the perspective on the Classical authors and especially on Ricardo in a way that passes 'unnoticed' by the readers (ibid., p. 1371, fn 28). Apparently, Porta judges Sraffa's papers by the *Gestalt* he sees of Sraffa. And about the latter there can be no doubt: Sraffa had a mission, which he carried out untiringly during his entire lifetime as an intellectual.

What is the knowledge Porta has at his disposal that allows him, or so he thinks, to arrive at a better reconstruction of Sraffa's motivation as an intellectual and of its scholarly manifestation over time? It is a quite innocent piece of information, which he has not dug out himself, but taken from a contribution by Nerio Naldi: Sraffa was exposed to 'socialist ideals' when at school in Milan and Turin. This is enough for Porta to put forward the remarkable contention that Sraffa was 'an accomplished intellectual of a socialist persuasion' (ibid., p. 1379, fn. 44) 'ever since his young years and that he had an immense knowledge of various strands of the relevant literature' (ibid., p. 1379). But not only this: Sraffa knew his role from early on, viz. his 'absolute dedication to a specific research programme developed over the entire course of his life' (ibid., p. 1360). Obviously it was 'a "Marxian research programme"' that 'formed the basis of Sraffa's search for a new foundation of economics' (ibid.). Porta adds: 'Sraffa's notion of surplus approach has a distinctive Marxian flavour and is read in this paper as an offspring of Marxianism [*sic*]' (ibid., p. 1365). This 'conjecture', we are told, seems at least to be 'perfectly natural, given that it can be gauged from a close reading of his literary remains' (ibid., p. 1360).

To Porta there can be no doubt that it was in Sraffa's 'formative years [in Milan and Turin], when his *conception of classical economics* took shape' (ibid., p. 1358, emphasis added). However, in order to carry out his research programme, which is said to have involved as a crucial element the reinterpretation of Ricardo along Marxian lines, he had to '*pull* back *to Ricardo* Marx's own attack on the vulgar [economists]' (ibid., p. 1363). In this way Sraffa sought to provide 'firm ground for a new classicism' erected upon Marxian foundations (ibid., p. 1363), a pedigree constructed *ab ovo*. Sraffa was 'an upholder of the Marxian idea of classicism in economics' (ibid., p. 1361) – from his early beginnings as an intellectual to the very end. The influence Sraffa was exposed to as a schoolboy decided his life as an economic theorist. There were no major shifts in Sraffa's thinking, no substantial changes in his perception of the Classical authors, no turning points, because 'his conception of Classical economics' stood firm. Possessed of such a conception right at the beginning of his academic life, in combination with his 'specific research programme', how could there be anything but continuity in his intellectual endeavour? To Porta this is, of course, a rhetorical question; its answer is all too obvious to him.[35]

Assessed against the background of Section 9.4 above, Porta's 'conjecture' is far from being 'perfectly natural'; in fact it is untenable. As we saw in that section, Sraffa conceived his analysis as firmly rooted in the approach advocated by Petty and the physiocrats. And while in his view the contributions of the British Classical economists and Marx clearly belonged to the tradition in economics established by these earlier authors, which differed in fundamental respects from the later marginalist one, he insisted that they had 'corrupted' the concepts of cost and value. Sraffa saw the 'corruption' under consideration first and foremost as the result of a mismatch between the sophisticated analytical concepts these authors had developed (production as a circular flow with a surplus product and inputs advanced at the beginning of the production period consisting of heterogeneous commodities) and the primitive tools at their disposal to deal with them in a coherent way (see Kurz, 2003). Lacking the knowledge of the mathematical tool of simultaneous equations and how to solve them, the Classical authors attempted to cope with the problem of the heterogeneity of commodities as best as they could by trying to reduce them to a common measure. Since labour was considered an indispensable input in the production of all commodities, labour was identified as the common measure (or, in the case of Marx, even as the 'substance') of value. Marx's analysis did not only belong to the 'Classical' tradition, it was arguably by far the most advanced one. Therefore it should come as no surprise that Sraffa felt that reconstructing the Classical theory rigorously from its original physical real-cost foundation in terms of simultaneous equations would eventually lead to a set of analytical propositions, which paralleled to some extent (to what extent precisely was unclear to him in the late 1920s) the propositions elaborated by Marx. *This* appears to be the deeper reason why Sraffa would conjecture, for example, in late 1927 'that the ultimate result will be a *re*statement of Marx' (D3/12/4: 15, emphasis added) – a remark that understandably enough caught the eye of several interpreters. However, its true meaning and significance appear to be insufficiently understood. The sought-after *re*statement necessitated Sraffa to start from what he considered to be the original and *noncorrupted* beginnings of the Classical approach – the 'loaf of bread' of Petty – and not from its later, but corrupted versions – the labour magnitudes invoked by Smith, Ricardo, and Marx. To argue that things are otherwise involves turning Sraffa's analytical project upside down.

These considerations, and the evidence provided in their support especially in Section 9.4 (and elsewhere in papers I wrote alone or together with Christian Gehrke and Neri Salvadori), show that Porta got it wrong. There was neither the need nor the possibility for Sraffa of telescoping, so to speak, Marx's analysis into the analyses of Petty, the physiocrats, or Ricardo. There was, rather, the need *and* possibility of telescoping the physical real-cost approach of Petty and the physiocrats into the analyses of Smith, Ricardo, and Marx. In other words, there was the need of starting afresh and of purging their analyses from the corruption under consideration. Contrary to Porta, we may say that 'Sraffa's notion of surplus approach has a distinctive physiocratic flavour' and that Sraffa was keen to reinterpret Smith, Ricardo, and Marx in terms of this approach rather than the earlier authors in terms of Marx's.

Porta's argumentative strategy necessitates one further remark. One might suppose that Porta cannot possibly consider the few lines on Sraffa's early education in Milan and Turin (ibid., p. 1379) to carry the weight of his story. But strangely enough, he does. In fact he even feels the need to warn those interpreters who take Sraffa at his 'own words' that they run a dangerous risk. For 'if one shuns the comprehensive approach [!] suggested in this paper [!] … then reading Sraffa's notes and jottings and going "behind the curtain" can turn into a *very dangerous exercise* indeed, as a result of severing the exercise itself from any contextual considerations' (ibid., pp. 1379–1380, emphasis added). This is a truly remarkable statement. Porta recommends elevating some little and conjectural evidence concerning Sraffa's formation as a youngster at school to the highest authority in interpreting the development of Sraffa's thinking. He contends that his interpretation simply supports that advanced by Luigi Pasinetti: 'The present essay, *in content and method*, endorses the line of inquiry pursued by Pasinetti' (Porta, 2012, p. 1359, see also Pasinetti, 2012a). In content and method, to be clear! Porta thus maintains that Pasinetti also advocates the view that Sraffa was a 'magnificent stage director', being at his best 'behind the scenes', etc. etc. Porta goes out of his way to praise and flatter Pasinetti in a manner that is rare in scholarly contributions. Can at least Porta be taken at 'face value'? Interestingly, later in his paper he contradicts the statement just cited and explicitly claims that Pasinetti endorses his, Porta's, line, when he speaks about 'the comprehensive approach suggested in this paper *and adopted by Pasinetti*' (Porta, 2012, p. 1379, emphasis added). The readers may consult Pasinetti (2012a and 2005) and decide for themselves whether Pasinetti has adopted Porta's approach or not. According to my reading he positively and definitely has not. In particular, Pasinetti writes about Sraffa's Introductions to Ricardo's *Works* that they 'have opened up the way to a clearer and deeper understanding than has ever been the case before of classical economic theory' (Pasinetti, 2012a, p. 1310). And as regards the concept of 'classical economic theory' employed, Pasinetti (ibid., pp. 1305–1306) says things that match perfectly with what Sraffa in a document from 'End of November 1927', titled 'Principio', had put in the following way:

> I shall begin by giving a short 'estratto' of what I believe is the essence of the classical theories of value, i.e. of those which include W. Petty, Cantillon, Physiocrats, A. Smith, Ricardo and Marx. This is not the theory of any one of them, but an extract of what I think is common to them. I state it of course, not in their own words, but in modern terminology, and it will be useful when we proceed to examine their theories to understand their portata {delivery capacity} from the point of view of our present inquiry. It will be a sort of 'frame', a machine, into which to fit their own statements in a homogeneous pattern, so as to be able to find what is common in them and what is the difference with the later theories.
>
> (D3/12/4: 12)

9.8 The labour theory of value and all that

Bellofiore wishes to provide 'a conjectural history of Sraffa's relationship to Marx' (Bellofiore, 2012, p. 1385). Much of what he says is based on material contained and interpreted in papers by Christian Gehrke, Neri Salvadori, and me, and in a couple of instances he even expresses agreement with what we have written. However, he contends that in recent papers of mine alone or together with the aforementioned 'there is a shift in emphasis relative to the earlier Kurz papers' (ibid., p. 1392) and that my earlier papers (Kurz, 1998, 2002) 'conflict' with 'the new evidence' provided by us (Bellofiore, 2012, p. 1396). He provides no evidence in support of his contentions. He also maintains that a paper he has written together with Potier on the Sraffa archive 'appears definitely [!] more faithful to Sraffa's relationship to Marx, in all its complexities … than Kurz's early papers published in 1998–2002' (ibid., p. 1393, fn 8). This may well be true, but it does not say what is wrong with what I have written. I do not imply, of course, that my own understanding of Sraffa's papers and their subtle architecture has not changed, and hopefully improved, since my first publications on them. But it seems that I was more risk-averse than others, who swiftly came forward with more or less bold speculations. My earlier papers, to which I went back on this occasion, did not strike me as containing misleading statements.

What I find striking, however, is the way Bellofiore introduces some of the propositions contained in recent papers by Gehrke, Salvadori, and me and the evidence we laid out in support of them. The reader is told that we 'have to recognise …' (ibid., p. 1396), 'cannot but confirm …' (ibid., p. 1392), now 'admit …' (ibid., p. 1393), etc., as if at long last and reluctantly we abandoned earlier views of ours, forced to this step by evidence we could no longer ignore or suppress or compelling criticisms put forward against us. Nothing of this sort! He even contends that in Gehrke and Kurz (2006) we argue that 'Sraffa's admiration towards Marx' is 'misdirected' (Bellofiore, 2012, p. 1392). He forgets to provide any evidence in support of his contentions.

As regards Bellofiore's attempt to relate Sraffa's work and the so-called 'new interpretation' of Marx, a few remarks must suffice (see also Kurz and Salvadori, 2012). The new interpretation is said to have 'rescued Marx's internal analytical consistency, though at the price of some circularity in the argument' (Bellofiore, 2012, p. 1387). The remarkable adjunct does not prevent Bellofiore from claiming that in this way 'unquestionable progress has been made' (ibid., p. 1388). I wonder wherein that progress consists. Bellofiore who rightly insists that one should care for the faithfulness of the interpretation of Sraffa given, with regard to the new interpretation of Marx appears to abandon this criterion. Yet this is not my main difficulty with his treatment of the new interpretation and his advocacy of the labour theory of value. He and some other Marxists convey the impression that the surplus-based approach stands or falls with the labour theory of value. However, this is not the case. Marx was convinced that he was already possessed of a *fully* correct theory, centred on the 'law of value'. He was wrong. Had he been right, all attempts by Marxists to salvage his labour value-based approach would have been unnecessary and futile.

Those who, like Bellofiore, insist on the importance and in fact indispensability of the labour theory of value typically contend that it is needed in order to demonstrate the 'exploitative' nature of profits (ibid., p. 1397). But 'exploitation' is just an evocative term. When Marx was writing, i.e., before marginal productivity theory began to filter into the academic and public discourse, one might still have been content with the observation that positive profits presuppose a positive surplus value (or surplus labour). But once marginalist theorists had argued that profits do not express exploitation but rather the productivity-enhancing effects of the employment of capital, an entirely new situation emerged. What if marginal productivity theory happened to be correct? Then it could no longer be maintained that the existence of 'surplus labour' by itself expresses that there is exploitation. Interestingly, Paul Samuelson's concept of the 'surrogate production function' shows that marginal productivity theory and the labour theory of value need not be incompatible with one another (Samuelson, 1962). Therefore some modern Marxists, preoccupied as they are with the labour theory of value, do not seem to see clearly what the real problem is: if one wishes to argue that workers do not get what their labour contributes to the product, then one has to demonstrate that marginal productivity theory in its various forms cannot be sustained.

In this context it is perhaps useful to draw attention to the fact that in a remarkable note written as early as 16 January 1946, Sraffa had anticipated *ante litteram* the flaw in Samuelson's attempt to defend the marginalist theory in term of the surrogate production function and also in that of Marxists, who cling to the labour theory of value:

> The Irony of it is, that if the '*Labour Theory of Value*' applied exactly throughout, *then, and only then, would the 'marginal product of capital'* theory work!
>
> It would require that all products had the same org.{anic} comp.{osition}; and that at each value of *r* {rate of interest or profits} *each* comm.{odity} had an 'alternative method', and that the relations within each pair should be the same (i.e. that marg.{inal} prod{uct}s. should be the same; & also the elasticities should be the same); so that, even when the System is switched, and another Org. Comp. came into being, it should be the same for all products.
>
> Obviously this would be equivalent to having only one means-product (wheat).
>
> Then, commodities would *always* be exchanged at their Values; and their relative Values would not change, even when productivity of labor [*sic*] increased.
>
> (D3/12/16: 34, passages that are underlined in Sraffa's manuscript are italicised here)

9.9 'Listening to silences'

Sinha puts forward a 'new interpretation' of Sraffa (1960) which, inter alia, 'for the first time [!]' purports to render clear 'the nature and significance of the first chapter of Sraffa's book' (Sinha, 2012, p. 1331), i.e., Sraffa's first equations. He says to have derived his inspiration from listening to 'Sraffa's silences'. What can one expect to hear, when listening to silences – one's own inner voice? As Bernheim put it (see Section 9.2), 'one then hears and reads from the sources what in the sense of an already assumed position one has hoped and expected to hear and read in them'. In fact, Sinha's paper too goes against all the maxims reported in Section 9.2 above. In particular, his entire argument is based on the premise that Sraffa was silent on certain issues, whereas in fact he was not. Sinha's paper abounds with what I consider to be elementary misunderstandings. Due to constraints of time and space, I restrict myself to a few remarks only.[36]

Wherein consists the 'new interpretation'? Sinha stresses 'that it is precisely the classical distinction between the "market" and "natural" prices and the theory of gravitation that are challenged by our interpretation of Sraffa's theory'. He adds:

> The *real question* is whether Sraffa's prices are supposed to be the *actual prices* at which industries exchange their products in the annual market *or whether they are the prices that would prevail when all the industries* [*sic*] *supplies would be equal to their respective effectual demands?*
>
> (Sinha, 2012, p. 1331, emphases added)

Sinha's answer is: 'The later [*sic*] position involves reasoning in terms of counterfactuals. Sraffa, however, consistently refrains from counterfactual reasoning' (ibid., p. 1335). Following this logic, Sraffa is said to have conceived his prices as those *actually* ruling in the market.

As we have seen in Section 9.4, the contention that Sraffa 'consistently refrained' from counterfactual reasoning is simply false. It is also simply false to contend that the prices Sraffa discusses 'are completely independent of demand considerations or the condition of equilibrium of demand and supply' (ibid., p. 1323, see also p. 1331 *et passim*). While Sraffa rejected the *marginalist* theory of demand and supply, it was of course clear to him that 'effectual demand' and thus gross output levels matter in ascertaining prices and the unknown distributive variable. He said so explicitly and repeatedly in his papers throughout the three periods of his constructive work, in his 1960 book and later. See, for example, the first system of equations discussed in Section 9.4 above, in which, interestingly enough and contradicting Sinha's contention, Sraffa stressed also that the values 'are *not* necessarily the ratios, in which exchange will *actually* take place in any community' (D3/12/5: 2, emphases added). In a note written in 1942 Sraffa expounded:

> This paper deals with an extremely elementary problem; so elementary indeed that its solution is generally taken for granted. The problem is that of *ascertaining the conditions of equilibrium of a system of prices & the rate of profits*, independently of the study of the forces which may

> bring about such a *state of equilibrium*. Since a solution of the second problem carries with it a solution of the first, that is the course usually adopted in modern theory. The first problem however is susceptible of a more general treatment, independent of the particular forces assumed for the second; & in view of the unsatisfactory character of the latter, there is advantage in maintaining its independence.
>
> (D3/12/15: 2, emphases added)

In a note composed on 20 February 1955, he wrote about his equations: 'It may be noted that they do not represent only the cost of production: they equally show *the use, or disposal, of each product*' (D3/12/2: 31, emphasis added). And it will surely not have escaped Sinha's attention that in Sraffa's book, in the context of joint production (with two products), Sraffa stressed that typically 'two methods of producing them in different proportions will be necessary for obtaining the *required proportion* of the two products through an appropriate combination of the two methods' (1960, p. 43, n. 2, emphasis added). And after the book was published, Sraffa in a letter dated 9 December 1964, wrote to the Indian economist Arun Bose, who had contended in a paper sent to Sraffa that in the latter's equations consumers' demand plays a 'purely passive role': 'Never have I said this … Nothing, in my view, could be more suicidal than to make such a statement. You are asking me to put my head on the block so that the first fool who comes along can cut it off neatly – Whatever you do, *please* do not represent me as saying such a thing' (C32: 3).[37]

The evidence put forward should suffice to see that it is pure fiction to contend, as Sinha does, that the system from which Sraffa begins his investigation into its mathematical properties is not characterised by a balancing of effectual demands and levels of outputs. The fact that Sraffa avoided the term 'demand' because he felt that it might all too easily and wrongly be read as involving an endorsement of the marginalist theory and the 'forces' it invokes, must not mislead one to think that 'requirements for use' play no role in Sraffa's theory.

9.10 Concluding remarks

This comment scrutinises critically some of the propositions contained in those papers in this Special Issue that deal with Piero Sraffa's intellectual development. In my capacity as the remaining general editor of the unpublished papers and correspondence of Piero Sraffa I was invited to read carefully all the papers in this Special Issue and comment on them. For obvious reasons the focus of attention is on Sraffa's gradual reformulation of the Classical approach to value and distribution, which culminated in his 1960 book, the kind of 'objectivism' Sraffa advocated, and the relationship of his analysis to the sciences, on the one hand, and to the analyses of William Petty, the physiocrats, Adam Smith, David Ricardo, and Karl Marx, on the other. Except for some minor points I am fully in agreement with what Luigi Pasinetti wrote in his paper and, with a single exception, I am also in agreement with John Davis. I have difficulties with some of Roberto Scazzieri's argument. My conclusions are very different, on some points radically different, from those put forward by Bellofiore and, in particular, by Porta and Sinha. In some cases I felt that Sraffa was treated ill. It is now up to the readers to make up their minds.

Notes

1 References to Sraffa's papers follow the catalogue prepared by Jonathan Smith. Unless otherwise stated, all emphases are in the original. Additions by me are in curly brackets, {}.

2 A first version of Garegnani's paper was given at the 2009 ASSA conference in San Francisco, co-organised by AEA and URPE; I was then a commentator of his paper and that of Christopher Bliss.

3 The Italian original reads: '*Quistione di metodo.* Se si vuole studiare la nascita di una concezione del mondo che dal suo fondatore non è stata mai esposta sistematicamente (e la cui coerenza essenziale è da ricercare non in ogni singolo scritto o serie di scritti ma nell'intiero sviluppo del lavoro intellettuale vario in cui gli elementi della concezione sono impliciti) *occorre fare preliminarmente un lavoro filologico minuzioso e condotto col massimo scrupolo de esattezza, di onestà scientifica, di lealtà intellettuale, di assenza di ogni preconcetto ed apriorismo o partito preso.* Occorre, prima di tutto, ricostruire il processo di sviluppo intellettuale del pensatore dato, per identificare gli elementi divenuti stabili e "permanenti", cioè che sono stati assunti come pensiero proprio, diverso e superiore al "materiale" precedentemente studiato e che ha servito di stimolo; solo questi elementi sono momenti essenziali del processo del sviluppo' (Gramsci, 1948, p. 76, second emphasis added).

4 It seems unlikely that Sraffa could study Gramsci's notebooks before the end of World War II, with the exception of a few hours in 1937. But between 1935 and 1937, when Gramsci was subjected to police surveillance in a private clinic, Sraffa could meet him several times and on these occasions they could talk about the content of the notebooks and Sraffa's work on Ricardo and the methodological questions involved. I am grateful to Nerio Naldi for instructing me on this.

5 Not all interpreters share this assessment. Porta, for example, denies that Sraffa was scientifically honest and contends that his interpretation of Ricardo was preconceived and served an ideological purpose.

6 William Cunningham (1892) in a paper titled 'A Plea for Pure Theory' had confronted the different views of Petty and Marshall. Sraffa probably sometime in the period from May to July 1928 excerpted and commented on the following lines from it: '"Prof. Marshall describes economics as the science of *measurable motives* (Present Position, p. 31). This … seems to me to be the very gist of the difference in treatment" C. is opposed to this and agrees with W. Petty. He wants to deal with "external phenomena" "laying a solid foundation of fact." "But when we start from motives, we loose all this advantage. What actually weighs with a man and determines him in any course of conduct, is not a thing we can observe … Motives are not obvious and we are likely to be mistaken about them"' (D3/12/9: 18).

7 Pasinetti (2012a, p. 1307) gives 1928 as the year when Sraffa began to formulate his theory in terms of equations and adds: 'But in the late 1920s he had barely been able to satisfactorily go beyond the "equations without a surplus". In 1941–1944 he really makes a breakthrough'. See, however, the following account.

8 It is only fair to point out that Gilibert aptly called his interpretation a 'speculation'.

9 Gilibert also refers to some other documents in Sraffa's papers, which he takes to corroborate his view, including a note from July 1928, which Bellofiore cites (Bellofiore, 2012, p. 1390). The reader will notice that the note was composed *after* Sraffa had elaborated his first layers of systems of equations without and with a surplus.

10 Sraffa used the term 'things' as a *terminus technicus* in his early works, meaning items 'bearing a label "private", according to law' (D3/12/6: 5). In the Italian economics literature he consulted, especially Pareto (1906) (and Pantaleoni), Sraffa annotated the term 'cose'; see, e.g., Sraffa's library, item 699.

11 The above system served as a kind of workhorse in much of Sraffa's early analysis. For example, the same set of first equations is also to be found at the beginning of document D3/12/11: 77–78, titled 'With surplus equations'. In the document Sraffa refers to the surplus of iron as 'the *physical* difference between the iron consumed by all industries and the iron produced by the iron industry' (ibid., p. 77, emphasis added). See also D3/12/9: 45 in which the with-surplus equations are discussed and Sraffa distinguishes between 'productive' and 'improductive [*sic*]' industries (the latter being identified with the surplus-using, luxuries producing industries). On the role of 'unproductive' industries in Sraffa's early work, see Subsection 9.4.6.

12 The translations of the remark next to the tabulation and the following text read: 'This is a *determinant.* Moreover the vertical sums are equal to the horizontal sums'. And: 'It is to be seen whether one can apply to this determinant the method of Volterra (Chini, p. 35) in order to find the number of "independent components" of the system. This might perhaps help: a) when not all goods entered as factors into each one. b) when there is a surplus, that is considering the various surpluses as different commodities (assuming therefore that as soon as the surplus emerges, one continues to produce the same quantity of "corn" as before, and the residual resources are all going to be dedicated to produce jewellery and other "unproductive" things)'.

13 As regards Sraffa's reference to a 'determinant' in D3/12/11: 87, he perhaps simply wanted to express that the system of equations is square and therefore the corresponding matrix has a determinant, as discussed by Chini (1923).

14 The English translation reads: 'When one has a certain number of substances of determinate chemical composition, each one of them may be taken in an arbitrary quantity, then it is clear that the various simple elements that enter and are a part of such a system cannot themselves be all prefixed in arbitrary quantities, but this will generally be possible only for a certain number of them. The quantities (masses) of the remaining elements will instead be completely determined by those fixed already of the first ones; these will be called the *independent components* of the system'. And: 'In order to obtain the number of these components (of which one can make use, for example, when one wants to apply to a heterogeneous complex the so-called *phase rule* [of Gibbs]), Prof. Volterra, in one of his publications … has indicated the following method'.

15 Interestingly, there are two markers in Chini's book relating to pp. 80–81 and 132–133. While these markers may have been left purely accidentally

in the places indicated, it deserves to be mentioned that on the pages under consideration Chini discusses how a *given* physical system – a piece of metal or a gas – responds to a rise or fall in temperature: the metal will expand or shrink, the pressure and volume of the gas will increase or decrease. However, there are limits to these induced changes. Analogously, the properties of a with-surplus economy with a *given* system of production are not fully determinate independently of the state of the distribution of the surplus (or, if we may use the metaphor, the 'heat' created in the conflict over the distribution of income). In some of his notes Sraffa had recourse to this analogy.

16 At the time the more popular works of physicists (and other natural scientists) were widely read by social scientists, and Sraffa was no exception to this. He, in all probability, came across, for example, the works of Hertz and Helmholtz when reading Labriola (1922, p. 326). Sraffa's annotations in his copy of the book (Sraffa 3577) are most interesting, not least because of his remarks in his own index at the end of the book. For example, with reference to E. Picard's *La science moderne et son état actuel* (Paris, 1905), he stressed: 'gli econ. mat. {the reference is to the mathematical economists like Walras and Pareto} hanno negligés des masses cachées 326'. Hertz and other physicists and chemists are also mentioned in Poincaré (1902; see Sraffa 3137).

17 On atomic theory in contemporary biology, chemistry, and physics, see also Sraffa's annotation in his copy of Whitehead (1926, p. 141). On the materialist conception of history, see Sraffa's annotations in his copy of Gramsci (1948, p. 161).

18 In the French edition of *Theorien über den Mehrwert*, which Sraffa read in the summer of 1927, he noted carefully all passages in which Marx distanced himself explicitly from an approach that proceeds exclusively in terms of commodities or 'use values'; and on the flyleaf at the end of Volume VI, we find in Sraffa's own index the entry 'Marx against physical cost 122' (Marx, 1924–1925, vol. VI). It was apparently later that he came across Engels's remark in his preface to Volume II of *Capital*: 'Marx stands in the same relation to his predecessors in the theory of surplus-value as Lavoisier stood to Priestley and Scheele' in chemistry (Marx, 1956, p. 16). See also the inside back cover of Marx (1961; Sraffa 3248), where Sraffa refers to Engels's comparison and adds: 'cioè *fecondità* di un'ipotesi'.

19 Sraffa soon saw, of course, that this involves an abstraction, because not all inputs enter the product, but some exit the process as waste.

20 When Sraffa in 1942 resumed work on his systems of equations he also specified the notation adopted; in a note composed in August of that year he stressed that in the equations '+' means 'with' and '=' means 'produce'; see D3/12/20: 4. And on 20 October 1942 he introduced the symbol '⟶' to describe production; see D3/12/23: 1. The problem of the (ir)reversibility of the process of production concerned Sraffa quite a bit in his papers. He argued that while single processes are irreversible, systems of production exhibit reversibility: by means of steel, etc. a lorry can be produced, and by means of a lorry, etc. steel.

21 English translation: 'is based on the essentially physiocratic point of view that value is a quantity that is intrinsic to the objects, almost a physical or chemical quality'.

22 In Sraffa (1960, p. 3) we will eventually read that 'such values spring directly from the methods of production'.

23 In a document contained in 'Notes' dated 'Michaelmas Term, 1928', Sraffa related his above approach of making the surplus disappear to the '"Method of exhaustion" v. E.B., 14, 535d' (D3/12/10: 41). The reference is apparently

to the entry 'Infinitesimal Calculus' by A. E. H. Love in *The Encyclopædia Britannica*, 11th edn, vol. XIV, p. 535, right-hand column (d = destra). The passage Sraffa appears to have in mind concerns 'Greek methods' and reads: 'The Greek geometers made little progress with the problem of tangents, but they devised methods for investigating the problem of quadratures. One of these methods was afterwards called the "method of exhaustions", and the principle on which it is based was laid down in the lemma prefixed to the 12th book of Euclid's *Elements* as follows: "If from the greater of two magnitudes there be taken more than its half, and from the remainder more than its half, and so on, there will at length remain a magnitude less than the smaller of the proposed magnitudes." The method adopted by Archimedes was more general'. See also Sraffa's reference to Archimedes in an entry in his *Cambridge Pocket Diary* on 9 December 1927 (E 1).

24 It deserves mention that this idea was still present when in summer 1942 Sraffa jotted down a list of topics (for the planned contents of the book he was to write) in D3/12/15: 1. It contains, among other things: '2) With profits – everything a necessity'.

25 See, in this context, also a note left in Sraffa's copy of Volume I of *Capital* (the copy he read in September 1940 while he was in the Metropole Internment Camp on the Isle of Man) containing a quotation from a paper by John Maurice Clark published in 1924. In the paper Clark maintained that in the last instance profits are due to private property of the means of production: the 'power to produce cannot exist apart from the power to withhold'; see Marx (1938b; Sraffa 3731). As Sraffa noted elsewhere, also Pareto entertained such a view.

26 However, he soon found out that this was not the case (see below). He overcame the impasse in which he found himself by introducing a new variable, the 'rate of surplus' or 'rate of interest' (or rather the interest factor), which was then determined simultaneously with the values of commodities; see, e.g., D3/12/6: 17.

27 Porta's contention that Neri Salvadori and I regard 'the young Sraffa as essentially a philosopher of science who enjoyed assuming the guise of an economist [!]' (Porta, 2012, p. 1359) is pure imagination on his part.

28 A major reason for the retardation of the Ricardo edition and *a fortiori* of Sraffa's constructive work was his difficulties with Jacob Hollander, who tried to sabotage the editorial project (see Gehrke and Kurz, 2002). For the great number of serious analytical difficulties Sraffa encountered on his long and winding way towards his 1960 book, see Gehrke and Kurz (2006) and Kurz and Salvadori (2005b).

29 On the origin of the 'corn model' in Smith, see the paper by Vianello (2012); see also Kurz and Sturn (2012, part 3). During his studies at the LSE especially with Edwin Cannan in 1921–1922, Sraffa read carefully Cannan's works, in particular Cannan (1893), and also *The Wealth of Nations*, which is reflected in numerous references to it in Sraffa's papers.

30 For a discussion of Ricardo's theory of profits and Sraffa's reformulation of it, see Kurz (2011).

31 Bellofiore (2012, p. 1391, fn 4) is right in this regard.

32 Sraffa put a straight line in the margin of the quotation.

33 The Italian versions of the two notes read: 'Quando si dice che l'essere determina la coscienza, non si intende stabilire un rapporto (causale) fra i due universali. Ciò non avrebbe senso, perché il rapporto causale può reggere solo fra particolari: l'enunciare un rapporto fra universali significa che questo rapporto si verifica sempre entro le coppie di particolari che compongono la

coppia di universali – ma non fra i due membri di questa coppia universale stessa. Inoltre il rapporto di determinazione è una forma speciale del rapporto di causalità: ci deve essere una corrispondenza (p. es. una somiglianza) fra i due membri del rapporto, in modo che si possa stabilire una legge specifica, che permetta di riconoscere/identificare la causa dato l'effetto (o viceversa); non una causalità astratta che in ogni caso particolare può essere conosciuta solo a posteriori (p. es. le "cause" di un avvenimento imprevisto, e magari imprevedibile [caso, accidente]). Così, fra un modo di produzione e la ideologia che gli corrisponde, c'è un rapporto di determinazione, c'è una somiglianza. Ma quando la ideologia diventa causa di cambiamenti nel modo di produzione, non vi è alcuna somiglianza fra la vecchia ideologia e il nuovo modo di produzione – essa è una causa astratta, ma non si può dire che lo determina (? è "causa essendi" ma non "causa cognoscendi")'. And: 'Un esempio di questo rapporto di determinazione è il rapporto fra i corpi e le loro ombre. Il corpo determina l'ombra nello stesso senso che l'essere determina la conoscenza {*sic*}: e non vi è reciprocità. Ma poi l'ombra è anch'essa un oggetto materiale e può a sua volta essere causa di altre cose, p. es. un albero fa un'ombra, e questa fa nascere un fungo. Però fra l'albero e la sua ombra c'è una somiglianza, una determinazione, che non sussiste fra quell'ombra e il fungo: in quest'ultimo caso vi è bensì una "somiglianza" o relazione fra ombra e fungo – ma è non fra *quell*'ombra e il fungo, ma l'ombra in generale, qualunque ombra. Inoltre, M. dice (in German Ideology, engl. tr. p. 14) che le ideologie (morale, religione, ecc.) e le correspondenti forme della coscienza: "They have no history, no development; but men, developing their material production and their material intercourse, alter, along with this their real existence, their thinking & the products of their thinking. Life is not determined by consciousness, but consciousness by life." Lo stesso, identicamente, vale per i corpi e le ombre: i primi hanno un proprio movimento e una propria storia – le ombre non fanno che riprodurre il movimento e la storia dei primi'.

34 See, however, Pasinetti, who maintains that Sraffa 'does not mention any kind of "economic agent"' (Pasinetti, 2012a, p. 1312).

35 Thus Porta calls Garegnani's 2005 paper a 'close-knit investigation' and 'an extremely valuable analysis' (Porta, 2012, p. 1362). This does not prevent him from rejecting it as 'highly problematic' and 'insufficient as a realistic description of Piero Sraffa's early intellectual development' (ibid., p. 1362). Obviously, to Porta no reason in support of this verdict is needed.

36 Without mentioning Kurz and Salvadori (1993), Sinha (see Sinha, 2012, Section 5) apparently deals with our work on Sraffa's Standard commodity, which he fundamentally misunderstands. The reader is asked to consult our piece and compare it with what Sinha has to say on this concept.

37 See Salvadori (2000) on the treatment of the problem of 'demand' in Sraffa.

Bibliography

Allen, H. S. 1928. The quantum theory, *Nature*, Supplement, no. 3084, December 8

Anonymous. 1821. *An Inquiry into those Principles Respecting the Nature of Demand and the Necessity of Consumption, Lately Advocated by Mr Malthus, from which it is Concluded, that Taxation and the Maintenance of Unproductive Consumers can be Conducive to the Progress of Wealth*, London, R. Hunter (Sraffa 1488)

Barba, A. and G. De Vivo. 2012. An 'unproductive labour' view of finance, *Cambridge Journal of Economics*, vol. 36, no. 6, 1479–1496

Bellofiore, R. 2012. The 'tiresome objector' and Old Moor: a renewal of the debate on Marx after Sraffa based on the unpublished material at the Wren Library, *Cambridge Journal of Economics*, vol. 36, no. 6, 1385–1399

Bernheim, E. 1894. *Lehrbuch der historischen Methode und der Geschichtsphilosophie*, Berlin, Duncker & Humblot

Cannan, E. 1893. *A History of the Theories of Production and Distribution in English Political Economy from 1776–1848*, London, P.S. King (Sraffa 1145, 7929)

Chini, M. 1923. *Corso speciale di matematiche con numerosi applicazioni ad uso principalmente dei chimici e dei naturalisti*, 6th edn, Livorno, Raffaello Giusti (Sraffa 3204)

Cunningham, W. 1892. A plea for pure theory, *Economic Review*, vol. 2, 25–41

Davidson, D. (ed.) 1970. *Essays on Actions and Events*, Oxford, Oxford University Press

Davis, J. B. 2012. The change in Sraffa's philosophical thinking, *Cambridge Journal of Economics*, vol. 36, no. 6, 1341–1356

De Vivo, G. 2003. Sraffa's path to *Production of Commodities by Means of Commodities*: an interpretation, *Contributions to Political Economy*, vol. 22, 41–62

Garegnani, P. 2005. On a turning point in Sraffa's theoretical and interpretative position in the late 1920s, *European Journal of the History of Economic Thought*, vol. 12, no. 3, 453–492; reprinted pp. 79–118 in Kurz, H. D., Pasinetti, L. L. and Salvadori, N. (eds), *Piero Sraffa:The Man and the Scholar—Exploring his Unpublished Papers*, London, Routledge

Garegnani, P. 2012. On the present state of the capital controversies, *Cambridge Journal of Economics*, vol. 36, no. 6, 1417–1432

Gehrke, C. and Kurz, H. D. 2002. Keynes and Sraffa's 'difficulties with J.H. Hollander': a note on the history of the RES edition of *The Works and Correspondence of David Ricardo*, *European Journal of the History of Economic Thought*, vol. 9, no. 4, 644–671; reprinted pp. 93–119 in Kurz, H. D. and Salvadori, N. 2007. *Interpreting Classical Economics: Studies in Long-period Analysis*, London, Routledge.

Gehrke, C. and Kurz, H. D. 2006. Sraffa on von Bortkiewicz: reconstructing the classical theory of value and distribution, *History of Political Economy*, vol. 38, no. 1, 91–149

Gilibert, G. 2003. The equations unveiled: Sraffa's price equations in the making, *Contributions to Political Economy*, vol. 22, 27–40

Gramsci, A. 1948. *Il materialismo storico e la filosofia di Benedetto Croce, papers 1929–1934*, Milan, Einaudi (Sraffa 3979)

Kurz, H. D. 1998. Against the current: Sraffa's unpublished manuscripts and the history of economic thought, *European Journal of the History of Economic Thought*, vol. 5, no. 3, 437–451; reprinted pp. 652–656 in Kurz, H. and Salvadori, N. (eds) 2003. *The Legacy of Piero Sraffa*, vol. II, Cheltenham, Edward Elgar Publishing

Kurz, H. D. 2002. Sraffa's contributions to economics: some notes on his unpublished papers, pp. 177–196 in Nisticó, S. and Tosato, D. (eds), *Competing Economic Theories: Essays in Memory of Giovanni Caravale*, London, Routledge

Kurz, H. D. 2003. The surplus interpretation of the classical economists, pp. 167–183 in Samuels, W., Biddle, J. and Davis, J. (eds), *The Blackwell Companion to the History of Economic Thought*, Oxford, Blackwell

Kurz, H. D. 2006. The agents of production are the commodities themselves: on the classical theory of production, distribution and value, *Structural Change and*

Economic Dynamics, vol. 17, 1–26; reprinted pp. 131–158 in Kurz, H. D. and Salvadori, N. 2007. *Interpreting Classical Economics: Studies in Long-period Analysis*, London, Routledge

Kurz, H. D. 2011. On David Ricardo's theory of profits: the laws of distribution are 'not essentially connected with the doctrine of value', *History of Economic Thought*, vol. 53, no. 1, 1–20

Kurz, H. D. and Salvadori, N. 1993. The 'standard commodity' and Ricardo's search for an 'invariable measure of value', pp. 95–123 in Baranzini, M. and Harcourt, G. C. (eds), *The Dynamics of the Wealth of Nations: Growth, Distribution and Structural Change—Essays in Honour of Luigi Pasinetti*, London, Macmillan; reprinted pp. 123–147 in Kurz, H. D. and Salvadori, N. 1998. *Understanding 'Classical' Economics: Studies in Long-period Theory*, London, Routledge

Kurz, H. D. and Salvadori, N. 1995. *Theory of Production: A Long-period Analysis*, Cambridge, Cambridge University Press

Kurz, H. D. and Salvadori, N. 2001. Sraffa and the mathematicians: Frank Ramsey and Alister Watson, pp. 187–216 in Cozzi, T. and Marchionatti, R. (eds), *Piero Sraffa's Political Economy: A Centenary Estimate*, London, Routledge; reprinted pp. 187–216 in Kurz, H. and Salvadori, N. 2003. *Classical Economics and Modern Theory: Studies in Long-period Analysis*, London, Routledge

Kurz, H. D. and Salvadori, N. 2004. Man from the moon: on Sraffa's objectivism, *Économies et Sociétés*, vol. 35, 1545–1557; reprinted pp. 120–130 in Kurz, H. D. and Salvadori, N. 2007. *Interpreting Classical Economics: Studies in Long-period Analysis*, London, Routledge

Kurz, H. D. and Salvadori, N. 2005a. Removing an 'insuperable obstacle' in the way of an objectivist analysis: Sraffa's attempts at fixed capital, *European Journal of the History of Economic Thought*, vol. 12, no. 3, 493–523; reprinted pp. 119–149 in Kurz, H. D., Pasinetti, L. L. and Salvadori, N. (eds) 2008. *Piero Sraffa: The Man and the Scholar—Exploring his Unpublished Papers*, London, Routledge

Kurz, H. D. and Salvadori, N. 2005b. Representing the production and circulation of commodities in material terms: on Sraffa's objectivism, *Review of Political Economy*, vol. 17, no. 3, 69–97; reprinted pp. 249–277 in Kurz, H. D., Pasinetti, L. L. and Salvadori, N. (eds) 2008. *Piero Sraffa: The Man and the Scholar—Exploring his Unpublished Papers*, London, Routledge

Kurz, H. D. and Salvadori, N. 2009. Sraffa and the labour theory of value: a few observations, pp. 187–213 in Vint, J., Metcalfe, J. S., Kurz, H. D., Salvadori, N. and Samuelson, P. A. (eds), *Economic Theory and Economic Thought: Festschrift in Honour of Ian Steedman*, London, Routledge

Kurz, H. D. and Salvadori, N. 2012. On the 'vexata questio of value': Ricardo, Marx and Sraffa, Chapter 12 in Taylor, L., Rezai, A. and Michl, T. (eds), *Analytical Insights and Social Fairness: Economic Essays in the Spirit of Duncan K. Foley*, London, Routledge, to be published

Kurz, H. D. and Sturn, R. 2012. *Die größten Ökonomen: Adam Smith (1723–1790)*, Stuttgart, Lucius und Lucius

Labriola, A. 1922. *Il valore della scienza economica: introduzioni a una critica dell'economia politica*, Naples, Alberto Morano (Sraffa 3577)

Lewis, C. S. 1960. *Studies in Words*, Cambridge, Cambridge University Press

Marx, K. 1924–1925. *Oeuvres complètes de Karl Marx: Histoire des doctrines économiques*, 8 vols, translated by J. Molitor, Paris, Alfred Costes (Sraffa 3699)

Marx, K. 1938a. *The German Ideology*, London, Lawrence & Wishart
Marx, K. 1938b. *Capital, vol. I*, London, George Allen & Unwin (Sraffa 3731)
Marx, K. 1956. *Capital, vol. II*, Moscow, Progress Publishers
Marx, K. 1961. *Teorie del plus valore,* vol. I, in *I classici del marxismo*, Rome, Editori Reuniti
Mill, J. 1826. *Elements of Political Economy*, 3rd edn, London, Henry G. Bohn
Naldi, N. 2012. Two notes on Piero Sraffa and Antonio Gramsci, *Cambridge Journal of Economics*, vol. 36, no. 6, 1401–1415
Pareto, V. 1906. *Manuale di economia politica con una introduzione alla scienza sociale,* Milan, Società editrice libreraria (Sraffa 699)
Panico, C., Pinto, A. and Puchet Anyul, M. 2012. Income distribution and the size of the financial sector: a Sraffian analysis, *Cambridge Journal of Economics*, vol. 36, no. 6, 1455–1477
Pasinetti, L. L. 2001. Continuity and change in Sraffa's thought: an archival excursus, pp. 139–156 in Cozzi, T. and Marchionatti, R. (eds), *Piero Sraffa's Political Economy: A Centenary Estimate*, London, Routledge
Pasinetti, L. L. 2005. The Sraffa-enigma: introduction, *European Journal of the History of Economic Thought*, vol. 12, no. 3, 373–378; reprinted in Kurz, H. D., Pasinetti, L. L. and Salvadori, N. (eds) 2008. *Piero Sraffa: The Man and the Scholar—Exploring his Unpublished Papers*, London, Routledge
Pasinetti, L. L. 2012a. Piero Sraffa and the future of economics, *Cambridge Journal of Economics*, vol. 36, no. 6, 1303–1314
Pasinetti, L. L. 2012b. A few counterfactual hypotheses on the current economic crisis, *Cambridge Journal of Economics*, vol. 36, no. 6, 1433–1453
Petty, W. 1986. *The Economic Writings of Sir William Petty, 2 vols*, edited by C. H. Hull; originally published in 1899, Cambridge, UK, Cambridge University Press; reprinted in one volume, NewYork, Kelley
Picard, E. 1905. *La science moderne et son état actuel*, Paris, Ernest Flammarion Poincaré, J. H. 1902. *La science et l'hypothèse*, Paris, Ernest Flammarion (Sraffa 3137)
Porta, P. L. 2012. Piero Sraffa's early views on classical political economy, *Cambridge Journal of Economics*, vol. 36, no. 6, 1357–1383
Ricardo, D. 1951–1973. Sraffa, P. (ed.) with the collaboration of M. H. Dobb, *The Works and Correspondence of David Ricardo,* 11 vols, Cambridge, UK, Cambridge University Press
Salvadori, N. 2000. Sraffa on demand: a textual analysis, pp. 181–197 in Kurz, H. D. (ed.), *Critical Essays on Piero Sraffa's Legacy in Economics*, Cambridge, Cambridge University Press
Samuelson, P. A. 1962. Parable and realism in capital theory: the surrogate production function, *Review of Economic Studies*, vol. 29, 193–206
Scazzieri, R. 2012. The political economy of *Production of Commodities by Means of Commodities*: a note on Pasinetti and Sraffa, *Cambridge Journal of Economics*, vol. 36, no. 6, 1315–1322
Sen, A. 2003. Sraffa, Wittgenstein, and Gramsci, *Journal of Economic Literature*, vol. XLI, no. 4, 1240–1255
Sinha, A. 2012. Listen to Sraffa's silences: a new interpretation of Sraffa's *Production of Commodities*, *Cambridge Journal of Economics*, vol. 36, no. 6, 1323–1339
Smith, A. 1976. *An Inquiry into the Nature and Causes of the Wealth of Nations*, two vols, in Campbell, R. H. and Skinner, A. S. (eds), *The Glasgow Edition of the Works and Correspondence of Adam Smith*, Oxford, Oxford University Press

Smith, J. 2012. Circuitous processes, jigsaw puzzles and indisputable results: making best use of the manuscripts of Sraffa's *Production of Commodities by Means of Commodities*. *Cambridge Journal of Economics*, vol. 36, no. 6, 1291–1301

Sraffa, P. 1960. *Production of Commodities by Means of Commodities*, Cambridge, Cambridge University Press

Vianello, F. 2012. The Smithian origin of Ricardo's corn ratio theory of profits: a suggested interpretation, pp. 239–268 in Ciccone, R., Gehrke, C. and Mongiovi, G. (eds), *Sraffa and Modern Economics*, vol. 1, Routledge, London

Whitehead, A. N. 1926. *Science and the Modern World, Lowell Lectures 1925*, Cambridge, Cambridge University Press

Wilkinson. F. 2012.Wages, economic development and the customary standard of life, *Cambridge Journal of Economics*, vol. 36, no. 6, 1497–1534

10 Besicovitch, Sraffa, and the existence of the standard commodity

Neri Salvadori

Original paper: Neri Salvadori (2011) Besicovitch, Sraffa, and the existence of the Standard commodity in Neri Salvadori and Christian Gehrke (eds), *Keynes, Sraffa and the Criticism of Neoclassical Theory: Essays in honour of Heinz Kurz*, 113–131. London: Routledge.

10.1 Introduction

At the end of summer 1996, Heinz Kurz, just back from a period of time spent at the Wren Library to work on the Sraffa papers, informed me that there was a lot of material on the relationship between Sraffa and the 'mathematical friends' he thanks in the Preface of *Production of Commodities by means of Commodities*. He also proposed to write a joint paper on 'Sraffa and the mathematicians', on the basis of this material. Shortly after I went to Cambridge and I agreed with my frequent coauthor to write such a paper. The deadline came from a Conference to be held at the Fondazione Einaudi at Turin in 15–18 October 1998. We committed ourselves to that title and started working.

I remember that first of all we prepared an Excel file to put the material in some order: one field was, obviously, the date (each single day from the 1920s to the 1950s); another field the content of Sraffa's diaries during that period; other fields were devoted to lists of documents in Sraffa papers which were either written or commented or amended during the period, either by Sraffa directly or by other scholars. This allowed the material to be read in the appropriate order.

What little material there was concerning Frank Ramsey proved very interesting: we were able to infer the essence of the meeting that the two friends had on 26 June 1928. It was a very fruitful meeting for Sraffa. Similarly we were able to reconstruct the talks that Sraffa and Alister Watson had in several occasions both during the writing of the book and while correcting the proofs. But we soon realised that it would be impossible to complete our original project since the material concerning Abram S. Besicovitch was enormous. So we added a subtitle to our original title and left the material concerning Besicovitch to another occasion (Kurz and Salvadori, 2001).

DOI: 10.4324/9781003138709-13

The occasion came when the Accademia dei Lincei organised a conference on Sraffa, held on 11–12 February 2003. Of the four sessions, one was devoted to '*Production of Commodities by means of Commodities* and Mathematics' and was chaired by the well-known mathematician Edoardo Vesentini, at that time the President of the Academy. We promised the Besicovitch part of our original project. We implemented our database and divided the material concerning Besicovitch into seven items, but we were able to deal with only two of these items (Kurz and Salvadori, 2004). A third item was added when Guglielmo Chiodi and Leonardo Ditta invited us to another conference on Sraffa (Kurz and Salvadori, 2008). Hence four items are still missing and I hope that Heinz and I will be able to complete our project in the near future.

The present chapter is strongly related to that project, but it is different in spirit. In those contributions Heinz and I tried to reconstruct the talks between Sraffa and his 'mathematical friends' and to locate their contributions within the development of Sraffa's thought. This chapter, instead, has its origin in the fact that the proof of the existence of the Standard commodity contained in Sraffa's book (§ 37) was recently debated. Lippi (2008) has argued that the algorithm in section 37 of Sraffa's book is not precisely stated and does not need to converge to the desired eigenvalue and eigenvector. The first part of the proposition has been known since the proof-reading stage of Sraffa's book when it was sustained by Alister Watson (cf. Kurz and Salvadori, 2001, pp. 272–273). But the second part escaped the attention of all commentators before Lippi. Indeed, examples can be found in which an algorithm corresponding to the description provided by Sraffa converges to a vector which is not an eigenvector and it is certainly to Lippi's credit that he uncovered the problem. In Appendix A, I report the example provided in a paper in which I investigated the properties that an algorithm needs to have in order to converge to the desired eigenvalue and eigenvector (cf. Salvadori, 2008). In an appendix to his paper Lippi (2008) provided a complete proof of the existence of the Standard commodity by using a very special algorithm from among all the algorithms corresponding to the description of section 37 and another special algorithm was provided, without proof, by Kurz and Salvadori (2001, p. 284). The fact that Sraffa did not choose a particular algorithm may suggest that he was convinced that any algorithm would do the job. This is wrong but, as I proved elsewhere (Salvadori, 2008), the job can actually be done by any algorithm based on a continuous function which can start from any feasible point.

In this paper I want to shed some more light on the issue from an historical perspective. Sraffa was provided a proof of the existence of the Standard commodity by Besicovitch on 21 September 1944. This proof has not yet been discussed in the literature. In Appendix B there is a transcription of the file D3/12/39: 42 that includes it. In this paper I will show that also the proof by Besicovitch is incomplete, but it can easily be completed. Once complete, this proof concerns a family of algorithms as well, but all the algorithms in question converge to the desired eigenvalue and eigenvector. Why did Sraffa not use this proof in his book? Section 10.5 tries to provide an answer.

10.2 Sraffa's Section 37

Sraffa starts section 37 of his book with the following two paragraphs.

> That any actual economic system of the type we have been considering can always be transformed into a Standard system may be shown by an imaginary experiment.
>
> (The experiment involves two types of alternating steps. One type consists in changing the proportions of the industries; the other in reducing in the same ratio the quantities produced by all industries, while leaving unchanged the quantities used as means of production.)

What Sraffa calls an 'imaginary experiment' is clearly what mathematicians call an algorithm: given an initial state, a definite list of well-defined instructions is given to proceed through a well-defined sequence of successive states, eventually terminating in an end-state. In order to formally reconstruct Sraffa's argument, let us introduce the square nonnegative matrix $\mathbf{A} = \left[a_{ij}\right]$ and the positive vector $\mathbf{l} = [l_1, l_2, \ldots, l_n]^T$ as the material input matrix and the labour input vector, on the assumption that the output matrix is the identity matrix **I**. Matrix **A** is assumed to be also indecomposable, that is, all non-basic commodities are explicitly not considered. Let us continue our reading of section 37.

> We start by adjusting the proportions of the industries of the system in such a way that of each basic commodity a larger quantity is produced than is strictly necessary for replacement.
>
> Let us next imagine gradually to reduce by means of successive small proportionate cuts the product of all the industries, without interfering with the quantities of labour and means of production that they employ.
>
> As soon as the cuts reduce the production of any one commodity to the minimum level required for replacement, we readjust the proportions of the industries so that there should again be a surplus of each product (while keeping constant the quantity of labour employed in the aggregate).

The initial state of the algorithm is the 'actual economic system'. This is able to produce a surplus, but does not need to produce a surplus consisting of all (basic) commodities, so the first step consists in determining

$\mathbf{x}_0 \in \{\mathbf{x} > \mathbf{0} | \mathbf{x}^T\mathbf{1} = \beta, \mathbf{x}^T[\mathbf{I} - \mathbf{A}] > \mathbf{0}^T\}$ and then building up two sequences: $\{\mathbf{x}_t\}$ and $\{\lambda_t\}$, where

$$\lambda_t = \lambda(\mathbf{x}_{t-1}) = \max_j \frac{\mathbf{x}_{t-1}^T\mathbf{A}\mathbf{e}_j}{\mathbf{x}_{t-1}^T\mathbf{e}_j}$$

so that $\mathbf{x}_{t-1}^T[\lambda_t\mathbf{I} - \mathbf{A}] \geqq \mathbf{0}^T$ and $\mathbf{x}_{t-1}^T[\lambda_t\mathbf{I} - \mathbf{A}] \ngtr \mathbf{0}^T$, and $\mathbf{x}_t$ $(t > 0)$ is a vector such that $\mathbf{x}_t > \mathbf{0}$, $\mathbf{x}_t^T\mathbf{1} = \beta$ and $\mathbf{x}_t^T[\lambda_t\mathbf{I} - \mathbf{A}] > \mathbf{0}^T$. Sraffa comments 'This is always feasible so long as there is a surplus of some commodities and a deficit of none'. However he does not provide a proof of this sentence. As we will see, this proof is an immediate consequence of the first three theorems provided by Besicovitch. Then Sraffa proceeds to the end-state of the algorithm.

> We continue with such an alternation of proportionate cuts with the re-establishment of a surplus for each product until we reach the point where the products have been reduced to such an extent that all-round replacement is just possible without leaving anything as surplus product.

The 'imaginary experiment' concludes, in Sraffa's opinion, when $\mathbf{x}_\infty > \mathbf{0}$, $\mathbf{x}_\infty^T\mathbf{1} = \beta$ and $\mathbf{x}_\infty^T[\lambda_\infty\mathbf{I} - \mathbf{A}] = \mathbf{0}^T$. Sraffa never states that the algorithm may need an infinite number of steps, but we know indeed that this is so. Finally, we have the last paragraph of section 37.

> Since to reach this position the products of all the industries have been cut in the same proportion we are now able to restore the original conditions of production by increasing the quantity produced in each industry by a uniform rate; we do not, on the other hand, disturb the proportions to which the industries have been brought. The uniform rate which restores the original conditions of production is *R* and the proportions attained by the industries are the proportions of the Standard system.

Hence we arrive at the equation

$$\mathbf{x}_\infty^T[\mathbf{I} - (1 + R)\mathbf{A}] = \mathbf{0}^T$$

where, obviously, $1 + R = 1/\lambda_\infty$. As Alister Watson, Kurz and Salvadori (2001), and Lippi (2008), among others, have remarked, the algorithm is not well defined since there are infinitely many ways to define $\mathbf{x}_t$. Completing the definition of the algorithm means defining a function $\phi(\mathbf{q})$ such that $\mathbf{x}_t = \phi(\mathbf{x}_{t-1})$, at each t. To be more precise, we introduce the sets

$$\mathrm{R} = \left\{ \mathbf{q} \in \Re^n \middle| \, \mathbf{q} \geq \mathbf{0}, \, \mathbf{q}^T \mathbf{1} = \beta, \, \mathbf{q}^T [\mathbf{I} - \mathbf{A}] \geq \mathbf{0}^T \right\}$$

$$\mathrm{R}\star = \left\{ \mathbf{q} \in \Re^n \middle| \, \exists \rho \geq 0 \, : \, \mathbf{q} \geq \mathbf{0}, \, \mathbf{q}^T \mathbf{1} = \beta, \, \mathbf{q}^T [\rho \mathbf{I} - \mathbf{A}] = \mathbf{0}^T \right\}$$

$$\mathrm{S} = \mathrm{R} - \mathrm{R}\star$$

and the set of functions

$$\mathrm{Z}(\mathrm{S}_0) = \left\{ \phi \, : \, \mathrm{S}_0 \to \mathrm{R} \middle| \, \forall \mathbf{q} \in \mathrm{S}_0 \, : \, \phi(\mathbf{q}) \in \mathrm{S}_0 \cup \mathrm{R}\star, \lambda(\mathbf{q})\phi(\mathbf{q}) - \mathbf{A}^T \phi(\mathbf{q}) > \mathbf{0} \right\}$$

where S_0 is any subset of S. Each function of the set $\bigcup_{\mathrm{S}_0 \subseteq \mathrm{S}} \mathrm{Z}(\mathrm{S}_0)$ defines a different algorithm which corresponds to Sraffa's description.

If function $\phi(\mathbf{q})$ has a fixed point in S, then sequence $\{\mathbf{x}_t\}$ may converge on the fixed point of function $\phi(\mathbf{q})$. As a consequence, sequence $\{\lambda_t\}$ may converge to a number which does not even need to be close to the eigenvalue of matrix **A**. This cannot hold if function $\phi(\mathbf{q})$ has the mentioned inequality properties in the whole S, and therefore the set of functions to be considered must be

$$\mathrm{Z} = \mathrm{Z}(\mathrm{S}) = \left\{ \phi{:}\mathrm{S} \to \mathrm{R} \middle| \, \forall \mathbf{q} \in \mathrm{S}{:}\, \phi(\mathbf{q}) \geq \mathbf{0}, \, \lambda(\mathbf{q})\phi(\mathbf{q}) - \mathbf{A}^T \phi(\mathbf{q}) > \mathbf{0}, \, \mathbf{1}^T \phi(\mathbf{q}) = \beta \right\}$$

and not $\bigcup_{\mathrm{S}_0 \subseteq \mathrm{S}} \mathrm{Z}(\mathrm{S}_0)$. This is the extra assumption found by Salvadori (2008). The interpretation is close at hand: the function $\phi(\mathbf{q})$ is such that $\phi(\mathbf{q}) \geq \mathbf{0}$, $\lambda(\mathbf{q})\phi(\mathbf{q}) - \mathbf{A}^T \phi(\mathbf{q}) > \mathbf{0}$, $\mathbf{1}^T \phi(\mathbf{q}) = \beta$, whatever is point $\mathbf{q} \in \mathrm{R}$ and not just in the support of sequence $\{\mathbf{x}_t\}$, as Sraffa's description may be interpreted. In the following two sections I will show that Besicovitch proposed a better defined algorithm and proved that the algorithm converges to the desired solution (apart from a small point to be completed).

10.3 Towards Besicovitch's proof

Besicovitch's proof is divided into four 'theorems'. Only the last is the required proof. The first three prepare the field. In this section we discuss the first three theorems. Besicovitch does not follow the matricial notation we used above to achieve a more compact presentation.

The first theorem of file D3/12/39: 42 reads in plain English: *With positive prices any distribution of the net outputs can be attained.* This theorem starts from the assumption that there is a system with no profits and positive prices and a positive wage rate. The aim is to prove that industries can be operated in such a way that any proportion in which the surplus is distributed among industries is feasible. The no profit assumption is not necessary, but probably follows the exercise that Sraffa is performing. Obviously the rate of profit must be lower than the maximum one since the wage rate must be positive and this is really what is needed. In modern notation the first theorem states:

$$\exists \mathbf{p} > \mathbf{0}, w > 0 : \mathbf{A}\mathbf{p} + w\mathbf{l} - \mathbf{p} \rightarrow \exists \mathbf{x} \geq \mathbf{0} : \mathbf{x}^T = \mathbf{x}^T \mathbf{A} + \mathbf{y}^T \ \forall \mathbf{y} \geq \mathbf{0}.$$

Obviously the semipositive vector $\mathbf{y}$ is the vector of what Besicovitch calls 'the Surplus outputs' (net outputs in the above). In order to obtain this result it is enough to prove that matrix $\mathbf{I} - \mathbf{A}$ is invertible and its inverse is positive, and we know that this is the case when matrix $\mathbf{A}$ is indecomposable and there is a positive vector $\mathbf{p}$ such that $[\mathbf{I} - \mathbf{A}]\mathbf{p} \geq \mathbf{0}$, because of the Perron-Frobenius Theorem. However, Besicovitch makes no reference to the latter Theorem and indeed the proof of the existence of the Standard commodity can be interpreted as a proof of the Perron-Frobenius Theorem (see Kurz and Salvadori, 1993).

The proof provided by Besicovitch is very ingenious, but may need some explanation. Like the Gauss-Jordan elimination way to solve a linear system of equations it is based on consecutive applications of two elementary steps: (i) multiplication of an equation by a non-zero scalar, and (ii) addition to an equation of non-zero scalar multiples of other equations. Besicovitch proves that since prices are positive the *non-zero* scalar multiplications involved in both steps are indeed *positive* scalar multiplications. Let us follow step by step this recursive proof. In the first step only the last industry, n, is considered. Since

$$a_{n1}p_1 + \ldots + a_{nn}p_n + l_n w = p_n$$

and since $a_{n1}p_1 + \ldots + a_{nn-1}p_{n-1} + l_n w > 0$, then $1 - a_{nn} > 0$. Hence it is possible to find a positive λ_n such that $\lambda_n(1 - a_{nn})$ can take any positive value.

In the second step the last two industries are considered. Taking account of the equations

$$a_{n-1,1}p_1 + \cdots + a_{n-1,n-1}p_{n-1} + a_{n-1,n}p_n + l_{n-1}w = p_{n-1}$$
$$a_{n1}p_1 + \cdots + a_{nn-1}p_{n-1} + a_{nn}p_n + l_n w = p_n$$

and using the first step, we can multiply the latter by a λ_n such that $\lambda_n(1 - a_{nn}) = a_{n-1,n}$ so as to obtain that the surplus of industry n equals the input of commodity n into industry $n-1$:

$$a_{n-1,1}p_1 + \cdots + a_{n-1,n-1}p_{n-1} + a_{n-1,n}p_n + l_{n-1}w = p_{n-1}$$
$$\frac{a_{n-1,n}}{1-a_{nn}}a_{n1}p_1 + \cdots + \frac{a_{n-1,n}}{1-a_{nn}}a_{nn-1}p_{n-1} + \frac{a_{n-1,n}}{1-a_{nn}}a_{nn}p_n + \frac{a_{n-1,n}}{1-a_{nn}}l_n w = \frac{a_{n-1,n}}{1-a_{nn}}p_n$$

As a consequence, by summing up the two equations we obtain

$$\left(a_{n-1,1} + \frac{a_{n-1,n}}{1-a_{nn}}a_{n1}\right)p_1 + \ldots + \left(a_{n-1,n-1} + \frac{a_{n-1,n}}{1-a_{nn}}a_{nn-1}\right)p_{n-1} +$$
$$\left(l_{n-1} + \frac{a_{n-1,n}}{1-a_{nn}}l_n\right)w = p_{n-1}$$

since

$$a_{n-1,n} + \frac{a_{n-1,n}}{1-a_{nn}} a_{nn} = \frac{a_{n-1,n}}{1-a_{nn}} .$$

Once again, since

$$\left(a_{n-1,1} + \frac{a_{n-1,n}}{1-a_{nn}} a_{n1} \right) p_1 + \ldots + \left(a_{n-1,n-2} + \frac{a_{n-1,n}}{1-a_{nn}} a_{nn-2} \right) p_{n-2} + \left(l_{n-1} + \frac{a_{n-1,n}}{1-a_{nn}} l_n \right) w > 0$$

then

$$1 - \left(a_{n-1,n-1} + \frac{a_{n-1,n}}{1-a_{nn}} a_{n,n-1} \right) = \frac{\det \begin{bmatrix} 1-a_{n-1,n-1} & -a_{n-1,n} \\ -a_{n,n-1} & 1-a_{nn} \end{bmatrix}}{1-a_{nn}} > 0.$$

Hence we can find two positive scalars λ_n and λ_{n-1} such that $\lambda_{n-1} - \lambda_n a_{n,n-1} - \lambda_{n-1} a_{n-1,n-1}$ can take any positive value and $\lambda_n - \lambda_n a_{nn} - \lambda_{n-1} a_{n-1,n} = 0$, that is, we can proportion the two equations in such a way that the output of commodity n equals the sum of the inputs of commodity n in the last two industries and the output of commodity $n-1$ is any desired positive number. In a similar way we can proportion the two equations in such a way that the output of commodity $n-1$ equals the sum of the inputs of commodity $n-1$ in the last two industries and the output of commodity n is any desired positive number. Thus the two equations can be so proportioned that there is the desired surplus of the last two commodities.

The third step analyses the last three industries. By using the second step we can proportion the last two equations in such a way that the outputs of the last two commodities equal the sum of their inputs in the last three industries.

$$a_{n-2,1} p_1 + \ldots + a_{n-2,n-1} p_{n-1} + a_{n-2,n} p_n + l_{n-2} w = p_{n-2}$$

$$\frac{\Delta_1}{\Delta} a_{n-1,1} p_1 + \ldots + \frac{\Delta_1}{\Delta} a_{n-1,n-1} p_{n-1} + \frac{\Delta_1}{\Delta} a_{n-1,n} p_n + \frac{\Delta_1}{\Delta} l_{n-1} w = \frac{\Delta_1}{\Delta} p_{n-1}$$

$$\frac{\Delta_2}{\Delta} a_{n1} p_1 + \ldots + \frac{\Delta_2}{\Delta} a_{nn-1} p_{n-1} + \frac{\Delta_2}{\Delta} a_{nn} p_n + \frac{\Delta_2}{\Delta} l_n w = \frac{\Delta_2}{\Delta} p_n$$

where

$$\Delta = \det \begin{bmatrix} 1-a_{n-1,n-1} & -a_{n-1,n} \\ -a_{n,n-1} & 1-a_{nn} \end{bmatrix}, \Delta_1 = \det \begin{bmatrix} a_{n-2,n-1} & -a_{n-1,n} \\ a_{n-2,n} & 1-a_{nn} \end{bmatrix},$$

$$\Delta_2 = \det \begin{bmatrix} 1-a_{n-1,n-1} & a_{n-2,n-1} \\ -a_{n,n-1} & a_{n-2,n} \end{bmatrix}.$$

By adding up, we obtain

$$\left(a_{n-2,1}+\frac{\Delta_1}{\Delta}a_{n-1,1}+\frac{\Delta_2}{\Delta}a_{n1}\right)p_1+\cdots+\left(a_{n-2,n-2}+\frac{\Delta_1}{\Delta}a_{n-1,n-2}+\frac{\Delta_2}{\Delta}a_{n,n-2}\right)p_{n-2}$$
$$+l_{n-2}w=p_{n-2}$$

since

$$a_{n-2,n-1}+\frac{\Delta_1}{\Delta}a_{n-1,n-1}+\frac{\Delta_2}{\Delta}a_{n,n-1}=\frac{\Delta_1}{\Delta},\quad a_{n-2,n}+\frac{\Delta_1}{\Delta}a_{n-1,n}+\frac{\Delta_2}{\Delta}a_{n,n}=\frac{\Delta_2}{\Delta}.$$

Once again, since prices are positive, we obtain that there is a surplus of commodity $n-2$, that is,

$$1-\left(a_{n-2,n-2}+\frac{\Delta_1}{\Delta}a_{n-1,n-2}+\frac{\Delta_2}{\Delta}a_{n,n-2}\right)$$
$$=\frac{\det\begin{bmatrix}1-a_{n-2,n-2} & -a_{n-2,n-1} & -a_{n-2,n}\\ -a_{n-1,n-2} & 1-a_{n-1,n-1} & -a_{n-1,n}\\ -a_{n,n-2} & -a_{n,n-1} & 1-a_{nn}\end{bmatrix}}{\Delta}>0$$

and that multipliers can be found such that the surplus of commodity $n-2$ can take any positive value, whereas the outputs of the last two commodities equal the sum of their inputs in the last three industries. This is enough to find multipliers such that there is the desired surplus of commodity $n-2$, the desired surplus of commodity $n-1$, and the desired surplus of commodity n. And so on.

The second theorem reads in plain English: *If the wage is positive and prices are positive, then net outputs cannot be all nought and, therefore, there is a surplus of at least one commodity.* In modern notation the second theorem states:

$$\exists\mathbf{p}>\mathbf{0},w>0:\mathbf{Ap}+w\mathbf{l}=\mathbf{p}\Rightarrow\mathbf{x}^T\neq\mathbf{x}^T\mathbf{A}\ \forall\mathbf{x}\geq\mathbf{0}$$

If not, we obtain $\mathbf{x}^T\mathbf{Ap}+w\mathbf{x}^T\mathbf{l}=\mathbf{x}^T\mathbf{p}=\mathbf{x}^T\mathbf{Ap}$, and therefore $w\mathbf{x}^T\mathbf{l}=0$, which is not possible. The proof by Besicovitch does not need a *reductio ad absurdum*. If $\mathbf{x}^T\mathbf{Ae}_i=\mathbf{x}^T\mathbf{e}_i$ each $i\neq j$, where $\mathbf{e}_i$ is the i-th unit vector, then

$$\mathbf{x}^T\mathbf{Ap}+w\mathbf{x}^T\mathbf{l}=\mathbf{x}^T\mathbf{Ae}_j\left(\mathbf{e}_j^T\mathbf{p}\right)+w\mathbf{x}^T\mathbf{l}+M=\mathbf{e}_j^T\mathbf{p}+M$$

where $M=\sum_{i\neq j}\mathbf{x}^T\mathbf{Ae}_i\left(\mathbf{e}_i^T\mathbf{p}\right)=\sum_{i\neq j}\mathbf{e}_i^T\mathbf{p}$ and since $w\mathbf{x}^T\mathbf{l}>0$, we have $\mathbf{x}^T\mathbf{Ae}_j<1$ as required.

The third theorem reads in plain English: *If the surplus of a commodity is positive and that of the others is nought then the prices are positive.* Note that it is always implicit that the wage rate is positive. The aim is to prove that if there is a positive surplus of at least one commodity (and a negative surplus of none), then the wage is positive and prices are positive. Also in this case it is enough to prove that matrix $\mathbf{I}-\mathbf{A}$ is invertible and its inverse is positive. In modern notation the third theorem states:

$$\exists \mathbf{x} \geq \mathbf{0} : \mathbf{x}^T \geq \mathbf{x}^T \mathbf{A} \Rightarrow \exists \mathbf{p} > \mathbf{0} : \mathbf{A}\mathbf{p} + w\mathbf{l} = \mathbf{p}$$

However, in the document D3/12/39: 42 of 21 September 1944, this theorem is not proven. What is proven is that if there is a surplus in one commodity and no surplus in all the others, then the equations can be proportioned in such a way that a surplus is obtained in every commodity (even this proof is incomplete: if the input matrix were decomposable, the statement would be false; the proof does not show why the statement holds when the input matrix is indecomposable). However, in the document D3/12/39: 42 there is a note by Sraffa saying: 'Refer to blue page 1'. The reference is no doubt to D3/12/39: 7, which is written on a blue piece of paper and contains a proof by Besicovitch of the fact that if there is a surplus in every commodity, then prices are positive.[1] The transcription of this document is reported below in Appendix C.

Before arguing the proof of the third theorem, I will discuss the proof in D3/12/39: 7. The statement in modern notation is:

$$\mathbf{e}^T > (1+r)\mathbf{e}^T \mathbf{A}, \quad (1+r)\mathbf{A}\mathbf{p} + w\mathbf{l} = \mathbf{p}, \quad w > 0 \Rightarrow \mathbf{p} > \mathbf{0}$$

where $\mathbf{e}$ is the sum vector of the appropriate size, that is a vector of 1's. Note that the above equation always admits a solution since it is homogeneous in $(\mathbf{p}, w)$. However, we are assuming here something more, i.e., that a solution with a positive w exists. We will deal with this problem soon. Suppose that in this solution some price (at least one) is negative or nought, and all the others (possibly none) are positive. With no loss of generality assume that the prices of the first h commodities are negative or nought, $1 \leq h \leq n$, and the last $n-h$ are positive. Then, with obvious meanings of symbols,

$$(1+r)\mathbf{A}_{12}\mathbf{p}_2 + w\mathbf{l}_1 = [\mathbf{I} - (1+r)\mathbf{A}_{11}]\mathbf{p}_1$$

which is impossible since $\mathbf{e}^T [\mathbf{I} - (1+r)\mathbf{A}_{11}]\mathbf{p}_1 \leq 0$ whereas $(1+r)\mathbf{e}^T \mathbf{A}_{12}\mathbf{p}_2 + w\mathbf{e}^T \mathbf{l}_1 > 0$. Note that this proof holds even if matrix $\mathbf{A}$ is decomposable, and therefore some commodities are non-basic, provided that labour enters directly into the production of all commodities and, therefore, $\mathbf{l}_1 > \mathbf{0}$ (it still holds if labour enters directly or indirectly into the production of all commodities, but I will not deal with this issue here). But what happens if all solutions to the system $(1+r)\mathbf{A}\mathbf{p} + w\mathbf{l} = \mathbf{p}$ have a zero w? Indeed the same proof can be slightly modified to prove that in this case $\mathbf{p} = \mathbf{0}$ and therefore the unique solution would be the trivial one. This being impossible, there are solutions with $w \neq 0$ and therefore with $w > 0$.[2]

Now we can discuss the proof of the third theorem in the document D3/12/39: 42. With no loss of generality assume that the first h commodities have a positive surplus, $1 \leq h \leq n$, whereas the last $n-h$ have no surplus (and no loss). Therefore $\mathbf{e}^T > \mathbf{e}^T\mathbf{A}_{11} + \mathbf{e}^T\mathbf{A}_{12}$ and $\mathbf{e}^T = \mathbf{e}^T\mathbf{A}_{12} + \mathbf{e}^T\mathbf{A}_{22}$ (note that in these and in the following formulas the vectors $\mathbf{e}$ involved have different sizes). Therefore, Besicovitch maintains, if u is a real number lower than 1, but so close to 1 that $u\mathbf{e}^T > u\mathbf{e}^T\mathbf{A}_{11} + \mathbf{e}^T\mathbf{A}_{12}$ still holds, then by necessity $\mathbf{e}^T > u\mathbf{e}^T\mathbf{A}_{12} + \mathbf{e}^T\mathbf{A}_{22}$. However, this is not necessarily true. Indeed, if matrix $\mathbf{A}$ is decomposable and $\mathbf{A}_{12} = \mathbf{0}$, this is certainly false. It is reasonable to suppose that Besicovitch assumed that all commodities are basic and, therefore, matrix $\mathbf{A}$ is indecomposable. Even in this case, however, the proof is incomplete ($\mathbf{e}^T\mathbf{A}_{12}$ is semi-positive, but does not need to be positive) since we may need to iterate the process to bring home the result. In fact, if matrix $\mathbf{A}$ is indecomposable, we are sure that $\mathbf{e}^T \geq u\mathbf{e}^T\mathbf{A}_{12} + \mathbf{e}^T\mathbf{A}_{22}$ and therefore the number of commodities with a positive surplus is increased and still no commodity has a negative surplus. Further, since at any iteration of the process the number of products with a positive surplus increases, the number of iterations needed to obtain a surplus in all commodities is certainly finite since it is lower than $n-h$.

The first three theorems of file D3/12/39: 42 are intended to support two facts. First, if there is a surplus of any type, industries may be proportioned in such a way as to get the surplus anywhere it is needed. Second, there is a surplus if, and only if, prices are positive and the wage rate is positive. The relationship with section 37 of the book by Sraffa (1960) is obvious. One of the two steps of the algorithm introduced there consists exactly in 'adjusting the proportions of the industries of the system in such a way that of each basic commodity a larger quantity is produced than is strictly necessary for replacement'. The fourth theorem concerns the existence of the Standard commodity and will be analysed in the next section.

10.4 Besicovitch's proof

The fourth theorem reads in plain English: *If prices are positive, then there exist positive multipliers $q_a, \ldots, q_k$ such that the net output is proportional to the total of every kind of raw material.* The proof is similar to that provided by Sraffa, but is more detailed and closer to the description of an algorithm. It starts by assuming that there is a surplus with regard to all commodities. If there were a surplus only in some industries, then we could find a starting point with a surplus in all industries, $\mathbf{x}_0 \in \left\{\mathbf{x} > \mathbf{0} \middle| \mathbf{x}^T\mathbf{1} = \beta, \mathbf{x}^T[\mathbf{I} - \mathbf{A}] > \mathbf{0}^T\right\}$, since the assumption of Theorem 1 holds. Then the second step used by Sraffa is applied. That is, it is found that

$$\lambda_1 = \lambda(\mathbf{x}_0) = \max_j \frac{\mathbf{x}_0^T\mathbf{A}\mathbf{e}_j}{\mathbf{x}_0^T\mathbf{e}_j}$$

so that $\mathbf{x}_0^T[\lambda_1\mathbf{I}-\mathbf{A}]\geq\mathbf{0}^T$ and $\mathbf{x}_0^T[\lambda_1\mathbf{I}-\mathbf{A}]\ngtr\mathbf{0}^T$. Then all the equations of commodities for which there is a surplus are multiplied by a common scalar lower than 1. Besicovitch thinks this is enough to obtain that all commodities are in surplus, but this does not need to be true since input coefficients are not all positive. However, since all commodities are assumed to be basic, the input matrix **A** is indecomposable and therefore we can get the desired result by iterating the same procedure, as seen above, in the analysis of the third theorem by Besicovitch. Let us consider the point in a more formal way.

Let $\mu\in\Re$ and $\mathbf{x}\in S$ be such that $\mu\mathbf{x}^T\geq\mathbf{x}^T\mathbf{A}$ and let us define the set of indices

$$\mathrm{I}_{\mu\mathbf{x}}=\left\{i\in\{1,\ 2,\ \dots,\ n\}\,\middle|\,\mu x_i>\sum_{j=1}^{n}x_ja_{ji}\right\}$$

$$\hat{\mathrm{I}}_{\mu\mathbf{x}}=\left\{i\in\{1,\ 2,\ \dots,\ n\}\,\middle|\,\mu x_i=\sum_{j=1}^{n}x_ja_{ji}\right\}$$

The aim of this step consists in finding an intensity vector $\phi(\mathbf{x})$ such that $\mathrm{I}_{\mu\phi(\mathbf{x})}=\{1,\ 2,\ \dots,\ n\}$ and, as a consequence, $\hat{\mathrm{I}}_{\mu\phi(\mathbf{x})}=\varnothing$. Besicovitch considers that this can be obtained if $\phi(\mathbf{x})$ is the function $\mathbf{g}(\mu,\mathbf{x})$, where

$$g_i(\mu,\mathbf{x})=\begin{cases}x_i & \text{if } i\in\hat{\mathrm{I}}_{\mu\mathbf{x}}\\ \eta x_i & \text{if } i\in\mathrm{I}_{\mu\mathbf{x}}\end{cases}$$

where η is a scalar lower than 1, but so close to 1 that

$$\mu(\eta x_i)>\sum_{j\in\hat{\mathrm{I}}_{\mu\mathbf{x}}}x_ja_{ji}+\eta\sum_{j\in\mathrm{I}_{\mu\mathbf{x}}}x_ja_{ji}\ \text{each } i\in\mathrm{I}_{\mu\mathbf{x}}.$$

That is,

$$\max_{i\in\mathrm{I}_{\mu\mathbf{x}}}\frac{\sum_{j\in\hat{\mathrm{I}}_{\mu\mathbf{x}}}x_ja_{ji}}{\mu x_i-\sum_{j\in\mathrm{I}_{\mu\mathbf{x}}}x_ja_{ji}}<\eta<1.$$

As mentioned above, this is not enough to obtain that $\mathrm{I}_{\mu\mathbf{g}(\mu,\mathbf{x})}=\{1,\ 2,\ \dots,\ n\}$ because some a_{ji} may be nought. However, by construction, $i\in\mathrm{I}_{\mu\mathbf{x}}$ implies that $i\in\mathrm{I}_{\mu\mathbf{g}(\mu,\mathbf{x})}$ and therefore $\mathrm{I}_{\mu\mathbf{g}(\mu,\mathbf{x})}\supseteq\mathrm{I}_{\mu\mathbf{x}}$. On the other hand, $\mathrm{I}_{\mu\mathbf{g}(\mu,\mathbf{x})}=\mathrm{I}_{\mu\mathbf{x}}$ if, and only if, $a_{ji}=0$, each $i\in\mathrm{I}_{\mu\mathbf{x}}$ and each $j\in\hat{\mathrm{I}}_{\mu\mathbf{x}}$. But then matrix **A** would be decomposable. This being impossible, we obtain that

$I_{\mu \mathbf{g}(\mu,\mathbf{x})} \supset I_{\mu \mathbf{x}}$. This is enough to say that the procedure can be iterated for a number of times lower than the (finite) number of commodities (also because if $I_{\mu \mathbf{x}} = \{1,2,\ldots,\}$, then $\mathbf{g}(\mu,\mathbf{x})$ is proportional to $\mathbf{x}$). Hence we can define:

$$\begin{aligned}
&\mathbf{h}_1(\mathbf{x}) = \mathbf{g}(\lambda(\mathbf{x}),\mathbf{x}) \\
&\mathbf{h}_j(\mathbf{x}) = \mathbf{g}(\lambda(\mathbf{x}),\mathbf{h}_{j-1}(\mathbf{x})) \quad j = 2,\ldots,n-1 \\
&\phi(\mathbf{x}) = \mathbf{h}_{n-1}(\mathbf{x}).
\end{aligned}$$

There is one further aspect considered by Besicovitch. In a remark he argued that 'we may keep one of our industries intact' in order to avoid all multipliers becoming zero. With no loss of generality, assume that the industry in question is industry 1. Therefore function $\mathbf{g}(\mu,\mathbf{x})$ must be redefined as

$$g_i(\mu,\mathbf{x}) = \begin{cases}
x_i & \text{if } i \in \hat{I}_{\mu \mathbf{x}} \text{ and } 1 \in \hat{I}_{\mu \mathbf{x}} \\
\eta x_i & \text{if } i \in I_{\mu \mathbf{x}} \text{ and } 1 \in \hat{I}_{\mu \mathbf{x}} \\
\frac{1}{\eta} x_i & \text{if } i \in \hat{I}_{\mu \mathbf{x}} \text{ and } 1 \notin \hat{I}_{\mu \mathbf{x}} \\
x_i & \text{if } i \in I_{\mu \mathbf{x}} \text{ and } 1 \notin \hat{I}_{\mu \mathbf{x}}
\end{cases}$$

Further, this function has the property that if $\mathbf{I}_{\mu \mathbf{x}} = \{1,2,\ldots,n\}$, then $\mathbf{g}(\mu,\mathbf{x}) = \mathbf{x}$. As seen in Section 10.2, Sraffa followed a different, but equivalent, strategy to avoid all multipliers becoming zero. He kept the amount of labour fixed. If we follow this strategy, then function $\mathbf{g}(\mu,\mathbf{x})$ must be redefined as

$$g_i(\mu,\mathbf{x}) = \begin{cases}
\theta x_i & \text{if } i \in \hat{I}_{\mu \mathbf{x}} \\
\theta \eta x_i & \text{if } i \in I_{\mu \mathbf{x}}
\end{cases}$$

where

$$\theta = \frac{\beta}{\sum_{j \in \hat{I}_{\mu \mathbf{x}}} x_j l_j + \eta \sum_{j \in I_{\mu \mathbf{x}}} x_j l_j}.$$

Also this function has the property that if $\mathbf{I}_{\mu \mathbf{x}} = \{1,2,\ldots,n\}$, then $\mathbf{g}(\mu,\mathbf{x}) = \mathbf{x}$

Also in Besicovitch's proof there is a family of potential algorithms involved. In order to have a proper algorithm we must have a way to define how η is chosen. For example, if we chose η in the middle of the range in which it can vary, we would have

$$\eta = \frac{1}{2} + \frac{1}{2} \max_{i \in I_{\mu \mathbf{x}}} \frac{\sum_{j \in \hat{I}_{\mu \mathbf{x}}} x_j a_{ji}}{\mu x_i - \sum_{j \in I_{\mu \mathbf{x}}} x_j a_{ji}}$$

and in general any possible choice could be defined as a choice of $0<\alpha<1$ in the expression

$$\eta=\alpha+(1-\alpha)\max_{i\in \mathrm{I}_{\mu\mathbf{x}}} \frac{\sum_{j\in \hat{\mathrm{I}}_{\mu\mathbf{x}}} x_j a_{ji}}{\mu x_i-\sum_{j\in \mathrm{I}_{\mu\mathbf{x}}} x_j a_{ji}}.$$

For each sequence $\{\alpha_i\}$, $0<\alpha_i<1$, we have a different algorithm; but whatever sequence $\{\alpha_i\}$ is chosen, it is easily proved that the conditions stated by Salvadori (2008) hold and therefore all the potential algorithms considered by Besicovitch converge to the desired result. In fact, for any given sequence $\{\alpha_i\}$ function $\phi(\mathbf{x})$ is continuous and can start from any point in S.

10.5 Sraffa and Besicovitch

Sraffa did not use the function $\phi(\mathbf{x})$ used by Besicovitch. He recognised that what is important is 'adjusting the proportions of the industries of the system in such a way that of each basic commodity a larger quantity is produced than is strictly necessary for replacement' and that at each step the desired result is closer, but he did not consider the fact that the 'imaginary experiment' may work through an infinite number of steps without approaching the Standard commodity.

Why did Sraffa not use the proof available to him and provided by Besicovitch in September 1944? A simple answer could be that Sraffa thought that the exposition of the proof could be simplified and that he failed to carry out the simplification required. This is a possible interpretation. However, there are other cases in which Sraffa made no use of an available proof by Besicovitch. For instance when in the 1950s Sraffa was faced with the need to define basics and non-basics in joint production, he conceived a definition in terms of a tax on the production of single commodities (a tithe). A tax on the production of a basic commodity affects all prices and the wage rate (for a given rate of profit), whereas a tax on the production of a non-basic commodity affects only prices of some non-basic commodities (if the numeraire is fixed only in terms of basic commodities). He was convinced to use the linear dependence definition we find in the book (§ 58) by Besicovitch (the whole story is told by Kurz and Salvadori, 2004). The tax argument appears in the book (§ 65), but it is a consequence, not the definition. Interestingly, Besicovitch proved three months after Sraffa had accepted the definition in terms of linear dependence that Sraffa's original idea was correct and that actually the definition could be given in terms of the tax. However, the proof is extremely demanding in terms of mathematical calculations (see Kurz and Salvadori, 2004). Sraffa made no mention of this proof by Besicovitch in his book.

Both the proof of the existence of the Standard commodity and the distinction between basic and non-basic commodities recall the concluding remarks in Sraffa's Preface of his book:

> It will be only too obvious that I have not always followed the expert advice that was given to me – particularly with regard to the notation adopted, which I have insisted on retaining (although admittedly open to objection in some respects) as being easy to follow for the non-mathematical reader.

Despite his interest in the existence of a proof, Sraffa was keen to provide one only if it was 'easy to follow for the non-mathematical reader'. He thought that the non-mathematical reader would understand his argument in section 37. If the mathematical reader were to find it incomplete, then such a reader would also be able to find a complete proof, which Sraffa knew existed.

10.6 Conclusion

In this paper I explored the relationship between the proof of the existence of the Standard commodity contained in section 37 of Sraffa's (1960) book and the proof supplied to Sraffa by Besicovitch on 21 September 1944, and investigated the completeness and consistency of such a proof. I also postulated some reasons which led Sraffa to omit this proof in his book in favour of an incomplete argument.

Appendix A: An example

Let

$$\mathbf{A} = \begin{bmatrix} 0 & h \\ k & 0 \end{bmatrix} \quad \mathbf{1} = \begin{bmatrix} \frac{1}{2} \\ \frac{1}{2} \end{bmatrix} \quad \beta = 1 \quad 0 < h < k < 1$$

It is easily calculated that the eigenvalue of maximum modulus of matrix $\mathbf{A}$ is $\sqrt{hk}$ and that the left eigenvector associated with this eigenvalue normalised by the condition $\mathbf{x}^T\mathbf{1} = \beta$ is

$$\begin{bmatrix} \frac{2\left(k - \sqrt{hk}\right)}{k - h} & \frac{2\left(\sqrt{hk} - h\right)}{k - h} \end{bmatrix}$$

It is easily recognised that

$$\mathrm{R} = \left\{ \mathbf{q} \in \Re^2 \middle| \ \frac{2k}{1+k} \le q_1 \le \frac{2}{1+h},\ q_2 = 2 - q_1 \right\}.$$

Finally, let us consider the function

$$\phi(\mathbf{q}) = \begin{bmatrix} 1 \\ 1-2\varepsilon \end{bmatrix} + \varepsilon\mathbf{q} \tag{1}$$

with

$$0 < \varepsilon < \frac{1}{2} - \frac{1}{2}\sqrt{\frac{h}{k}} \tag{2}$$

From inequalities (2) we obtain the inequality

$$\frac{1}{1-\varepsilon} < \frac{2\left(k-\sqrt{hk}\right)}{k-h}$$

from which we obtain[3] that $\lambda(\mathbf{q})\phi(\mathbf{q}) - \mathbf{A}^T\phi(\mathbf{q}) > \mathbf{0}$ for each $\mathbf{q} \in \mathrm{S}_1$, whereas this property does not hold for $\mathbf{q} \in \mathrm{S}_2$, where

$$\mathrm{S}_1 = \left\{ \mathbf{q} \in \mathrm{S} \,\middle|\, q_1 < \frac{1}{1-\varepsilon} \right\}$$

$$\mathrm{S}_2 = \left\{ \mathbf{q} \in \mathrm{S} \,\middle|\, \frac{1}{1-\varepsilon} \le q_1 < \frac{2\left(k-\sqrt{hk}\right)}{k-h} \right\}$$

Further, it is easily verified that $\mathbf{q} \in \mathrm{S}_1 \Rightarrow \phi(\mathbf{q}) \in \mathrm{S}_1$. Therefore each element of any sequence defined by the conditions

$$\mathbf{q}_0 \in \mathrm{S}_1,\ \mathbf{q}_{t+1} = \begin{cases} \mathbf{q}_t & \text{if } \lambda(\mathbf{q}_t)\mathbf{q}_t - \mathbf{A}^T\mathbf{q}_t = \mathbf{0} \\ \phi(\mathbf{q}_t) & \text{if } \lambda(\mathbf{q}_t)\mathbf{q}_t - \mathbf{A}^T\mathbf{q}_t \neq \mathbf{0} \end{cases}$$

satisfies the conditions stated by Sraffa, but

$$\lim_{i\to\infty} \lambda(\mathbf{q}_i) = (1-2\varepsilon)k > \sqrt{hk}$$

$$\lim_{i\to\infty} \mathbf{q}_i = \begin{bmatrix} \dfrac{1}{1-\varepsilon} \\ \dfrac{1-2\varepsilon}{1-\varepsilon} \end{bmatrix} \neq \begin{bmatrix} \dfrac{2\left(k-\sqrt{hk}\right)}{k-h} \\ \dfrac{2\left(\sqrt{hk}-h\right)}{k-h} \end{bmatrix}$$

The last limit is the unique fixed point of function (1).

Appendix B: D3/12/39: 42

Besic.: – **21.9.44**: (42) 1–4:

'Th 1 If prices are +ve, any distribution of the Surplus outputs can be attained'

Proof

(i) $A_k p_a + ... + K_k p_k + l_k w = K p_k$

obviously any desirable surplus of K can be produced since $K > K_k$ (∵ of +ve prices).

$$\text{(ii)} \begin{cases} A_j p_a + ... + J_j p_j + K_j p_k + l_j w = J p_j \\ A_k p_a + . \qquad . \qquad . \qquad = K p_k \end{cases}$$

Let the surplus of the *K*-industry be K_j. Then *J* industry produces some Surplus. Multiply{in}g both =ions {equations} by the Same factor the *J* surplus may take any assigned value. S{imilar}ly we can make *J* not to have any Surplus & *K* to have any assigned surplus. Then add{in}g the two firs{t} =ions {equations} & the two second ones we get an assigned Surplus of *J* & f{o}r *K*, a. s.o., q.e.d.

'Th 2 If the prices are +ve {positive} and the surplus of *B*,..., *K* is 0 then the surplus of *A* is +ive {positive}.

Proof

For take the surplus of *B*,..., *K* (wrt {with respect to} *B*... *K*) to be B_a,..., K_a. Then the surplus f{o}r *B*,... *K* wrt {with respect to} *A*,..., *K* is 0. Write

$$A_a p_a + ... + l_a w = A p_a$$

$$\overline{\qquad\qquad}$$

$$A_k p_a + ... + l_k w = K p_k$$

& add them & drop *B*,..., *K* terms from both sides as they are = {equal}. The result is

$$(A_a + ... + A_k) p_a + (l_a + ... + l_k) w = A p_a \,.$$

i.e. $A_a + ... + A_k < A$, q.e.d.

'Th 3 If the Surplus of *A* is +ve {positive} & of *B*,..., *K* is 0 then the prices are +ve {positive}.

For multiplying *A*=ion {equation A} by *u* (< 1) sufficiently near 1 we shall still have the surplus of *A* +ve {positive} & we shall make surplus of *B*,..., *K* +ve {positive}.

{Addition by Sraffa on bottom of page: (Refer to blue page 1)}

'Th 4 If prices are +ve {positive} there exist +ve {positive} multipliers q_a,..., q_k such that the Surplus output is proportional to the total of every kind of raw materials.

Proof.

$$A_a p_a + ... + 1_a w = A p_a$$

(1).........

$$\mathrm{A}_k P_a + ... = K p_k$$

assuming the surplus for each to be +ve {positive}, i.e.

$$A_a + ... + A_k < A$$

(2).......

$$K_a + ... + K_k < K$$

Consider

$$A_a + \ldots + A_k < Au$$
$$(3) \ldots\ldots\ldots\ldots\ldots$$
$$K_a + \ldots + K_k < ku$$

The ≠ties {inequalities} remain true as u decreases from 1 until it reaches a certain value $u_0 > 0$ for which some of the ≠ties {inequalities} become =ties {equalities}, f.i {for instance} the first two. Then we multiply the $C, \ldots, K$ = ions {equations} by $k < 1$ but near 1, so that the surplus of $C, \ldots, K$ still remain positive. This will release a surplus of A & B. Then (3) will be true wrt {with respect to} the reformed system for $u = u_0$. Now we decrease u beyond u_0 a.s.o. In this way we shall reach as System

$$q_a \left(A_k P_a + \ldots\ldots\ldots\right) = q_a A p_a$$
$$\ldots\ldots\ldots\ldots$$
$$q_a \left(\ldots\ldots\ldots\ldots\ldots\right) = q_a K p_k$$

for which

$$q_a A_a + \ldots q_k A_k < q_a A u$$
$$\ldots\ldots\ldots\ldots\ldots$$
$$q_a K_a + \ldots\ldots\ldots < q_k K u$$

for $u_1 < u \leq 1$,& when $\mathrm{u} = \mathrm{u}_1$ all the ≠ies {inequalities} become =ies {equalities}.

Remark.

All $q_a, \cdots, q_k$ cannot become 0 since in all our adjustments we may keep one of our industries intact, f. i A, & from this it follows that $u_1 \geq A_a / A$(∴ 1st =ion {first equation} of (3)).

Appendix C: D3/12/39: 7

$$\left(A_a p_a + \cdots + k_a p_k\right)(1+r) + L_a w = A p_a$$
$$\ldots\ldots\ldots\ldots$$
$$\left(A_k p_a + \cdots + k_k p_k\right)(1+r) + L_k w = K p_a$$

If r is such that

$$\left(A_a + \ldots + A_k\right)(1+r) < A$$
$$\left(K_a + \ldots + K_k\right)(1+r) < K$$

then all prices are positive, assuming $w > 0$

Proof.

Suppose not. Let $p_a < 0, p_b < 0$, the rest > 0. Then adding the first two equations and taking to the right A and B terms we shall have

$$\left\{\left(c_a + c_b\right) p_c + \ldots + \left(K_a + K_b\right) p_k\right\}(1+r) + \left(L_a + L_b\right) w$$
$$= \left\{A - \left(A_a + A_b\right)(1+r)\right\} p_a + \left\{B - \left(B_a + B_b\right)(1+r) p_b\right.$$

which is impossible, since the expression on the left hand side is > 0, and on r. h. side < 0.

ASB

Notes

1 D3/12/39: 8 is also written on a blue piece of paper and contains a proof by Besicovitch, but on a different issue.

2 If $w=0$, with no loss of generality assume that the prices of the first h commodities are positive, $1 \leq h \leq n$, and the last $n-h$ are either negative or zero. Then, with obvious meanings of symbols,

$$(1+r)\mathbf{A}_{12}\mathbf{p}_2 + w\mathbf{l}_1 = [\mathbf{I} - (1+r)\mathbf{A}_{11}]\mathbf{p}_1$$

which is impossible since $\mathbf{e}^T[\mathbf{I} - (1+r)\mathbf{A}_{11}]\mathbf{p}_1 > 0$ whereas $(1+r)\mathbf{e}^T\mathbf{A}_{12}\mathbf{p}_2 + w\mathbf{e}^T\mathbf{l}_1 \leq 0$. Hence no price can be positive. Similarly it is proved that no price can be negative.

3 If $q_1 \leq 2\left(k - \sqrt{hk}\right)(k-h)^{-1}$, then $\lambda(\mathbf{q}) = k(2-q_1)q_1^{-1}$. Further $\lambda(\mathbf{q})\mathbf{e}_1^T\phi(\mathbf{q}) - \mathbf{e}_1^T\mathbf{A}^T\phi(\mathbf{q}) > 0$ if and only if $q_1 < (1-\varepsilon)^{-1}$ whereas $\lambda(\mathbf{q})\mathbf{e}_2^T\phi(\mathbf{q}) - \mathbf{e}_2^T\mathbf{A}^T\phi(\mathbf{q}) > 0$ for $q_1 \leq 2\left(k - \sqrt{hk}\right)(k-h)^{-1}$, provided that inequalities (2) hold.

References

Kurz, H. D. and Salvadori, N. (1993) The 'Standard Commodity' and Ricardo's Search for an 'invariable measure of value', in M. Baranzini and G. C. Harcourt (eds), *The Dynamics of the Wealth of Nations. Growth, Distribution and Structural Change*, London: Macmillan. Reprinted in Kurz, H. D. and Salvadori, N. (1998) *Understanding Classical Economics*, London and New York: Routledge, 123–147.

Kurz, H. D. and Salvadori, N. (2001) Sraffa and the Mathematicians: Frank Ramsey and Alister Watson, in T. Cozzi and R. Marchionatti (eds), *Piero Sraffa's Political Economy. A Centenary Estimate*, London and New York: Routledge, 254–284. Reprinted in Kurz, H. D. and Salvadori, N. (2003) *Classical Economics and Modern Theory*, London and New York: Routledge, 187–214.

Kurz, H. D. and Salvadori, N. (2004) On the collaborarion between Sraffa and Besicovitch: the cases of fixed capital and non-basics in joint production, in *Piero Sraffa*, Rome: Accademia Nazionale dei Lincei, 255–301. Reprinted in Kurz, H. D. and Salvadori, N. (2007) *Interpreting Classical Economics*, London and New York: Routledge, 159–200.

Kurz, H. D. and Salvadori, N. (2008) On the collaboration between Sraffa and Besicovitch: the 'Proof of Gradient', in G. Chiodi and L. Ditta (eds) *Sraffa or an Alternative Economics*, Houndmills: Palgrave Macmillan, pp. 260–274. Reprinted in Kurz, H. D. and Salvadori, N. (2015) *Revisiting Classical Economics*, London and New York: Routledge, 125–141.

Lippi, M. (2008) Some observations on Sraffa and mathematical proofs, in G. Chiodi and L. Ditta (eds) *Sraffa or an Alternative Economics*, Houndmills: Palgrave Macmillan, pp. 243–252.

Salvadori, N. (2008) On a proof of Sraffa's, in G. Chiodi and L. Ditta (eds) *Sraffa or an Alternative Economics*, Houndmills: Palgrave Macmillan, pp. 253–259. Reprinted in Kurz, H. D. and Salvadori, N. (2015) *Revisiting Classical Economics*, London and New York: Routledge, 93–101.

Sraffa, P. (1960) *Production of Commodities by Means of Commodities*, Cambridge: Cambridge UP.

11 Piero Sraffa's early work on joint production

Probing into the intricacies of multiple-product systems

Heinz D. Kurz and Neri Salvadori

Original paper: Heinz D. Kurz and Neri Salvadori (2014) Piero Sraffa's early work on joint production: probing into the intricacies of multiple-product systems in Fabrice Tricou and Daniella Leeman (eds), *Économie mathématique et Histoire: Hommage à Christian Bidard*, 55–73. Paris: Presses universitaires de Paris Ouest.

11.1 Introduction

In his essay 'Is von Neumann square?' Christian Bidard (1986) showed that, flukes apart, in the von Neumann model (von Neumann 1945) the number of processes operated equals the number of commodities the prices of which have to be ascertained and are positive. Christian variously compared the von Neumann approach to joint production with that of Sraffa (1960) and pointed out similarities and differences. Sraffa had dealt with cases of joint production as early as the late 1920s, but at the time within the framework of Marshall's demand and supply analysis. Marshall ([1890] 1920: see Chap. VI, §§4 and 6, and Mathematical Appendix, Note XX) had closed the system in terms of given functions or schedules of the (relative) demand for the two products that were produced jointly in fixed or variable proportions, the case of two joint products being the conventional workhorse of the analysis. (See also Sraffa's reference to Marshall in Section 11.2 below.) In this case the system is closed, that is, it has as many equations as unknowns to be determined, even if there is only a single process available producing jointly two products: the demand side conceived of as given demand functions based on utility considerations steps in to close the system (see Kurz 1986).

Sraffa, as is well known, felt that Marshall's approach to value and distribution was flawed. In his view the Classical *physical real cost* approach had been prematurely abandoned and replaced by a theory, in which the 'forces' of demand and supply were seen to determine price and quantity. However, it was Sraffa's conviction that this theory could not be sustained. He was keen to reformulate the Classical approach by shedding the weaknesses in the form in which it had been handed down by authors from Adam Smith to David Ricardo and by elaborating on its strengths.

DOI: 10.4324/9781003138709-14

A litmus test of the quality of the reformulated theory was whether it was able to deal with all cases of material production, including joint production proper, fixed capital, and the use of renewable and exhaustible resources, in a coherent way.

A bit more should perhaps be said about the analytical context in which Sraffa at first referred to joint products in his own reconstructive work. It was right at the time when he turned from his '1st equations', which concerned the case of single production without a surplus (that is, an economy that produces just as much as it necessarily uses up), to his '2nd equations', which were designed to cover the case of an economy with a surplus. In a note dated November 1927, he wrote:

> If we try to introduce surplus, the equations become contradictory, because the sum of the terms on the left is greater than the sum on the left {sic}: there is no solution for the system. This means that the problem is overdetermined {sic}: we must either drop one of the equations or add an unknown (*either an industry has joint products*, one of them being the surplus, so that we can drop an equation{,} or we add as an unknown the rate of interest: if this is feasible we can have different surpluses in different industries.)
>
> (D3/12/11: 17; emphasis added)[1]

In the margin of the conditional Sraffa added a bold straight line and the remark 'THE SOLUTION'. The first possibility allowed him, or so he thought, to tuck away the surplus product and thus reduce the system to one which by construction has no surplus (see on this Kurz 2012: Section 4). The second one was the one he eventually adopted, thus putting the joint products approach in systems with single production on one side. The marginalist approach to joint production is mentioned in the following document, which was probably composed at around the same time as the one just referred to. What is interesting with respect to it is that Sraffa there invoked the *Rule of Free Goods*:

> Joint products: they are always assumed to be slightly variable, and therefore to have a marg. cost (both cover the whole: Wicksteed, or Euler){.} Well, as we are in const. returns, that is the cost of each. If absolutely invariable, probably only one would have a price: the one which is not wanted (at whatever price) in that amount, would be gratis.
>
> (D3/12/11: 25)

Sraffa worked on the reformulation of the Classical theory of value and distribution essentially during three periods. He began his (re-)constructive work in the second half of the 1920s and began to formulate his systems of equations in the autumn and winter of 1927–1928. He had to interrupt his work when around the turn of 1931 he decided to devote all his energy to the Ricardo edition. To this task the Royal Economic Society had appointed him at the beginning of 1930. Sraffa had then been working on the problems of fixed capital and land. He intended to return to them as soon as possible after having accomplished the editorial task.[2] In the works of Marshall, Marx, Malthus, and James Mill he had come across the idea that what is left of a fixed capital good at the end of the production period could be considered a joint product to the main product. However, he at first rejected this idea because he felt that it blurred the concepts of physical real cost and thus of surplus (see Kurz and Salvadori 2005). When Sraffa in 1942 eventually was able go back to his old notes and take up the argument where he had left it, he quickly saw that he had prematurely set aside the idea under consideration. Between 1942 and the late summer of 1943 he managed to solve the problem of durable instruments of production to his satisfaction with the help of his 'mathematical friend' Abram S. Besicovitch, developing the joint products approach (see Kurz and Salvadori 2005).

Simultaneously Sraffa began to ponder the case of joint production proper of the 'wool and mutton, or wheat and straw' variety (Sraffa 1960, p. 63).[3] This he did from November 1942 onwards (see Sraffa Papers, folder D3/12/28). He saw quickly that the case of multiple-product industries was a great deal more difficult than the case of single-product industries and exhibited certain remarkable properties not encountered in the latter. He worked hard on the case of joint production proper up until around 1946, when he had to abandon his project once again on behalf of the Ricardo edition. It was only in the second half of the 1950s that he could return to his respective studies. He then saw that in important respects his earlier analysis could not be sustained and that a deeper investigation of the problems was necessary. For a detailed account of the development of Sraffa's thoughts on the matter, see Kurz and Salvadori (2004).

In this chapter we scrutinise Sraffa's early work on joint production. We show that already in the first half of the 1940s he arrived at results that would enter into chapter VII, 'Joint Production', and chapter IX, 'Other Effects of Joint Production', of his 1960 book. While he also started to work on the Standard system with joint production, the theme of chapter VIII, he did not arrive at a convincing solution. In particular he did not see that the distinction between basic and non-basic products had to be newly defined in the case of joint production. This he accomplished only in the third period of his reconstructive work in the second half of the 1950s (see Kurz and Salvadori 2004: Section 5).

Before we enter into a discussion of the issues at hand two facts deserve mentioning. First, Sraffa had the habit of re-reading his manuscripts at later dates and adding comments on them. Thus we find jottings from the 1950s in his papers and notes written in the 1940s. Second, during his internment in a prisoner of war camp on the Isle of Man in 1940 Sraffa read the reprint of the English translation by S. Moore and E. Aveling of the third German edition of volume I of *Das Kapital* (Marx 1938). He was apparently struck by the parallelism between his work and that of Marx, which is reflected in his use of Marxian concepts such as 'value' (as opposed to price) or 'constant capital' (produced means of production).

It is now useful to summarise briefly the content of the second part of Sraffa's 1960 book, which is devoted to multiple-product industries. This allows us to specify, which sections of the book are covered by the notes we will review here. (For the reader's convenience, we will refer also to other papers by us, in which we discuss other notes by Sraffa that contribute to a better understanding of the making of *Production of Commodities*.)

Part II of *Production of Commodities* is subdivided in five chapters and altogether 42 sections. The last two chapters (X and XI) are devoted to Fixed Capital and Land, respectively (see Kurz and Salvadori 2004, Section 4, and 2005, for a reconstruction of the role played by Besicovitch in the elaboration of Chapter X). Chapter VIII deals with the construction of the Standard system in joint production. This required a new definition of basic and non-basic commodities (see Kurz and Salvadori 2004, Section 5, again for the role Besicovitch played in this). The material we review in the present paper relates to Chapters VII and IX. Chapter VII introduces the problem of joint production. In particular in Section 50 Sraffa argues that the number of processes should be equal to the number of commodities. This argument took shape in 1942-1943 as the material below shows and was partly confirmed by the literature subsequent to the publication of Sraffa's 1960 book (see also Bidard 1986). Chapter IX is devoted to the following problems: (i) the specification of the quantities of labour embodied in jointly produced commodities (Sections 66 and 67); (ii) the Reduction to dated quantities of labour (Section 68, but Section 79 of Chapter X is also relevant in this respect); (iii) the possibility of negative prices (Sections 69–72), where special attention is given to (iv) the perplexing case of negative quantities of labour (Section 70).

11.2 Closing the system of production equations

The first document of interest to us Sraffa drafted on 2 November 1942. He wrote:

> Joint Products
>
> If one branch of production produces more than one commodity, some additional conditions are required to determine the necessary price.
>
> But it should be noticed that the problem is not merely that of splitting up the joint cost of production and allotting to each of the [joint] products [its due] the proportion that belongs to it.[4] This would be so only in the case that all the commodities jointly produced entered only into human consumption, and not in the production of other commodities. But that, in general is not the case. All the costs of

commodities in the production of which directly or indirectly there enter jointly produced commodities become indeterminate; and in general all prices will become indeterminate if there are a number of jointly produced commodities.

Thus a sheep farmer produces sheep that he sells to the butcher and wool that he sells to the wool merchant /spinner/. Of these sheep are among the commodities that he uses for production, but wool is not; therefore it is impossible to determine the joint cost of the sheep and wool produced in a year without knowing at the same time the separate cost of the sheep.[5]

On the back of the page Sraffa added:

> In so far as this is a criticism of Marshall, it fails.[6] For, if 2 commodities were rigidly jointly supplied, he would have, for n commods., n demand equations + $n - 1$ supply equations, to determine n prices and $n - 1$ (*not* n) quantities: for, given the quantity of one of the two joint commods., the other follows directly from the fixed proportion in which they are produced.
>
> (D3/12/28: 3)

On 12 January Sraffa composed the following note, in which he raised a number of questions, which he tackled in the following months:

> Joint Products + Fixed Cap.
>
> Q. How do we deal with these?
>
> A. By the compounding equations.
>
> Q. And how do we carry out Reduction?
>
> A. By solving for $r = 0$ and thereby finding the true quantities of L {labour}.
>
> Q. But solving for $r = 0$ gives only the total quantities of the Ls, not the distribution of each among the ns. Cannot this be found?
>
> A. It ought to be possible to find it. And the reason is this. Suppose that (our hypothesis being verified) the compounding equations are solved for *all* the possible values of r. Then we know the p of each commodity as a function of r. Now such a function can, in general, correspond to only *one* particular distribution of the L among the ns; therefore, given the function, the distribution is determined. The problem thus has two steps: 1st, give a method for actually finding this distribution, by using the function obtained by the solutions for all values of r; 2nd, find this distribution *independently* of the solution for all values of r.
>
> Now such an independent solution is obtained, in the simple case of circ. cap., by substitution. But this method is not available with joint products (including Fix. Cap. in compound. eq.^{s})
>
> (D3/12/30: 84)

The next day he turned to the problem of defining the value of a commodity, that is, the quantity of labour needed in its production, and pointed out a difference between the case of single and that of joint production. He stated:

> Quantity of Labour + Value (Define)
>
> In the original scheme I have two independent ways for measuring the q. of lab. contained in a commodity: 1) "tracing back" (+ finding the quant. of lab. used directly + indirectly (i.e. Reduction); and 2) solving the equations for $r = 0$.
>
> Consequently I can say that the q. of lab. (measured according to 1) determines value (measured acc. to 2).
>
> But with Joint Products the matter is different. The method 2 is still open, but method 1 is not. Therefore, if I continue to speak of q. of lab. determining value, I am making a tautology, for the two things are not measured independently.

Actually, Sraffa's proposition turned out to be wrong: while method 2 is still possible, provided the number of processes of production equals the number of prices of products to be ascertained, method 1, the Reduction to dated quantities of labour does not work any longer, as Sraffa was to discover soon. He continued:

> Quantity of Labour: Definition.
>
> I must now put my cards on the table.
>
> What we do is this:
>
> First, we take the ordinary notion of "quantity of labour contained in a commodity", when it is produced by "unaided" labour.
>
> Then we extend it to the case of a commodity produced by labour + other commodities (say, raw materials), which however in their turn are produced by unaided labour. And we call it the quantity of labour "directly + indirectly" entering into that commodity.
>
> Then we extend it to the case where all commodities are made by labour with other commodities. Here the "tracing back" operation has no end – it involves us in the summation of an infinite series. And we call "q. of labour" the limit of this sum.
>
> This is quite a big step + is on the very borderline of the ordinary notion: in fact it can be said to have one foot inside it + the other outside. For what we do is this. We set up a system of equations, in which each comm. produced is equated to the quantities of labour + commod.[s] used in its production. Then our "tracing back" process consists in successive substitutions of the commodities with their equations; when carried to the limit this is a method of solution of the system of equations. And we define the *ratios* (?) of the

solutions as the quantities of labour. This method of solution has an evident resemblance with the "ordinary notion" definition of q. of lab. as used in the preceding examples; + the extension appears quite natural.

But there is another, direct, method of solution of the system of equations, which gives of course the same results, but by a shorter route. This however has no resemblance with the "ordinary notion"; yet, the ratios of the roots, by whatever method obtained, are defined as the quantities of labour. These ratios are also the values at which the products must be exchanged if the process has to be reproduced. Thus the proposition: "the values when $r = 0$ are proportional to the quantities of labour contained in the various commodities" is a definition of the quantities of labour; or, alternately, a definition of the values. (It may be noted that the fact that they are defined in terms of one another does not imply that value + q. of lab. are "the same thing" – any more than the kilogram + the litre are "the same thing" for being defined in terms of one another.)

[In this I should have brought in *r*, Reduction, and solution for $r = 0$ as equivalents. Here, with circ. cap. the "tracing back" still corresponds

We must notice that in this case the actual "tracing back" is impossible. Yet, the limit is accepted as the measure of the labour contained.

Having gone so far, we now extend the definition to all cases, including those in which the "ordinary notion" cannot be applied accurately, or not even imagined: the quantity of labour contained in a commodity is proportional to the roots of the equations of production for $r = 0$, in other words to its value.

When we come to the next extensions, to fixed capital and to joint products, a greater effort of abstraction is required. There is however a difference between the two cases: for fixed capital, some people may think that there is no insuperable (great) difficulty in accepting the idea that the quantity of labour that passes into the product of a machine lasting *n* years with constant efficiency is $1/n$ of that originally contained in the machine. While for joint products no intuitive support is available. However, Wicksell finds an "insuperable" difficulty in applying the principle of "previously done labour" (Lect. I, 260) in the case of fixed capital.[7] "Clearly {it is then quite impossible to decide how much of the previously invested labour resources still remain 'stored-up' in the capital-good.} in f.n., with W's last sentence.[8] (It is remarkable how W. readily accept {sic} a "concrete significance" in the differential as a measure of the quantity of labour. Clearly it is a question of mental habit, + it would be idle to try + persuade another man that a notion is "intuitive". But one can prove whether it is self-contradictory.)

On 22 January 1943 he added:

> N.B. The solutions of the equations are a set of numbers. These numbers measure: a) the values for $r = 0$, b) the quantities of labour for all cases [which, of course, are independent of *r*].
>
> To say that the values, for $r = 0$, are proport. to quantities of labour is only an equivalent expression for the above.
>
> But the two interpretations of the solutions are not on the same footing. The first corresponds to a real event which *only* actually takes place in the one case when $r = 0$. The second corresponds to a real event (q. of lab. performed) which *always* takes place, whatever the *r*. – Thus the solution of the equations for $r = 0$ has a totally different importance from the solution for *r* equal to any other one number, say.06 or 6 per cent.[9] This solution only represents an event when *r* actually is.06.
>
> (D3/12/33: 83 (1–6))

11.3 Is the system square?

The question of whether, and on which grounds, it can be assumed that there are as many equations as there are unknowns to be ascertained kept bothering Sraffa. On 11 March 1943 he wrote:

> It may be objected: You say "If 2 commodities are produced jointly we need 2 independent equations, i.e. the pair must be produced by 2 different methods, each of which produces the two in different proportions." Now I quite see that that would suit you, that it would enable you to solve your problem: but there is nothing to allow you to assume that you will be so lucky, that you will find that in fact there are 2 equations, just as required, neither more nor less. Why could'nt {sic} there be 3, or 4, or 26? And why couldn't there be only one?

To emphasise the importance of these questions he put a straight red line in the margin of the passage.

> Now, as to the 1st question, it can be proved that there cannot be more than 2: i.e. that if the conditions of equal profits + equal prices are to be satisfied not more than two methods of production can be employed – of three or more methods, all, except two, will be less profitable + therefore will not be employed, at any one moment (i.e. at any one value of *r*).
>
> As to the second question, it is conceivable that only one method is known: therefore the thing can only be shown to be probable. Ruling out "impossible" methods, i.e. methods which at *all* values of *r* are less profitable, it can be shown that if there are two possible methods, they

will be compatible over a certain range of values of r [range which is the wider, the wider the difference in proportion of the two commodities produced by the two methods?]; and if a limited number of alternative methods are known they will easily cover all values of r.[10]

Note that this depends on the fact that until two methods are not found the two prices are variable: + they are adjusted, up to the limit of possibility, so as to make two methods equally profitable.

Note also that it involves a much smaller number of methods known than does the drawing of a continuous supply curve (which involves an "infinite" number).

[N.B. This calls for the consideration of the problem: if various possible methods of production are known, how is the solution found? i.e. how can the methods {be} determined *before* (i.e. simultaneously with) the prices are known?]

(D3/12/28: 2)

The answer is, of course, that methods and prices are determined together with one another. This Sraffa establishes in the following period. At the time he is keen to reformulate the joint-products equations in such a way that they can be compared to single-product equations, not least in order to see whether the properties of the latter carry over to the former. The main property under consideration is whether the 'Reduction to dated quantities of labour' can be applied to them. In a note composed on 22 March 1943 he writes:

I have said somewhere[11] that wool is not necessary to produce sheep but sheep are necessary to produce wool: therefore that the determination of value does not consist in separating (allotting) a given joint cost, for the cost is not "given" until we know the value of sheep.

Along this passage there is a red straight line in the margin. Sraffa continues:

Now it is not exact that wool does not "enter into the cost" of sheep – it enters negatively: in effect to produce a sheep, some wool must be produced while it grows up, as a bye-product, inevitably: this must be sold + its proceeds deducted from the cost of the sheep – thus a negative "cost".

Thus we can write the two equations (both for sheep + wool, in different proportions) in this form: in one we transfer the wool produced, from the right to the left with minus sign – in the other we transfer the sheep produced, from right to left making it negative. If we abstract from the sign (which does not affect the procedure of solution) each of these two equations for sheep + wool is in every respect similar to the equation for any ordinary commodity (not jointly produced). Or rather, they are similar to the two equations of two

> commodities which are produced separately (i.e. have each an equation of its own)[12] but which enter into one another's production – e.g. coal + iron. The same difficulties are found in these, since the cost of production of coal includes the price of coal (through iron). The equations are solved in the same way. And in the same way it is possible to apply Reduction to joint products, only having negative terms.
>
> (D3/12/28: 1)

He clearly saw that there will be negative terms in the Reduction equation. Does this in the end render this method inapplicable in the case of joint production? For a while he thought that this was not the case. He was, in fact, not easily prepared to give up this method, because it was the only one, he was convinced, that allowed one to ascertain the direct and indirect amounts of labour needed to produce one unit of a commodity in a direct and clear manner; he in fact called it 'the source of the identification of Values with quantities of labour' (see D3/12/36: 7(1) dated 8 March 1944). The other methods – the solution of the system of equations for $r = 0$ and the sub-system method (which he traced back to Marx; see D3/12/35: 35) – while yielding the same result, lacked that concreteness and vividness that is characteristic of the Reduction method.

11.4 The inapplicability of the Reduction method

This point is a delicate one. The problem Sraffa raises in the notes we review here is something we could call the imputation of the prices of commodities to dated quantities of labour. Sraffa attempted to tackle it in terms of what he called the 'Reduction method'. After long disquisitions he convinced himself that the method, which performed well in the case of single production, cannot be applied in the case of joint production, because it did not lead to a sequence that would converge. Actually, the problem of imputation can be solved even if the Reduction has no solution. Here is the obvious solution.

Start from, in obvious notation,

$$\mathbf{Bp} = (1+r)\mathbf{Ap} + w\mathbf{l}$$

to obtain

$$\mathbf{p} = (1+r)\mathbf{B}^{-1}\mathbf{Ap} + w\mathbf{B}^{-1}\mathbf{l}$$

(assuming that $\mathbf{B}^{-1}$ exists) and then

$$\mathbf{p} = w\mathbf{B}^{-1}\mathbf{l} + w(1+r)\mathbf{B}^{-1}\mathbf{AB}^{-1}\mathbf{l} + w(1+r)^2\left(\mathbf{B}^{-1}\mathbf{A}\right)^2\mathbf{B}^{-1}\mathbf{l} + \ldots$$
$$+ w(1+r)^t\left(\mathbf{B}^{-1}\mathbf{A}\right)^t\mathbf{B}^{-1}\mathbf{l} + \ldots$$

The problem of imputation thus has a solution. But the Reduction may not work, since $\lim_{t\to\infty}(1+r)^t\left(\mathbf{B}^{-1}\mathbf{A}\right)^t$ may not exist, or may be different from **0**, or, in any case, the series is not converging. The Sraffa of 1960 was aware of this and, in fact, produced, in Section 79, an example involving fixed capital in which the labour coefficients are alternately positive and negative, but increasing in absolute value.[13]

However, Sraffa eventually, in the 1950s after a long struggle with the subject, convinced himself that the method could not be sustained in the joint-products case. Doubts to this effect are sounded as early as 30 July 1943. Joint products (the reference is to the case with just two jointly produced things), he stresses,

> involve always that there are two methods of production (two equations) in which the two commodities are produced in different proportions.
>
> The first difficulty, with sheep + wool, is that sheep "enter into" their cost, + wool does not. The solution for $r = 0$ seems to provide an answer to this, for we now know how much labour is contained "separately" in a sheep. This, however{, } is not enough, as we do not know its distribution by Periods of Rotation. ^{m}See Note on page b_2 {see below (9)}^{m} {Adds to para:} {There are really 2 difficulties: a) we don't know how the labour in a sheep is distributed by Periods; b) we don't know how a unit of labour is distrib. between sheep + wool}[14]
>
> The simplest supposition that offers itself, is to assume that each unit of labour that enters the joint product is distributed between the two products according /in proportion to/ their value.
>
> There are 2 equations for sheep plus wool, + we shall call them I and II.
>
> Take I + carry out the solution and Reduction according to this rule; whenever in the cost we find a sheep we reduce it according to equation I itself. Thus we obtain a result which may appear satisfactory. We note however that it is based on Values obtained by the solution of the system of equations, including II: thus although in the Reduction we have not used II, the result is not independent of II – in fact it entirely depends on it: if II were different we should have obtained a different result in the Reduction of I.
>
> (D3/12/34: 8)

Sraffa continues:

> These are two separate problems:
>
> 1) The first arises in the general case' even if both the commodities jointly produced are used only for consumption, so that neither enters directly or indirectly in the joint production.
>
> In this case the aggregate cost of production of each of the two methods is determined *independently* of the way in which it is divided and allotted separately to the two products. In other words, given *one*

> of the two equations + the general conditions of the system, its cost /i.e. Q. of Lab./ (i.e. its Reduction) can be calculated independently of the other equation (i.e. *whatever* this other equation may be, on condition that it does not vary the system – + this allows a range of variation for the form of that equation).
>
> 2) The second arises if one, or both, of the two joint products enter directly or indirectly in their own production.[15] In this case it is clear that the aggregate cost (i.e. Quantity of Labour, i.e. Reduction) directly *depends* on the distribution of the cost between the two products. And since this depends on both equations, the Quantity of Labour contained in one method (the method being unchanged) will vary with variations in the form of the other equation.
>
> (D3/12/34: 9)

Sraffa then argues that we do have two reduction equations for sheep and two for wool, which 'contain (that is our starting point) equal Qs. of L.', which, however, 'are differently distributed among P{eriod}s of Rot{ation}. This does not affect their values (for $r = 0$) which are equal'. He adds:

> But, here is the question: will their prices, calculated from the Reductions, be equal for all values of *r*? for clearly these are affected by the distribution among P. of Rot.
>
> Obviously they will not be equal: thus the result we get via solution for $r = 0$ and Reduction is different from that which we obtain by direct solution for the various values of *r* – for by this method the two prices of sheep were always equal.
>
> The reason for the discrepancy is this: The Reduction, for each equation, gives the same identical distribution for sheep + for wool, it does so ex hypothesi, for that is the method we have adopted. Therefore the relative price of sheep + wool is the same for all values of *r*.
>
> But this is contrary to the basis of the system, which requires variability of this relative price. For, equations I + II represent two different methods, + therefore for different *r*s their aggregate products will have different relative prices: and the equality of the two separate prices of sheep and of their two separate prices of wool is secured by varying the relative price of sheep in terms of wool.
>
> E.g. suppose that method I produces a larger proportion of sheep to wool than does II; and suppose also that with the increase of *r* the aggregate price of I rises relatively to II: it follows that the equality of the two prices of sheep will be maintained when *r* increases by an increase in the price of sheep relatively to wool.
>
> Thus the Reduction is worthless.
>
> (D3/12/34: 10–11)

Yet in a note added on 5 February 1955 to the document he seems to have still not been convinced that this is in fact the case.

Sraffa's above considerations appear to have led him to the finding that (labour) values need not be strictly positive. In a folder with notes composed between September 1943 and January 1944 he discusses this problem and the possibility of having only one joint products equation but two equations using one of the joint products in single-products processes of production. We deal only with Sraffa's discussion of the case of negative values, which foreshadows §66 of his 1960 book.

11.5 Negative values

As Sraffa stressed, when two methods are used by means of which two products can be produced jointly, no assumption as to their 'productiveness' is made. However, if $r = 0$ the lack of competitiveness of one of the methods is reflected in a negative value of one of the products. This does not mean that the two methods cannot be employed side by side for values of $r > 0$. Sraffa is of the opinion that in order to explain the compatibility of the two methods at some levels of r and their incompatibility at some other levels one needs the Reduction method. It allows one to trace back the value ($r = 0$) or price ($r > 0$) of the products to sequences of dated quantities of labour spent in the production of the products, which have to be discounted forward at the given rate of profits ($r \geq 0$). This is why Sraffa wishes to hold firmly to the Reduction method. He expounds on 27 September 1943 in a note entitled 'negative Values':

> So long as we consider a system where each commodity is produced by a separate process, and where all capital is circulating capital, there is no difficulty in supposing that r may take the value 0,[16] or any other arbitrary value – in spite of the fact that this particular technical system of production exists in a situation in which r has a particular value which is different from the one arbitrarily assumed. We can do this, because it involves no *internal* contradiction. It is true that, if r actually had the arbitrarily assumed value, different technical methods would be adopted; but these alternative methods exist only as hypothetical possibilities, and they are therefore not part of the actual system of production, which alone is represented by the system of equations.

Sraffa puts a straight line in the margin of the last two sentences. A few days later, on 2 October, he adds:

> When we consider joint products however the position is different. The two methods of production which are used to produce jointly two commodities are compatible with one another over a certain range of values of r. But outside that range they are inconsistent, in the sense that there is no pair of prices for the two products which, given w, will give the same rate of profits to the two capitals employed in the two methods.

> This difficulty has nothing to do with the fact that there may be alternative methods which, at any value of *r* different from the one ruling in the circumstances considered, would be cheaper than one or both {of} the methods described by the equations, + consequently would be adopted. The difficulty would arise if no such hypothetical alternative methods were available at all. It arises when we assume that, while *w* is varied, no change takes place in the coefficients of our equations, i.e. in the methods of production. It arises therefore purely from the internal conditions of our system of equations, which appear to become self-contradictory when the value of *r* moves outside the range in which the two methods of production are compatible.

There is a straight line in the margin of the last sentence. Sraffa continues:

> This can be shown best by an example.
>
> Suppose that by method I, for each sheep produced for slaughter, there are produced 30 lb of raw wool; and by method II, for each sheep produced, there are 25 lb of wool.
>
> And that, by solving the equations for $r = 0$ {later he adds: [This *must* be obtained by Reduction, *not* by solution]}, we find that the quantity of labour embodied in the aggregate product of method I is less than the quantity embodied in that of method II.
>
> It is clear that the two methods are only compatible when the aggregate price of the product of method I is larger than that of the product of method II: and if this happens, say, for the range of *r* comprised between 5% and 10%; that is because the component parts of the two quantities of labour are distributed in time in such ways that give that result.

In the margin of this passage he adds the following *nota bene*:

> N.B. Here, instead of this, an example should be used which involves *only* circ. cap., + not fixed as sheep inevitably do. Then, we can talk at once, without begging the question, of labour embodied in aggreg. product.

The main text continues:

> When $r = 0$, and the commodities exchange at values which are proportional to the q. of lab. contained, it becomes impossible to continue producing under method II. Our system becomes contradictory.
>
> This contradiction however arises from the fact that we are imagining that the exchange may actually take place under methods which in fact exist in circumstances in which *r* has a particular (?not determined) value different from 0. However, while the picture of

exchange actually taking place at $r = 0$ facilitates our understanding, its possibility is not essential to our argument.

We require the Values, in the first place, as an auxiliary for the solution of the equations: in this capacity they form only an intermediate step in our calculation + they disappear from the final result.

Now, so long as we think of Values as ratios at which commodities are in fact exchanged in the market, they must obviously be all positive. But when we use them only as auxiliaries in a calculation there can be no difficulty in admitting that they may be negative numbers.

As soon as we admit negative Values the contradiction is resolved. In the example above, if wool is regarded as having a negative Value, then it is possible for the aggregate product of method I to be smaller than that of method II. And there will be a particular negative Value of wool which will make the two aggregate values proportional to the two quantities of labour. (34 (3))[17]

In the second place we require the Values as a measure of the relative quantities of labour contained in commodities.

After having considered in the above case [when corrected] Joint Products neither of which is used in *own* production, now examine the case when one of the products (sheep) is also used as constant capital. The difficulty is that Reduction is impossible, without having first the solution; and after solution, it becomes unnecessary.

(D3/12/35: 34(1–3); emphases added)

Sraffa does not leave things at that, but in the following weeks is, inter alia, keen to provide a more intuitively accessible explanation of negative values. On 29 November 1943 he asks:

What does it mean that a commodity has a negative value? If the commod. is taken in isolation, nothing. But if it is produced jointly with other commodities, and a given quantity of labour is bestowed on their joint production, and it is found that the *other* commodities, taken by themselves, are found to contain more labour than has been bestowed on the lot, then the excess must be equal to the negative value of the first commodity. So that, taken as a whole, the group of jointly produced commodities contain exactly as much labour as has been spent on their production.

[N.B. The above must assume that the "neg.-value-commodity" is *not* used in the production of itself – otherwise it begs the question. This extension must be made later, by analogy]

But suppose that the neg.-value-commodity is also used, as means of production in the production of another commodity. Suppose society is composed of two branches of production, in one, 15 men (without any constant capital) produce jointly commodities A and B: the product A has a negative value of – 5 man-years, and the product

> B a positive value of 20 man-years: the sum of values, 15 man-years, agrees with the input. In the other branch of production 15 men, using as constant capital a quantity of *a* equal to A, produce the product C, which therefore has a value of 10 man-years. The aggregate product of society is thus 25 man-years: and it may be asked, how is it possible out of this product to pay the full wages of 30 men for a year?
>
> The answer is that only commodities *b* and *c* go into their consumption, and the aggregate value of these two is 30 man-years. We can visualise the exchange taking place thus. The first branch must sell to the second its whole output of *a*. As this has a negative value it will "receive a negative payment" for it; that is, it will have to make a positive payment. In order to deliver A (value – 5) it will have to give at the same time a value of 5 man-years of *c*: it will thus remain with 15*c*, with which it will pay its own wages. The second branch will use the – 5 man years contained in A to replace its constant capital, and will use its own product (C = 10 man years) plus the 5 man years of B received, or a total of 15 man-years to pay the wages of its own 15 men.
>
> (D3/12/35: 34(7–8))

Disenchanted with the finding that the Reduction method cannot be used in the case of joint production, Sraffa was on the lookout for an alternative. This 'third method' he found was what he later called the 'Sub system', which, he writes on 4 October 1943, 'is the one used by Old Moore' (D3/12/35: 35). (His friends called Marx that way because of his dark complexion.) In the same document Sraffa notices that it was not an independent new method, but that it actually replaced the method of simultaneous solution of the system of price equations. The latter, he insists, 'is not really a method for finding the quantity of labour: it gives numbers, which we find are *equal* to the quantities of labour given by Reduction, + so we conclude that it gives Q. of labour. But, in + by itself, it does not give them. On the other hand, the present method does give them – once we accept that Const. Cap. only reproduces its own value' (D3/12/35: 35-36).

In January 1944 (no precise date is given) Sraffa composes a note that foreshadows §70 of his 1960 book. The example of liability and debt he was to employ in the context of negative quantities in the Standard commodity in §56.

> Suppose that we say that the aggregate wealth of two brothers is £100, of which the elder has £150, and the second has a debt of £50 which he owes to his elder. We don't thereby assume the existence of "negative wealth". There is an aggregate wealth, necessarily positive, which we can measure directly. It is distributed among a number of individuals. In the distribution negative parts may appear.
>
> *The same for labour distributed between the joint products.*
>
> (D3/12/35: 40; emphasis added)

11.6 Concluding observations

The selection of passages from Sraffa's unpublished manuscripts in the beginning of the second period of his constructive work bear witness to his early probing steps into the difficult area of joint production. It shows that his treatment of pure joint production grew out of his analysis of durable instruments of production after he had adopted the joint-products method in 1942. In this year and the following Sraffa succeeded in elaborating several of the propositions contained in Chapter VII–IX of his book, including the possibility of negative (labour) values vis-à-vis strictly positive prices. As regards other problems, including the determination of relative prices and the maximum rate of profits, the Standard system and the distinction between basic and non-basic commodities, Sraffa was less successful and in important respects we have to wait until the second half of the 1950s to see him master some of the intricate problems with the help of his 'mathematical friend', Besicovitch (see Kurz and Salvadori 2004). It is interesting to note, however, that the necessity to deal with the problem of the choice of technique in systems with joint production (and fixed capital) made him see a possibility, which later, in the capital controversies of the 1960s and 1970s, became known as 'reverse capital deepening' or 'capital reversing'.[18] As early as 19 January 1944 Sraffa emphasises:

> The most important point in this discussion is the proof that the new method need not "employ more capital (however measured) + less labour" than the old one, as a result of fall in *r*. This contradicts the marg. prod. of capital theory.
>
> (D3/12/35: 7 (7))

Notes

1 References to the Sraffa Papers, which are kept at Trinity College, Cambridge, follow the catalogue prepared by Jonathan Smith, archivist. Since in his text Sraffa typically used both round and square brackets, all additions by us will be in wavy brackets, {}.

2 As we know, Sraffa at the time held the overly optimistic expectation that he would have to interrupt his re-constructive work, which culminated in his 1960 book (Sraffa 1960), only for a short period of time, three years at most. It was only in 1951 that he eventually managed to publish volumes I–IV of *The Works and Correspondence of David Ricardo.*

3 The wool and mutton case involved, of course, fixed capital (that is, sheep of different age), as Sraffa was to notice.

4 There are two straight lines in the margin along this statement.

5 There is straight line in red in the margin along the second statement.

6 The reference is to Marshall's discussion of joint production. Marshall had argued that demand schedules will bridge the gap, that is, satisfy the condition 'that our theory has as many equations as it has unknowns, neither more nor less' (Marshall 1922, Mathematical Appendix, note XXI).

7 The reference is to Wicksell (1934, vol. I, p. 260; SL 2095).

8 Sraffa does not provide the full quotation, but indicates where it has to be placed. The quotation reads: 'It is only at the margin of production that these quantities can be differentiated and have a concrete significance assigned to them' (Wicksell, 1934, vol. I, p. 260).
9 There are two straight lines in the margin of the last two sentences.
10 See also the remark added to the following document on 25 January 1955.
11 See note of 9 November 1942 (D3/12/28: 3–4) above.
12 There is a straight line in the margin of the preceding expression.
13 It may be interesting to note that Schefold (1976) has proved that for small levels of *r* another series converges (at least in the case of fixed capital with no jointly utilised machines):

$$\mathbf{p} = w(\mathbf{B}-\mathbf{A})^{-1}\mathbf{1} + wr(\mathbf{B}-\mathbf{A})^{-1}\mathbf{A}(\mathbf{B}-\mathbf{A})^{-1}\mathbf{1}$$
$$+wr^2\left((\mathbf{B}-\mathbf{A})^{-1}\mathbf{A}\right)^2(\mathbf{B}-\mathbf{A})^{-1}\mathbf{1}+$$
$$+\ldots+wr^t\left((\mathbf{B}-\mathbf{A})^{-1}\mathbf{A}\right)^t(\mathbf{B}-\mathbf{A})^{-1}\mathbf{1}+\ldots$$

14 Here the wavy brackets are Sraffa's.
15 {Sraffa appends the following footnote:} 'With the exception of the case in which they enter into each of the two methods of production in the same proportions as they are produced in that method: for this reduces to the case (1) + the cost of each method is independent of the distribution of the cost between the two products'.
16 {Sraffa adds the following footnote:} 'Here, and below, I really mean "that the rate of S{urplus}.V{alue}. is zero"; and therefore should say "that *w* is at its maximum".'
17 {Sraffa added two notes to this:} '*Note* 1 The larger the negative value of wool, the larger will be the positive value of sheep, so that the sum of the two will be proportional to the aggregate quantity of labour embodied'. {See, however, the remark of 6 February 1955 below.} '*Note* 2. If the quantity of labour embodied in the products of the two methods is equal, the Value of wool is 0.'
18 On capital reversing, see the discussion in Bidard (2004, chap. 9).

References

Bidard, Christian (1986). Is von Neumann square? *Journal of Economics*, 46(4): 407–419.

Bidard, Christian (2004). *Prices, Reproduction, Scarcity*. Cambridge: CUP.

Kurz, Heinz D. (1986). Classical and early neoclassical economists on joint production. *Metroeconomica*, 38(1): 1–37. Reprinted in H. D. Kurz, *Capital, Distribution and Effective Demand*, London 1990: Polity Press.

Kurz, Heinz D. (2012). Don't treat too ill my Piero! Interpreting Sraffa's papers. *Cambridge Journal of Economics*, 36: 1535–1569.

Kurz, Heinz D. and Salvadori, Neri (2004). On the Collaboration between Sraffa and Besicovitch: The Case of Fixed Capital and Non-Basics in Joint Production. *Atti dei Convegni Lincei* 2000, Accademia Nazionale dei Lincei, Rome, pp. 255–301. Reprinted in H.D. Kurz and N. Salvadori, *Interpreting Classical Economics*, Abingdon: Routledge, 2007, pp. 159–200.

Kurz, Heinz D. and Salvadori, Neri (2005). Removing an 'insuperable obstacle' in the way of an objectivist analysis: Sraffa's attempts at fixed capital. *European Journal of the History of Economic Thought*, 12(3): 493–523. Reprinted in H. D.

Kurz, L. L. Pasinetti and N. Salvadori (eds), *Piero Sraffa: The Man and the Scholar. Exploring his Unpublished Papers*, London: Routledge, 2008, pp. 119–149.

Marshall, Alfred ([1890] 1922). *Principles of Economics*, 8th edn., 1920. Reprinted 1922. London: Macmillan.

Marx, Karl (1938). *Capital*, vol. I, London: George Allen & Unwin. (SL 3731)

Neumann, John von (1945). A model of general economic equilibrium, *Review of Economic Studies*, 13: 1–9.

Schefold, Bertram (1976). Reduction to dated quantities of labour, roundabout processes, and switches of techniques in fixed capital systems, *Metroeconomica*, 28: 1–15.

Sraffa Piero (1960). *Production of Commodities by Means of Commodities*, Cambridge: Cambridge University Press.

Wicksell, Knut (1934). *Lectures on Political Economy*, vol. I, London: George Routledge & Sons. (SL 2095).

IV

Competition and monopoly

12 The Classical notion of competition revisited[1]

Neri Salvadori and Rodolfo Signorino

Original paper: Neri Salvadori and Rodolfo Signorino (2013) *The Classical notion of competition revisited*, History of Political Economy, 45:1, 149–175, DOI: 10.1215/00182702-1965222. Durham, North Carolina: Duke University Press.

The gravitation of market prices toward natural prices in all markets characterised by free competition was widely affirmed by the Classical authors, despite the lack of a formal proof. In the wake of the revival of interest in Classical economics fostered by the publication of *Production of Commodities by Means of Commodities* (Sraffa 1960), since the mid-1970s, a vast literature has blossomed concerning the stability of long-period equilibrium within multisectoral models of Classical inspiration. (For a survey of this literature, see Bellino 2011.) Besides the formal results achieved on the subject of stability, the debate on gravitation has stimulated an in-depth investigation of the Classical notion of market competition (Arena 1978; Semmler 1984; Steedman 1984; Dumenil and Levy 1987). This investigation has also highlighted some unsatisfactory aspects in the latter, particularly the actual process of market price determination in a situation of market disequilibrium:

> Little is said concerning the actual process [that governs the functioning of the market for commodities]. For example, it is not clear who is changing prices, what information is used, when this change occurs, what the outcome is on the market etc.
>
> (Dumenil and Levy 1987, p. 136)

> [L'originalita della teoria classica della libera concorrenza] non è pero in grado di nascondere certe insufficienze: l'economia politica classica si scontra infatti con il problema centrale dell'articolazione tra prezzi di mercato e prezzi naturali. La soluzione di queste difficolta richiede una nuova definizione di questa articolazione.
>
> (Arena 1978, p. 323)[2]

The aim of this chapter is to detect and highlight those elements present in Classical texts that may be fruitfully employed to overcome the above

DOI: 10.4324/9781003138709-16

drawbacks of the Classical view of market competition. Moreover, as recent commentators on Classical economics have emphasised, in a situation of disequilibrium, when the quantity of a given commodity brought to the market differs from Smithian effectual demand, the likely outcome is that of a dispersion of prices:

> Whereas natural price is by definition a singular magnitude for each kind of commodity, the competitive processes whereby market prices deviate from natural price under conditions of market imbalance are consistent with, indeed likely to cause, transactions at nonuniform prices. That is to say, market price as literally the actual prices at which transactions occur when there is such market imbalance, is not in general a singular magnitude.
>
> (Aspromourgos 2009, p. 72; see also pp. 85 and 88)

Accordingly, we claim that the Classical theory of market prices gives scope to the analysis of the behaviour of the agents acting in situations of market imbalance through some of the analytical tools and formal results achieved by the modern game-theoretic approach to oligopoly theory, namely, the notion of mixed (i.e., nondeterministic) price strategy.

In what follows, we distinguish and compare two different conceptions of market competition: the Walrasian notion of perfect competition and the Classical notion of free competition, focusing in particular on Adam Smith and Karl Marx. We stress that while the Walrasian notion may be described as an equilibrium state in which atomistic agents treat prices parametrically, the Classical notion is a situation in which agents employ their market power by setting prices strategically. The absence of a price-taking assumption in the Classical authors is the main reason why the theoretical difficulties besetting the Walrasian notion outside market-clearing equilibrium do not plague the Classical notion as well. Yet though for the Classical authors price undercutting and outbidding are the typical phenomena that occur in any market characterised by free competition, it is fair to say that they went no farther than to provide only some unsystematic guidelines on how to analyse in due detail the competitive process of market price determination. Among other things, we show that Marx's extensive use of metaphors and numerical examples hides the modern taxonomy of buyers' market, sellers' market, and mixed strategy equilibrium in the capacity space of a standard Bertrand duopoly model. In particular, we argue that Marx was conscious that between the buyers' market, in which the price is determined by the reservation price of sellers, and the sellers' market, in which the price is determined by the reservation price of buyers, there is something in which the price is not unique and any equilibrium can concern only distributions of probability (mixed strategies) on the behaviour of the traders. We substantiate this fact by using a formalism derived from the contemporary analysis of Bertrand competition. (The elements required to identify a necessary and sufficient condition to separate these three different market outcomes are sketched in an appendix.) We are aware that our analysis, once duly developed, needs to be related to the contemporary gravitation literature. Yet we defer investigation of this issue to a future paper.[3]

The structure of the article is as follows. Section 12.1 compares two different notions of the concept of market competition, the Classical notion of free competition and the neo-classical notion of perfect competition, and highlights some problematic aspects of the latter, absent in the former. Sections 12.2 and 12.3 assess the Classical theory of free competition, as developed by Adam Smith and Karl Marx, with particular concern for market price determination. Section 12.4 investigates how the Classical notion of competition has percolated into the modern literature on so-called Bertrand competition. Section 12.5 concludes.

12.1 Two different notions of market competition or just one?

Few commentators would disagree with the following statement: 'Although the concept of competition has always been central to economic thinking... it is one that has taken on a number of interpretations and meanings, many of them vague' (Vickers 1995, p. 3). In particular, John Vickers distinguishes the notion of perfect competition – a 'seemingly tranquil equilibrium state in which well-informed agents treat prices parametrically' from the 'original and "real" concept' of competition, a 'rivalrous behaviour with respect to prices and other variables in a world characterized by flux, uncertainty and disequilibrium' (p. 7).

Despite the differences between these two notions, many authors have come (more or less explicitly) to consider the Classical notion of free competition nothing but a primitive and pre-analytical version of the neo-classical theory of perfect competition, a version still imbued with casual empiricism:

> It is a remarkable fact that the concept of competition did not begin to receive explicit and systematic attention in the main stream of economics until 1871. This concept... was long treated with the kindly_ casualness with which one treats of the intuitively obvious 'Competition' entered economics from common discourse, and for long it connoted only the independent rivalry of two or more persons.
>
> (Stigler 1957, p. 1)

Such an interpretation has deeply influenced many of the leading exponents of neo-classical economics. (See, e.g., Arrow and Hahn 1971, in particular chapter 1, 'Historical Introduction', and Samuelson 1978.) Even outside the neo-classical camp this interpretation has found supporters such as Nicholas Kaldor (1972, p. 1241), when he claims that

> one can trace a more or less continuous development of price theory from the subsequent chapters of Smith [the fourth chapter of the *Wealth of Nations]* through Ricardo, Walras, Marshall, right up to Debreu and the most sophisticated of present-day Americans.

Vickers (1995, p. 7) himself concludes that 'the claim that there are two concepts of competition is somewhat misleading'.

Nonetheless, historians of economic thought who have endorsed an alternative point of view have not been lacking. Paul McNulty (1967, p. 397) not only argued that the Classical notion of competition as a behavioural process is radically different from the neo-classical notion of competition as an equilibrium state but also went so far as to claim that the neo-classical assumption of individual price-taking behaviour is entirely alien to the Classical analysis:[4] 'Smith's concept of competition was decidedly not one in which the firm was passive with respect to price but was, rather, one in which the market moved toward equilibrium through the active price responses of its various participants'. Therefore, what in the previous interpretation appears simply as a process of analytical refinement, in McNulty's view is no less than 'a basic conceptual change' (p. 397). Moreover, unlike Stigler, McNulty holds that the Classical notion of competition is far from being derived from casual empiricism. Smith is the great systematiser of the analysis of the concept of market competition carried out by a series of authors before him (most notably, Cantillon and Turgot), and his specific contribution was to raise the concept of competition to a 'general organizing principle of economic society. After Smith's great achievement, the concept of competition became quite literally the *sine qua non* of economic reasoning' (McNulty 1967, pp. 396–397; see also McNulty 1968, pp. 646–647).[5]

McNulty's interpretation raises the matter of investigating the theoretical conditions that have led to such a dramatic change of meaning in the original notion of competition. A first step in this direction may be found in the distinction between two different notions of economic science: (1) economics as the science that studies a system of forces and (2) economics as the science that studies a system of relations – a distinction introduced by Marco Dardi (1983) that was recently emphasised by Nicola Giocoli (2005):

> According to the system-of-forces (SOF) view, economics is a discipline whose main subject is the analysis of the economic processes

> generated by market and not-market forces, including-but by no means exclusively-the processes leading the system to an equilibrium. According to the system-of-relations (SOR) view, economics is a discipline whose main subject is the investigation of the existence and properties of economic equilibria in terms of the validation and mutual consistency of given formal conditions, but that has little if anything to say about the meaningfulness of these equilibria for the analysis of real economic systems.
>
> (Giocoli 2005, p. 180)

According to Giocoli, the SOF view was the dominant vision up to the years between the two world wars, while the SOR view gained popularity only in the second postwar period when considerable intellectual effort was devoted to the project of a full axiomatisation of economic science (p. 180). Similarly, in a series of papers, Blaug (1997, 2002, and 2003) indicated in the formalist revolution of the 1950s and the parallel rise to dominance of the Walrasian general equilibrium theory the two driving forces that led to the decline of the Classical (and early neo-classical) notion of competition as a process and its replacement with the modern notion of competition as an end-state (with the associated first and second fundamental theorems of welfare economics).

Thus it may be claimed that the semantic shift in the notion of competition is part of a more general process of redefining central categories and concepts of economic analysis started in the 1930s with the rediscovery of Walrasian general equilibrium theory (Donzelli 1990, chap. 9) and fully accomplished in the late 1970s with the rediscovery of the Nash equilibrium concept (Giocoli 2003, chap. 5): the Classical notion of market competition makes little sense outside the SOF view, while the Walrasian notion of competition perfectly fits the theoretical standards set by the SOR view.

There are at least two reasons why the distinction between the Classical notion of competition and the neo-classical one and a careful analysis of the theoretical domain of the latter is not simply a historiographical exercise:

1 The neoclassical theory of perfect competition carries with it some theoretical difficulties alien to the Classical notion of free competition.
2 The Classical notion of competition can be made analytically precise in terms of the modern concept of mixed strategies equilibrium.

The final part of this section is devoted to substantiating point 1 above, while we defer analysis of point 2 to Section 12.4.

As pointed out by Jerry Green (1974), every market equilibrium concept requires the specification of a consistent set of behavioural postulates that prescribe what happens in equilibrium and what happens outside equilibrium. In the Walrasian framework, the behavioural postulates that define the situation of equilibrium differ from those that define the adjustment mechanism in disequilibrium. As regards the former, the behavioural postulate is that every agent assumes market prices as parametrically given and, on the basis of such prices and other constraints, maximises his or her own objective function. By contrast, in disequilibrium, the behavioural postulate is that a meta-agent, the auctioneer, determines market prices according to market excess demands. Moreover, no transactions among the agents are allowed to take place during the adjustment process.[6] As a consequence, the price-taking behaviour assumption implies that each individual firm in a given market has no incentive to set a price different from the ruling market price and has no incentive to carry on transactions at a price other than the Walrasian market-clearing price. Thus, such an assumption drastically reduces the theoretical domain of the theory to equilibrium, market-clearing situations.[7]

To our knowledge, Kenneth Arrow (1959) was the first to highlight the logical difficulties besetting the neo-classical theory of perfect competition:

> the Law [of supply and demand, Arrow's equation 3: $dp/dt = h(S - D)$ with $h' < 0$ and $h(0) = 0$] is not on the same logical level as the hypotheses underlying equation 1 [$D = f(p)$ and $S = g(p)$]. It is not explained whose decision it is to change prices in accordance with equation 3.
>
> Each individual participant in the economy is supposed to take prices as given and determine his or her choices as to purchases and sales accordingly; there is no one left over whose job it is to make a decision on price.
>
> (Arrow 1959, p. 43)[8]

In short, for Arrow, in the perfect competition setup there is no place left for 'a rational decision with respect to prices', thus implying the conclusion that 'perfect competition can really prevail only at equilibrium' (p. 41). The solution proposed by Arrow to study market price dynamics outside market-clearing equilibrium consists in turning to the theory of monopoly: 'When supply and demand do not balance, even in an objectively competitive market, the individual firms are in the position of monopolists as far as the imperfect elasticity of demand for their products is concerned' (p. 46). However, Arrow claims that standard monopoly theory must be modified so as to remove the assumption that monopolists know perfectly their own demand curve (besides their own cost curves): 'Uncertainty [as to the demand curve] is a crucial consideration in the theory of monopolistic price adjustment' (p. 44). In such circumstances, monopolists will vary their own price, in a process of trial and error, until they find the price that maximises their expected profits.

For our purpose, the salient points of Arrow's analysis are the following:

1 Jevons's law of indifference, which states that there is only one price ruling in a competitive market, ceases to be valid in disequilibrium: 'Although the broad tendency will be for prices to rise when demand exceeds supply, there can easily be a considerable dispersion of prices among different sellers of the same commodity' (pp. 46–47).
2 By assuming that competition takes place on both sides of the market, that is, competition among sellers and competition among buyers, a buyers' market may be distinguished from a sellers' market:

> By a parallel argument each buyer on a market with an inequality between supply and demand can be regarded as a monopsonist....
>
> *In disequilibrium, the market consists of a number of monopolists facing a number of monopsonists.* The most general picture is that of a shifting set of bilateral monopolies In general, it is reasonable to suppose that if the selling side of the market is much more concentrated than the buying side, the main force in changing prices will be the monopolistic behavior of the sellers Similarly, if the buying side of the market is the more concentrated, as in non-unionized labor markets, the dynamics will come from that side.
>
> (p. 47; emphasis added)

In the following two sections we make it clear that these two elements of Arrow's contribution may be found in Smith's and, even more explicitly, in Marx's treatment of market prices, thus paving the way for a restatement of the Classical notion of competition through contemporary game-theoretic analysis.[9]

12.2 The Classical notion of free competition: Adam Smith

George Richardson (1975, pp. 350–351) has convincingly argued that

> competition features within *The Wealth of Nations* in two different contexts; first, in the account given of the balancing of supply and demand in particular markets, and, secondly, in the explanation of structural and technological development. Smith offers us in effect both a theory of economic equilibrium and a theory of economic evolution; and in each of these competition has a key role to play.

In what follows we concentrate on the static aspect of the Smithian notion of market competition, concerned with market price determination, leaving aside its dynamic aspect (see Lavezzi 2003).

As far as the Classical notion of market competition is concerned, the locus classicus is book 1, chapter 7, of Smith's ([1776] 1976) *Wealth of Nations (WN)*.[10] Smith's working assumption is that it is possible to classify the economic forces in action in a given moment into two broad categories, (1) those erratic and short-lived forces that determine the market values both of commodity prices and of the distributive variables and (2) those systematic and persistent forces that determine the natural values of the same magnitudes. Classical economists generally hold the view that only the latter can be the proper subject of scientific inquiry (Ciccone 1999, p. 70).[11]

The data from which the Smithian argument starts are the natural rates of wages, profits, and rents that, sectoral specificities apart, depend mainly on the conditions of prosperity of the economic system under scrutiny, its 'advancing, stationary, or declining condition' (*WN* I.vii.I). The natural price of (re)production of the various commodities derives from the summation of these three elements. The natural price is therefore a magnitude that is not immediately formed in the market but that, given some appropriate conditions, may come true in the market. Indeed, the natural price constitutes a sort of a floor for the market price in the sense that the latter cannot remain for long below the former without seriously jeopardising the reproduction of the commodity in question:

> The competition of the different dealers obliges them all to accept of [the natural price], but does not oblige them to accept of less.
>
> … The natural price, or the price of free competition,... is the lowest which can be taken, not upon every occasion, indeed, but for any considerable time together. ... [It] is the lowest which the sellers can commonly afford to take, and at the same time continue their business.
>
> (*WN* 1.vii.11, 27)

The theoretical importance of natural prices consists in providing a guide to the theorist for explaining the dynamic path followed by market prices:

> The natural price, therefore, is, as it were, the central price, to which the prices of all commodities are continually gravitating. Different accidents may sometimes keep them suspended a good deal above it, and sometimes force them down even somewhat below it. But whatever may be the obstacles which hinder them from settling in this center of repose and continuance, they are constantly tending towards it.
>
> (*WN* 1.vii.15)

To study the genesis of market prices and the existing relations between market prices and natural prices, Smith introduces the concept of *effectual demand*, that is, 'the demand of those who are willing to pay the natural price of the commodity' (*WN* I.vii.8.) It is to be stressed that the relationship between the quantity brought to the market and the effectual demand determines only the market price of a commodity and not also its natural price.[12] Moreover, 'demand' and 'supply' are treated by Smith as given quantities and not as functional relationships between price and quantity characterised by well-defined formal properties, as they would be in the neo-classical theory (Garegnani 1983; Aspromourgos 2009, pp. 83–84).[13]

Given the unplanned nature of market economies, at the end of a productive cycle, entrepreneurs may not face in the market a demand able to absorb the whole of their production at the natural price (at least). This requires the specification of an adjustment mechanism powerful enough to bring about effective convergence to a situation in which the produced quantity coincides with the effectual demand: in the absence of such a mechanism, natural prices may not constitute a reliable guide to explain the movements of market prices.[14]

In short, the adjustment mechanism envisaged by Classical authors is as follows. At the end of a productive cycle, the entrepreneur brings to the market a given quantity of produced commodity resulting from the production decisions taken at the beginning of the cycle just concluded. Of course, this quantity cannot be modified to adjust to the demand actually encountered on the market. Thus the adjustment variable is constituted by the commodity's selling price. Smith assumes that, in the presence of a gap between production and effectual demand, a sort of auction starts among the agents that happen to be on (what we today would call) the long side of the market: such agents are prepared to offer higher and higher prices (in case of excess demand) or lower and lower prices (in the case of excess supply).

Once the market price of any commodity happens to be different from its natural price, this causes an imbalance in the distributive sphere in the sense that the remunerations of those people who have contributed to the production of the commodity prove different from their respective natural values. In the absence of entry/exit barriers and in the presence of market transparency, the difference between the market price and the natural price brings about (1) an intersectoral reallocation of economic resources in search of the highest market remuneration and (2) a variation in the produced quantity of the commodity in the following periods. This process comes to a halt only when the produced quantity and demanded quantity balance in correspondence of the natural price and the market values of wages, profits, and rent equal their respective natural values.[15] Therefore the imbalance in the sphere of circulation (the discrepancy between the natural price and market price of a commodity) spills over to the sphere of distribution (the discrepancy between natural values and market values of wages, profits, and rent) and, finally, to the sphere of production (the intersectoral reallocation of productive resources and variation in quantities produced in the following periods).

The assumed tendency of market values toward their respective natural values is based on two assumptions: (1) the owners of the employed inputs consider, besides the outlay costs, also the opportunity costs in their decisions as to where to allocate their economic resources (Aspromourgos 2009, pp. 67, 98) and (2) there are but negligible barriers to the intersectoral mobility of economic resources (p. 91):

> When the price of any commodity is neither more nor less than what is sufficient to pay the rent of the land, the wages of the labour, and the profits of the stock employed in raising, preparing, and bringing it to market, according to their natural rates, the commodity is then sold for what may be called its natural price.
>
> The commodity is then sold precisely for what it is worth, or for what it really costs the person who brings it to market; for *though in common language what is called the prime cost of any commodity does not comprehend the profit of the person who is to sell it again, yet if he sell it at a price which does not allow him the ordinary rate of profit in his neighbourhood, he is evidently a loser by (he trade; since by employing his stock in some other way he might have made that profit…* .
>
> Though the price, therefore, which leaves him this profit is not always the lowest at which a dealer may sometimes sell his goods, it is the lowest at which he is likely to sell them for any considerable time; at least where *there is perfect liberty, or where he may change his trade as often as he pleases.*
>
> (*WN* l.vii.4–6; emphases added)

The above shows that Smith devotes much care to determining natural values and to the gravitation process of market magnitudes to their natural counterparts. The same cannot be maintained as regards the question of market price determination, particularly when the market is not in a situation of long-period equilibrium. Taking stock of Smith's sparse hints on this subject, it is possible to point out what follows.

First, in those markets in which competition is not free (e.g., because of legal monopoly and/or the presence of a guild, a collusive agreement, a law or a rule that somehow prevents economic agents allocating their resources in the sector they prefer) or where there are industrial secrets, entrepreneurs voluntarily limit the produced quantity so that the market is left understocked and the market price stays artificially high:

> The exclusive privileges of corporations, statutes of apprenticeship, and all those laws which restrain, in particular employments, the competition to smaller number than might otherwise go into them,

> have the same tendency, though in a less degree. They are a sort of enlarged monopolies, and may frequently, for ages together and in whole classes of employments, keep up the market price of particular commodities above the natural price, and maintain both the wages of the labour and the profits of the stock employed about them somewhat above their natural rate.
>
> (*WN* l.vii.28)

Conversely, where competition is free and industrial secrets absent, price undercutting starts as soon as at least two competitors are present in the market. This process is amplified by increasing the number of competitors, since this fact makes the establishment of a collusive agreement more unlikely:

> The quantity of grocery goods, for example, which can be sold in a particular town, is limited by the demand of that town and its neighbourhood. The capital, therefore, which can be employed in the grocery trade cannot exceed what is sufficient to purchase that quantity. If this capital is divided between two different grocers, their competition will tend to make both of them sell cheaper, than if it were in the hands of one only; and if it were divided among twenty, their competition would be just so much the greater, and the chance of their combining together, in order to raise the price, just so much the less.
>
> (*WN* II.v.7)

Second, Smith's explanation for the determination of market prices in situations of disequilibrium includes not only elements that are seemingly the fruit of casual observation and that he does not analyse in greater detail (the wealth of the buyers and their desire to get the commodity *versus* the necessity of the sellers to dispose of their own commodities) but also elements that he instead systematically applies in his analysis of the various markets. Of the latter, the most significant is the relative number of sellers and buyers and their relative ability to make a binding agreement. The market price will be high or low depending on whether buyers are more numerous than sellers (and vice versa): the buyers 'bid against one another' offering higher and higher prices, the sellers 'bid against one another' offering lower and lower prices. The relative number of the buyers in relation to the sellers is therefore the crucial element: every time that the agents on one side of the market are few and are able to communicate (e.g., because they operate in the same place such as a town) while the agents on the other side of the market are many and are unable to communicate (e.g., because they are isolated and scattered in the countryside), the bargaining from which the market price springs will obviously be more favourable to the former. This is particularly evident in Smith's analysis of the labour market:

> What are the common wages of labour depends every where upon the contract usually made between those two parties, whose interests are by no means the same. The workmen desire to get as much, the masters to give as little as possible. The former are disposed to combine in order to raise, the latter in order to lower the wages of labour.
>
> It is not, however, difficult to foresee which of the two parties must, upon all ordinary occasions, have the advantage in the dispute, and force the other into compliance with their terms. The masters, being fewer in number, can combine much more easily; and the law, besides, authorises, or at least does not prohibit their combinations, while it prohibits those of the workmen....
>
> When in any country the demand for those who live by wages; · labourers, journeymen, servants of every kind, is continually increasing; when every year furnishes employment for a greater number than had been employed the year before, the workmen have no occasion to combine in order to raise their wages. The scarcity of hands occasions a competition among masters, who bid against one another, in order to get workmen, and thus voluntarily break through the natural combination of masters not to raise wages.
>
> (*WN*I.viii.11–12, 17)

In the following section we show how Marx draws on and develops these elements of Smith's treatment of market prices.

12.3 The Classical notion of free competition: Karl Marx

In Chapter 3 of *Wage-Labour and Capital* (Marx [1847] 1933) it is possible to find a vivid description of price determination in the market for a raw material, cotton. We think that such a description provides a clue to the young Marx's view of the competitive process. The chapter bears the title 'By what is the price of a commodity determined?' and Marx's answer is the quite conventional one: 'By the competition between buyers and sellers, by the relation of the demand to the supply, of the call to the offer' (p. 21). Yet, immediately after, he adds that 'the competition by which the price of a commodity is determined is *threefold*' (ibid.; emphasis added). The first element highlighted by Marx is competition among the sellers:

> Whoever sells commodities of the same quality most cheaply, is sure to drive the other sellers from the field and to secure the greatest market

> for himself. ... [It is competition among the sellers] which forces down the price of the commodities offered by them.
>
> (ibid.)

The second element is competition among the buyers that 'causes the price of the proffered commodities to rise' (ibid.). These two aspects of competition are *not* considered sufficient to fully determine the outcome of the competitive process. In fact, Marx adds a third and last element:

> Finally, there is *competition between the buyers and the sellers:* these wisp to purchase as cheaply as possible, those to sell as dearly as possible. The result of this competition between buyers and sellers will depend upon the relations between the two above-mentioned camps of competitors–i.e., upon whether the competition in the army of sellers is stronger. Industry leads two great armies into the field against each other, and each of these again is engaged in a battle among its own troops in its own ranks. The army among whose troops there is less fighting, carries off the victory over the opposing host.
>
> (ibid.)[16]

We claim that the metaphor of the two armies that, at one and the same time, are engaged in fighting one another and in their own ranks, coupled with the suggestion that the result of the battle is eventually decided by the interplay of these two levels of fighting, paves the way to an interesting analytical intuition. In our view, Marx's rhetoric foreshadows the modern notion of a mixed strategy equilibrium: the outcome of market competition need not be univocally determined, even if optimal (mixed) strategies are.

To clarify his thought, Marx goes on to provide a concrete example. Marx's choice of a raw material market for this didactic purpose is illuminating. In the market of a consumption good it is quite obvious to assume a multitude of atomistic buyers. In such a case, competition among buyers would be reduced to their reservation prices and, eventually, described through a demand curve. It may not be so in the case of a raw material market, where the number of buyers may exceed that of sellers, and, in some cases, it is even possible to reverse the image of atomistic buyers to that of atomistic sellers. Marx's example starts with the analysis of what, in modern terminology, is called a sellers' market: 'Let us suppose that there are 100 bales of cotton in the market and at the same time purchasers for 1,000 bales of cotton' (p. 21). The fact that the demand is many (ten!) times greater than the supply is very likely to be intentional: if there were 100 bales and purchasers for 110, conditions would have not been, in Marx's opinion, those of a sellers' market. On the contrary, 100 to 1,000 is considered enough to obtain that

> the cotton sellers, who perceive the troops of the enemy in the most violent contention among themselves, and who therefore are fully assured of the sale of their whole 100 bales, will beware of pulling one another's hair in order to force down the price of cotton at the very moment in which their opponents race with one another to screw it up high. So, all 'of a sudden, peace reigns in the army of sellers. They stand opposed to the buyers like one man, fold their arms in philosophic contentment and their claims would find no limit did not the offers of even the most importunate of buyers have a very definite limit.
>
> (p. 22)

Obviously, the ratio of 1 to 10 is, in itself, neither a necessary nor a sufficient condition. This is not the place to find a necessary and sufficient condition in general, yet an attempt to pinpoint the elements required for such a condition can be made with the help of a simple symbolism. This is attempted in a very special case in the appendix. Going back to the example, Marx continues by introducing the buyers' market: 'It is well known that the opposite case, with the opposite result, happens more frequently. Great excess of supply over demand; desperate competition among the sellers, and a lack of buyers; forced sales of commodities at ridiculously low prices' (p. 22). Marx's text reveals that, for him, the buyers' market and sellers' market are not contiguous in the sense that between them there is something, but apart from the metaphor of the two armies, his readers are just left with the obvious remark that 'in the same proportion in which [competition among the sellers] decreases, the competition among the buyers increases. Result: a more or less considerable rise in the prices of commodities' (p. 22).

The Marxian text continues by introducing long-period considerations, that is, the gravitation of market prices toward prices of production (here Marx uses the expression *costs of production)* as a consequence of capital migration from (into) those sectors where market prices are below (above) costs of production. Yet in Marx's view, market prices are not to be dismissed lightly as theoretically insignificant. Marx, in fact, goes so far as to claim that the typical market outcome is a market price above or below costs of production, while the equality between the two should be considered an exception:

> The determination of price by the cost of production is not to be understood in the sense of the bourgeois economists. The economists say that the average price of commodities equals the cost of production: that is the law. The anarchic movement, in which the rise is compensated for by a fall and the fall by a rise, they regard as an accident. We might just as well consider the fluctuations as the law, and the

> determination of the price by cost of production as an accident-as is, in fact, done by certain other economists. But it is precisely these fluctuations which, viewed more closely, carry the most frightful devastation in their train and, like an earthquake, cause bourgeois society to shake to its very foundations-it is precisely these fluctuations that force the price to conform to the cost of production. In the totality of this disorderly movement is to be found its order. In the total course of this industrial anarchy, in this circular movement, competition balances, as it were, the one extravagance by the other.
>
> (p. 24)

The reader might think that the elder Marx, equipped with an improved understanding of the Classical notion of prices of production and with a more mature version of his own theory of labour-value, would not have endorsed the foregoing analysis by the young Marx. We think that this is not the case, as witnessed by book 3, chapter 10, of *Capital* (Marx [1894] 1909). This chapter, bearing the title 'Compensation of the Average Rate of Profit by Competition. Market Prices and Market Values. Surplusprofit', is located in part 2, where Marx is confronted with the (insurmountable) problem of reconciling the origin of profit from surplus value with a uniform rate of profit and a uniform rate of surplus value among sectors. This is not the place to provide a thorough assessment of this chapter. It suffices to note the following.

After identifying in 11.X.14 the conditions to be met in order that 'the prices at which commodities are exchanged with one another may correspond approximately to their values', Marx adds in 11.X.15: '[The fact that] the commodities of the various spheres of production are sold at their value implies, of course, only that their value is the center of gravity around which prices fluctuate, and around which their rise and fall tends to an equilibrium'. This sentence has been often quoted in the modern literature on gravitation. However, it is not clear whether Marx thinks that the price is unique at each moment of time or, rather, that there is a constellation of prices at each moment of time. The difference is substantial. If sellers and buyers follow mixed strategies instead of pure strategies, there is clearly a constellation of prices at each moment of time. Marx also identifies two simple cases. In the first, 'demand is so strong that it does not let up when the price is regulated by the value of commodities produced under the most unfavorable conditions' (II.X.16); in this case these conditions determine the market value. In the second, 'the mass of the produced commodities exceeds the quantity which is ordinarily disposed of at average market-values' and, as a consequence, 'the commodities produced under the most favorable conditions regulate the market value' (II.X.16). Marx is more interested in the result of this process than in the analysis of less simple cases.[17] However, in 11.X.51 he claims:

> That side of competition, which is momentarily the weaker, is also that in which the individual acts independently of the mass of his competitors and often works against them, whereby the dependence of one upon the other is impressed upon them, while the stronger side always acts more or less unitedly against its antagonist. If the demand for this particular kind of commodities is larger than the supply, *then one buyer outbids another,* within certain limits, and thereby raises the price of the commodity for all of them above the market-price, while on the other hand *the sellers unite in trying to sell at a high price.* If, vice versa, the supply exceeds the demand, some one *begins to dispose of his goods at a cheaper rate* and the others must follow, while the buyers *unite in their efforts to depress the market-price as much as possible below the market-value.* The common interest is appreciated only so long as each gains more by it than without it. And common action ceases, as soon as this or that side becomes the weaker, when each one tries to get out of it by his own devices with as little loss as possible.
>
> (emphases added)

Here we find a clear echo of the argument used by the young Marx in *Wage-Labour and Capital.* It is also clear that the price is *not* unique at each moment of time: on the contrary, there is a constellation of prices at each moment of time. This fact supports our claims that the process needs to be analysed under the assumption that buyers and sellers follow mixed strategies instead of pure strategies.

12.4 Classical competition and Bertrand competition

In the previous sections we outlined the Classical notion of competition with particular concern for market price determination. In this section we try to answer the following question: has the Classical notion of competition percolated into modern theory? A positive answer to such a question would allow us to make use of some recent results in order to extend the analysis of market competition within Classical economics.

As is well known, in 1883 the mathematician Joseph Louis François Bertrand wrote a review of Leon Walras's *Theorie mathematique de la richesse sociale* (published in 1883) and Augustin Cournot's *Recherches sur les principes mathematiques de la theorie des richesses* (published in 1838).[18] Bertrand was highly skeptical of the then recent blossoming of mathematical economics. In particular, he poured scorn on Cournot's book:

> [Cournot's] formulae, written only in letters, bristle with unknown functions; [Cournot] would consider it outside his field if he were to be more specific. Practical economists must feel that it would be of little value to study such formulae, be they true or false, so they escape from this study by merely closing the book. If Cournot's theory of

> wealth... has failed to attract any serious attention over the past century, it is because the ideas are lost under the profusion of algebraic signs.
>
> (quoted in Magnan de Bornier 1992, p. 647)

As concerns Cournot's duopoly model, Bertrand claimed that, pace Cournot, it admitted 'no solution under this assumption' (p. 647), that is, under the assumption that each duopolist tries to undercut the rival in order to attract buyers and stops doing that only when he or she has nothing more to gain from reducing his or her prices. (Note that for Bertrand it is Cournot himself who assumed price competition between the two sellers.) In short, the gist of Bertrand's criticism is that Cournot failed to acknowledge that the envisaged downward movement of prices was limited only by the marginal cost.[19] A somewhat similar charge of indeterminacy was raised 16 years later by a distinguished economist, Francis Ysidro Edgeworth, in a paper originally published in Italian in 1897 and translated with some modifications into English in 1925. Edgeworth went beyond Bertrand insofar as he claimed that the duopoly model admits a continuous price cycle in the presence of diminishing returns:

> [The case of two identical articles] is treated by Cournot as the first step in the transition from monopoly to perfect competition. He concludes that a determinate proposition of equilibrium defined by certain quantities of the articles will be reached. Cournot's conclusion has been shown to be erroneous by Bertrand for the case in which there is no cost of production; by Professor Marshall for the case in which the cost follows the law of increasing returns; and by the present writer for the case in which the cost follows the law of diminishing returns. *In the last case there will be an indeterminate tract through which the index of value will oscillate, or rather will vibrate irregularly for an indefinite length of time.*
>
> (Edgeworth 1925, pp. 117–118; emphasis added)

To defend this claim, Edgeworth produced a numerical example in which two firms compete on prices, but they have capacity constraints. Edgeworth showed there is no (pure strategy) equilibrium in his example and formulated a sort of dynamic solution: firms undercut each other until the price becomes so low that it is convenient for a firm to quote a high price and sell only to the residual demand instead of undercutting the price quoted by the rival. As Edgeworth wrote:

> At every stage in the fall of price, and before it has reached its limiting value..., it is competent to each monopolist to deliberate whether it will pay him better to lower the price against his rival as already described, *or rather to raise it to a higher, perhaps the initial,* level for that

> remainder of customers of which he cannot be deprived by his rival (owing to the latter's limitation of supply). Long before the lowest point has been reached, that alternative will have become more advantageous than the course first described.
>
> (p. 120)

With the development of game theory and its application to oligopoly models, the so-called Bertrand-Edgeworth competition, explicitly based on price undercutting, became a fruitful and extensively studied alternative to the price-taking competition embodied in the standard perfect competition model (see Baye and Kovenock 2008). Yet the contemporary Bertrand competition model is somewhat different from the original formulation and from the Classical notion of competition. First, it is a one-shot game with a mixed strategy equilibrium and not a dynamic process of price undercutting. This feature magnifies the relevance of two missing elements in Smith's and Marx's writings. First is the problem of firms quoting the same price: in the case of a tie the firms fixing the lowest prices must share total demand in one way or another. This requires the introduction of a specific assumption in this regard. Second is the problem of how demand is rationed when a firm's quantity demanded exceeds its capacity. The introduction of a demand rationing scheme is another assumption lacking in the Classical authors.

However, a comparison between modern Bertrand competition and Smith's notion of competition, and even more the story told by Marx in *Wage-Labour and Capital*, magnifies some deficiencies of the former. First, in the former there is a multitude of atomistic buyers described through a demand curve confronted with a given number of sellers, each defined by their costs (generally marginal costs are constant and uniform) and capacity. On the contrary, in Marx we find a sort of symmetry between sellers and buyers. It is certainly not difficult to extend the Bertrand competition model to investigate the case in which there is a multitude of atomistic sellers described through a supply curve confronted with a given number of buyers, each defined by their reservation price (possibly constant and uniform) and purchasing power. Generalisation to a symmetrical case in which a number of sellers with their costs and selling capacities are confronted with a number of buyers with their reservation prices and buying capacities is certainly less obvious. Second, Bertrand competition theorists have analysed quite extensively the case of duopoly with constant marginal cost. Few contributions have investigated the oligopoly (see De Francesco and Salvadori 2010 and the literature cited therein). When there are more than two competing firms, many changes are needed. In the case of two firms, any firm can either undercut the other or avoid doing so. In the case of three or more firms, any firm can either undercut all other firms or just some of the firms and not others, or none of them. For example, in the case in which there are two (either equal or not) large firms and a smaller firm, the latter can avoid high prices so that the two large firms are not interested in undercutting it when they undercut each other at higher prices. The small firm can take advantage of this protection from competition with larger firms (at high prices) to obtain a larger rate of profit (see De Francesco and Salvadori 2010, theorem 1(c)). The analysis provided in the appendix may give an idea of the problems involved.

12.5 Final remarks

In this article we attempted to assess the Classical notion of free competition in comparison with the Walrasian notion of perfect competition. We showed that the latter is plagued with some logical difficulties that drastically reduce its explanatory power to equilibrium situations. Such difficulties are absent in the Classical notion of competition, which, contrary to the Walrasian one, is not based on any kind of price-taking assumption. Yet the former also displays some unsatisfactory aspects. In particular, while the Classical authors extensively investigated long-period, natural values, and gravitation, they were more sketchy on market price determination in situations of market disequilibrium. To fill this lacuna we analysed Smith's and Marx's views on competition between buyers and sellers. We claim that, taking inspiration from the modern theory of Bertrand competition, it is possible both to render Smith's and Marx's hints formally precise and to provide interesting new questions for modern Bertrand competition theorists.

Appendix 1

Let N be the number of buyers. Their reservation price is p_b. Let $B_1 \geq B_2 \geq \ldots B_N$ be the different quantities of cotton they want to buy and let $B = B_1 + B_2 + \ldots + B_N$. Similarly, let M be the number of sellers and c be their reservation price. Let $S_1 \geq S_2 \geq \ldots S_M$ be the different quantities of cotton they want to sell and $S = S_1 + S_2 + \ldots + S_M$. Let us assume that $c < p_b$ (the case in which $c \geq p_b$ requires more accurate analysis) and that there are no buyers with a reservation price lower than p_b and no sellers with a reservation price higher than c (once again, a more accurate analysis would be required otherwise).

If $S < B_2 + \ldots + B_N$, that is, if all buyers *but the largest one* are willing to buy *more* than the existing amount of cotton, buyer 1 could be excluded from the purchase and, as a consequence, any other buyer 2, 3,..., N could be excluded too. Overbidding among buyers leads the price of cotton to rise to p_b. Therefore the best strategy for each buyer is to express a demand for cotton at her reservation price and the best strategy for each seller is to quote the price p_b. On the contrary, if $B > S > B_2 + \ldots + B_N$, that is, if all buyers *but the largest one* are willing to buy *less* than the existing amount of cotton even if all buyers are willing to buy *more* than the existing amount of cotton, buyer 1 knows that she will certainly buy some cotton. In the limiting case in which all buyers 2,...., N have purchased their desired amount of cotton, buyer 1 is a monopsonist in relation to the sellers who have not sold their cotton. Let p_m be this monopsony price. Obviously, $p_m = c$.[20] Clearly, if buyers 2, 3,..., N quote price p_b for cotton, buyer 1 will quote price $p_m < p_b$. But if buyer 1 quotes price p_m for cotton, (some of) the other $N-1$ buyers will outbid her instead of quoting p_b. Therefore buyer 1 will overbid on them, instead of quoting p_m. And so on, until the price goes up so much that buyer 1 will prefer again to quote price $p_m = c$ and buy only $S - (B_1 +... + B_N)$ units of corn. And so on and so forth. In this situation, sellers cannot 'stand opposed to the buyers like one man' and 'fold their arms in philosophic contentment': they must fight each other to sell at a higher price.

Similarly, if $B < S_2+... +S_M$ undercutting among sellers leads the price of cotton to drop to c. Therefore, the best strategy for each seller is to quote her reservation price and the best strategy for each buyer is to express a demand for cotton at price c. On the contrary, if $S > B > S_2+... +S_M$, no equilibrium price exists. Nor can an equilibrium price exist if $S = B$, since $S > B_2 +... + B_N$ and $B > S_2 +... + S_M$: the larger seller has a realistic possibility of selling part of her cotton at p_b and the larger buyer has a realistic possibility of buying part of the desired amount of cotton at c.

As a consequence, if $B + S_1 > S$ and $S + B_1 > B$, both armies, to use Marx's metaphor, are engaged in infighting. The best strategies for both buyers and sellers are not single (i.e., deterministic) prices but distributions of probability within a set of prices.

Determining such distributions of probability requires proper analysis, which is beyond the scope of this article. Besides, to make such calculations we need to make further assumptions not stated by Marx. In particular, we need to know how the residual demand (supply) is determined for sellers (buyers) quoting a price higher (lower) than that quoted by other sellers (buyers) and what happens in the event of a tie. What is certain is that buyer 1 will never quote a price lower than c (the monopsony price if all other buyers are served) or a price higher than p_{Mb}, defined by the condition that buyer 1 gets the same profit from buying min $\{S, B_1\}$ at price p_{Mb} and buying $S - (B_2 +... + B_N)$ at price c. But, as a consequence, no buyer will quote prices outside the range $[c, p_{Mb}]$. Similarly, seller 1 will never quote a price higher than p_b (the monopoly price if all other sellers are served) nor a price lower than p_{ms}, defined by the condition that seller 1 gets the same profit from selling $B - (S_2 +... + S_M)$ at price p_b and selling min $\{B, S_1\}$ at price p_{ms}. However, as a consequence, no seller will quote prices outside the range $[p_{ms}, p_b]$. Both arguments make sure that traders can quote only prices that are in both ranges $[c, p_{Mb}]$ and $[p_{ms}, p_b]$.

Notes

1 This article was prepared for the Italian National Research Project, co-financed by the Italian Minister of University, 'Heterogeneous Sectors, Growth, and Technical Change' (2007). A previous version of this article was presented at the thirteenth annual conference of the European Society for the History of Economic Thought, Thessaloniki, Greece, 23–26 April 2009, and at the seventh annual conference of the Italian Association for the History of Political Economy, Trento, Italy, 30 May–1 June 2010. We wish to thank Alain Alcouffe, Enrico Bellino, Stefano Fiori, Heinz D. Kurz, Manuela Mosca, Arrigo Opocher, and Maria Pia Paganelli for their comments. The usual caveats apply.

2 [The originality of the classical theory of free competition] is not, however, able to hide certain inadequacies: classical political economy clashes with the central problem of the articulation between market prices and natural prices. The solution of such difficulties requires a new definition of this articulation. [Our translation.]

3 The basic model used to represent the Classical gravitation process is the so-called cross-dual model, in which (1) sectoral outputs change in response to differentials in the rates of profit and (2) market prices change in response to excess demand of the various commodities. While the first adjustment process is widely accepted as a fair formalisation of the Classical principle of capital mobility, the second appears as a mechanical transposition of the Walrasian price adjustment process and is the ultimate culprit behind the intrinsic instability of cross-dual gravitation processes. The present article proposes a totally different market price formation and should be able to resolve the instability problem envisaged in this literature.

4 From this point of view, McNulty's interpretation is akin to those of Samuel Hollander (1973) and John Eatwell (1987). The former claims that 'the Smithian conception of competition must be carefully distinguished from the modern conception which envisages sellers (and consumers) as "price-takers" rather than "price-makers"' (126), while the latter points out that 'the characteristics of "perfect" competition (notably the conditions which ensure price-taking) are often read back, illegitimately, into Classical discussions of competition' (63). See also High 2001, xiv–xv; and Machovec 1995, chap. 8. While Blaug (2001, p. 153) defines Arrow and Hahn's 1971 tribute to Adam Smith as a forerunner of perfect competition (and Pareto optimality) analysis no less than 'a historical travesty', a more balanced position is endorsed by Michael Bradley (2010, p. 238), who argues that 'Smithian "liberty" contains the seeds of perfect competition, but perfect competition is different from "perfect liberty" in some critical respects, particularly the nature of competition and the role of entrepreneurs.'

5 McNulty (1967, pp. 395–396) provides a discussion of Cantillon and Turgot as forerunners of

Smith on competition. An extensive treatment of the evolution of the notions of price, cost, and competition before Smith may be found in Aspromourgos 2009, pp. 101–110.

6 From this perspective Edgeworth's concept of equilibrium *(core)* and his adjustment process in disequilibrium *(recontracting)* are superior to the Walrasian ones: 'The recontracting process ... is based on the same behavioral postulate, blocking by coalitions, that is used to define the solution concept, the core. [The core is defined to be the set of all unblocked allocations. That is, it is the set of all allocations such that no subset of the participants can improve the position of all its members by withdrawing from the system and using

only the resources of its members.] This seems to be a desirable property. It is, however, not shared by most studies of disequilibrium price dynamics because these involve price changes brought about by a market manager or other artificiality. Prices do not vary as a consequence of the maximizing behavior of individuals' (Green 1974, p. 22).

7 Current textbooks also acknowledge this fact: 'Strictly speaking, it is *equilibrium* market prices that [consumers and producers] will regard as unaffected by their actions For the price-taking assumption to be appropriate, what we want is that [consumers and producers] have no *incentive* to alter prices that, if taken as given, equate demand and supply (we have already seen that [consumers and producers] *do* have an incentive to alter prices that do not equate demand and supply)' (Mas-Colell, Whinston, and Green 1995, pp. 314nl, 315; emphasis added).

8 D (S) is the quantity demanded (supplied) of a given commodity X, p its price, and f(p) and $g(p)$ the demand and supply functions, respectively, while dp/dt = $h(S - D)$ is the time derivative that formalises the law of motion of market price in relation to market excess demand.

9 Arrow's 1959 contribution with its emphasis on the role of monopoly theory in explaining competitive price convergence is the ideal starting point for the subsequent neo-Walrasian literature on disequilibrium trading (see Donzelli 1990, chap. 9).

10 As is well known, David Ricardo (1951, p. 91) devotes to the distinction between natural and market magnitudes just the short chapter 4 of his *Principles*, where he explicitly refers to chapter 7 of *WN*, where 'all that concerns this question is most ably treated'.

11 Ricardo (1951, pp. 91–92) clearly states that the *focus* of his analysis is only natural magnitudes: 'Having fully acknowledged the temporary effects which, in particular employments of capital, may be produced on the prices of commodities, as well on the wages of labour, and the profits of stock, by accidental causes, without influencing the general prices of commodities, wages or profits, since these effects are equally operative in all stages of society, we will leave them entirely out of consideration, whilst we are treating of the laws which regulate natural prices, natural wages and natural profits, effects totally independent of these accidental causes.'

12 See Ricardo's (1951, p. 382) rejection of the opinion that price depends solely on the proportion between these two quantities.

13 Differences between the classical and the neo-classical theories of value and distribution have been emphasised by such authors as Krishna Bharadwaj (1978), Alessandro Roncaglia (1978), and Pierangelo Garegnani (1984). Nonetheless, historiographical controversies are still very much alive: see Blaug (1999, 2009) versus Kurz and Salvadori (2002, 2010).

14 This consideration may explain Ricardo's (1951, p. 90; emphasis added) emphasis on the effectiveness of the adjustment mechanism: 'When we look to the markets of a large town, and observe how regularly they are supplied both with home and foreign commodities, in the quantity in which they are required, under all circumstances of varying demand ... without often producing either the effect of a glut from too abundant a supply, or an enormously high price from the supply being unequal to the demand, *we must confess that the principle which apportions capital to each trade in the precise amount that is required, is more active than is generally supposed.*'

15 However, Classical economists were perfectly aware of the existence of profit and wage rate differentials. For a modern treatment, see Kurz and Salvadori 1995, chapter 11.

16 Marx's treatment of competition in this passage echoes James Steuart's notion of double competition. Marx was well acquainted with the work of Steuart, with whom he often took issue (Denis 1999). On Steuart's notion of double competition, see Menudo and Tortajada 2009.

17 'No matter what may be the way in which prices are regulated, the result always is the following: 1) The law of value dominates the movements of prices, ... 2) The average profit which determines the prices of production must always be approximately equal to that quantity of surplus-value, which falls to the share of a certain individual capital in its capacity as an aliquot part of the total social capital' (II.X.17–18). (All references to *Capital* give part number, chapter number, paragraph number.)

18 An English translation of Bertrand's text, originally in *Journal des Savants* volume 48, pp. 499–508, is provided in the appendix of Magnan de Bornier 1992.

19 In Bertrand's wording, 'without limits', but this is only because in Cournot's original example the marginal cost is zero. This is not the place to discuss whether Bertrand's interpretation of Cournot is well grounded or whether Cournot actually used prices instead of quantities as strategic variables: see Magnan de Bornier (1992, 2001), Dimand and Dore (1999), and Morrison (1998, 2001).

20 Note that if buyers with a reservation price larger than *c* exist, the monopsony price is larger than *c*.

References

Arena, R. 1978. "Note sulla concezione classica della concorrenza." *Economia e Lavoro,* no. 2:323–352.

Arrow, K. J. 1959. "Toward a Theory of Price Adjustment." In *The Allocation of Economic Resources*, edited by M. Abramovitz, 41–51. Stanford: Stanford University Press.

Arrow, K. J., and F. H. Hahn. 1971. *General Competitive Analysis.* San Francisco: Holden Day.

Aspromourgos, T. 2009. *The Science of Wealth: Adam Smith and the Framing of Political Economy.* London: Routledge.

Baye, M. R., and D. Kovenock. 2008. "Bertrand Competition." *The New Palgrave: A Dictionary of Economics*, edited by J. Eatwell, M. Milgate, and P. Newman. London: Macmillan.

Bellino, E. 2011. "Gravitation of Market Prices towards Natural Prices." In *Sraffa and Modern Economics,* edited by R. Ciccone, C. Gehrke, and G. Mongiovi, 58–75. London: Routledge.

Bharadwaj, K. 1978. *Classical Political Economy and the Rise to Dominance of Supply and Demand Theories.* New Delhi: Orient Longmans.

Blaug, M. 1997. "Competition as an End-State and Competition as a Process." In *Not Only an Economist: Recent Essays by Mark Blaug*, 66–86. Cheltenham: Edward Elgar.

———. 1999. "Misunderstanding Classical Economics: The Sraffian Interpretation of the Surplus Approach." *History of Political Economy* 31:213–236.

———. 2001. "No History of Ideas, Please, We're Economists." *Journal of Economic Perspectives* 15:145–164.

———. 2002. "Ugly Currents in Modern Economics." In *Fact and Fiction in Economics: Models, Realism, and Social Construction*, edited by U. Maki, 35–56. Cambridge: Cambridge University Press.

———. 2003. "The Formalist Revolution of the 1950s." *Journal of the History of Economic Thought* 25:145–156.

———. 2009. "The Trade-Off between Rigor and Relevance: Sraffian Economics as a Case in Point." *History of Political Economy* 41:219–247.

Bradley, M. E. 2010. "Adam Smith's System of Natural Liberty: Competition, Contestability, and Market Process." *Journal of the History of Economic Thought* 32:237–262.

Ciccone, R. 1999. "Classical and Neoclassical Short-Run Prices: A Comparative Analysis of Their Intended Empirical Content." In *Value, Distribution, and Capital: Essays in Honour of Pierangelo Garegnani,* edited by G. Mongiovi and F. Petri, 69–92. London: Routledge.

Dardi, M. 1983. "Piero Sraffa (1898–1983)." *Quaderni di Storia dell' Economia Politica* 3:3–14.

De Francesco, M.A., and N. Salvadori.'2010. "Bertrand-Edgeworth Games under Oligopoly with a Complete Characterization for the Triopoly." http://mpra.ub.uni-muenchen.de/18766/.

Denis, H. 1999. "Marx's Polemics against Steuart." In *The Economics of James Steuart,* edited by R. Tortajada, 76–83. London: Routledge.

Dimand, R. W., and Mohammed H. I. Dore. 1999: "Cournot, Bertrand, and Game Theory: A Further Note." *Atlantic Economic Journal* 27:325–333.

Donzelli, F. 1990. "The Concept of Equilibrium in Neoclassical Economic Theory: An Inquiry into the Evolution of General Competitive Analysis from Walras to the 'Neo-Walrasian Research Programme.'" PhD diss., University of Cambridge.

Dumenil, G., and D. Levy. 1987. "The Dynamics of Competition: A Restoration of Classical Analysis." *Cambridge Journal of Economics* 11:133–164.

Eatwell, J. 1987. "Classical Competition." *The New Palgrave: A Dictionary of Economics,* edited by J. Eatwell, M. Milgate, and P. Newman. London: Macmillan.

Edgeworth, F. Y. 1897. "La teoria pura del monopolio." *Giornale degli Economisti* 40:13–31.

———. 1925. "The Pure Theory of Monopoly." In *Papers Relating to Political Economy,* 1:111–142. London: Macmillan.

Garegnani, P. 1983. "The Classical Theory of Wages and the Role of Demand Schedules in the Determination of Relative Prices." *American Economic Review* 73:309–313.

———. 1984. "Value and Distribution in the Classical Economists and Marx." *Oxford Economic Papers* 36:291–325.

Giocoli, N. 2003. *Modeling Rational Agents: From Interwar Economics to Early Modern Game Theory.* Cheltenham: Edward Elgar.

———. 2005. "Modeling Rational Agents: The Consistency View of Rationality and the Changing Image of Neoclassical Economics." *Cahiers d'Economie Politique,* no. 49:177–208.

Green, J. 1974. "The Stability of Edgeworth's Recontracting Process." *Econometrica* 42:21–34.

High, J. 2001. "Introduction: Split Personality; A Brief History of Competition in Economic Theory." In *Competition,* edited by J. High, xiii–xv. Critical Ideas in Economics. Cheltenham: Edward Elgar.

Hollander, S. 1973. *The Economics of Adam Smith.* Toronto: University of Toronto Press.

Kaldor, N. 1972. "The Irrelevance of Equilibrium Economics." *Economic Journal* 82:1237–1255.

Kurz, H. D., and N. Salvadori. 1995. *Theory of Production: A Long-Period Analysis.* Cambridge: Cambridge University Press.

———. 2002. "Mark Blaug on the 'Sraffian Interpretation of the Surplus Approach.'" *History of Political Economy* 34:225–236.

———. 2010. "In Favor of Rigor *and* Relevance: A Reply to Mark Blaug." *History of Political Economy* 43:607–616.

Lavezzi, A. 2003. "Smith, Marshall, and Young on Division of Labour and Economic Growth." *European Journal of the History of Economic Thought* 10:81–108.

Machovec, F. M. 1995. *Perfect Competition and the Transformation of Economics.* London: Routledge.

Magnan de Bornier, J. 1992. "The 'Cournot-Bertrand Debate': A Historical Perspective." *History of Political Economy* 24:623–656.

———. 2001. "Magnan de Bornier on Cournot-Bertrand: A Rejoinder to Clarence Morrison." *History of Political Economy* 33:167–174.

Marx, K. (1847) 1933. *Wage-Labour and Capital.* New York: International Publishers.

———. (1894) 1909. *Capital.* Vol. 3. Chicago: Charles H. Kerr.

Mas-Colell, A., M. Whinston, and J. Green. 1995. *Microeconomic Theory.* New York: Oxford University Press.

McNulty, P. 1967. "A Note on the History of Perfect Competition." *Journal of Political Economy* 75:395–399.

———. 1968. "Economic Theory and the Meaning of Competition." *Quarterly Journal of Economics* 82:639–656.

Menudo, J. M., and R. Tortajada. 2009. "Double Competition and Market Stability in Sir James Steuart." WP ECON 09.06. http://ssrn.com/abstract=1408122. Published as "Sir James Steuart on Double Competition and Market Stability." *History of Economic Ideas* 23:39–58.

Morrison, C. 1998. "Cournot, Bertrand, and Modern Game Theory." *Atlantic Economic Journal* 26:172–174.

———. 2001. "Magnan de Bornier on Cournot-Bertrand." *History of Political Economy* 33:161–165.

Ricardo, D. 1951. *The Works and Correspondence of David Ricardo.* Vol. 1, *Principles of Political Economy and Taxation.* Edited by Piero Sraffa, with the collaboration of Maurice Dobb. Cambridge: Cambridge University Press.

Richardson, G. B. 1975. "Adam Smith on Competition and Increasing Returns." In *Essays on Adam Smith,* edited by A. S. Skinner and T. Wilson, 350–360. Oxford: Oxford University Press.

Roncaglia, A. 1978. *Sraffa and the Theory of Prices.* Chichester: John Wiley.

Samuelson, P.A. 1978. "The Canonical Classical Model of Political Economy." *Journal of Economic Literature* 16:1415–1434.

Semmler, W. 1984. "On the Classical and Marxian Theories of Competition, Value, and Prices of Production." *Australian Economic Papers* 23:130–150.

Smith, A. (1776) 1976. *An Inquiry into the Nature and Causes of the Wealth of Nations.* Vol. 2 of *The Glasgow Edition of the Works and Correspondence of Adam Smith,* edited by R.H. Campbell and A. S. Skinner. Oxford: Oxford University. Press.

Sraffa, P. 1960. *Production of Commodities by Means of Commodities: A Prelude to a Critique of Economic Theory*. Cambridge: Cambridge University Press.
Steedman, I. 1984. "Natural Prices, Differential Profit Rates, and the Classical Competitive Process." *Manchester School* 52:123–140.
Stigler, G. 1957. "Perfect Competition, Historically Contemplated." *Journal of Political Economy* 65:1–17.
Vickers, J. 1995 "Concepts of Competition." *Oxford Economic Papers* 47:1–23.

13 Adam Smith on monopoly theory

Making good a lacuna[1]

Neri Salvadori and Rodolfo Signorino

Original paper: Neri Salvadori and Rodolfo Signorino (2014) Adam Smith on monopoly theory. Making good a lacuna, *Scottish Journal of Political Economy*, 61:2, 178–195, DOI: https://doi.org/10.1111/sjpe.12040. Hoboken, New Jersey: Wiley, on behalf of the Scottish Economic Society.

13.1 Introduction

Historians of economic analysis usually acknowledge the French *ingénieurs-économistes* of the first half of the nineteenth century as being the forerunners of the formal theory of monopoly (Blaug, 1997a, pp. 331ff; Mosca, 1998; Ekelund and Hebert, 1999). By the same token, Adam Smith's contribution to the subject of monopoly has been by and large underrated or even passed over without comment. Yet, the author of *The Wealth of Nations* (*WN* hereafter) discusses, often at length, a number of issues pertaining to monopoly. Such a situation involves an exegetical dilemma. Is Smith's analysis of monopoly not worthy of a particular mention since it is intrinsically defective or largely inferior to that later elaborated by the French school? Or did Smith leave his analysis of monopoly in an embryonic form, and the majority of scholars assess it on the basis of wrong premises? By 'wrong premises' we mean different premises from those which Smith (implicitly) used in his approach.[2]

In this article, we follow the latter route and propose a rational reconstruction of Smith's theory of monopoly. Our contribution clashes with the conventional view that Smith had little or nothing analytically interesting to say on this subject, and may be summarised as follows. The first question we tackle concerns the terminology: the word 'monopoly' is generally used by Smith to refer to a heterogeneous collection of market outcomes, besides that of a market in which there is just one seller. (Yet, Smith also analysed this kind of market). Moreover, while it is commonly thought that Smith's theory of monopoly, if there is such a thing, is to be found first and foremost in Book I, Chapter 7, 'Of the Natural and Market Price of the Commodities', of *WN*, we show that this is not actually so. Smith devotes this chapter to illustrating his theory of natural prices and their role as attractors of market prices in all those markets where

DOI: 10.4324/9781003138709-17

there is free competition: monopoly is merely a side issue. By contrast, an extensive discussion regarding monopoly can be found in several chapters in Book IV, 'Of Systems of Political Economy', and Book V, 'Of the Revenue of the Sovereign or Commonwealth'. In these two books, Smith takes issue with a panoply of government measures concerning international trade, colonial trade, and the exclusive privileges of trading companies, measures enacted over time under the influence both of mercantilist authors and various pressure groups. We thus focus on these two books as the proper place to look for Smith's theory of monopoly. We show that Smith's account of monopolists' behaviour is a good deal richer than that provided by later theorists. In our view, Smith's monopolists follow a three-step strategy: (i) enforcement of their barriers to entry, (ii) choice of the quantity of the commodity to be brought to the market, and (iii) market price fixing, taking due account of the results actually achieved in the previous two steps. (Note that step (iii) is not redundant since Smith assumes no Walrasian-like price mechanism.) We also show that Smith was aware of the growth-retarding effect of monopoly and, accordingly, urged state regulation.

The structure of the chapter is as follows. In Section 13.2, we assess some contributions that underestimate the Classical theory of monopoly or even deny its existence: we focus on the premises on which these contributions are generally based. In Section 13.3, we present our rational reconstruction of Smith's theory of monopoly, based on a different set of assumptions. Section 13.4 concludes.

13.2 Smith's theory of monopoly: the conventional view

To the best of our knowledge, Leon Walras was the first to express the view that Classical economists, including Adam Smith, were virtually silent regarding monopoly theory. In Lecture 41, 'Price fixing and monopoly', of his *Elements of Pure Economics* Walras claims that Antoine Augustin Cournot (1838 [1897]) and Jules Dupuit (1844 [1952], 1849 [1962]) were the founders of the formal theory of monopoly. In addition, Walras stresses that economists have usually failed to follow the analytical path opened up by Cournot and Dupuit. The consequence of this unfortunate choice has been, as far as monopoly theory is concerned, a conceptual muddle which has led to terminological bedlam. According to Walras, economists in fact

> have given the name of monopoly to enterprises [i.e. industries] which are not under a single control, but under the [divided] control of a limited number of persons. And, by analogy, they have even applied the term monopoly to the ownership of certain productive services that are limited in quantity like, for example, land.
>
> (Walras (1874–1877, [1954]), pp. 435–436)

Walras does not explicitly mention Smith in this context; yet, his wording seems to paraphrase sentences such as the following:

> The exclusive privileges of corporations, statutes of apprenticeship, and all those laws which restrain, in particular employments, the competition to a smaller number than might otherwise go into them, [...] are a sort of enlarged monopolies...
>
> (*WN* I.vii.28)

> The rent of land, therefore, considered as the price paid for the use of the land, is naturally a monopoly price. It is not at all proportioned to what the landlord may have laid out upon the improvement of the land, or to what he can afford to take; but to what the farmer can afford to give.
>
> (*WN* I.xi.5)

More recently, the lack of a sound theory of monopoly in Smith has been forcefully supported by Stigler (See also Kurz and Salvadori, 1995, p. 17, and Dutt, 1998):

> Adam Smith, that great manufacturer of traditions, did not fail us in the area of monopoly, for he created or rendered authoritative three traditions that were faithfully followed in English economics for almost 100 years. The first tradition was to pay no attention to the formal theory of monopoly.
>
> (Stigler, 1982, p. 1)

As an explanation for the lack of a theory of monopoly in *WN*, some commentators point out that, at Smith's time, the Industrial Revolution was just at the onset: industrial sectors characterised by significant scale economies or high capital requirements were still exceptions, not the norm (Blaug, 1997a, p. 35). As a consequence, in the second half of the eighteenth century in England 'most monopolies were the effect of collusion, which was favoured either by the guild system or by the small extent of the market. Or else they were common in branches of trade dominated by regulated or joint-stock companies' (De Roover, 1951, p. 523). It is thus not a mere coincidence that '[Smith's] blast against monopolies is aimed at the exclusive privileges, first, of the guilds or corporations and, next, of the regulated and joint-stock companies' (ibid.).

An alternative explanation is offered by those commentators who argue that (i) the adoption of the method of long-period positions led Classical economists, including Smith, to focus on the long-period consequences of actual entry and that (ii) the analysis of market competition in the presence of sizeable entry barriers was not high on their agenda (Hovenkamp, 1989; Ciccone, 1999). The logical implication of this line of reasoning is that monopoly is basically a short-term phenomenon, worthy of only passing attention, provided that the forces of free competition are not annihilated by an explicit government measure. This explanation is dubious in the presence of significant and persistent entry/exit barriers. Smith points out plainly that market prices stay above their relative natural levels for a very long timespan or even forever (*WN* I.vii.20, 24 and 28). He maintains that this applies particularly in the cases of natural productions which 'require a singularity of soil and situation' and of 'exclusive privileges of corporations, statutes of apprenticeship, and all those laws which restrain, in particular employments, the competition to a smaller number than might otherwise go into them'. Hence, in these latter cases it is the very text of *WN* that bars interpreters from invoking the non-persistence argument as an excuse for a lack of a general theory of market prices.

From the above we draw the conclusion that, as regards monopoly, a lacuna exists within the exegetical literature on Smith. In the following section, we scrutinise the text of *WN* in search of hints which may prove valuable to set out a rational reconstruction of Smith's theory of monopoly.

13.3 Adam Smith on monopoly

The claim that Smith has no theory of monopoly is usually based (more or less consciously) on the following two working assumptions: (i) the proper definition of 'monopoly' is the literal (or Cournot-Walrasian) one, which is a form of market characterised by the presence of a single producer who does not fear entry from outsiders and (ii) the proper place to look for Smith's theory of monopoly is Book I, Chapter 7, of *WN*. We think that both assumptions are unduly restrictive and stand in the way of an accurate reconstruction of Smith's views on monopoly.

As concerns the meaning of the word 'monopoly', it needs to be stressed that Smith attaches very different meanings to the words 'competition' and 'monopoly' from those currently used today. In Smith's time, 'competition' and 'monopoly' were not considered specific items within a well-defined taxonomy of market structures. They were not classified on the basis of number and dimensions of incumbent firms, typology of entry/exit barriers, coefficient of demand elasticity, space and timing of strategic moves, etc. In *WN* the word 'competition' is synonymous with freedom of trade; while the word 'monopoly' is synonymous with restrictions to such freedom. While there is one freedom, there are many restrictions and usually (but not always) they derive from an act of government or are tolerated by the government.[3] Moreover, unlike the Cournot-Walrasian notion of perfect competition, the Smithian notion of free competition does not require a continuum of infinitesimal agents, each taking a market equilibrium price as a parametric datum (Hovenkamp, 1989 and Blaug, 1997b).[4]

As we show in this section while free competition is the way market transactions are usually structured within a 'system of natural liberty' for Smith, the various concrete instances of monopoly are the way market transactions are usually structured within the 'systems either of preference or of restraint' (*WN* IV.ix.51). From this perspective, the Smithian notion of monopoly is akin to that elaborated, long before *WN*, by the Scholastic authors. As highlighted by De Roover (1951, 1955), the Scholastic authors employed the word 'monopoly' in relation to a heterogeneous collection of market outcomes characterised by the fact that a single agent or a cartel obtains the control of the supply of a given commodity. This also includes unlawful or unethical trade practices such as engrossing, forestalling, and regrating, which were considered marketing offences within English common law. This explains the stigma of *turpe lucrum* attached to monopoly profits. For Scholastic authors, as well as Smith, monopolists aim to create an artificial dearth in their own markets to establish and keep prices at a higher level and thus gain higher profits than those obtained in a situation of free competition. In Smith's words:

> The monopolists, by keeping the market constantly understocked, by never fully supplying the effectual demand, sell their commodities much above the natural price, and raise their emoluments, whether they consist in wages or profit, greatly above their natural rate.
>
> (*WN* I.vii.26)

> The government of towns corporate was altogether in the hands of traders and artificers; and it was the manifest interest of every particular class of them, to prevent the market from being over-stocked, as they commonly express it, with their own particular species of industry; which is in reality to keep it always under-stocked.
>
> (*WN* I.x.c.18)

Let us now turn to the second assumption: the proper place to find Smith's theory of monopoly. In Book I Chapter 7 of *WN*:

1. Smith refers broadly to monopolies as market outcomes resulting from a plurality of restrictions on the intersectoral mobility of capital and labour;
2. Smith claims that the monopoly price 'is upon every occasion the highest which can be got [...] the highest which can be squeezed out of the buyers, or which, it is supposed, they will consent to give' (WN I.vii.27), and; finally,
3. Smith classifies the circumstances that make market prices persistently higher than the natural level into three broad categories: 'particular accidents' (industrial or trade secrets), 'natural causes' (e.g., the very specific nature of French vineyards), and 'particular regulations of

> police' (the legal monopoly granted to an individual or trading company, the exclusive privileges of corporations, statutes of apprenticeship, etc.).

In short, in Book I Chapter 7 of *WN,* Smith's remarks regarding monopoly are scattered and unsystematic. It is no wonder that scholars looking for a fully fledged theory of monopoly have not found anything there! At this juncture it must be stressed that in the text of *WN,* the word 'monopoly' appears only in 11 paragraphs in the first three books; whereas in Book IV, 'Of Systems of Political Economy', and Book V, 'Of the Revenue of the Sovereign or Commonwealth', it appears in 84 and 16 paragraphs respectively.[5] In these two latter books, Smith uses the word 'monopoly' in relation to government measures concerning international trade, colonial trade, and the exclusive privileges of trading companies.[6] It is Smith himself who emphasises the strict connection between monopoly and mercantilist measures:

> Monopoly of one kind or another, indeed, seems to be the sole engine of the mercantile system.
>
> (*WN* IV.vii.c.89)

Leaving aside the specific details of each individual measure, the element common to all is the artificial exclusion of outsiders from a given market. The following passages concerning two of Smith's favourite instances of monopoly, the exclusive privileges of corporations and trade companies, are thus revealing:

> The exclusive privilege of an incorporated trade necessarily restrains the competition, in the town where it is established, to those who are free of the trade. To have served an apprenticeship in the town, under a master properly qualified, is commonly the necessary requisite for obtaining this freedom. The bye-laws of the corporation regulate sometimes the number of apprentices which any master is allowed to have, and almost always the number of years which each apprentice is obliged to serve. *The intention of both regulations is to restrain the competition to a much smaller number than might otherwise be disposed to enter into the trade.*
>
> (*WN* I.x.c.5, emphasis added)

> The object, besides, of the greater part of the bye-laws of all regulated companies, as well as of all other corporations, is not so much to oppress those who are already members, as *to discourage others from becoming so*; which may be done, not only by a high fine, but by many other contrivances. The constant view of such companies is always to raise the rate of their own profit as high as they can; to keep the market, both for the goods which they export, and for those which they

> import, as much understocked as they can: which can be done only by restraining the competition, or by *discouraging new adventurers from entering into the trade.*
>
> (*WN* V.i.e.10, emphasis added)

The consequence of this banishment is that incumbents are able to determine the quantity of a given commodity available at the marketplace *in the long run*. Consider the following passage concerning colonial trade:

> Some nations have given up the whole commerce of their colonies to an exclusive company, of whom the colonists were obliged to buy all such European goods as they wanted, and to whom they were obliged to sell the whole of their own surplus produce. It was the interest of the company, therefore, not only to sell the former as dear, and to buy the latter as cheap as possible, but to buy no more of the latter, even at this low price than what they could dispose of for a very high price in Europe. It was their interest, not only to degrade in all cases the value of the surplus produce of the colony, but in many cases *to discourage and keep down the natural increase of its quantity.*
>
> (*WN* IV.vii.b.22, emphasis added)

Thanks to these artificial barriers to entry, incumbents may take actions which would not have been profitable in conditions of free competition. In game theory jargon, it is possible to claim that the incumbents' strategy space depends, inter alia, on the presence or absence of artificial barriers to entry. Smithian incumbents follow a three-step strategy. In the first step, incumbents invest resources to enforce the entry barrier created by the governmental measure. In the second step, they choose the productive capacity and determine the quantity of the commodity to bring to the market. In the third and final step, they set the price of the commodity brought to the market. In the following we examine each of these three steps in turn.

13.3.1 Enforcement of entry barriers

Regarding the first step, note that the mere enactment of a government measure is no guarantee for incumbents that public enforcement would be sufficient to prevent unlawful entry into the market. As a case in point, consider colonial trade. As is well known, in the aftermath of the discovery of the New World many European countries granted the exclusive right to companies to carry out colonial trade. Smith underlines that the great distance between the mother country and the colonies and the extension of coasts favoured smuggling, which was often an effective way to circumvent the exclusive privileges granted to trading companies (see *WN* IV.iv.10 and IV.vii.b.12; see also *WN* IV.viii.32 and 40 on the illegal exportation of wool and Arabic gum respectively). Whenever public enforcement does not provide the incumbents' desired level of entry discouragement, incumbents must invest a part of their own resources to supplement public enforcement of the entry barrier. Consider colonial trade again. To justify the grants of exclusive privileges to trade companies, a literature flourished supporting the claim that these companies provided public goods by building and maintaining forts and garrisons yielding protection against attacks by natives and pirates. As any public good, forts and garrisons suffered from free riding: hence the necessity to back up company profits by granting a legal monopoly (Anderson and Tollison, 1983). In the case of oceanic trade, Smith is not hostile to the granting of a legal monopoly, taking due consideration of the high capital requirement and risk coefficient involved in this kind of trade and the benefits for the country. However, he insists that the monopoly should only be temporary, and forts and garrisons should come into public hands when the monopoly right expires:

> But upon the expiration of the term, the monopoly ought certainly to determine; the forts and garrisons, if it was found necessary to establish any, to be taken into the hands of government, their value to be paid to the company, and the trade to be laid open to all the subjects of the state.
>
> (*WN* V.i.e.30)

In any case, Smith shows no sympathy for the claim that forts and garrisons are public goods. According to Anderson and Tollison (1982, p. 1248),

> forts and garrisons provided a mechanism for the enforcement of the cartel rights of the chartered companies against the interlopers. [...] It is not that free riding was not taking place; it was. It is that the relevant free riding was with respect to monopoly price and not company provision of public goods. A simple extension of Smith's analysis and a consideration of the historical relevance of the forts reveal the interlopers for what they surely were – competitive entrants on legally sanctioned monopoly rights.

What is relevant for our purposes is the fact that trade companies, notwithstanding the grant of a monopoly right, were conscious of the potential competition by outsiders (Smith's interlopers) and, accordingly, took the decision to invest in entry-deterring activities to privately enforce their publicly granted monopoly right.

13.3.2 Choice of productive capacity and produced quantity

Regarding the second step of the incumbent's strategy, it must be stressed that, in the absence of effective entry barriers, incumbents have no control over the quantity actually brought to the market *in the long run*. In several passages of *WN*, Smith iterates that, in freely competitive markets, the quantity of a given commodity actually brought to the market 'naturally suits itself' to its effectual demand (see *WN* I.vii.12 and 16, IV.i.12 etc.). Whenever the market price is higher than the natural price, new firms enter the market and, thus, overall production increases to equate with effectual demand. When the entry process comes to an end, market and natural prices coincide and all producers (new and old) earn the same rate of profit: the natural rate. Hence, to gain extra-profits *in the long run*, incumbents must keep the market price persistently above its natural level. To achieve this, they must be able to create and maintain an artificial dearth, that is, bring to the market a persistently less amount of the commodity than the effectual demand. In the absence of natural barriers (such as in the case of fine French wines) and artificial barriers (such as legal monopolies), no incumbent has the incentive to voluntary reduce its own production to create an artificial dearth in the long run. Such a decision would be thwarted by the entry of outsiders as soon as a market-natural price discrepancy appeared.[7] By contrast, in the presence of entry barriers, given an effectual demand, incumbents are able to, and thus have an incentive to, create an artificial dearth by a voluntary reduction in their individual production or even in their individual production capacity. In this regard consider the following passages where Smith mentions the cases of colonial monopolists destroying plantations (and thus reducing production capacity) or burning up part of the annual harvest:

> Our tobacco planters [in Virginia and Maryland], accordingly, have shown the same fear of the super-abundance of tobacco, which the proprietors of the old vineyards in France have of the super-abundance of wine. By act of assembly they have restrained its cultivation to six thousand plants, supposed to yield a thousand weight of tobacco, for every negro between sixteen and sixty years of age. Such a negro, over and above this quantity of tobacco, can manage, they reckon, four acres of Indian corn. To prevent the market from being overstocked too, they have sometimes, in plentiful years, we are told by Dr. Douglas, (I suspect he has been ill informed) burnt a certain quantity of tobacco for every negro, in the same manner as the Dutch are said to do of spices. If such violent methods are necessary to keep up the present price of tobacco, the superior advantage of its culture over that of corn, if it still has any, will not probably be of long continuance.
>
> (*WN* I.xi.33)

> In the spice islands the Dutch are said to burn all the spiceries which a fertile season produces beyond what they expect to dispose of in Europe with such a profit as they think sufficient. In the islands

> where they have no settlements, they give a premium to those who collect the young blossoms and green leaves of the clove and nutmeg trees which naturally grow there, but which this savage policy has now, it is said, almost completely extirpated. Even in the islands where they have settlements they have very much reduced, it is said, the number of those trees. If the produce even of their own islands was much greater than what suited their market, the natives, they suspect, might find means to convey some part of it to other nations; and the best way, they imagine, to secure their own monopoly is to take care that no more shall grow than what they themselves carry to market.
>
> (*WN* IV.vii.c.101)

What clearly emerges is that, in Smith's view, monopolists do believe that a permanent reduction in market quantity leads to a permanent increase in market price. In modern terminology, this amounts to saying that Smith's monopolists clearly perceive that they face an inverse price-quantity relationship in terms of demand. This result needs to be stressed since it helps in clearing up the common misunderstandings concerning Garegnani's controversial 1983 reconstruction of the role of demand schedules within the Classical value theory. In the light of our reconstruction of Smith's view of monopoly, Garegnani's effectual demand can only be an analytical tool forged to analyse market price dynamics in competitive markets outside equilibrium, given the natural values of the distributive variables. By the same token, Garegnani (1983) should not be (mis)interpreted as implying that the Classical value theory has no room for demand schedules (albeit different from the well-behaved schedules of neo-classical economics).[8]

13.3.3 *Setting the price*

Once the effective enforcement of the monopoly right has been achieved and an artificial dearth created, the last step of the incumbents' strategy is their price setting policy. If a monopolist knew the height and slope of its market demand function perfectly, price fixing would be trivial, once produced quantity is known. However, these are not Smith's assumptions: monopolists decide both the quantity to bring to the market and the initial selling price, while the 'market' determines whether demand equals supply or whether a shortage or a surplus is obtained at the price initially fixed by the monopolists. In the case of excess demand or supply, monopolists will accordingly revise prices up or down. To clarify Smith's view, we now study the price setting policy of inland corn dealers after a bad harvest. Although a natural, non-artificial form of dearth, a bad harvest is still a form of dearth. Smith's analysis of inland corn dealers' price strategy in the years of a bad harvest may thus provide useful insights into Smith's view on the incumbents' price setting policy in the presence of an artificial dearth such as that caused by Smithian monopolists, who intentionally keep their market constantly understocked.

The price setting policy of inland corn dealers after a bad harvest is analysed by Smith in a long section entitled, 'Digression concerning the Corn Trade and Corn Laws', in the middle of Book IV, Chapter V, 'Of Bounties'. At first reading this section does not seem appropriate for a rational reconstruction of Smith's theory of monopoly. In Smith's view, in fact, both supply and demand make the emergence and persistence of a monopoly highly unlikely in the corn market of a developed country:

> As in every civilized country [corn] is the commodity of which the annual consumption is the greatest, so a greater quantity of industry is annually employed in producing corn than in producing any other commodity. When it first comes from the ground, too, it is necessarily divided among a greater number of owners than any other commodity; and these owners can never be collected into one place like a number of independent manufacturers, but are necessarily scattered through all the different corners of the country. These first owners either immediately supply the consumers in their own neighbourhood, or they supply other inland dealers who supply those consumers. The inland dealers in corn, therefore, including both the farmer and the baker, are necessarily more numerous than the dealers in any other commodity, and their dispersed situation renders it altogether impossible for them to enter into any general combination.
>
> (*WN* IV.v.b.4)

Hence, according to Smith, an artificial scarcity of corn may seldom or never be intentionally created in the corn market of a developed country:[9]

> Were it possible, indeed, for one great company of merchants to possess themselves of the whole crop of an extensive country, it might, perhaps, be their interest to deal with it as the Dutch are said to do with the spiceries of the Moluccas, to destroy or throw away a considerable part of it in order to keep up the price of the rest. But it is scarce possible, even by the violence of law, to establish such an extensive monopoly with regard to corn; and, wherever the law leaves the trade free, it is of all commodities the least liable to be engrossed or monopolized by the force of a few large capitals, which buy up the greater part of it. (*ibidem*)

Yet, what the above does not imply is that the corn market of a developed country is never plagued by any form of dearth: a great variety of natural causes, in fact, cyclically cause a bad corn harvest. How do inland corn dealers set the price of corn in the years of bad harvest? The relevant passage is the following:

> It is his interest to raise the price of his corn as high as the real scarcity of the season requires, and it can never be his interest to raise it higher. By raising the price he discourages the consumption, and puts everybody more or less, but particularly the inferior ranks of people, upon thrift and good management. If, by raising it too high, he discourages the consumption so much that the supply of the season is likely to go beyond the consumption of the season, and to last for some time after the next crop begins to come in, he runs the hazard, not only of losing a considerable part of his corn by natural causes, but of being obliged to sell what remains of it for much less than what he might have had for it several months before. If by not raising the price high enough he discourages the consumption so little that the supply of the season is likely to fall short of the consumption of the season, he not only loses a part of the profit which he might otherwise have made, but he exposes the people to suffer before the end of the season, instead of the hardships of a dearth, the dreadful horrors of a famine.
>
> (*WN* IV.v.b.3)

The inland corn dealers set the price of corn so as to meet these two conditions: (i) to sell all their corn before the next harvest and (ii) to maximise profits. To achieve these two targets inland corn dealers have to estimate accurately the relevant portion of the corn demand function and set the price accordingly. The only difference between the inland corn dealers who set the price in a year of bad harvest and incumbents enjoying a legal monopoly is the different source (natural vs. artificial) of dearth.

13.3.4 Macrodynamic consequences of monopoly and the need for state regulation

In this chapter, we have concentrated on the microeconomic side of Smith's analysis of monopoly. However, we are aware that Smith was greatly interested in the macrodynamic consequences of monopoly. In his view, monopolies (particularly those created by an act of government) cause a subversion of the 'natural distribution' of labour and capital stock among the various sectors of a given economy, that is, a different allocation of economic resources from that which would have been established by free competition (see *WN* IV.vii.c.92 and ff). Since for Smith, a competitive allocation of resources is wealth maximising, Smith's analysis implies that economies beset by monopolies are poorer and grow more slowly than competitive economies.

Such detrimental macroeconomic consequences of monopoly (in the Smithian sense of artificial restrictions to free competition) were present in Smith's mind ever since the *Lectures on Jurisprudence*. There Smith maintains that

> The wealth of a state consists in the cheapness of provisions and all other necessaries and conveniences of life; that is, the small proportion they bear to the money payd, considering the quantity of money which is in the state; or in other words that they should be easily come at. Its poverty again consists in the uncomeatibleness or difficulty with which the severall necessaryes of life are procured. Now all monopolies evidently tend to promote the poverty or, which comes to the same thing, the uncomeatibleness of the thing so monopolized. Thus for example if one should get an exclusive privilege of making and selling all the silk in the kingdom, he would as he had it at his own making greatly increase the price; he would perhaps lessen the quantity made to a tenth part of that now in use; and would raise the price nearly in proportion; and by this means he would make great profit at a less expense of materialls and labour than can be done when many have the same liberty. The price of the commodity is by this means raised, and the quantity of this necessary, ornament, or conveniency of life is at the same time lessened.
>
> (*LJ* (A) ii.33–34)

And he adds:

> The establishment of corporations and other societies who have an exclusive right is equally detrimental. The severall corporations in towns have all an exclusive privilege of exercising that trade within the liberties of the town, (no one being allowed to take up a business but who has served an apprenticeship in the town; formerly no one but whose father had been a burgher.) Now, e.g., the corporation of butchers have the sole liberty of killing and selling all the flesh that is brought to market. Here, the privilege is not vested in the person of one man, but as the number is fixt they will readily enter into compacts to keep up the price of the commodity and at the same time supply the market but very indifferently with flesh.
>
> (*LJ* (A) ii.34–35)

Smith underlines two consequences deriving from the pervasive presence of monopolies. One is demographic. Consider a closed economy (say a given town) where several markets have been monopolised. Since the expenditure flows of the various monopolists are closely interlinked – the members of each corporation sell their commodity at a supra-competitive price, but, at the same time, they buy all other monopolised commodities for an equally high price – the general price level of such an economy turns out to be higher than would be ideally obtained in a freely competitive environment. Accordingly, fewer people would choose to live in the town and many more would choose to live elsewhere (say in the countryside), thus reducing the potential outlet market for the commodities produced in the town:

> Besides by these corporations the number of inhabitants is greatly diminished; and any who would settle in the city are hindered from so doing. By this means there are generally two or three large villages in the neighbourhood of every city. If a corporation lessens the number of rivalls, it also lessens the number of customers.
>
> (*LJ*(A) ii.36–37)

The other important consequence is Smith's plea for state regulation in monopolised markets:

> [butchers, brewers, bakers, etc.] prevent a concourse and by that means raise the price of their commodities. And accordingly there is generally a magistrate who settles the price of all these commodities.
>
> (*LJ*(A) vi.88–89)

On the contrary 'as there is no corporation of the dealers in cloth there is no one who regulates the price of it' (ibid.). Smith adds that state regulation is aimed at achieving a kind of second best, the first best being achieved by a freely competitive economy:

> It is the same thing to a baker whether he makes £50 by making 1000 or 100000 loaves in the year. And when there are few in any branch of business they can easily agree amongst themselves to do this. There is therefore a magistrate or clerk of the market appointed who regulates the price of this according to that of corn or oats in the neighbourhood. This expedient, tho necessary where corporations are allowed, does not answer the end of a plentiful market in any shape so well as that of allowing a free concurrence.
>
> (*LJ*(A) vi.89)

It is interesting that Smith allows state regulation also for very special commodities such as coined gold:

> The Master of the Mint should not however be allowed to take any price he inclined for the coinage, for it is necessary that he should be the only coiner and have a monopoly of the coinage. It is therefore necessary that here, as in all other monopolies, there should be a fixed or assized price.
>
> (*LJ*(A) vi.150–151)

The reference to the Master of the Mint makes it clear that state regulation is also needed when there is a recognised public interest in preserving a monopoly. Although Smith rarely misses an occasion to report the evils of monopoly, he was not blind to the possibility that a temporary monopoly could further a social aim. In the case of patents and copyrights, as well as in the case of opening new roads to international trade, the grant of a temporary monopoly is envisaged by Smith as a necessary means to induce the required inflow of capital into innovative but costly and hazardous enterprises:

> When a company of merchants undertake, at their own risk and expense, to establish a new trade with some remote and barbarous nation, it may not be unreasonable to incorporate them into a joint-stock company, and to grant them, in case of their success, a monopoly of the trade for a certain number of years. It is the easiest and most natural way in which the state can recompense them for hazarding a dangerous and expensive experiment, of which the public is afterwards to reap the bene fit. A temporary monopoly of this kind may be vindicated upon the same principles upon which a like monopoly of a new machine is granted to its inventor, and that of a new book to its author.
>
> (*WN* V.i.e.30)

Moreover, Smith was aware of the political dangers of allowing free competition (particularly foreign competition) in all those sectors tied to 'the defence of the country':

> The defence of Great Britain, for example, depends very much upon the number of its sailors and shipping. The Act of navigation therefore, very properly endeavours to give the sailors and shipping of Great Britain the monopoly of the trade of their own country in some cases by absolute prohibitions and in others by heavy burdens upon the shipping of foreign countries.
>
> (*WN* IV.ii.24)

Finally, Smith pleaded for caution in implementing deregulation or a pro-competitive policy aimed at eliminating legal entry barriers. By anticipating the sunk costs argument, which was subsequently developed by Ricardo in Chapter 19, 'On Sudden Changes in the Channels of Trade', of his *Principles of Political Economy and Taxation*, Smith noted that monopolists usually employ a significant amount of fixed capital in their trades. The value of this form of capital would be highly depreciated in the case of a sudden repeal of the legal monopoly:

> The undertaker of a great manufacture, who, by the home-markets being suddenly laid open to the competition of foreigners, should be

> obliged to abandon his trade, would no doubt suffer very considerably. That part of his capital which had usually been employed in purchasing materials and in paying his workmen might, without much difficulty, perhaps, find another employment. But that part of it which was fixed in workhouses, and in the instruments of trade, could scarce be disposed of without considerable loss. The equitable regard, therefore, to his interest requires that changes of this kind should never be introduced suddenly, but slowly, gradually, and after a very long warning. The legislature, were it possible that its deliberations could be always directed, not by the clamorous importunity of partial interests, but by an extensive view of the general good, ought upon this very account, perhaps, to be particularly careful neither to establish any new monopolies of this kind, nor to extend further those which are already established. Every such regulation introduces some degree of real disorder into the constitution of the state, which it will be difficult afterwards to cure without occasioning another disorder.
>
> (*WN* IV.ii.44)

13.4 Final remarks

This chapter has proposed a rational reconstruction of Smith's theory of monopoly. We have started from the premise that interpreters granting low marks to Smith as a monopolist theorist have been misled, partly by the fact that Smith uses the term 'monopoly' in a very different way from current usage, and partly by the fact that they have looked for a Smithian theory of monopoly in the wrong place, that is, in Chapter 7 of Book I of *WN*. We have shown that for Smith monopoly refers to a variety of market outcomes whose common feature is that the entry of new firms is persistently forestalled. In addition, we have focused on Books IV and V of *WN* as the proper place to find useful clues of a theory of monopoly along Smithian lines.

We hope to have shown that Smith's account of monopolists' behaviour is richer than that provided by later theorists. In Smith's view, monopolists' behaviour is based on a deliberate manipulation of their productive capacity and the quantity brought to the market to achieve a higher market price than the competitive level. This behaviour makes sense provided that Smith's monopolists are assumed to perceive demand as an inverse price-quantity relationship. We believe that this result may help in clarifying the controversial role of the demand within rational reconstructions of the Classical theory of value.

Acknowledgements

We wish to thank Ghislain Delplace, Heinz D. Kurz, Manuela Mosca, Ferdinando Meacci, and Nathalie Sigot for their comments. Usual caveats apply. Financial support from PRIN 2009 'Growth and Structural Change' is gratefully acknowledged.

Notes

1 A previous version of this manuscript was presented at the 17th Annual Conference of the European Society for the History of Economic Thought, Saint-Petersburg, Russia, 17–19 May 2012 and at IX Annual Conference of the Italian Association for the History of Political Economy (STOREP), Padua, Italy, 1–3 June 2012.

2 Exegetical dilemmas of this kind are not uncommon within the historiography of economic analysis. To give just one example, Kurz and Salvadori (2009) show that Ricardo's *Principles of Political Economy and Taxation* implicitly encompasses an economic theory of exhaustible resources and even the Hotelling Rule, notwithstanding the fact that Ricardo did not treat royalties as anything different from profits. Ricardian interpreters have generally been misled by their search for a Ricardian theory of exhaustible resources in the wrong place, that is, in Chapter III, 'On the Rents of Mines', of Ricardo's *Principles*. By contrast, Kurz and Salvadori's focus is on Chapter XXIV, 'Doctrine of Adam Smith concerning the Rent of Land'.

3 To the best of our knowledge, the first Classical economist to make use of the word 'monopoly' mainly in the contemporary meaning of 'sole producer' was William Nassau Senior (1854, Chapter 4).

4 Salvadori and Signorino (2012) provide a detailed analysis of the theoretical differences between the Classical notion of free competition and the neo-classical notion of perfect competition.

5 The computing was carried out using the online version of *WN* available at The Library of Economics and Liberty: http://www.econlib.org/library/Smith/smWN.html.

6 As is well known, Smith charges mercantilist authors with having fallaciously equated the wealth of a nation with the quantity of gold and silver circulating in it and, accordingly, with having recommended government measures aimed at the creation of an artificial surplus of the balance of trade. Such measures amounted to high customs duties or absolute prohibitions to discourage the importation of foreign commodities and drawbacks, bounties, advantageous treaties of commerce with foreign states, and the establishment of colonies to encourage the exportation of domestic commodities (see *WN* IV.i.35). As to the ability of pressure groups to influence public policy, Smith goes so far as to claim that the very foundation and maintenance of the British Empire was a political project 'extremely fit for a nation whose government is influenced by shopkeepers' (*WN* IV.vii.c.63).

7 Differences in emphasis apart, Classical economists took for granted that market and natural prices would coincide on average whenever there is free competition. Ricardo, in particular, was very confident that 'the principle which apportions capital to each trade in the precise amount that it is required, is more active than is generally supposed' (*Works* I.iv.4).

8 Garegnani (1983) starts from the claim that within neo-classical economics, the relative prices of all commodities, both consumption goods and factors of production services, are determined simultaneously by the interplay of well-defined demand and supply functions. Yet, 'the role of demand functions in determining [consumption goods] prices depends on their role in determining distribution by means of the "relative scarcity" of the "factors of production"'. (*idem*, p. 309). By contrast, for Garegnani, both the idea of factors of

production prices determined by their relative scarcity and the perfect logical symmetry between income distribution and value theory are entirely alien to Classical economics. Adam Smith and David Ricardo studied the relative prices of consumption goods, taking as given the real wage rate that had already been determined in another part of their theories. This is why, according to Garegnani, Smith and Ricardo thought of demand not as a function endowed with well-defined formal properties but rather as a point, the point of effectual demand, i.e., the quantity of a given commodity demanded at the natural price. The analytical role of effectual demand is to give a clue to scholars as to the dynamics of market prices in situations of market disequilibrium: 'the prices corresponding to quantities below (above) the normal quantity q_n would be determinate only in that they are higher (lower) than the nor mal price p_n. If we wished to represent this notion [in the familiar price-quantity diagram], we would find two areas, North-West (*NW*) and South-East (*SE*) of the normal price-quantity point *P*, where *NW* indicates where the price is likely to be found when the quantity supplied has fallen accidentally short of q_n, and *SE* indicates where it is likely to be in the opposite case' (ibid.).

9 Smith's analysis of the corn market involves a well-defined policy prescription: since artificial dearth due to monopolists' deliberate action is unlikely, *laissez-faire* is the best policy option in the corn market. For Smith, government interventions are more often than not the real cause of the evils (corn scarcity and famines) they are intended to cure: see (*WN* IV.v.b.5 ff). Smith's positive and prescriptive views on this subject are questionable. Since medieval times local and national authorities all around Europe have enacted and enforced severe measures against engrossers creating artificial scarcity of victuals (see De Roover, 1958, p. 428 ff), a proof of the fact that foodstuff engrossing was not as unlikely as Smith thought it to be. Rashid (1980) assesses Smith's analysis of the price setting policy of inland corn dealers and provides evidence that, in Smith's time, England's corn market was not as atomistic as Smith alleged it to be.

References

Anderson, G. M. and Tollison, R. D. (1982). Adam Smith's analysis of joint-stock companies. *Journal of Political Economy*, 90, 6, pp. 1237–1256.

Anderson, G. M. and Tollison, R. D. (1983). Apologiae for chartered monopolies in for eign trade 1600–1800. *History of Political Economy*, 15, 4, pp. 549–566.

Blaug, M. (1997a). *Economic Theory in Retrospect*, 3rd edn. Cambridge: Cambridge University Press.

Blaug, M. (1997b). Competition as an end-state and competition as a process. In M. Blaug (ed.), *Not Only an Economist. Recent Essays by Mark Blaug*. Cheltenham, UK/Brookfield: Edward Elgar, pp. 66–86.

Ciccone, R. (1999). Classical and Neoclassical Short-Run Prices. A comparative analysis of their intended empirical content. In G. Mongiovi and F. Petri (eds), *Value, Distribution and Capital. Essays in honour of Pierangelo Garegnani*. London: Routledge, pp. 69–92.

Cournot, A. A. (1838 [1897]). *Recherches sur les principes mathe'matiques de la the'orie des richesses. Translated by N. Bacon as Researches into the Mathematical Principles of the Theory of Wealth*. London: Macmillan.

De Roover, R. (1951). Monopoly theory prior to Adam Smith: a revision. *The Quarterly Journal of Economics*, 65, 4, pp. 492–524.

De Roover, R. (1955). Scholastic economics: survival and lasting influence from the sixteenth century to Adam Smith. *The Quarterly Journal of Economics*, 69, 2, pp. 161–190.

De Roover, R. (1958). The concept of the just price: theory and economic policy. *The Journal of Economic History*, 18, 4, pp. 418–434.

Dupuit, J. (1844 [1952]). De la mesure de l'utilit'e des travaux publics. *Annales des Ponts et Chausse'es. English translation by R.H. Barback as "On the Measurement of the Utility of Public Works". International Economic Papers*, 2, pp. 83–110. London: Macmillan.

Dupuit, J. (1849 [1962]). De l'influence des p'eages sur l'utilit'e des voies de communication. *Annales des Ponts et Chausse'es. English translation by E. Henderson as "On Tolls and Transport Charges". International Economic Papers*, 11, pp. 7–31. London: Macmillan.

Dutt, A. K. (1998). Monopoly. In H. D. Kurz and N. Salvadori (eds), *The Elgar Companion to Classical Economics. Volume II: L Z.* Cheltenham, UK/Northampton, MA: Edward Elgar, pp. 141–145.

Ekelund, R. B. and Hebert, R. F. (1999). *Secret Origins of Modern Microeconomics: Dupuit and the Engineers.* Chicago: University of Chicago Press.

Garegnani, P. (1983). The classical theory of wages and the role of demand schedules in the determination of relative prices. *The American Economic Review*, 73, 2, pp. 309–313.

Hovenkamp, H. (1989). The Sherman Act and the classical theory of competition. *Iowa Law Review*, 74, pp. 1019–1065.

Kurz, H. D. and Salvadori, N. (1995). *Theory of Production. A Long-Period Analysis.* Cambridge: Cambridge University Press.

Kurz, H. D. and Salvadori, N. (2009). Ricardo on exhaustible resources, and the Hotelling Rule. In A. Ikeo and H. D. Kurz (eds). *A History of Economic Theory. Essays in Honour of Takashi Negishi.* London: Routledge, pp. 68–79.

Mosca, M. (1998). Jules Dupuit, the French "ingénieurs économistes" and the Société d'Economie Politique. In G. Faccarello (ed.). *Studies in the History of French Political Economy: From Bodin to Walras.* London: Routledge, pp. 254–283.

Rashid, S. (1980). The policy of Laissez-Faire during scarcities. *The Economic Journal*, 90, 359, pp. 493–503.

Ricardo, D. (1951). *On the Principles of Political Economy and Taxation, 3rd edn 1821, Vol. I of The Works and Correspondence of David Ricardo, edited by P. Sraffa with the collaboration of M.H. Dobb.* Cambridge: Cambridge University Press. In the text quoted as Works, volume number, chapter number, paragraph number.

Salvadori, N. and Signorino, R. (2016). Competition. G. Faccarello and H. D. Kurz (eds). *Handbook of the History of Economic Analysis*, Vol. 3. Cheltenham, UK and Northampton, MA, USA: Edward Elgar, pp. 70–81.

Senior, N. W. (1854). *Four Introductory Lectures on Political Economy*, 3rd edn. London: Richard Griffin and Co.

Smith, A. (1976). *An Inquiry into the Nature and Causes of the Wealth of Nations, 1st edn 1776, Vol. II of The Glasgow Edition of the Works and Correspondence of Adam Smith, edited by R.H. Campbell and A.S. Skinner.* Oxford: Oxford University Press. In the text quoted as WN, book number, chapter number, paragraph number.

Smith, A. (1978). *Lectures on Jurisprudence. Edited by R. L. Meek, D. D. Raphael and Peter Stein, Vol. V of The Glasgow Edition of the Works and Correspondence of Adam Smith*, edited by R.H. Campbell and A.S. Skinner. Oxford: Oxford University Press. In the text quoted as LJ, A or B report, manuscript number, paragraph number.

Stigler, G. J. (1982). The economists and the problem of monopoly. *The American Economic Review*, 72, 2, pp. 1–11.

Walras, L. (1874–1877 [1954]). *E'le'ments d'e'conomie politique pure, ou the'orie de la richesse sociale. English translation by W. Jaffe' as Elements of Pure Economics or The Theory of Social Wealth*. London: Allen and Unwin.

14 Adam Smith on markets, competition, and violations of natural liberty

Heinz D. Kurz[1]

Original paper: Heinz D. Kurz (2016) Adam Smith on markets, competition and violations of natural liberty, *Cambridge Journal of Economics*, 40:2, 615–638, DOI: https://doi.org/10.1093/cje/bev011. Oxford: Oxford University Press, on behalf of the Cambridge Political Economy Society.

14.1 Introduction

Adam Smith advocated a socio-economic system in which large parts of economic life are coordinated via interdependent markets in conditions of free competition. Such a system, he was convinced, favoured 'equality, liberty and justice' (WN IV.ix.3) in society and therefore was a good thing. He did *not* argue, as is often contended, 'that nothing but selfishness is necessary to yield socially beneficial outcomes' (Schotter, 1985, p. 2). He encountered the dark sides of ruthless selfishness, greed, and rapacity on a large scale in the time in which he lived and he saw that a main effort of selfish people was directed at narrowing and eventually abolishing competition. He deplored time and again 'the wretched spirit of monopoly' (WN IV.ii.21) that permeated what he called the 'mercantile system' with its privileges, preferences, and concentration of economic and political power in a few hands. This system was beneficial to those few at the cost of the many and decelerated economic development and growth. The East India Companies of Great Britain and the Netherlands were scary cases in point

1 Presented at the conference 'Die Philosophie des Marktes', Philosophical Seminar of the Technical University of Braunschweig, 13–15 February 2014, at the Research Seminar of the Faculty of Social and Economic Studies, University of Graz, 9 April 2014 and at the 'International Conference on New Thinking in Economic Theory and Policy', Meiji University, Tokyo, 13–15 September 2014. I am grateful to Tony Aspromourgos, Christian Gehrke, Geoff Harcourt, Manfred Holler, Neri Salvadori, Takashi Yagi, and two anonymous referees for valuable comments on an earlier draft of this paper, to Corinna Blasch and Andreas Rainer for preparing the figures in the paper and to the participants of the conferences and the seminar for useful discussions. I benefited a great deal from the joint work with Richard Sturn on Smith during the past couple of years. All remaining errors and misconceptions are, of course, entirely my responsibility.

DOI: 10.4324/9781003138709-18

of the enormous damage that unfettered selfish behaviour could bring about. Clearly, selfishness alone did *not* yield socially beneficial outcomes. Checks and balances were needed in order to channel selfish behaviour in directions that were socially beneficial and prevent it from developing its dark and destructive sides. These checks and balances included several elements, from the rule of law to moral norms, particularly self-restraint, and conceived of liberty essentially as the security of the individual. In order for self-regard to be able to properly work for the general benefit, the Scottish moral and political philosopher put forward a substantial list of things that played a role in this. He insisted, among other things, that the constitution of a country, its law, and institutions, made a good deal of difference and exemplified this with respect to North America, on the one hand, and the East Indies, on the other:

> The difference between the genius of the British constitution which protects and governs North America, and that of the mercantile company which oppresses and domineers in the East Indies, cannot perhaps be better illustrated than by the different state of those countries.
>
> (WN I.viii.26)

In *The Fable of the Bees* (1723), Bernard Mandeville had argued that vice, not virtue, engenders prosperity and is thus socially beneficial. He poetised: 'The Worst of all the multitude Did something for the common good' and 'T'enjoy the World's Conveniences, Befamed in War, yet live in Ease Without great Vices is a vain Eutopia seated in the Brain' (Mandeville, [1723] 1924, pp. 68, 76). Smith (and before him David Hume) strongly disagreed with Mandeville and in *The Theory of Moral Sentiments* (1976a) called the latter's views 'in almost every respect erroneous' (TMS, p. 451). Containing vicious behaviour need not, as Mandeville had contended, entail a cumulative downturn of the economy because of dwindling levels of demand, with the result that locksmiths would no longer produce locks, lawyers and judges would go out of business, standing armies become superfluous, etc. Since according to Smith 'the desire of bettering our condition … comes with us from the womb, and never leaves us till we go into the grave' (WN II.iii.28), there is no fear that the productive resources that are no longer needed to protect a man's property will not eventually be used in other activities:

> The uniform, constant, and uninterrupted effort of every man to better his condition, the principles from which publick and national, as well as private opulence is originally derived, is frequently powerful enough to maintain the natural progress of things toward improvement.
>
> (WN II.iii.31)

Hence good government, which controls and retrenches the dark sides of selfishness, will not lead to poverty and misery. On the contrary, it will stimulate diligence, industry, and creativity. The 'science of the legislator', Smith had elaborated, was designed to show the way to good government.

What was missing was a demonstration of the working of markets in conditions of free competition. Pursuing one's self-interest in a decentralised economy through a network of interdependent markets did not imply chaos and anarchy, as several economists and social philosophers had argued. It did not imply a *bellum omnium contra omnes*, unless Leviathan, the absolutist state, would intervene with an iron fist and keep the desires and avidities of individuals at bay, as Thomas Hobbes had argued. No Leviathan was required and if there was one it was detrimental to the well-being of the large majority of the people. But good government was badly needed. It had to provide an institutional and regulatory framework that involved incentives, which channelled selfishness in directions that were not only individually but socially beneficial. And it had to establish and preserve competitive conditions.

This chapter is composed as follows. Section 14.2 deals with Smith's view as to the origin of man's propensity 'to truck, barter and exchange', i.e., to organise markets and carry out most of his economic transactions by means of this medium. Section 14.3 turns to Adam Smith's distinction between 'market' and 'natural' prices and expounds the determination of the latter within a simple analytical framework. Smith considers natural prices as the more fundamental magnitudes and conceives of them as centres of gravitation of market prices. Section 14.4 turns to his idea of the gravitation of market prices towards, or oscillation around, their natural levels and what in Smith's view spoke in their favour. Clearly, if there was no such gravitation (or oscillation) the concept of natural price could be said to be void and Smith's view of markets and their allegedly remarkable properties, without any foundation. A simple model will be used to discuss Smith's view, the difficulties it faces and how they can perhaps be overcome. Section 14.5 deals briefly with the centripetal forces unleashed by competition: the introduction of 'improvements' and innovations – new methods of production and new goods – and how they are absorbed into the economic system. Section 14.6 addresses the problem of the information upon which sellers and buyers in markets base their decisions and act. It will be argued that Smith was perfectly well aware of the fact that information is asymmetrically distributed among market participants, a fact that gives rise to the phenomena of moral hazard and adverse selection. This will be illustrated in terms of the banking trade, which Smith identified as being particularly prone to malfunctioning and instability. The danger that selfish and unscrupulous people might endanger the security of the whole society makes him advocate regulations of the banking trade, notwithstanding the fact that this involves a violation of natural liberty. Section 14.7 contains some observations on the 'wretched spirit of monopoly', which is permanently on the lookout for means and ways to abandon competition in the interest of abnormal profits. Section 14.8 concludes.

Before I turn to the main argument of this paper, it should be mentioned that our understanding of the Classical economists has been substantially revised and improved thanks to Piero Sraffa's reformulation of the 'standpoint … of the old classical economists from Adam Smith to Ricardo', a standpoint that had been 'submerged and forgotten since the advent of the "marginal method"' (Sraffa, 1960, p. v). This standpoint has then been further elaborated by, among others, Pierangelo Garegnani, Luigi Pasinetti, Bertram Schefold, and Ian Steedman. It has brought back to life the extraordinary richness, depth, and basic coherence of the Classical economists' analysis, which differs in important respects from the marginalist one. The following disquisition shows that many of the insights Smith had into the structure of the economic system and its working have been lost sight of in much of modern theory. The paper thus also throws into doubt the widespread view that the market for economic ideas is a perfectly functioning selection mechanism that preserves everything that is sound and valid and eliminates everything that is misleading and wrong. For example, had Smith's analysis of the banking and financial system been absorbed into the mainstream, the recent financial crisis would not have been met with surprise and disbelief in large parts of the economics profession.

14.2 Men's natural faculties, the propensity to exchange, and markets

The starting point of Smith's analysis of markets is an empirical and philosophical anthropology of man's nature and disposition, his innate characteristic features, his urges and desires, his physical, mental and emotional faculties, etc. In *The Theory of Moral Sentiments*, Smith had displayed his view of man in great detail. In *The Wealth of Nations* (1976b) he focused on those characteristics of man that are of special importance in economic life. A benign 'Providence', he was convinced, had endowed man with faculties and motives that conditioned him towards association, cooperation and competition, development and growth. Smith discerned 'a certain propensity in human nature … to truck, barter, and exchange one thing for another' (WN I.ii.1). He added:

> Whether this propensity be one of those original principles in human nature, of which no further account can be given; or whether, as seems more probable, it be the necessary consequence of the faculties of reason and speech, it belongs not to our present subject to enquire. It is common to all men, and to be found in no other race of animals, which seem to know neither this nor any other species of contract.
> (WN I.ii.2)

But man is not only able to communicate, truck, barter and exchange, he is also in need of it: 'In civilized society he stands at all times in need of the cooperation and assistance of great multitudes, while his whole life is scarce sufficient to gain the friendship of a few persons' (WN I. ii.2). From this Smith concludes that:

> man has almost constant occasion for the help of his brethren, and it is in vain for him to expect it from their benevolence only. He will be more likely to prevail if he can interest their self-love in his favour, and shew them that it is for their own advantage to do for him what he requires of them. Whoever offers to another a bargain of any kind, proposes to do this. Give me that which I want, and you shall have this which you want, is the meaning of every such offer; and it is in this manner that we obtain from one another the far greater part of those good offices which we stand in need of.
>
> (WN I.ii.2)

He exemplifies what we nowadays call the *double coincidence of wants* in one of the best-known passages of *The Wealth of Nations*:

> It is not from the benevolence of the butcher, the brewer, or the baker, that we expect our dinner, but from their regard to their own interest. We address ourselves, not to their humanity but to their self-love, and never talk to them of our own necessities but of their advantages.
>
> (WN I.ii.2)

Finally, he also sees the division of labour – which in his construction is the source of opulence – rooted in the propensity under consideration:

> As it is by treaty, by barter, and by purchase, that we obtain from one another the greater part of those mutual good offices which we stand in need of, so it is this same trucking disposition which originally gives occasion to the division of labour.
>
> (WN I.ii.3)

Within a few pages, Smith establishes two crucial axioms upon which his entire analysis rests:

i The market is a natural form of organising economic affairs, because it reflects natural faculties of man.

ii Man's well-being depends on the proper exertion of his trucking disposition and thus on the functioning of markets, because they lead to an ever-deeper division of labour, increase labour productivity and raise income per capita, Smith's measure of the wealth of a nation.

According to Smith, markets perform their role best in conditions of *free competition*, i.e., in the absence of barriers to entry into and exit from the various markets. Competition activates both what may be called centripetal and centrifugal forces. The former are supposed to make market prices gravitate towards (or oscillate around) their natural levels and thus actually establish what is nowadays called a long-period position of the economic system with respect to commodity prices and income distribution, which is ascertained independently of the process of gravitation. The latter involve a disruption of that position and its replacement by a new one as a consequence of technical and organisational change. While in the former case the battle of competition is fought with respect to prices, given technical knowledge, in the latter case it is fought with respect to new technical knowledge – new methods of production and new goods, i.e., 'improvements' or innovations. In the second case, competition may be compared to a whip propelling the economic system to higher and higher levels of productivity and a growing variety of goods. It refers to the non-equilibrium, evolutionary, and developmental side of competition. In both cases the emphasis is on the rivalry between agents and the behavioural process it engenders.[1]

Here we focus first on the centripetal forces of competition. They give order and coherence to the economy by disciplining the market participants: 'good management', Smith insists, 'can never be universally established but in consequence of that free and universal competition, *which forces every body to have recourse to it for the sake of self-defence*' (WN I.xi.b.5; emphasis added).[2] Good management is considered the *conditio sine qua non* of survival in competitive markets. For example, firms underbid one another as regards the price of the product in order to increase their sales and they overbid one another as regards the wages paid to workers in order to attract more workers when the economy is in an 'advancing condition' (WN I.vii.1) and employment is high. Competition and markets, Smith was convinced, accomplish effectively and at a small cost what a Leviathan could accomplish, if at all, only much less effectively and at a much higher cost.[3]

Free competition forms the basis of what Smith called 'a system of natural liberty', because it is seen to realise as best as possible the principles of 'equality, liberty and justice'.[4] Free competition involves the absence of any legal or other barriers to entry into or exit from a market: where there is 'perfect liberty', Smith writes, a producer or proprietor of capital, land, or capacity to work 'may change his trade as often as he wishes' (WN I.vii.6). However barriers to mobility play an important role in the mercantile system with its 'particular regulations of police' (WN I.vii.20), such as legal monopolies, privileges, preferences, guilds, statutes of apprenticeship, etc. Smith was highly critical of such barriers and opted for their abolition, but he allowed for several exceptions to natural liberty. An obvious case is when the integrity of the state itself is threatened.

He thus defended the Act of Navigation, which gave the sailors and shipping of Great Britain the monopoly of the trade of their own country, on the grounds that 'defence is of much more importance than opulence' (WN IV.ii.30). But in Smith we find also several examples of purely economic justifications for legal interventions and regulations. See in this regard the detailed list in Aspromourgos (2009; see also Aspromourgos, 2013) and the important instances discussed in Section 14.6 below.

Smith's remarkable advocacy of the monopoly privileges of the Bank of England is to be seen in connection with his dictum regarding defence versus opulence. The Bank of England, he was convinced, played an important role in financing public expenditures by advancing taxes to be paid to the Crown at an interest in times of peace and by contracting public debt in times of war (see WN V.iii.4). The Bank of England was 'the backbone of the country's fiscal strength, and thus of its international power'.[5] See on this Goodacre (2010).

Setting aside these exceptions, let us turn to the case of free and unbridled competition, Smith's ideal state of affairs. This state of affairs, Smith was clear, did not mimic the reality of the time in which he lived – the distortions caused by the mercantilist policy were still visible in almost each and every part of the economy. It was the state Smith advocated as the first best solution if assessed in terms of economic performance – the size of the social product in a given year, its growth over time, and its distribution among the different ranks of people. When he nevertheless carried out much of his abstract analysis of the working of markets on the premise of free competition, he did so because he wished to demonstrate the superior properties of the system of natural liberty and its self-regulating, homeostatic nature.

So how do markets function in Smith's view? What kind of results do they generate? And, perhaps most important, are they *stable*? Can one entrust the destiny of large parts of social life to their care? This brings us to an investigation of Smith's view of the formation of prices and the determination of income distribution as it is contained in chapter VII of book I of *The Wealth of Nations*.

14.3 Market prices and natural prices

Smith distinguishes between 'market prices' and 'natural prices'. About the former he writes:

> The market price of every particular commodity is regulated by the proportion between the quantity which is actually brought to market, and the demand of those who are willing to pay the natural prices of the commodity, or the whole value of the rent, labour, and profit, which must be paid in order to bring it thither. Such people may be called the effectual demanders, and their demand the *effectual demand*;

since it may be sufficient to effectuate the bringing of the commodity to market.

(WN I.vii.8, emphasis added)

The distinction between market and natural prices corresponds to that between all kinds of forces affecting prices in a given place and time, including forces that are temporary, accidental, and non-systematic, on the one hand, and forces that are persistent and systematic, on the other. Natural prices reflect only persistent and systematic forces. These include:

i The system of production actually adopted by cost-minimising producers.
ii Real wages paid to workers.

Real wages depend in turn, inter alia, on whether the economy is in a declining, stagnant, or growing state (see, e.g., WN I.vii.33). Given independent variables or data (i) and (ii), the dependent variables (a) the rate of profits and the rents of land and (b) natural prices can be ascertained (see below). 'The competition of the different dealers', Smith writes, 'obliges them all to accept of this [natural] price, but does not oblige them to accept of less' (WN I.vii.11). He insists that the natural price is the lowest price in the long run, 'which sellers can commonly afford to take, and at the same time continue their business': it covers their costs of production and yields them the ordinary rate of return on capital.

14.3.1 Natural prices

Setting aside the problem of land and the rent of land (a very weak part in Smith's analysis, as Ricardo was to point out; see also Kurz and Sturn, 2013a, 2013b), the system of *natural price* equations is characterised by a uniform (net) rate of profits r on the capital advanced in each sector of the economy.[6] For the sake of achieving greater analytical clarity, we may formalise Smith's argument. In the simple case of m single product industries and thus circulating capital only, and normalising gross outputs as unity, we can write the natural price equations of Classical derivation as:

$$\mathbf{p} = (1+r)\mathbf{A}\mathbf{p} \tag{14.1}$$

where $\mathbf{p}$ is the m-dimensional price vector $(p_1, p_2, \ldots, p_m)^T$,r is the general rate of profits and $\mathbf{A}$ is the matrix of material inputs per unit of output, where the vector of inputs needed by an industry to produce its gross output of one unit is given by the respective row of the matrix (see Kurz and Salvadori, 1995, ch. 4). Each coefficient of $m \times m$ matrix $\mathbf{A}$ gives the amount of a particular commodity used up as a means of production in the production of a particular commodity plus the amount of that commodity needed in the support of the workers producing it. We may split up matrix **A** into a matrix giving only the material means of production **M** and a matrix giving the necessary subsistence of workers **S**. On the simplifying assumption of a uniform real wage per unit of labour employed in production, given by vector $\mathbf{w}^T = (w_1, w_2, \ldots, w_m)$, and denoting the quantities of (direct) labour needed per unit of output in the different industries by $\mathbf{l} = (l_1, l_2, \ldots, l_m)^T$, we have:

$$\mathbf{A} = \mathbf{M} + \mathbf{S} = \mathbf{M} + \mathbf{l}\mathbf{w}^T$$

and therefore

$$\mathbf{p} = (1+r)(\mathbf{M} + \mathbf{l}\mathbf{w}^T)\mathbf{p} \tag{14.2}$$

With **M**, **l**, and **w** given and taking the bundle of non-negative quantities of the different commodities $\mathbf{b}^T = (b_1, b_2, \ldots, b_m)$ as the standard of value or numeraire, i.e., setting its value equal to unity:

$$\mathbf{b}^T \mathbf{p} = 1 \tag{14.3}$$

the general rate of profits r and the natural prices in terms of the standard **b** can be ascertained. No other data or known variables are needed to determine the unknowns.

This is a formalisation of the concept of natural prices proposed by Smith in WN I.vii.[7] Here the real wage **w** and the rate of profits r designate what Smith called the 'natural rate of wages' and the 'natural rate of profits'. At natural prices **p**, the real wage **w** translates into a nominal wage w in terms of the standard of value:

$$w = \mathbf{w}^T \mathbf{p} \tag{14.4}$$

14.3.2 Market prices

For a given real wage, Smith considers natural prices **p** and rate of profits r as *centres of gravitation* of market or actual prices:

> The natural price, therefore, is, as it were, the central price, to which the prices of all commodities are continually gravitating. Different accidents may sometimes keep them suspended a good deal above it, and sometimes force them down even somewhat below it. But whatever may be the obstacles which hinder them from settling in this center of repose and continuance, they are constantly tending towards it.
>
> (WN I.vii.15)

Market prices are also said to 'oscillate' around their natural levels.[8]

Why do market prices happen to deviate from their natural levels? Because there is no presumption that the quantity of a commodity that is actually brought to market equals the effectual demand for it, i.e., that quantity which will find a sufficient, and just sufficient, demand if the natural price of the commodity prevails. Smith conceives both of the quantity brought to market and effectual demand as given quantities and not as schedules or functions relating price and quantity as in marginalist theory with its concepts of the forces of 'demand' and 'supply' (see Garegnani, 1983). The deviation of market prices from their natural levels reflects the fact that many economic transactions in market economies are typically not settled ahead of time (in terms of existing future markets) or coordinated *ex ante* by some central authority. The question then is by means of which mechanism is coordination achieved over time? What Smith has to show is that such deviations are self-correcting: whenever they emerge, they swiftly activate forces from within the economic system that tend to remove them and bring the system back to its natural, normal or long-period position. Since this self-correcting process is supposed to work quickly and efficiently, Smith concludes that it is admissible to focus attention on natural prices and their determinants and consider market prices only incidentally, when short-run considerations are appropriate. This applies, for example, to the case of a public mourning, which 'raises the price of black cloth (with which the market is almost always understocked upon such occasions) and augments the profits of the merchants who possess any considerable quantity of it'. At the same time, 'It sinks the price of coloured silks and cloths, and thereby reduces the profits of the merchants who have any considerable quantity of them upon hand' (WN I.vii.19). In other cases, substantial and time-consuming processes of the reallocation of capital, labour, and land will take place. Self-interested behaviour, Smith is convinced, will bring about these processes and thereby effectuate the gravitation of market prices and of distributive variables (profits, wages, and rent) towards their natural levels.

While Smith talks most of the time about *the* market price of a commodity (as opposed to its natural price), as if it was a single price, he is well aware of the fact that different circumstances of firms and customers will typically be reflected in a multiplicity of actual prices, i.e., a dispersion of market prices. In the following we set aside this aspect of market imbalances.

The view of Smith and the subsequent Classical economists that the process of gravitation works rather smoothly is based on two premises:

i Whenever the quantity of a commodity brought to market is smaller (larger) than effectual demand, the market price will be above (below) the level of the natural price of the commodity. This implies that the sectoral (commodity-specific) rate of profit (and/or the wage rate and/or the rents paid) will be above (below) their natural level.

ii Profit-seeking producers will decrease (increase) the quantity of the commodity brought to market, if the sectoral (commodity-specific) rate of profit is below (above) the level in other (adjacent) sectors of the economy.

Are these premises necessary and sufficient to support Smith's conviction that the vector of natural prices is, in modern terms, a stable fixed point (an attractor)? This question received considerable attention in the aftermath of the publication of Piero Sraffa's *Production of Commodities by Means of Commodities* (Sraffa, 1960), which was explicitly designed to reformulate and revive 'the standpoint of the old classical economists from Adam Smith to Ricardo' (Sraffa, 1960, p. v). However apart from providing some allusions and hints, Sraffa in his book did not deal with the gravitation problem; he rather assumed that gravitation works. Could an analysis of it be elaborated that supplements Sraffa's reformulation and rectification of the Classical theory of value and distribution and thereby base Smith and the Classical economists' view on more solid ground?

14.4 The problem of gravitation

A rich literature on gravitation blossomed in the 1980s and 1990s, but the results were not conclusive. Depending on the kind of formalisation chosen, prices either gravitated or they did not. Here is not the place to provide a detailed summary account of this literature (see Bellino, 2011). It suffices to point out why some of the results were negative, doubting or denying gravitation, whereas others were positive, basically confirming Smith's intuition – an intuition shared by a large number of economists, including Ricardo, John Stuart Mill, Marx, and basically also all marginalist authors working within a long-period framework of the analysis, such as Eugen von BöhmBawerk, Knut Wicksell, Léon Walras, Vilfredo Pareto, und Gustav Cassel.

The majority of models were of the 'cross-dual dynamics' variety. In these models it was assumed that relative prices react upon sectoral output proportions and vice versa.[9] More precisely, the rates of change of actual prices respond to deviations of effectual demand from the quantity brought to the market and the rates of change of sectoral output proportions respond to deviations of sectoral from the average (or natural) rate of profits.

The formalisation of gravitation typically starts from a given fixed point $(\mathbf{x}^\star, \mathbf{p}^\star, r^\star)$, characterised by a uniform rate of profits:

$$r_1 = r_2 = \ldots = r_m = r^\star$$

and the equality between effectual demand and actual supply in each and every market

$$\mathbf{d}^\star = \mathbf{s} = \mathbf{x}^\star$$

where $\mathbf{d}^\star = (d_1{}^\star, d_2{}^\star, \ldots, d_m{}^\star)$ gives the vector of effectual demands, $\mathbf{s} = (s_1, s_2, \ldots, s_m)$ gives the vector of actual supplies and $\mathbf{x}^\star$ indicates the quantities corresponding to $\mathbf{p}^\star$ and $r^\star$. Then the two premises of Smith's view were modelled in the following way. Premise 1 was taken to imply with regard to commodity $j\,(j = 1, 2, \ldots, m)$ that there exists a continuous and sign-preserving function f_j that translates differences between $d_j{}^\star$ and s_j to an instantaneous change of actual price p_j:

$$dp_j / dt = f_j\left(d_j^\star - s_j\right) \tag{14.5}$$

where dp_j/dt gives the time derivative of the market price of commodity j. Premise 2 concerns a change in output and supply of commodity j as a consequence of capital (and labour) movements between sectors triggered by a difference between sector j's profit rate and the rates yielded in adjacent sectors. This difference was seen to follow from a difference between commodity j's market price and its natural price. The mechanism contemplated was translated into a continuous and sign-preserving function:

$$ds_i / dt = g_i\left(p_i - p_i^\star\right) \tag{14.6}$$

where ds_j/dt gives the time derivative of the supply of commodity j. Movements of prices respond to differences of quantities and vice versa; this is the basic logic of the cross-dual models of gravitation.

Alas, it turned out that equations (14.5) and (14.6) were not sufficient to establish gravitation in the given context. Hence in order to overcome the impasse, various authors added to these equations further *ad hoc* assumptions, including for example the assumption that the vector of effectual demands does not change over time or the assumption that it changes in a given manner (e.g., it grows proportionately at a given rate of growth). In the first case both wages and profits are consumed, whereas in the second case in normal or natural conditions and assuming that there is no saving and investment out of wages, all profits are saved and invested in the sector in which they have been made.

This did not, however, settle the issue. While in a two-sectoral framework there is an equivalence between $p_j - p_j^\star > 0\left(p_j - p_j^\star < 0\right)$ and $r_j > r^\star\left(r_j < r^\star\right)$, in an m-sectoral framework ($m > 2$) this is not necessarily the case. While the market price of a commodity may be larger (smaller) than its natural price, the sectoral (commodity-specific) profit rate need not be larger (smaller) than that of an adjacent sector or the average rate in the economy as a whole, $r_ø$: it may be the case that the market prices of one or several of the sector's inputs are above their natural levels, with the effect that the rate of profit of the sector under consideration is below (above) the natural and the average rate in the system as a whole (see Steedman, 1984). Obviously it is not acceptable to look just at the situation in a single sector – a partial analysis will not suffice. Rather, one has to look at all sectors and their interdependences and all prices and output levels in order to be able to assess sectoral profit rates.

The problems indicated are illustrated in Figures 14.1 and 14.2, where Figure 14.1 deals with the two-commodity case and Figure 14.2 with the *m*-commodity case. In the first case (see Figure 14.1) F gives the long-period position of the sector producing commodity *j*. If the amount of commodity *j* (j = 1, 2) brought to market s_j^0 is larger than effectual demand $x_j^\star$, the actual price of commodity *j*, p^0, will be smaller than its natural price $p^\star$; correspondingly, the actual rate of profit r_j^0 will be lower than the natural rate $r^\star$ and the rate in the other sector. Now assume that,

AU. Please note that the images will be placed in the proofs.

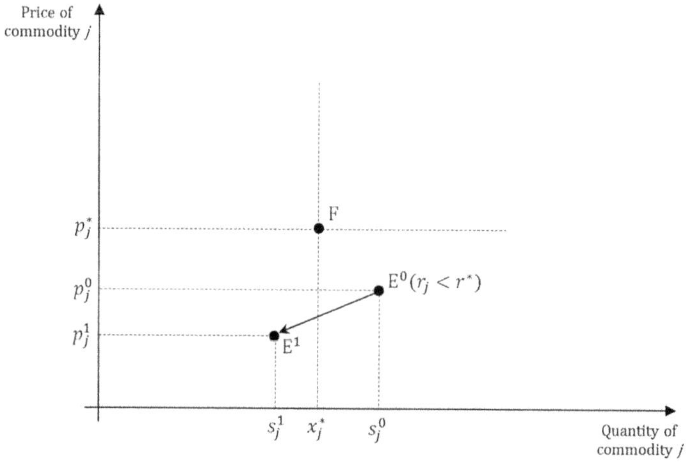

Figure 14.1 The two-sector case.

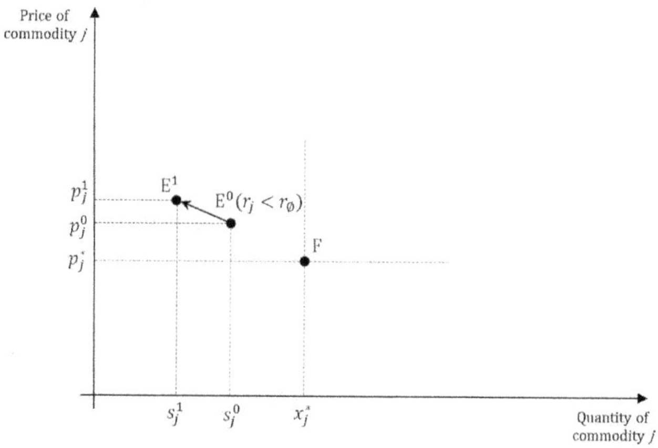

Figure 14.2 The m-sector case.

according to the particular specification of the adjustment equations (14.5) and (14.6), the actual price quantity constellation happens to move from E^0 to E^1. Clearly, actual output has to decrease and so it does. This part of the story appears to be all right. But the other part is not: the momentum of a falling price of the product, implied by the initial constellation, is still overwhelming and leads to a further drop of the price and, correspondingly, an even larger deviation of the sectoral profit rate from the natural one and the one obtained in the other sector. Hence the output of commodity *j* would have to fall even further, because $r_j^1 < r^\star$, and this despite the fact that commodity *j* is already in short supply compared with effectual demand.

In the *m*-sectoral case depicted in Figure 14.2, a quantity brought to market of commodity *j* is supposed to fall short of effectual demand, which is reflected in an actual price of commodity *j* that is higher than the natural level of it; see point E^0 in Figure 14.2. However, for the reason given in the above, this does not necessarily mean that the commodity-specific rate of profit is higher than the natural rate or an average of the rates obtained in the other sectors. If the rate of profit in sector *j* happens to be smaller than these other rates, this would involve capital and labour leaving the sector, thereby decreasing output and thus further increasing the deviation from the long-period position. Instead of reducing the deviation from the long-period position, it acerbates it with respect to commodity *j*. Comparing E^1 and F: while the price response seems to be satisfactory, the higher market price is not reflected in a higher (i.e., above-average) commodity-specific rate of profit. Therefore, more capital and labour will be withdrawn from the sector, implying a further decrease in output and, correspondingly, a further increase in commodity *j*'s market price and thus an even greater deviation from the long-period position.

Hence the dynamics of the cross-dual models of gravitation imply that the process is inherently unstable. Does this imply that there is no reason to trust in Smith's basic idea and, *a fortiori*, in the importance of the concept of a long-period position $(\mathbf{x}^\star, \mathbf{p}^\star, r^\star)$? After all, what would be the worth of an economic state – a long-period position – that is not an attractor or centre of gravitation of actual magnitudes?

According to some commentators the negative conclusions drawn by certain contributors to the debate were premature. First, the negative results obtained are not as negative as they seem initially. Second, the cross-dual models can be said not to formalise the idea of gravitation in a way that is faithful to Smith and other Classical economists. If the formalisation is adapted accordingly, stability results in well-specified conditions.

Garegnani (1990) has put forward the following argument in support of gravitation. His point of reference was Sraffa's (1960) multisector analysis of the production of commodities by means of commodities. In such a framework, while the situation displayed in Figure 14.2 may apply in some sectors, it cannot simultaneously apply in all sectors. In a system in which each commodity enters directly or indirectly into the production of all commodities, when a positive deviation of the market price of a particular commodity is accompanied by a negative deviation of the rate of profit, then the same opposition of signs cannot be true for at least one of the means of production that enters directly or indirectly into that commodity. For that means of production, both the rate of profit and the market price deviation will have to be positive. Hence the rise in its output will tend to reduce its market price, leading directly or indirectly to an increase in the rate of profit of the commodity. This increase in the rate of profit will then reverse 'the initial "perverse" [fall] in output' (Garegnani, 1990, p. 331).

As regards the second point, if one replaces adjustment equation (14.5) by a mechanism in which the levels (rather than the rates of change) of market prices relative to natural prices respond to differences between effectual demand and quantities brought to market, it can be shown that the processes may converge to a long-period position (see Bellino and Serrano, 2011).

Finally, Salvadori and Signorino (2014) argue that Smith (but also, e.g., Marx) refers to market prices not as a single price holding at a given moment of time, but as a constellation of prices that reduce to a single one only in the special cases of a buyers' market or a sellers' market, and that market prices could be studied using probability distributions as students of Bertrand competition have done. With respect to gravitation, they argue that the difficulties encountered in the respective literature are probably related to the erroneous concept of market price as a single magnitude. It will still have to be investigated whether the difficulties might perhaps be overcome by starting from dispersed prices, as Smith had suggested.

Related to this, a few further observations on Smith's analysis are apposite. He stressed that reactions of prices in different sectors will typically be different, reflecting differences in the characteristic features of the sectors, the needs and wants of people, their wealth, etc. And he stressed that a deficient supply will trigger competition among buyers (so-called sellers' market), whereas an excess supply will trigger competition among sellers (so-called buyers' market): competition will thus be ignited on what is nowadays dubbed the 'long' side of the market. For example, Smith emphasised that consequent upon a deficiency of actual supply compared with effectual demand:

> A competition will immediately begin among them, and the market price will rise more or less above the natural price, according to as either the greatness of the deficiency, or the wealth and wanton luxury of the competitors, happen to animate more or less the eagerness of the competition. Among competitors of equal wealth and luxury the same deficiency will generally occasion a more or less eager competition, according as the acquisition of the commodity happens to be or

> more or less importance to them: Hence the exorbitant price of the necessities of life during the blockade of a town or in a famine.
> (WN I.vii.9)

In the case of the quantity exceeding effectual demand:

> The market price will sink more or less below the natural price, according as the greatness of the excess increases more or less the competition of the sellers, or according as it happens to be more or less important to them to get immediately rid of the commodity. The same excess of the importation of perishable, will occasion a much greater competition than in that of durable commodities; in the importation of oranges, for example, than in that of old iron.
> (WN I.vii.10)

Translating Smith's reasoning into a formalisation in which the levels of prices and the levels of output will be affected by deviations of outputs and prices from their natural levels allows one to discuss Smith's intuition of the stabilising role played by the mobility of capital (and labour).

This section may be concluded by stating that while the stability issue is far from being settled, in the light of some recent studies it appears to look less disquieting than it did some time ago. In the following we rely on Smith's idea of the stability of commodity markets in the sense that in competitive conditions actual prices can be taken to converge towards, or oscillate around, their natural levels.

We now turn briefly to what we called the centrifugal force of competition: the rivalry in a race makes producers seek to defend themselves from competitors by introducing new methods of production and new goods. Competition, the story goes, is responsible for what was later called the restlessness of the capitalist economy, continuously generating change from within.[10]

14.5 Improvements

Here it suffices to draw attention to the following elements of Smith's analysis.[11] First, Smith saw improvements taking place in all sectors of the economy. The successful innovator is said to make extra profits for a while until, as a consequence of imitation and the diffusion of the improvement across the economy, the extra profits of the pioneer will erode and a new long-period position emerge. Smith pointed out:

> The establishment of any new manufacture, of any new branch of commerce, or of any new practice in agriculture, is always a speculation, from which the projector promises himself extraordinary profits. These profits sometimes are very great, and sometimes, more

> frequently, perhaps, they are quite otherwise; but in general they bear no regular proportion to those of other old trades in the neighbourhood. If the project succeeds, they are commonly at first very high. When the trade or practice becomes thoroughly established and well known, the competition reduces them to the level of other trades.
> (WN I.x.b.43)

Second, while innovations unleash centrifugal forces, which displace the old long-period position of the economy $(\mathbf{x}^{\star}, \mathbf{p}^{\star}, w^{\star}, r^{\star})$ and define a new one $(\mathbf{x}^{\star\star}, \mathbf{p}^{\star\star}, w^{\star\star}, r^{\star\star})$, they at the same time activate the centripetal forces of competition that move the system towards the latter.

Third, a part and parcel of the ever-deeper division of labour induced by competition is the emergence of what nowadays is called the research and development sector of the economy. Smith observes:

> All the improvements in machinery … have by no means been the inventions of those who had occasion to use the machines. Many improvements have been made by the ingenuity of the makers of the machines, when to make them became the business of a peculiar trade; and some by that of those who are called philosophers or men of speculation, whose trade it is, not to do any thing, but to observe every thing; and who, upon that account, are often capable of combining together the powers of the most distant and dissimilar objects. *In the progress of society, philosophy or speculation becomes, like every other employment, the principal or sole trade and occupation of a particular class of citizens.*
> (WN I.i.9; emphasis added)

Philosophy or speculation, i.e., science, percolates ever-more-modern society and becomes the foundation of its material metabolism and surplus creation. Two hundred and fifty years before the invention of the term 'knowledge society', Smith insists that 'the quantity of science' available to a society decides its members' productivity and wealth (WN I.i.9).

Fourth, it is interesting to note that Smith uses the combinatory metaphor to describe novelty: new economically useful knowledge derives from the combination of reconfigured bits of known particles of knowledge, a definition that involves the path dependency of progress in knowledge. Interestingly, Schumpeter (1912) and several other economists after him adopted the metaphor.

Fifth, the unintended consequences of self-seeking behaviour are an important theme in Smith's analysis. By pursuing their profit interests, capitalists are said to trigger a process that eventually, 'behind their backs' as Marx was to say, improves the lot of the many, i.e., increases also the incomes of the 'labouring poor' (WN I.i.1) and is thus beneficial to society as a whole. This is Smith's main argument in favour of a market economy. The criticism of selfishness, greed, and rapacity from a purely moral point of view by the canonists and schoolmen focuses attention on individual motives, but ignores largely the effects that according to Smith follow from actions based upon such motives. In a *well-governed society*, self-interested behaviour is seen to generate largely socially beneficial results. A narrowly moral point of view prevents one from forming a solid judgement on the subject matter.[12]

In the following two sections we take into account additional aspects of the problem at hand. We begin with a discussion of the problems of what nowadays are called asymmetric information, moral hazard, and adverse selection in Section 14.6, with the focus being on banking and financial markets. It is interesting to see that Smith's analysis foreshadows these concepts. Then, in Section 14.7, we turn briefly to 'the wretched spirit of monopoly', which Smith considered to be the greatest danger to a regime of 'natural liberty' and which in his view dominated the mercantilist system.

14.6 Asymmetric information, moral hazard, and adverse selection

Above we have dealt only with markets for commodities such as agricultural products and manufactures, i.e., commodities that can be used as means of production and means of subsistence or luxuries. Smith was very well aware of the fact that especially financial and money markets are very different from commodity markets.

The introduction of paper money on a large scale in France at the beginning of the eighteenth century, which was arguably one of the greatest innovations in the entire history of money and finance, was widely discussed at the time. Smith understood very well that the way it was done brought France to the brink of collapse and was accompanied by what is known as the 'Mississippi Bubble'. The introduction of paper money under the Duke of Orléans, the regent of France, was carried out following (at least partly) plans elaborated by John Law, a Scotsman like Smith and an excellent mathematician and gambler. It was meant to reduce the enormous debt the French King had accumulated. Law had argued that there was no danger of inflation and instability, because the countervalue to paper money consisted in (parts of) the land possessed by the King.

Interestingly, Smith approved of the introduction of paper money and compared it explicitly to 'some improvements in mechanicks' (WN II.ii.39), i.e., technical progress, because it allowed the replacement of gold and silver, highly precious metals, by a material whose production costs were close to nil. However he also saw the dangers associated with the new financial instrument. While 'The gold and silver money which circulates in any economy may very properly be compared to a highway', on which commodities are transported, paper money represents instead 'a sort of waggon-way through the air'. The commerce and industry of a country,

Smith warned, 'cannot be altogether so secure, when they are thus, as it were, suspended upon the *Daedalian wings of paper money*, as when they travel upon the solid ground of gold and silver' (WN II.ii.86, emphasis added).

He dubbed the plans of the 'famous Mr. Law ... splendid, but visionary' (WN II.ii.78). What was needed was an implementation of paper money by a 'judicious operation of banking' (WN II.ii.86). In a single paragraph the concept of judicious or 'prudent' operation of banking is mentioned four times! Yet even if all bankers were 'people of undoubted credit' (WN II.ii.95), this would not be enough to ban all dangers. Smith expounded:

> Over and above the accidents to which they [i.e. commerce and industry] are exposed from the unskilfulness of the conductors of this paper money, they are liable to several others, *from which no prudence or skill of those conductors can guard them.*
>
> (WN II.ii.86, emphasis added)

His pessimism was rooted in phenomena we nowadays call *asymmetric information, moral hazard*, and *adverse selection*. These are widespread if not ubiquitous and even the most judicious regulations of the banking system can only restrict, but not entirely eliminate, them.

14.6.1 Asymmetric information and moral hazard

'Mean people' will have a particular incentive to become bankers, Smith observed, if they are allowed to issue bank notes for very small sums. As several examples in history show, this triggered large increases of the circulation of paper money, economic crises, and the bankruptcy of many banks. The 'beggarly bankers', Smith warned, may cause 'a very great calamity to many poor people who had received their notes in payment' (WN II.ii.90). From this he concluded that the issuance of bank notes for very small sums ought to be prohibited by law. Notes for large sums ought to be used in transactions among merchants, whereas ordinary people ought to use only coins and thus travel upon the solid ground of silver and gold. His proposal implied the co-existence of two circuits of money that were supposed not to communicate with one another.

Smith was clear that to restrain a banker from issuing small notes 'is a manifest violation of that natural liberty which it is the proper business of law, not to infringe, but to support'. He added:

> Such regulations may, no doubt, be considered as in some respect a violation of natural liberty. But those exertions of the natural liberty of a few individuals, which might endanger the security of the whole society, are, and ought to be, restrained by the laws of all governments; of the most free, as well as of the most despotical. The obligation of

> building party walls, in order to prevent the communication of fire, is a violation of natural liberty, exactly of the same kind with the regulations of the banking trade which are here proposed.
>
> (WN II.ii.94)

Information asymmetries permeate *The Wealth of Nations*. Smith even classifies the three grand orders of men – landlords, workers, and capitalists – according to their members' access to information and knowledge. (i) Landlords, he writes, receive revenue (rent) that 'costs them neither labour nor care, but comes to them … independent of any plan or project of their own'. This makes them indolent and 'renders them too often, not only ignorant, but incapable of that application of mind which is necessary in order to foresee and understand the consequences of any publick regulation' (WN I.xi.p.8). (ii) Things are worse with respect to the second order of people: the worker's 'condition leaves him no time to receive the necessary information, and his education and habits are commonly such as to render him unfit to judge even though he was fully informed'. The worker is most in danger of being manipulated: 'In the publick deliberation, therefore, his voice is little heard and less regarded, except upon some particular occasions, when his clamour is animated, set on, and supported by his employers, *not for his, but their own particular purposes*' (WN I.xi.p.9, emphasis added). (iii) The people that are best informed in economic and political matters are merchants and master manufacturers, who 'during their whole lives … are engaged in plans and projects' and who therefore 'have frequently more acuteness of understanding than the greater part of country gentlemen' (WN I.xi.p.10). These men, possessed of a 'superior knowledge of their own interest', are on the one hand the source of economic development. Their selfishness may, however, be detrimental to the interests of the other classes and society at large. Smith insists with special reference to the 'dealers' or market intermediaries:

> The interest of the dealers, however, in any particular branch of trade or manufactures, is always in some respects different from, and even opposite to, that of the publick. To widen the market and to narrow the competition, is always the interest of the dealers. To widen the market may frequently be agreeable enough to the interest of the publick; but *to narrow the competition must always be against it, and can serve only to enable the dealers, by raising their profits above what they naturally would be, to levy, for their own benefit, an absurd tax upon the rest of their fellow-citizens.*

Smith continues in an alarming tone:

> The proposal of any new law or regulation of commerce which comes from this order, ought always to be listened to with great precaution,

> and ought never to be adopted till after having been long and carefully examined, not only with the most scrupulous, but with the most suspicious attention. *It comes from an order of men, whose interest is never exactly the same with that of the publick, who have generally an interest to deceive and even to oppress the publick, and who accordingly have, upon many occasions, both deceived and oppressed it.*
>
> (WN I.xi.p.10, emphases added)

Those who are better informed – dealers, merchants, manufacturers, and moneyed men – may use their superior knowledge to the detriment of others, whether in discussions of political matters or in economic transactions. Their counterparts – customers, consumers, and in general, workers – are in danger of being 'pulled over the barrel', as the proverb says: they are exposed to moral hazard. Smith stressed especially that bankers are willing to take risks, knowing that in case of failure the potential costs of their decisions will be borne by others.[13]

14.6.2 Adverse selection

Smith stressed that projects that exhibit a higher expected profitability are typically also more risky.[14] As the recent financial crisis illustrated once again, many people ignored this fact. They fell victim to 'irrational exuberance' (Alan Greenspan). Smith's respective observations read like a commentary on the crisis. With the (occasionally hypertrophic) growth of a bank's business, bankers 'can know very little about [their debtors]'. They give money to:

> chimerical projectors, the drawers and re-drawers of circulating bills of exchange, who would employ the money in extravagant undertaking, which, with all the assistance that could be given them, they would probably never be able to compleat, and which, if they should be compleated, would never repay the expence which they had really cost.
>
> (WN II.ii.77)

The problem, Smith stressed, is that 'chimerical projectors' are willing to offer high rates of interest to banks because they expect very high profits from their 'extravagant undertaking' and, should the undertaking fail, do not intend to pay back the debt. The 'sober and frugal debtors', who 'might have less of the grand and the marvellous, [but] more of the solid and the profitable', on the contrary would, after careful calculation, be prepared to pay only a lower rate of interest. Banks can therefore be expected to go for the chimerical and not for the sober and frugal. This leads to an adverse selection, which transfers a great part of the capital of a country 'from prudent and profitable, to imprudent and unprofitable undertakings' (WN II.ii.77).

Smith opposed the prohibition of interest taking – the laws against 'usury' as they existed in several countries at his time. 'This regulation', he wrote:

> instead of preventing, has been found from experience to increase the evil of usury; the debtor being obliged to pay, not only for the use of the money, but for the risk which his creditor runs by accepting a compensation for that use. *He is obliged, if one may say so, to insure his creditor from the penalties of usury.*
>
> (WN II.iv.13, emphasis added)

Yet he advocated a legal upper boundary to the rate of interest, which 'ought not to be much above the lowest market rate'. If there was no such upper limit or if the legal rate was fixed at too high a level:

> the greater part of the money which was to be lent, would be lent to prodigals and projectors, who alone would be willing to give this high interest. Sober people, who will give for the use of money no more than a part of what they are likely to make by the use of it, would not venture into competition. A great part of the capital of the country would thus be kept out of the hands which were most likely to make a profitable and advantageous use of it, and thrown into those which were most likely to waste and destroy it. Where the legal rate of interest, on the contrary, is fixed but a very little above the lowest market rate, sober people are universally preferred, as borrowers, to prodigals and projectors. The person who lends money gets nearly as much interest from the former as he dares to take from the latter, and his money is much safer in the hands of one set of people, than in those of the other. A great part of the capital of the country is thus thrown into the hands in which it is most likely to be employed with advantage.
>
> (WN II.iv.15)

The argument shows that for Smith the question was not whether or not the banking trade ought to be regulated: the answer was a resounding yes. The question was rather which regulations would look after 'the security of the whole society' and at the same time leave enough room for the pursuit of self-interest and allow banks to provide the needed credit for doing so.

To conclude, we address briefly what in Smith's view constituted a major threat to competitive conditions and thus the system of natural liberty – the wretched spirit of monopoly.[15]

14.7 The 'wretched spirit of monopoly'

This spirit was constantly seeking possibilities to remove competition and establish monopolistic conditions. The monopolist does not have to fear competitors, who underbid his price and take away from him a part of the market and profits. Monopolies are able 'to keep up the market price, for a long time together, a good deal above the natural price' (WN I.vii.20). The difference between the monopoly and the natural price is pocketed as supernormal profit. Hence to stop competition is in the interest of the single merchant and master manufacturer because it is profitable to do so. Smith's concept of monopoly is much broader than the modern one, which restricts the term to the case in which there is basically only a single producer and seller. In Smith, a lasting difference between the market and the natural price is the characteristic feature of a monopoly, i.e., gravitation is blocked. In terms of our system of price equations (1), the competitive rate of profits r would have to be replaced by differential rates $r_1, r_2, \ldots, r_m$ – one for each sector, where $r_j > 0, j = 1, 2, \ldots, m$, and each set of (feasible) rates would typically be accompanied by a different set of relative prices. We may illustrate this in terms of just two sectors. In Figure 14.3 the real wage rate in terms of one of the commodities ω is measured along the vertical axis, whereas the sector-specific profit rates r_1 and r_2 are measured along the two axes on the bottom plane. At a given natural wage rate $\omega^\star$, the uniform competitive rate of profits $r^\star$ $(= r_1 = r_2)$ would be given by the intersection of the 45° line and the intersection of the r_1-r_2-ω relationship (also known as the 'wage frontier'; see Kurz and Salvadori, 1995, pp. 50–51) and the plane parallel to the level $\omega^\star$ of the real wage rate. If in one sector producers are able to pocket a higher rate of profit than the natural one, because of monopolistic privileges, and if

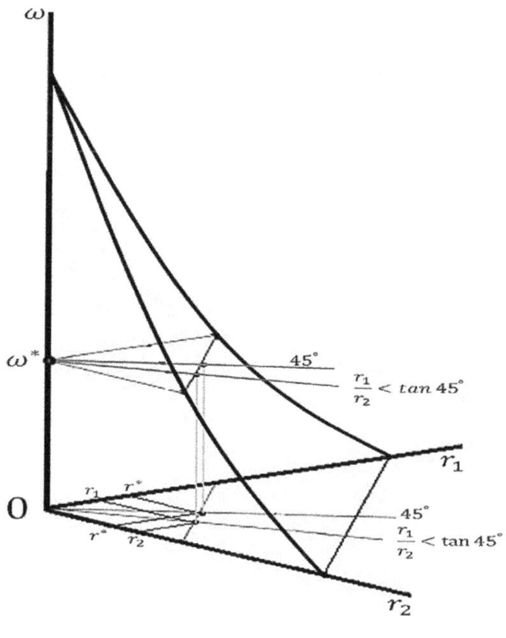

Figure 14.3 The wage frontier.

the real wage rate happens to be unaffected by this, then the rate of profit in the other sector will have to be smaller than the natural one. In Figure 14.3 such a constellation is given by $r_2 > r^\star > r_1$. Hence the three distributive variables are not independent of one another: given any one of them, the other two are inversely related.[16] Smith showed some awareness of this (although there are passages in *The Wealth of Nations* that shed doubt on his understanding). He also understood somewhat that changing income distribution, i.e., in the present analytical framework: hypothetically moving on the surface of the wage frontier, would be accompanied by changes in relative prices (see Kurz and Sturn, 2013a, section 2.6.3).

Smith distinguishes between natural and artificial monopolies. A particular French wine that grows only on land of a special location and quality and therefore is limited in supply, for example, may bring the proprietor of the land a monopoly rent, provided the demand for the wine is high and keeps the market price constantly above its natural level. Several cases, which in modern theory involve a natural monopoly, Smith mentions only in passing. His attention focuses instead on artificial monopolies as the result of economic policy measures. These monopolies can, in principle, be dissolved again and according to Smith they should, because 'The price of monopoly is upon every occasion the highest which can be got. The natural price, or the price of free competition, on the contrary, is the lowest which can be taken … for any considerable time together' (WN I.vii.27). Smith expounds:

> A monopoly granted either to an individual or to a trading company has the same effect as a secret in trade or manufactures. The monopolists, *by keeping the market constantly under-stocked, by never fully supplying the effectual demand*, sell their commodities much above the natural price, and raise their emoluments, whether they consist in wages or profit, greatly above their natural rate.
>
> (WN, I.vii.26, emphasis added)

Smith is not under any circumstances opposed to legal monopolies – see especially his endorsement of the Act of Navigation. But he insists that they must be temporary, subject to strict requirements, and severe supervision and control. The English East India Company and similar companies are forbidding examples of the enormous damage legal monopolies can cause:

> The constant view of such companies is always to raise the rate of their own profit as high as they can; to keep the market, both for the goods which they export, and for those which they import, as much understocked as they can: which can be done only by restraining the competition, or by discouraging new adventurers from entering into the trade.
>
> (WN V.i.e.10)

And elsewhere Smith observes:

> Some nations have given up the whole commerce of their colonies to an exclusive company, of whom the colonists were obliged to buy all such European goods as they wanted, and to whom they were obliged to sell the whole of their own surplus produce. It was the interest of the company, therefore, not only to sell the former as dear, and to buy the latter as cheap as possible, but to buy no more of the latter, even at this low price, than what they could dispose of for a very high price in Europe. It was their interest, not only to degrade in all cases the value of the surplus produce of the colony, but in many cases to discourage and keep down the natural increase of its quantity. Of all the expedients that can well be contrived to stunt the natural growth of a new colony, that of an exclusive company is undoubtedly the most effectual.
>
> (WN IV.vii.b.22)

The rule of such companies in the colonies was typically violent and cruel. And while Smith was a fervent advocate of free trade, he deplored the fact that 'The savage injustice of the Europeans rendered an event, which ought to have been beneficial to all, ruinous and destructive to several of those unfortunate countries' (WN IV.i.32).

Finally, we must discuss briefly Smith's view of the determination of wages in chapter VIII of book I of *The Wealth of Nations* and whether it is related to the problem of monopoly. Smith emphasised that there is a conflict over the distribution of income:

> What are the common wages of labour depends every where upon the contract usually made between those two parties, whose interests are by no means the same. The workmen desire to get as much, the masters to give as little as possible. The former are disposed to combine in order to raise, the later in order to lower the wages of labour.
>
> (WN I.viii.11)

He added:

> It is not, however, difficult to foresee which of the two parties must, upon all ordinary occasions, have the advantage in the dispute, and force the other into compliance with their terms. [1] The masters, being fewer in number, can combine much more easily; and [2] the law, besides, authorises, or at least does not prohibit their combinations, while it prohibits those of the workmen. We have no acts of parliament against combining to lower the price of work; but many against combining to raise it. In all such disputes the masters can hold out much longer. … [3] [Masters] could generally live a year or two

> upon the stocks which they have already acquired. Many workmen could not subsist a week, few could subsist a month, and scarce any a year without employment.
>
> (WN I.viii.12)

Because of the reasons [1]–[3] given, workers' bargaining position is weak and they must typically accept the conditions dictated by employers in the 'dispute' over wages. 'Masters', Smith observed,

> are always and every where in a sort of tacit, but constant and uniform combination, not to raise the wages of labour above their actual rate. To violate this combination is every where a most unpopular action, and a sort of reproach to a master among his neighbours and equals.

He added: 'We seldom, indeed, hear of this combination, because it is the usual, and one may say, *the natural state of things* which nobody ever hears of' (WN I.viii.13, emphasis added). It is only in conditions of swift economic expansion, when the growth of the demand for hands exceeds the supply that masters violate the combination:

> The scarcity of hands occasions a competition among masters, who bid against one another, in order to get workmen, and thus voluntarily break through the natural combination of masters not to raise wages.
>
> (WN I.viii.17)[17]

The combination of masters not to raise (and possibly even to reduce) wages Smith interestingly calls the 'natural state of things'. The success of masters in this regard would therefore lead to a lower real wage (**w** in Section 14.3 or ω in the present section), but not necessarily to a distortion of competitive conditions between different sectors reflected in differential profit rates.[18] In terms of Alfred Marshall's distinction between 'class conflicts' and 'trade conflicts' – i.e., the 'discords of interest among the several sections of a nation, and between each of those sections and the nation as a whole' (Marshall, 1920, p. 17) – we would have to speak of a class conflict. But in case monopolistic privileges of some industry impact negatively both on the profits of capitalists in other industries and on the wages of workers in general, we would have a superposition of both types of conflict and Smith's respective disquisition would have also a bearing on the theme dealt with in this section.

14.8 Concluding remarks

Markets and trade are, in principle, good things – provided there is competition. But competition is always in danger of being undermined and eroded, giving way to monopolies that are very comfortable and highly profitable to monopolists and may spell great trouble for many people.

In Smith's view, political economy – as an important, and perhaps even the most important, part of a kind of master political science, encompassing the *science of the legislator* – has the task to fight superstition and false beliefs in matters of economic policy, to debunk opinions that present individual interests as promoting the general good and to propose a regulatory framework for markets and institutions that helps to ward off threats to the security of society as a whole and provide incentives such that self-seeking behaviour has also socially beneficial effects.

The paper shows that the ideas of Adam Smith still may resonate and illuminate the problems of today and the theories that try to tackle them.

Notes

1 Smith was not the first author to advocate such a concept of competition. He was anticipated by Richard Cantillon and Anne Robert Jacques Turgot (see Kurz and Salvadori, 1995, pp. 37–40). Smith has rightly been called 'the great systematiser' in this area of analysis (as well as in others), who blended the insights of earlier authors and insights of his own into as coherent a whole as possible (McNulty, 1968, pp. 645–646).

2 Marx, echoing Smith's remark, was later to speak of the 'coercive law of competition'.

3 John Stuart Mill (1973, p. 242) maintained that 'Only through the principle of competition has political economy any pretension to the character of a science', because rents, profits, wages, and prices are determined by competition so that 'laws may be assigned for them'. It deserves to be stressed that the classical concept of free competition must not be confounded with the marginalist concept of perfect competition, as is frequently done in the literature. For a clear discussion of the differences between the two concepts, see McNulty (1968) and recently Salvadori and Signorino (2013, section 1).

4 Equality here means equal opportunity and rights of agents, not material equality.

5 I borrowed this expression from the report of one of the referees. As is well known, Ricardo did not share Smith's view and was highly critical of the Bank of England's privileges.

6 Here we set aside Smith's discussion (in WN, I.x) of systematic and permanent differences in profit rates due to differential risk, agreeableness of the business, etc. See, therefore, Kurz and Salvadori (1995, ch. 11).

7 There is some controversy about whether Smith saw the constraint binding changes in real wages and the general rate of profits, given the system of production in use. As is argued in Kurz and Sturn (2013a, pp. 90–112), Smith glimpsed the constraint in some passages of *The Wealth of Nations*, but then lost sight of it again in others. One of the reasons for this is to be seen in the fact that he tended to associate higher real wages with a higher labour productivity (see, e.g., WN I.viii.44). Hence he did not take the system of production to be independent of real wages. In this case the impact of an increase in wages on the rate of profits is not obvious. It was Ricardo who for good established the inverse relationship between real wages and the rate of profits, given the system of production.

8 It should come as no surprise that in the context of the problem of gravitation (see Section 4) Smith employs terms used by Sir Isaac Newton in astronomy, indicating a certain analogy seen by Smith between the types of phenomena

under consideration. What Smith appears to have in mind with respect to (**p**, *r*), paraphrased in terms of modern economic dynamics, is a stable fixed point that is not necessarily asymptotically stable; if it is not, it is a limit cycle (see, e.g., Shone, 2002).

9 Cross-dual gravitation models were introduced into the literature by Nikaido (1983) in the context of a discussion of Marx's view of competition. For a short summary account of the basic approach and problems, see Boggio (1986); for a more comprehensive account, see Bellino (2011).

10 The sung hero of 'new combinations', i.e., innovations, and the process of 'creative destruction' is of course Joseph A. Schumpeter (1912); see Kurz (2012) and Kurz and Sturn (2012). The unsung hero, one might add, is Marx.

11 For a more detailed discussion of Smith's view of technical change, its achievements, and shortcomings, see also Aspromourgos (2009), Kurz (2010) and Kurz and Sturn (2013a).

12 Smith appears to have been overly optimistic in this regard, because an increase in real wages was retarded for quite some time till after the Industrial Revolution had got in full swing, as studies in economic history show. Smith counted first and foremost upon capitalist dynamics, which he hoped would drive up wages despite workers' weak position in society. He indicated that a legal regulation of the labour contract could assist the 'natural' forces and improve the living conditions of workers (see Aspromourgos, 2013, p. 286). He did not foresee, however, the rise of trade unions and their impact on wages.

13 Interestingly, Robert Lucas Jr opined: 'I think of all progress in economic thinking, in the kind of basic core of economic theory, as developing entirely as learning how to do what Hume and Smith and Ricardo wanted to do, only better' (Lucas, 2004, p. 22). Can Smith (or Hume or Ricardo) be said to have entertained the view that a society whose members are characterised by conflicting interests and asymmetries in economic power and information levels be analysed in terms of a single 'representative agent'? Certainly not. Lucas's claim that his analysis is rooted in that of the Classical economists is without any foundation. What can at most be said is that the Classical economists contemplated the interplay of different representative agents, where each agent represents either a class of people (workers, capitalists, or landlords) or a group within a class (e.g., merchants, masters, or moneyed men).

14 With regard to different employments of capital, Smith stresses: 'The ordinary rate of profit always rises more or less with the risk' (WN I.x.b.33). He exemplifies this in terms of foreign trade, which may be considered to be more profitable, but also more risky. Caring for the security of his investment and being possessed of a risk-averse attitude, the typical investor, Smith surmises, can be expected to employ his capital at home. He thus supports domestic rather than foreign industry, 'led by an invisible hand to promote an end which was no part of his intention' (WN IV.ii.9). But there is also the other side of the coin: man typically shows 'contempt of risk and the presumptuous hope of success' (WN I.x.b.29), a fact around which the discussion above revolves.

15 For a comprehensive discussion of Smith's theory of monopoly, see Salvadori and Signorino (2014).

16 To provide a recent example: when the former CEO of Deutsche Bank, Josef Ackermann, requested a rate of return of 25% for his business, this should have been understood as a sort of declaration of war in the dispute over the distribution of income to the other industries in the economy and to workers. Clearly, for given technical conditions of production, one side can only gain at the cost of some other side(s).

17 In Smith, the level of the real wage rate is contingent upon the balance of power between workers and masters, which in turn depends, inter alia, on the rate of capital accumulation.

18 Smith's idea was picked up by several authors and may be seen to be at the origin of the concept of 'class monopoly' as it was advocated, for example, by the German economist Franz Oppenheimer and, following him, Erich Preiser and the Polish economist Michal Kalecki.

Bibliography

Aspromourgos, T. 2009. *The Science of Wealth: Adam Smith and the Framing of Political Economy*, London, Routledge

Aspromourgos, T. 2013. Adam Smith on labour and capital, pp. 267–289 in Berry, C. J., Paganelli, M. P. and Smith, C. (eds), *The Oxford Handbook of Adam Smith*, Oxford, Oxford University Press

Bellino, E. 2011. Gravitation of market prices towards natural prices, pp. 58–75 in Ciccone, R., Gehrke, C. and Mongiovi, G. (eds), *Sraffa and Modern Economics*, London, Routledge

Bellino, E. and Serrano, F. 2011. 'Gravitation Analysis: Beyond Cross-dual Models and Back to Adam Smith', unpublished paper

Boggio, L. 1986. Centre of gravitation, pp. 392–394 in Eatwell, J., Milgate, M. and Newman, P. (eds), *The New Palgrave: A Dictionary of Economics*, vol. 1, London, Macmillan

Garegnani, P. 1983. The classical theory of wages and the role of demand schedules in the determination of relative prices, *American Economic Review: Papers and Proceedings*, vol. 73, 309–313

Garegnani, P. 1990. On some supposed obstacles to the tendency of market prices towards natural prices, *Political Economy*, vol. 6, nos 1–2, 329–359

Goodacre, H. J. 2010. Limited liability and the wealth of 'uncivilised nations': Adam Smith and the limits to the European Enlightenment, *Cambridge Journal of Economics*, vol. 35, no. 5, 857–867

Kurz, H. D. 2010. Technical change, capital accumulation and income distribution in classical economics: Adam Smith, David Ricardo and Karl Marx, *European Journal of the History of Economic Thought*, vol. 11, 1183–1222

Kurz, H. D. 2012. Schumpeter's new combinations: revisiting his *Theorie der wirtschaftlichen Entwicklung* on the occasion of its centenary, *Journal of Evolutionary Economics*, vol. 22, no. 5, 871–899

Kurz, H. D. and Salvadori, N. 1995. *Theory of Production: A Long-period Analysis*, Cambridge, Cambridge University Press

Kurz, H. D. and Sturn, R. 2012. *Schumpeter für jedermann: von der Rastlosigkeit des Kapitalismus*, Frankfurt am Main, Frankfurter Allgemeine Buch

Kurz, H. D. and Sturn, R. 2013a. *Die größten Ökonomen: Adam Smith*, Konstanz, UVK

Kurz, H. D. and Sturn, R. 2013b. *Adam Smith für jedermann: Pionier der modernen Ökonomie*, Frankfurt am Main, Frankfurter Allgemeine Buch

Lucas, R. E. 2004. My Keynesian education, in de Vroey, M. and Hoover, K. (eds), *The IS–LM Model: Its Rise, Fall and Strange Persistence, annual supplement to vol. 36 of History of Political Economy*, vol. 36, no. 4, 12–24

McNulty, P. 1968. Economic theory and the meaning of competition, *Quarterly Journal of Economics*, vol. 82, 639–656

Mandeville, B. 1924. *The Fable of the Bees; or, Private Vices, Publick Benefits*, 2nd edn (1st edn 1723), Oxford, Clarendon Press

Marshall, A. 1920. *Industry and Trade*, 2nd edn (1st edn 1919), London, Macmillan

Mill, J. S. 1973. *Principles of Political Economy*, first published in 1848, vol. 2, Toronto, Toronto University Press

Nikaido, H. 1983. Marx on competition, *Zeitschrift für Nationalökonomie/Journal of Economics*, vol. 43, no. 4, 337–362

Salvadori, N. and Signorino, R. 2013. The classical notion of competition revisited, *History of Political Economy*, vol. 45, no. 1, 149–175

Salvadori, N. and Signorino, R. 2014. Adam Smith on monopoly theory: making good a lacuna, *Scottish Journal of Political Economy*, vol. 61, no. 2, 178–195.

Schotter, A. 1985. *Free Market Economics: A Critical Appraisal*, New York, Blackwell

Schumpeter, J. A. 1912. *Theorie der wirtschaftlichen Entwicklung*, Berlin, Duncker & Humblot

Shone, R. 2002. *Economic Dynamics*, 2nd edn, Cambridge, UK, Cambridge University Press

Smith, A. 1976a. The Theory of Moral Sentiments, first published in 1959, in Raphael, D. D. and Macfie, A. L. (eds.), *The Glasgow Edition of the Works and Correspondence of Adam Smith*, Oxford, Oxford University Press

Smith, A. 1976b. An Inquiry into the Nature and Causes of the Wealth of Nations, first published in 1776, in Campbell, R. H. and Skinner, A.S. (eds.), *The Glasgow Edition of the Works and Correspondence of Adam Smith*, two vols, Oxford, Oxford University. In the text referred to as WN, book number, chapter number, section number, paragraph number.

Sraffa, P. 1960. *Production of Commodities by Means of Commodities*, Cambridge, Cambridge University Press

Steedman, I. 1984. Natural prices, differential profit rates and the classical competitive process, *Manchester School*, vol. 25, no. 2, 123–140

Subject index

Note: Page numbers followed by "n" refer to end notes.

Name index

Note: Page numbers followed by "n" refer to end notes.

For Product Safety Concerns and Information please contact our EU representative GPSR@taylorandfrancis.com
Taylor & Francis Verlag GmbH, Kaufingerstraße 24, 80331 München, Germany

www.ingramcontent.com/pod-product-compliance
Ingram Content Group UK Ltd.
Pitfield, Milton Keynes, MK11 3LW, UK
UKHW022348190926
475702UK00015B/2166
9780367687069